DECORATED
ROMAN
ARMOUR

To all the Lovers of Roman Military History

DECORATED
ROMAN
ARMOUR

From the Age of the Kings
to the Death of
Justinian the Great

Raffaele D'Amato

and

Andrey Evgenevich Negin

FRONTLINE BOOKS

DECORATED ROMAN ARMOUR
From the Age of the Kings to the Death of Justinian the Great

This edition published in 2017 by Frontline Books,
an imprint of Pen & Sword Books Ltd,
47 Church Street, Barnsley, S. Yorkshire, S70 2AS

ISBN: 978-1-47389-287-3.

CIP data records for this title are available from the British Library

For more information on our books, please visit
www.frontline-books.com
email info@frontline-books.com
or write to us at the above address.

Printed in India by Replika Press Pvt. Ltd.

Typeset in 10.5 / 12.5pt Palatino

Contents

List of Plates   vi

Acknowledgements   vii

Introduction   xi

1 Decorated Armour in the Age of the Kings (753–509 BC)   1

2 Decorated Armour in the Age of the Consuls (509–27 BC)   22

3 Decorated Armour of the Principate (27 BC– AD 284)   55

4 Decorated Armour of the Principate in Archaeological Context   80

5 Decorated Armour of the Dominate (AD 284–565)   244

Notes   290

Bibliography   320

List of Plates

Plate 1 Salii priest in ceremonial armour, eighth century BC

Plate 2 Roman champion 'Oratius', seventh century BC

Plate 3 First-class (*classis preima*) hoplite, Romano-Etruscan aristocrat in battle armour, age of Tarquinius the Bold

Plate 4 Roman *Magister Equitum* – battle order 500 BC

Plate 5 Italic *Socius* warrior in Marcellina armour, fourth century BC

Plate 6 Consul Caius Flaminius Nepos, battle order, 217 BC

Plate 7 Consul in Rhodian Armour, second century BC

Plate 8 Caesarian *Centurio*, Gallic Wars, 58–52 BC

Plate 9 Thracian aristocratic auxiliary cavalryman from Vize, 45 AD

Plate 10 Quintus Lucius Faustus – *miles legio XIIII Geminae Martiae Victricis*

Plate 11 Batavian auxiliary cavalry, Marcianus, from Noviomagus, second half of the first century AD

Plate 12 Roman *Magister Equitum*, AD 117 (Nawa grave)

Plate 13 Roman officer of Osroene Cavalry, reign of Alexander Severus, AD 235

Plate 14 Cavalryman in *Hippika Gymnasia* armour, second–third century AD

Plate 15 *Draconarius* in *Hippika Gymnasia* armour, third century AD

Plate 16 Straubing 'Amazon' warrior on horseback, third century AD

Plate 17 *Draconarius* of the *Domestici Equitum Cataphractarii*, AD 356

Plate 18 *Cataphractarius* of *Schola Scutariorum secunda*, *Scholae Palatinae*, from the column of Arcadius, early fifth century AD

Plate 19 Justinian in the triumphal costume of Achilles

Acknowledgements

First, the authors would like express their gratitude to the colleagues and friends who have supplied the photos of the specimens listed in the catalogue and their permission to publish them in this book. In particular we would like to thank: Dr Andreas Pangerl, Dr Ernst Künzl, Dr László Kocsis (Magyar Nemzeti Múzeum), Dr Dan Isac, Dr Ivan Radman (Archaeological museum Zagreb), Alex Kyrychenko (Emory University), Dr László Borhy (Eötvös Loránd University), Martijn Wijnhoven, Dr Pascal Vipard (Université de Lorraine), Dr Petényi Sándor (Kuny Domokos Museum in Tata), Dr Thomas Fischer (Archäologischen Institut der Universität zu Köln), Dr Mike Bishop (School of Archaeology, University of Oxford), Stanimir Dimitrov, Nikolay Zubkov, Robert Cummins (Providence Academy, Plymouth), Dr Knight Delaval (Sotheby's), Dr Mark Merrony (Musée d'Art Classique de Mougins), Dr.ssa Marina Mattei (Musei Capitolini, Roma), Dr.ssa Laura Maria Vigna (Musei Capitolini, Roma), Dr Roberto Meneghini (Museo dei Fori Imperiali, Roma), Dr.ssa Barbara Mazzei (Pontificia Accademia); Dr.ssa Rita Paris (Museo delle Terme, Roma), Dr Gianfranco Gazzetti (Museo di Lucus Feroniae, Roma), Dr.ssa Giuseppina Ghini (Museo delle navi di Nemi, Nemi), the late Dr Gabriele Cateni (Archaeological National Museum, Volterra), Dr.ssa Gabriella Pantò (Museo di Antichità, Torino), Dr.ssa Patrizia Petitti (Museo di Antichità, Torino), Prof. Livio Zerbini (Università of Ferrara); Dr.ssa Giuseppina Carlotta Cianferoni (Museo Archeologico di Firenze), Dr Fiorillo Gaetano (Archeoclub of Alife), Dr Giuseppe Valentini (Archeoclub of Crecchio), Dr Antonio Gaetano (Teramo); Dr.ssa Maria Rita Sgarlata (Commissione di Archeologia Sacra, Siracusa) Dr.ssa Tatiana Bommara (Commissione di Archeologia Sacra, Siracusa), Prof. Vujadin Ivanišević (Archaeological Institute, Beograd); Dr.ssa Aleksandra Sojic (Beograd), Dr Kreuzmer Theresia (Prutting Church, Oberbayern); Dr Ashraf Nageh, (Coptic Museum of Cairo); Dr Hatice Deniz (Kars); Dr Umut Özgür Özel; Dr Valeri Yotov (Varna, Archaeological Museum); Dr Marina Persengieva (Varna).

We are also indebted to Don Francesco Grassi, priest of the church of Sts Cesidius and Rufinus, Trasacco, who with great kindness allowed one of the authors to inspect the place and take photo in very difficult conditions.

ACKNOWLEDGEMENTS

The warmest thanks are due to all the owners of important private European collections who opened their treasures to us. Their help and their permission to publish for the first time the items from their private museums in this book represent a great contribution to this branch of military history and to scientific research in general.

Second, it is our duty to thank the colleagues and friends who have supported us with material help and hospitality, giving us advices and further iconographical material for the preparation of the book: Dr.Massimo Bizzarri (Roma), Dr Fabrizio Crespini (Siena), Dr Andrea Salimbeti (Torino), Prof. Taxiarchis Kolias, Director of the Institute for Byzantine Research at the University of Athens; Professor Ewald Kislinger, of the Institut fur Byzantinistik und Neogräzistik, Vienna University; Prof. Georgios Theotokis, Fatih University, Istanbul; Dr Nejat Çuhadaroğlu (Hisart Müzesi, Istanbul).

Furthermore, we must thank the following institutions for the material they furnished: the DAI Library of Rome; the University of Pennsylvania Museum; the Metropolitan Museum of New York; the Paul Getty Museum, Malibu; the Royal Ontario Museum, Toronto; Christie's; Gerhard Hirsch; the Pontificia Accademia; the Soprintendenza Archeologica per i Beni Culturali della Sicilia; the Museo Archeologico Nazionale of Aquileia; the Musei Apostolici Vaticani; the Museo della Civiltà Romana, Roma; the Museo Archeologico Nazionale di Villa Giulia, Roma; the Museo of Palazzo Altems, Roma; the Museo Archeologico of Chiusi; the Museo of the Cattedrale, Chiusi; the Museo Archeologico Nazionale of Palestrina; the Museo Archeologico Nazionale of Umbria, Perugia; the Museo Nazionale of the Alto Medioevo, Crecchio; the Museo Archeologico Nazionale of Napoli; the Pompei Antiquarium; the Museo Archeologico Nazionale of Reggio Calabria; the Museo Provinciale of Catanzaro; the Historijski muzej Bosne i Hercegovine, Sarajevo; the Iron Gates Museum of Kladovo; the National Museum of Beograd; the Vojvodina Museum, Novi Sad; the Narodni Muzej of Ljubljana; the Muzej Slavonije of Osijek; the Muzej Brodskog Posavlja, Slavonski Brod; the Split Archaeological Museum; the Archaeological Museum of Dyrrachium (Durrës, Albania); the Benaki Museum, Athens; the Narodni Muzej, Bitola; the Archaeological Museum of Plovdiv; the Varna Archaeological Museum; the Archeological Museum of Novae; the Topči Museum, Razgrad; the Stara Zagora Regional Historical Museum; the Sofia National Historical Museum; the Natsionalen arheologicheski muzey of Sofia; the Silistra Local Historical Museum; the Regionalen Istoricheski Muzej, Pernik; the archaeological Museum of Pleven; Lovec, Istoritcheski Muzej; the Museum Freiburg im Breisgau, für Ur- und Frühgeschichte; the Odessa Archaeological Museum; the Hermitage Museum; the Muzeul National de Istorie a României, Bucharest; the Antická Gerulata of Rusovce; the Muzeul de Istorie, Turda; the Muzeul Naţional Brukenthal of Sibiu; Muzeul Ţării Făgăraşului Cincşor; the Muzeul de Istorie Naţională şi Arheologie, Constanţa; the Aiud Muzeul de Istorie; the Muzeul National de Istorie a Transilvaniei, Cluj-Napoca; the Muzeul National al Unirii, Alba Iulia; the Národní Muzeum of Praha; the Bâcs-Kiskun megyei müzeum of Kecskemét; the Aquincumi Múzeum, Budapest; the Magyar Nemzeti Mûzeum, Budapest; the Visegrad Matyas Kiräly Müzeum; the Kuny Domokos

Museum at Tata Castle; the National Archaeological Museum, Warsaw; the Slovenské Národné Museum, Bratislava; the Musée Fenaille of Rodez; the Musée Lapidaire de Narbonne; the Musée Dauphinois, Grenoble; the Musée archéologie nationale of Saint-Germain-en-Laye; the Musée de Vieux-la-Romaine; the Musée de la ville, Haguenau; the Musée Rolin, Autun; the Musée Archéologique of Strasbourg; the Museum of the Louvre, Paris; the British Museum, London; the Providence Academy, Plymouth; the Castle Museum of Norwich; the Peterborough Museum; the Omnium Museum, Cirencester; the Arbeia Roman Fort Museum; the Vindolanda Museum; the Abbey of Hexham; Leicestershire County Council; the National Museum of Scotland, Edinburgh; the National Museum of Wales, Cardiff; the Museo Arqueológico de Granada; the Museo de Arte Romano, Merida; the Museo Arqueológico Nacional of Madrid; the Musée National d'Histoire et d'Art of Luxembourg; the Musée du Cinquantenaire, Brüssel; the Rijksmuseum van Oudheden, Leiden; the Rotterdam Bureau Oudheidkundig Onderzoek; the Valkhof-Kam museum of Nijmegen; the Gemeentelijk Oudheidkundig Museum, Heerlen; the Utrecht Museum; the Kopenhagen Nationalmuseum; the Schleswig-Holsteinisches Landesmuseum für Vorgeschichte; the Museum für Ur- und Frühgeschichte Freiburg of Breisgau,; the Archäologische Staatssammlung München; the Staatliche Antike Sammlung and Glyptotheke Anschrift, München; the Württembergisches Landesmuseum, Stuttgart; the Mainz Römisch-Germanisches Zentralmuseum; the Mittelrheinisches Landesmuseum, Mainz; the Pergamon Museum, Berlin; the Deutsches Historisches Museum, Berlin; the Antikensammlung, Berlin; the Osnabrück Museum und Park Kalkriese; the Museum der Stadt of Regensburg; the Museum of Neuburg an der Donau; the Deutsches National Museum, Nurnberg; the Furstlich Hohenzollernsches Museum, Sigmaringen; the Römisch-Germanisches Museum, Köln; the Museumszentrum Burg Linn, Krefeld; the Bonn Rheinisches Landesmuseum; the Hessisches Landesmuseum of Darmstadt; the Brandenburgisches Landesamt für Denmalpflege und Arch. Landesmuseum of Wünsdorf; the Museumszentrum Burg Linn of Krefeld; der Stadt Museum, Regensburg; the Historisches Museum der Pfalz, Speyer; the Gäubodenmuseum of Straubing; the Museum of Ingolstadt; the Mittelrhein Museum of Koblenz; the Römermuseum of Augsburg; the Aschberg, Dillingen Museum; the Stadsmuseum of Woerden; the Limesmuseum Aalen; the Frankfurt, Museum für Vor- und Frühgeschichte; the Museum of Weißenburg, the Enns Museum; the Augustiner Chorherrenstift of Herzogenburg; the Landesmuseum für Vorgeschichte, Halle; the Eichstätt, Museum; the Schlossmuseum of Aschaffenburg; the Museum Hermagor; the Antikensammlung of Kunsthistorisches Museum, Vienna; the Vienna Österreichisches Archäologisches Institut; the Museum Carnuntinum; the Saalburg Museum; the Schweizerisches Nationalmuseum, Zurich; the Archaeological Museum in Istanbul; the Adana archaeological Museum; the Mardin Archaeological Museum; the Khutaya Archaeological Museum; the Gaziantep Glass Museum; the National Museum, Jerusalem; the National Museum of Damascus; the Musée Archéologique of Rabat; the Musée National des Antiquités, Alger; the Sabratha Archaeological Museum; Dr Jorge António (Município de Alter do Chão).

Introduction

Nowadays the interest of military historians and enthusiasts in the reconstruction of Roman arms and armour, and in the daily life of the Roman soldier, is very high. Recent archaeological excavations related to the military equipment of the Roman Empire have revealed a large amount of precious artefacts, often decorated with gold and silver: helmets, pieces of armour, shin guards, military decorations and horse harness.

The militarisation of Roman society was a inevitable consequence of the historical heritage derived from the training and development of the Roman community. Among the ancient nations such a level of involvement of citizens in military activity can perhaps be found only in Sparta, although one should not underestimate the influence the Romans received from Italic peoples such as the Samnites, whose military caste, characterised by a strong hierarchy, may even show similarities to those of the Indian Rajputs and the Japanese Samurai.

The Romans always considered the profession of arms as a necessary part of the education and instruction of every Roman citizen and always gave a big boost to military exercises. The military tradition of the Roman people in arms even survived into the Middle Ages, when the Roman state in the East continued as Byzantium.

The national and social importance of this tradition was also reflected in the decoration of arms, which were characterised by elements of religious and mythological significance, also reflecting the status of membership, wealth, prestige and the glory of the *gens*, of the *exercitus* and finally of the *Res Publica*. From the beginning of Roman history, military service was associated with the display of pride and virtue, also represented by the splendour of arms and equipment.

Particularly after the reforms of Marius, towards the end of the second century BC, when the ranks of the army were filled mainly by volunteers and a career in the army became a lucrative profession, the *miles pompaticus* (the soldier dressed for the Triumph) became the expression of the strength and power of the *Imperium* of the *Res Publica* and of the ambitious generals. This aspect was even more pronounced under Augustus, where the principle of voluntary recruitment – after further reforms of the Roman military occurred during the turbulent years of the end of the Consular Age – definitively transformed the army into a professional war machine. Higher pay and better standards of living were also reflected in weapons and their decoration. The soldiers invested their higher wages and benefits in their equipment and clothing, or decorated weapons were special gifts or imperial benefits. Plebeians and provincial representatives of the local nobility, princes or foreign refugees, and barbarian chiefs – no one escaped the desire to excel during the difficult challenges posed by the wars of the Empire, also using different kind of weapons that show to all, in battle and on parade, their status as members of a warrior elite.

The trainings, the entertainments, the martial races between horsemen on the Field of Mars and in all the training grounds in both camp and cities became opportunities for the legionaries to display weapons and armour of incomparable splendour and at the same time demonstrate the power and the glory of the Empire to their barbarian enemies. The military aesthetic became art and found its expression either on the monuments erected to celebrate the victories of the Empire, in the small gravestones and reliefs depicting soldiers, or in the production of weapons that fulfilled a double function, both aesthetic and practical. Military equipment became 'parade dress' and 'parade equipment' became an integral part of military life, even on the battlefield. This happened throughout the Empire, even in remote garrisons, which often give us the most beautiful examples of this armament. The artistic monuments – reflecting the splendour of such equipment – were far from being merely conventional, but portrayed the *milites* in their best 'military accoutrements'.

This aspect of the military life of Ancient Rome had a much more important role than that played by the decoration of weapons in modern armies. First, the decoration or the use of different weapons and special items helped to differentiate the units within the Roman army, the various ranks of the commanders and individual personalities: the ancient world gave the warrior great personal freedom in the choice of his individual equipment, the purchase of his personal weapons and armour and also – for those who had the opportunity – in the use of weapons of higher quality (than those mass-produced by the State *fabricae*), made with the use of precious metals, or at a higher cost. It should be remembered that the troops marched in close formation not only on parade but also on the battlefield, where several pieces of equipment, signs and colours could help to distinguish different units. The decoration of helmets, for instance, was a factor of this kind: for example, the *Legio Alaudae* created by Caesar, which had received its name from the characteristic twin feathers attached to the side of its helmets, or the regiment of the *Cornuti Seniores Auxilia Palatina* of Constantine the Great, recognisable by the feathers or horns on the front of their helmets. These details, among many others, helped to distinguish the troops on the battlefield and this – at a time when the concept of uniform did not exist – served the function of modern uniforms. It is perhaps no exaggeration to say that, for the warrior of antiquity, the beauty and decoration of arms was equivalent to, in modern semantics, the concept of uniform for modern armies. For example, commanders and officers could be recognised by parts of their equipment that differed from those of the rank and file (it is enough remember the silver helmets of the centurions with their particular transverse crest) and also for the richness of their decoration and their equipment. Secondly, the decorated weapons and armour, as well as the decorations worn in battle (*dona militaria*) were symbols showing the merit and high military status enjoyed by the owner. This should not only be evident in respect of his fellow soldiers, but – according to the mentality of the ancient world – was even more essential in battle when the Roman soldier, in the melee and in the various actions of war, was face to face with the enemy: it was therefore important to demonstrate to their opponents who they were dealing with, inspiring fear with the wealth and splendour of the equipment, thus demonstrating its superiority. This means that the decoration of weapons and their cost, without detracting from their functional quality, acquired a symbolic value and had a strong psychological impact on the battlefield, as in all warlike civilisations.

The decoration of arms thus became part of one of the highest artistic expressions of the Roman world, because its principles became an indissoluble element of taste, without losing their practical function. This was also married with one other great feature of Roman society, its predilection for mass military events, like the triumphs and the gladiatorial games. In the Roman world the appreciation the art of war and military ceremonies was not only the prerogative of a small minority: the taste for war contributed to the institutionalisation and to the creation of equipment and dress made for parades and trophies, and which was also used to perform some ceremonial aspects of military operations and their connected rituals.

The army, in addition to its daily routine tasks in peace and in war, exercised a propaganda function with its traditional military ceremonies held on different occasions: the payment of the troops, the distributing of rewards and gifts, the reviewing of the legions, the performance of sacred ceremonies in honour of the deities, the tournaments of chivalry, the parades and the triumphal processions. It was a visual embodiment which marked the transition from everyday to solemnity. The involvement of different degrees and types of people – mere spectators, army, civilian and religious authorities – in the military spectacles required a considerable coherence and capacity in a specific organisation. Costly public ceremonies had as a principal objective to demonstrate the greatness of Rome and the invincible force of its army to both subjects and citizens.

These factors were an essential part of military life. These solemn ceremonies, which gave an impression of battle array, represented the highlight of this spectacular idea: the marching of the troops, the glitter of the banners and the shine of the armour and weapons, the wealth and the decoration of the different equipment showed that the army was synonymous with the celebration of the warrior spirit of the people, an expression of cohesive discipline of the armed community which personified the power and glory of the *Res Publica*. It was an exceptional show to see and to hear: the marching troops, the raucous sound of *tubae* and *cornua*, the signals given by the flags and the *signa*, the shine and splendour of weapons and armour, the eagles of the legions gleaming in the sun, the sparkle of the signs of the various divisions and sub-divisions of the army and the waving of flags and bronze-headed dragons with silk bodies, the decoration of armour, the weapons painted in vivid colours and the *tabulae pictae* representing the army's deeds, the gleaming helmets of cavalrymen and their officers: all this was part of an unprecedented choreography of strength and power, designed to impress the onlookers, whether they were citizens or guests and foreign ambassadors. To all this was added the neighing of splendidly caparisoned horses, the sound of military footsteps led by experienced soldiers whose hobnailed *caligae* and *calcei* crunched ominously on the paved squares and streets of cities, or on the clay of fields of Mars. Here, in these parades, stood painted and decorated statues of the gods, who gave the ceremony a further dimension of the religious piety of the Roman state.

This combined study should provide a fairly complete representation of military objects considered here and commonly called 'parade' items. The purpose of this work is not only, however, to merely collect an near-complete catalogue of drawings, photographs and iconography of these objects – as well as those now preserved in museums and public collections or those in private collections around the world – to offer students, enthusiasts and scholars. An attempt will also be made in an original way to solve a number of technical problems such as the identification, the nature and evolution of face-mask helmets and their use on the battlefield, as well as the techniques of production of individual pieces of equipment. The armament of the *miles pompaticus*, that of the soldier of the Roman army equipped with the best and most beautiful weapons, is studied here in a whole new perspective, which contends that, in the history of arms and armies, it is necessary not only to analyse the archaeological data and the narrow context in which they were used, but also the mental and ideological structure of those who employed the objects that we find in excavations. Then you may find that the theory of the use of the term 'parade' for high-status weapons does not correspond to the truth at all and that such weapons were used not only in the triumphant ceremonies and inside the so-called *Hyppika Gymnasia* or in other martial games and parades, but also on the battlefield. We hope that this work is the starting point for the development of the study of this part of Roman armament in new directions and at the same time could be useful to scholars of classical culture as well as to students of military science. The study of the ancient sources must be joined today by the need to address this issue by an archaeological survey of the ancient monuments and artefacts that must be conducted with rigorous analysis and special methods, in order to make a reliable interpretation of the artefacts given to us by archaeology, a parallel and equally reliable and accurate reading of the monuments and images of soldiers and weapons represented on the tombstones, memorial pillars, arches, coins, sarcophagi and other funerary monuments is also necessary. It is clear that this analysis is often faced with specific difficulties and problems – often caused by bias owning to a flawed vision of roman art by certain scholars – that result in continuous debate among specialists who study roman weaponry. These discussions are intended to clarify, sometimes with success, the real identity of a item like a functional weapon, the characteristics of a particular type of weaponry and its use, its evolution in the general military-technical evolution of human history, under the influence of specific historical conditions and the demands of war, or under the influence of the fashions of the time to which they belong or that of the nations from which they were borrowed. From these discussions and investigations valuable results may emerge for the archaeological investigations that may also change stereotyped views of Roman culture.

Our analysis therefore will move for each chapter on different areas: the analysis of individual pieces of equipment through the publication of photographs or drawings (including some very rare ones), findings and the analysis of their iconographic representation, and the study of written sources about them. Furthermore, in addition to the necessary catalogue which will accompany the text, this study will also be supplemented, where necessary, with diagrams, maps and tables. Finally, nineteen colour plates by specialised artists will try to recreate a picturesque rundown of some possible models of *milites pompatici* in their most splendid equipment, in peace and in war.

The book was originally conceived as an English version of A. E. Negin's book *Roman Ceremonial and Tournament Armament* published in Russian in 2010. However, this work examined only the Roman armour of the Principate which is usually identified with parade and tournament armament (the latter being used for *hippika gymnasia*). Subsequently, however, we decided to expand the material by extending the time frame and covering the evolution of decorated armour throughout the history of Ancient Rome. With this approach, along with the parade and tournament armour, the book covers all known examples of decorated armament which could also be used in battle. It is often impossible to unambiguously interpret a given piece as a purely ceremonial one, so this definition is not included in the title of the book. Throughout the book, we will discuss the criteria to be used to attribute a particular item to the parade armour, but while in general the book deals with the evolution of all decorated Roman armour, it will focus mainly on armour, shields and helmets.

The book was written jointly by two authors. However, this does not mean the authors implicitly agree with all each other's hypotheses and interpretations. In some cases, the reader will see such a divergence of views in comments and footnotes. This is not accidental. The authors did not combine their efforts while working on the text and each of them was entirely free in his investigations while writing a certain part of the book. The part of the book, which describes the time of the Principate and deals, for the most part, with so-called tournament armour (for *hippika gymnasia*), is based on the text of the book published in Russia, which will be totally unfamiliar to an English-speaking reader. This text was significantly reworked and supplemented based on new archaeological finds. Thus, the reader is enabled to see the history of decorated armour throughout the whole history of Ancient Rome.

Andrey Negin
Raffaele D'Amato

1

DECORATED ARMOUR IN THE AGE OF THE KINGS

(753–509 BC)

THE ARMAMENT OF THE EARLY ROMAN WARRIOR

The panoply of the warrior of the Age of Romulus, as well as of the warriors of the Age of the Kings, was usually the military accoutrements of the European late Bronze Age warrior, but was sometimes of very elaborate pattern. Basically the defensive armament of the elite warrior, the aristocratic leader of a tribal contingent or of a warrior band, was composed of a shield, a helm and armour, the offensive of a spear and a sword. However, it was in the protective equipment that the Romans, under the influence of their neighbours, begin to apply particular care in the lavish decoration of their panoplies, linked with the sacred symbols of their primitive religion.

THE SHIELD

The shield or *scutum* was in use from the days of Romulus and according to Plutarch the first king of Rome replaced the bronze Argive shield (*aspis* or *clipeus*) with the Sabine shield or *thyréos* (Greek name for the *scutum*[1]), i.e. a bigger shield. On the other hand, Diodorus Siculus presented the *thyréos* as the first Roman shield. It is however very difficult to know if Plutarch saw with his own eyes ancient bronze shields in the *sacrarium* of Romulus and, considering the Roman shields of his own age, wished to attribute to Romulus the much more famous *scutum* or *thyréos*.[2] According to Dionysius[3] the *clipeus* was a copy of the Argive *aspis* and existed from the time of Romulus.

Contemporary bronze figurines[4] and decorative figures of warriors, in metal foil applied on fabric,[5] show how during the period of the early kings shield decorations were of Villanovan style. The bronze Argive shield mentioned by Plutarch should therefore be understood to be the extensively embossed and decorated shields of the Villanovan Age, of which Rome has provided some examples.

These defensive items, probably manufactured in Etruria, most likely in Tarquinii, were used both for ceremonial purposes and in battle[6] In ancient times

1

FIG. 1. Bronze shield from Corneto, identical to that from Esquiline grave 94, eighth century BC. (After Pinza, 1905, fig. 62)

so-called 'parade' equipment in reality displayed the wealth and power of the wearer to the enemy and moreover the practical purpose of the weapon always took precedence over any ceremonial use. Depictions of fighting warriors and deities from the Villanovan period also attest to the use of these shields in battle, without compromising their importance as signs of social status.[7]

These shields, as shown by the specimens found in *Tarquinia* (*Tomba del Guerriero*) and Verrucchio, were lined with leather.[8] This fact, as already emphasised by Saultner,[9] is further proof that the long-held opinion that shields made from bronze sheets would have been, as were some helmets, just parade items and not intended for practical use in action, was wrong. The presence of leather (or some other organic perishable fabric) under the bronze sheet to absorb the impact of blows shows the shield was meant to be used in hand-to-hand combat.[10] However, most modern scholars have tended to emphasise the purely ornamental function of such items, on the basis that, in some finds, the delicacy of the heavily-ornamented shield's bronze sheet is proof of its exclusively ceremonial use. Other scholars support the thesis that these shields were solely employed as decorative objects, considering that some of them, in the

FIG. 2. Bronze helmet from Rome, Esquiline grave 94, eighth century BC. (After Pinza, 1905, tav. XI, 11)

Villanovan-Etruscan milieu, were hung on the walls of graves.[11] Of course we cannot exclude an ornamental function for the shields placed – during the Orientalizing Period – in female graves (e.g. grave 70 of Laurentina or grave 17 of Pitino, near San Severino Marche). But this does not exclude the possibility that these shields could have been used in battle and then used to ornament the grave of a high-ranking woman, perhaps the wife of a prominent warlord.[12] In any case, for most ancient graves, especially those of warriors, this interpretation is rejected. In Iron Age Etruria, the graves of eminent persons are usually characterised by full panoply, comprising functional defensive as well as offensive weapons:[13] so there is not reason to exclude the possibility that these bronze shields also had a military use. In the passage from the earlier to the so-called Orientalising period, the military elements of some funerary contexts seems no more functional, so they have been interpreted as parade items by some authors, especially the helmets and the shields covered with bronze sheets, placed in the graves of South Etruria, on whose borders Rome lies.

In considering this point, we must remember that social evolution differed between northern and southern Etruria in precisely this Orientalising period, in aspects of social life associated with weapons: hunting, training, symposium.[14] These differences are visible also in the deposition of the weapons in graves: while in Northern Etruria the combination of weapons seems to mirror effective uses, in South Etruria and in Rome the weapons are rare, if not entirely absent, in some graves. In this singular situation, indeed, the wealth of the armament would have been only intended to legitimise the socio-economic hierarchy within the group.[15] However, this prestige would have not been of a value reflected outside the group, if we accept the theory that the Villanovan community would have brought into battle simple weapons of offense, or were only wearing modest garments made of perishable materials and devoid of metal components. Recent studies have shown how this metal protection was perfectly suited for battle,[16] although only the wealthiest men could afford the full panoply (helmet, shield, breastplate) fashioned from beaten bronze and with embossed decoration.[17]

Further support for the thesis that the bronze-sheet shields were used in actual combat is that it would not have been in the mentality of the ancients merely to use costly and beautiful weapons *domi* and not *bellique*, i.e. only during feasts or religious ceremonies in time of peace. Such weapons were also worn in wartime, to show the power and wealth of the wearer and of his community.[18]

The display on the battlefield and especially before of the enemy of symbols of wealth received originally also had a tribal collective value: the demonstration of well-being throughout the village, indicating its importance. Examples of this were the famous Roman bronze *ancilia* shields, derived from a model 'fallen' from heaven and preserved by the college of the Salii.[19] They were considered a collective treasure of particular religious value and as objects of fundamental importance for the entire community.

This Villanovan shield was formed of thin sheets of laminated bronze, decorated with repoussè ornamentation, fixed over, as in the Achaean and archaic Greek shields, with a padding of hardened leather or wood, all materials which generally perished over time.[20] Virgil, describing the archaic bronze Latin shields, speaks of a lining of seven layers of leather.[21] The bronze surface of the shield, whose structure recalled the Argive one, was embossed with geometrical patterns and figures.[22] The grip was riveted in the centre, with the rivets set in a decorative pattern on the front of the shield. To carry the shield on the march or when using two-handed weapons, four or five rings were attached for ropes or straps.[23] Bronze staples were fixed to these rings to produce noise, with the deliberate intention of causing a psychological impact upon the enemy.[24]

The Esquiline tombs[25] have furnished some splendid specimens of these round bronze round shields, some about 61cm in diameter, but another much larger. The Esquiline specimen of grave 94 was recovered in 118 fragments (fig. 1). It was a disc-shaped shield of bronze foil, decorated with dots and geometrical circles:[26] twenty-one of its fragments, when assembled, were clearly identified as belonging to the rim of the shield, showing as a part of the bronze foil was folded around a circle of iron, to confer on the whole structure the necessary resistance and stiffness.[27] This again is evidence against the often-proposed thesis that such shields were only used for parade purposes. Measuring the edges of each of these twenty-one fragments, you get a total length of 97cm: but since there are not even two such fragments that exactly match each other, it must be inferred that the circumference of the shield was much greater than the other Roman shields of the period that have been found.[28]

Indeed the curvature of the larger fragments suggest a diameter greater than a metre. Considering the miserable state to which the repoussé foil was reduced, all shattered, it was hard then and still difficult today to completely reconstruct the original decoration.[29]

For sure, it is possible to see a continuous embossed circle turned around the edge of the shield, followed by a second one of well-embossed buttons, then by a further concentric circle similar to the first. Other fragments make clear that this decoration did not stop at the edge of the shield: rather, towards the middle of the disk continuous lines were sometimes replaced by others of embossed dots,

FIG. 3. Proto-Corinthian helmet, from Lake Nemi, seventh century BC, Museum of the Nemi Ships. (Photo by A. E. Negin)

alternating with the bossed ones.[30] Some fragments, with pendants attached,[31] show straight continuous areas alternating with other areas filled with bosses, arranged usually with ones near the others. These areas were not probably part of the decoration of the central part of the shield but most probably parts of bronze sheets added to the inner surface of the shield.[32] Finally a fragment bears a stud impressed by punching, surrounded by concentric circles. As we will see, this decorative technique is typical of the Roman archaic period and corresponds with the pectoral found in graves 86 (fig. 4) and 14.[33]

FIG. 4. Fragments of bronze pectoral from Rome, Esquiline grave 86, eighth century BC. (After Pinza, 1905, tav. XV, 9)

The bronze pendants attached to the aforementioned fragments acted as staples. They were realized by melting them into a matrix or mould, closed by another piece having a flat surface.[34] The staples were decorated in relief on one side, left flat and smooth on the other. In total the Esquiline shield revealed six staples, some of them oxidized but attached together through their flat surface and some others welded to the sheet fragments of the shield.[35] Their position made clear that the decorated surface was mounted so as to adhere to the internal side of the shield's lamina. Similar shields, and particularly the one found in Corneto, show what was the original position of these staples: arranged in pairs they had to hang from rods or strips nailed to the inside of the shield, so as to serve their function which was not just ornamental.[36] So, considering that two of the staples were attached together through their flat faces, you can see that they were precisely matched in a way that, thanks to the movement of the shield, they could produce the martial clatter described above.

The proper bronze Argive *aspis* (Plate 3) was widely used in early Roman times starting from the Etruscan age and more properly from the early seventh century.[37] It was suitable to protect the hoplite fighting in phalanx and its lavishly decoration and ornament was copied in its entirety by the Etruscans. According to Servius this *clipeus* was made of ox leather and covered with bronze, carried on the left arm and was heavy.[38] Its dimensions varied from 1m to 80cm in diameter. Also the Roman phalanx, like the Greek one, decorated its round shields with lavishly-painted designs.[39] Livy offers no evidence for any standard blazon (*episemata*) used by the Romans, but we can suppose that the five totemic animals, represented also on *signa* (standards), were possibly used as shield devices: the eagle, the bull, the boar, the horse and, naturally, the she-wolf. In addition the inside of the *clipeus* was also lavishly decorated, as can be seen in a painted figurine from the Equiline hill (Plate 3).[40] Here the shield is painted on the inner side in dark violet, whereas the ropes for the suspension are coloured with geometrical chequered patterns in white, black and violet.

FIG. 5. (opposite) Helmet and cuirass from the tomb of the warrior in Lanuvium, turn of sixth–fifth century BC, Rome, Museo Nazionale Romano – Baths of Diocletian. (Photo by A. E. Negin)

THE HELMET

In his erudite *Origines*[41] Isidorus attests how in the earlier period the term *cassis* designated the metal helmet and *galea* the leather one; the former was a word of Etruscan origin whilst the latter derived from the term *galerus* or leather cap, derived from animal skins (*galeritus*):[42] such an explanation is confirmed by Varro.[43]

The metal helmet was common since the early Iron Age and was perhaps of Achaean origin. The excavations of Villanovan Rome have revealed to us a simple 'pot' helmet and a 'calotte' helmet, found in graves and huts of the Romulean period, or slightly later (eighth–seventh century BC)[44] (fig. 2). The 'pot' or 'bell' helmet, found as early as in an eighth-century coffer grave (*ad arca*) from the Esquiline and other graves,[45] was made of a bronze single-piece skull, while later Italic variants were fashioned from jointed plates.[46] Its skull was somewhat spherical and with a flared rim: this, in some Etruscan and Italic specimens, was riveted for strength.[47] The smooth surface of these kinds of helmet was intended to deflect blows. The 'calotte' helmets[48] from Rome appear to be variants of a similar helmet from Montegiorgio Piceno and from Montelparo (ex Zschille collection).[49] Some of them, like the helmet found in the Necropolis of Tolentinum, were decorated with rich engraving.

These practical helmets were probably furnished with a leather chinstrap, even though, a similar *galea*, found in the *Tomba del Duce* at Vetulonia,[50] dated in the first half of the seventh century, still had the remains of what was probably a bronze cheek-piece. As with the specimen from Vetulonia, the Roman helmet has two small bronze bosses on the skull.

The simple shape of these helmets does not exclude their decoration, mainly provided by the huge crest on top of them, which can be seen in contemporary Etruscan and Italic representations.[51] The helmets originally had a plumed crest, sometimes attached directly to the calotte (in the simple 'pot' helmet), or sometimes inserted in a metal crest holder.[52] The horsehair plume, in the Ancona, Vetulonia and Montegiorgio Piceno variants, was fixed among the two halves riveted onto the helmet's top:[53] the function of the huge crest was the intimidation of the enemy, by the increased height it gave to the wearer.[54]

Certainly, other helmets of the Villanovian type were in use after the eighth century BC. In the 'Certosa situla', Paleo-Venetians warriors of the sixth century BC are marching with different kinds of helmets, among them the 'pot' type furnished with a high crest.[55] New types of helmets were in the meantime introduced both from Etruria and *Magna Graecia*.

From the sacred area around the lake of Nemi, where slave-champions disputed the title of 'King of the Forest' (*Rex Nemorensis*),[56] one of the most ancient examples of proto-Corinthian helmets found on the Italic Peninsula has been recovered, which can be dated to the beginning of the seventh century BC (fig. 3). When used such helmets were brightly polished and very often, according to the Italiote costume, they were decorated with a fake horsehair beard attached to the lining (Plate 2). Such half-cultic aspects exaggerated the terrible appearance of the warrior, similar to the God of War.[57] At that time, the confrontation between Rome and Alba Longa (echoed in the legendary duel between *Oratii* and *Curiatii*) was at its peak and the Etruscan influence on the military accoutrements of the warriors of ancient Latium was increasing.

In the Servian age the Roman hoplite was protected by helmets of Greek type (Plate 3).[58] We cannot confirm if during the early period the Romans used the true Corinthian helmet, which is otherwise well attested in Southern Etruria and typical of the hoplite armies,[59] although the terracotta figures from Roman temples seem to suggest that this was the case.[60]Moreover, Corinthian helmets were used in Tarquinii, birthplace of the last Kings of Rome.[61]

We are, however more certain about the use of the so-called Etrusco-Corinthian or Apulo-Corinthian type, a lighter version of the Corinthian helmet used by Greeks, Etruscan and South Italic warriors.[62] The Etrusco-Corinthian type made its appearance early on the Attic vases of the sixth–fifth centuries BC, throughout Central Italy.[63] It is depicted also on figurines from Veii.[64] It was worn on the back of the head rather than covering the face, like the Corinthian specimens painted on Attic pottery.[65]

A splendid specimen of type E has survived from Vulci[66] and is preserved in the British Museum. Its eye-sockets, brows and nasal piece appear rather stylised. Sometimes a horizontal neck-guard was present whilst often the skull was decorated with incised figures.[67] This 'face-type' design was destined to be developed until the Late Imperial Age, in a merely ornamental way (figs 83, 175, 267, 268). Probably the fact that the representations of Mars and Minerva in Latium and in Etruria, as well as in South Italy, often show these gods wearing this type of helmet, could link its use to the invocation of divine protection.[68]

The crest or *crista* of the helmets was composed of feathers and a horse tail, being probably of Achaean origin: an example comes from painted fictile plaques from Palestrina. In the contemporary written regulations we do not find any description of such crests, but they are frequently depicted although these look rather stylised, making it difficult to make out any detail.[69] The plumes were possibly inserted by the stalk in a 'wooden box', while the 'bristle' horsehair was perhaps dressed up with grease. The horse tail would have hung free.[70] The regulations of Servius do not specify any colour for the crest but the hoplites from the Palestrina freeze show blonde horsehair crests with the upper part dyed red. The crest gave an imposing aspect to the hoplite[71] but it is unknown if it served as a badge of rank. However, the presence of a *crista transversa* on some helmets could suggest that, even in this early period, this kind of crest distinguished the officers. From the Age of the Kings, the presence of this particular plume placed transversally across the top of the helmet allows us to recognise the centurions in the iconography of ancient Etruscan-Roman art.[72]

Using a transversal crest to distinguish the officers was probably a Greek invention. This traditional system had passed to the Romans already by the Age of the Kings', introduced by the Etruscans, who probably derived it from the Greek or Italiote armies, whose officers very often, like those of the Spartan army, wore such crests.[73] The system was introduced by the Etruscans, as a badge of rank for their centurions, probably before the Age of Servius Tullius and remained the main distinctive symbol of Roman centurions until at least the first century AD.[74]

A terracotta temple figure from Caere (Cerveteri) shows a white *crista transversa* edged in red.[75]This mask '*antefissa*' is dated to the sixth century BC; this could be indicative that the *crista transversa* was already used by the centurions at that time, which is also confirmed, for ancient Latium, by terracotta *antefissae* found in *Satricum* and *Ardea*. The kind of helmet is a very particular one, completely covering the face and having the skull shaped like the face of a horned Silenus.[76] The helmet represented in the *antefissa* corresponds perfectly with an original specimen once preserved in the Archaeological Museum of San Marino (today maybe in a private collection in Milan), which has also been dated to the sixth century BC (fig. 168).

This last specimen introduces the topic of the use of masked helmets in the Roman army.[77] One theory says that the Romans borrowed them from the Etruscans, who could have used them in their ceremonial gladiatorial games, but probably also in battle. Also Livy[78] says that the Romans derived their military competitions and games from the Etruscans. Petrikovits tried to link the invention of such helmets with their use by the young Patricians in the mounted game called *Lusus Troiae*, or with the Roman custom of manufacturing masks of their ancestors.[79]

THE BODY ARMOUR

In the pre-Servian age, in the Etruscan-Latin area of the early Iron Age, the standard protection for the warrior's body was the squared bronze breastplate typical of the so-called Villanovan age.[80] This kind of protection was conceptually similar to the cuirass-disc of many areas of south-central Italy. Some of these bronze pectorals have been discovered in the Esquiline graves.[81] The Roman examples, from the mid-eighth century BC, are rectangular in shape with sides that curve inwards,[82] about 23cm long and 19cm wide. It is possible that this kind of protection could be related to the *kardiophylax* described by Polybius,[83] since the dimensions are very similar. This protection, designed (as the Greek name attests) to protect the heart, was an innovation which appeared in the Villanovian culture in around 760–720 BC, more and less contemporary to the introduction of the large circular shield made of bronze sheets. They were worn with the long side running vertically.[84] Four holes were made in the shorter sides for the attachment of a leather backing and straps to keep the pectoral in place. In the Roman examples there is no trace of a second protective plate fixed on the back, as in some Etruscan ones.[85]

The Roman pectorals belong to Type B of such squared protections, according to the classifications of the De Marinis, and their ornamentation is very similar to most ancient pectorals from Monterozzi, to which they are close also in size, about 12cm x 16cm. However, the sides of the Roman ones are all convex.[86]

The pectorals were decorated with geometrical patterns on their edges, while the central square part was ornamented by five bosses. Some of them, like that from grave 14,[87] had very simple decoration.[88] The pectoral of grave 14 is trapezoidal with projecting sides and curved corners. It consists of a solid bronze plate, reinforced on the short sides with a plate of the same metal cut like a tape, applied below the lamina along the edge and fastened to it by a series of decorative rivets.[89] The cover tapes are smooth, but the plate is decorated and perforated at the edge and on the sides by holes all around, for the fastening of the leather lining and fixing it to the breast. Only a short section of this granulated decoration on the short sides is visible today, in which can also be noticed two more parallel beams at the edge, bounded by lines incised by diagonal and opposite hatches.[90] Within the frame of the pectoral the main ornament consists of five small circles or diskettes, one at the centre and the others towards the corners. Each of them is surrounded by two punched-in concentric circles.[91]

Much more decorated is the pectoral from grave 86 (fig. 4) (the one from grave 87, surviving only as eight fragments, was probably of the same type): this one is a rectangular bronze plate, with falling sides and rounded corners, but, differently from the one of grave 14, there are only three holes and these are on the short sides. The short sides are reinforced with a strip of foil riveted on the bottom.[92] The decoration of the breastplate consists of a band of three lines of dots alternated with bosses along the edge of the plate. At the corners four large bosses with three concentric circles all around each boss can be seen: the main boss in the centre is equally surrounded by three concentric circles and from another external one.[93] The pectoral is of a rhomboid shape, with ornate corners, 14cm wide in the middle and 19cm high. The pectoral of find group 98, although it survives only in a fragmentary state (21cm., so that it was possible only to reconstruct one of the short sides and other parts), was reinforced on the rim by a nailed sheet and the sides were decorated with a double row of bronze bosses through which runs a punched row of points.[94] Maybe such armour comes from the Aegean war pectorals of the Achaean warriors.[95] The luxurious defensive equipment of the priests of Mars, the *Salii*, probably reflected that of the first Patrician warbands.[96] The breastplate (*aeneum pectoris tegumentum*) that was the main protection of these warrior-priests recalls the squared specimens from the Esquiline.

The introduction of the Greek-Etruscan military system in Rome by Servius Tullius determined the adoption, at least for the Patrician warriors of the first class, of heavy hoplite armour.[97] In a later period the types of body armour developed into a real cuirass composed by front and back plates, possibly conceived by the Greek armourers in the prototype 'bell-shape' from Argos.

The belly-cuirass of the Argos[98] type, already known in the previous century, was now widely used by the warriors of the first and second class: this is not only attested by the artistic monuments, like the frieze of Palestrina, but also confirmed by actual specimens recovered in Etruria and Latium. The shape of this cuirass is without any doubt the distinctive feature of the Praeneste warriors: it would confirm that such *loricae* were not unknown in Rome. This armour was composed of two halves on which were incised stylised muscles, with a lower rim raised at the bottom to protect the abdomen.[99] These corselets reached just to the waist and were encircled on their lower rim by a rolled-forward edge, today sometimes called 'bell-shaped' or 'gutter-shaped'[100] These edges had the function of stopping sliding blows and protecting the groin and legs. A similar edge protected the neck like a gorget. The early types of the bell-shaped cuirass were almost smooth in their design.[101]

Like other, similar body armours this cuirass (γυαλοθωραξ) was composed of two plates (γυαλα)[102] fastened with pins, rings and straps. The original corselets of this kind from Latium and Southern Etruria, like those preserved in the Vatican Museum, show a fastening system composed of a full-length hinge complete with pin on the right-hand side and fastening buckles and straps on the left.[103] This bell-shaped cuirass also appears on many pottery paintings,[104] bronze figurines[105] and bucchero-reliefs:[106] possibly it was used by the warriors of the first class, kings, praetors, etc. As with many Greek specimens, this armour was sometimes lavishly painted or had painted decorations.[107] This is again confirmed by the Palestrina terracotta fragments and by other Etruscan friezes of same type,[108] where the outline of the muscles on the corselet is painted in violet-purple.[109]

The body-protection was sometimes completed by greaves, leg-guards and arm-guards. Leg-guards or *ocreae* (expressly mentioned by Livy) of the Etruscan style were made of copper-alloy.[110] The colour of ancient bronze differed according to the alloy of copper and tin which composed it.The greaves reproduced the embossed muscles of the lower legs and were put around the calves by bending the metal.[111] Their embossed parts were often true works of art, like an example preserved in the Villa Giulia Museum decorated with embossed lions' heads[112] on the knees.

All these pieces of armour were lined with leather and sponge (*spongia*), usually glued on, to prevent chafing.[113] Some archaeological specimens still preserve fragments of this lining. The high cost of the whole panoply could be borne only by the first-class Patricians.[114] An interesting account by Plutarch in his life of King Numa Pompilius tells us how in the early Rome there were guilds of joiners, goldsmiths, dyers, shoemakers and potters, but there was a shortage of weavers and in particularly of blacksmiths[115] It is possible too that the armours were imported from more advanced centres of Latium such as Veii, Tarquinii and Praeneste.[116]

The sixth-century terracotta relief from the Louvre,[117] showing Etruscan warriors clad in highly decorated leather armour could be an indication that this kind of armour was already used by the early Romans, at least at the time of the Etruscan Kings. The stela of Avile Tites, from Volterra, shows the warrior armed with spear and axe, clad in a tunic beneath a *lorica* with painted shoulder-guards.[118] We have further evidence for the employment in Rome of the Greek *linothorax*, although of Etruscan shape: the above-mentioned torso of a warrior, once part of a decorative complex of a temple on the Esquiline, shows the employment by the Roman hoplites of such armour exactly on the eve of the expulsion of the last king (Plate 3).[119] The armour is lavishly painted and decorated with stars in *terra di Siena* and blue, which adorned the shoulder-guards (*humeralia*) while the surface of the *thorax* shows a belt painted with the same colours, made of geometrical interlacing motifs. The decoration of the armour is typically Etruscan and evokes similar armour in the terracotta reliefs of South Etruria and Latium.[120]

THE GRAVE OF A *MAGISTER EQUITUM*: THE LANUVIUM TOMB.

The rank of *Magister Equitum* came from the Etruscan *Maghister* and possibly also from the *Tribunus Celerum*, the tribune leading the 300 cavalrymen created by

Romulus and called *Celeres*. In the hierarchy the *Magister* was a senator and was associated with the *Praetores*. He was entitled to all the insignia of the Supreme Command, such the *Sella Curulis* (or commander's chair), the *toga* with the purple border (*praetexta*) and the escort of six *lictores*.[121] Dio Cassius (an historian of the third century AD) gives him the officer's side-sword or *xiphos parazomnisthes*. In a warrior burial from Lanuvium (near Rome) dated to the turn of the sixth–fifth century BC – more precisely the period between 509 BC and 475 BC – a panoply rather similar to that of the first class mentioned by Livy was discovered.[122] Within the general run of Latium sixth–fifth century graves, the 'tomb of the warrior' from Lanuvium remains an exception. It stands out because, though modest and without grave goods, it contains the body of a military commander, buried with his arms and athletic equipment (discus, strigil, pouch for sand, alabaster flask) in a rough peperino sarcophagus.[123] The combination of military and athletic ideals points to a strong Greek influence, hardly surprising in those years in which the cult of the Dioscuri, after spreading throughout Latium, appeared even in Rome.

The warrior buried in the grave was laid to rest with a long spear for cavalry fighting (*hasta*), javelins (*veruta*), an axe (*securis*), a curved single-edged sword (*gladius*) of *machaira* type andremains of a leather belt, but particularly with a shining panoply, composed of a helmet, a muscled cuirass and remains of a shield (Plate 4; fig. 5).[124] The armour of Lanuvium armours a real masterpiece of Roman metalwork and shows the importance of the patrician officer who was buried in the grave. The axe, or *secures*, may be an insignia of rank.[125] The *Magister Equitum* deliberately had such rank derived directly from the Etruscan officers, who held the double-axe symbolising together with the *fasces lictorii* the power of life and death over their own men, called an *imperium*. This, together with the elements of horse harness (a bronze ring-shaped bit), could help the identification of the Lanuvium warrior as a cavalry commander of very high rank.[126]

The metal helmet found in the grave is one of the types most used from the sixth to the fourth century in Central Italy: the Negau type, which developed from a simple bowl. The type, conventionally known as Negau from the Balkan site where several specimens were found, followed the design of a globe-shaped skull narrowed at the base.[127] Sometimes it had a streamlined shape or was embossed with curls which strengthened it. A brim was always fixed to the lower rim (figs. 5, 34).[128] The Lanuvium helmet is of the Vetulonia variant of the Negau type, made of silver and gilded bronze and lacking cheek-guards. The pushed-forward skull was about 16cm in height and had charming eyes of gold and enamel (glass paste), encircled in silver and surmounted by stylised eye-brows.[129] The rim at the middle of the skull was decorated by smart dots, ovules and curls with a small leaf. The decoration of the helmet with its wide-open eyes perhaps was intended to terrify enemies and it corresponds with a similar helmet from Lombardy (fig. 34).[130] Remains of very small figurines also made of silver were recovered from the burial, but at the moment nothing can be said about their position on the skull. Clearly such a precious helmet was suitable for a high-ranking officer: a similar later Etruscan helmet of the Negau class, adds a fine bearded mask (fig. 167).[131]

The helmet had the lower rim decorated with embossed feathers, which represented a stylised laurel wreath. The presence of possible holders for real feathers on the sides was supposed because, when the helmet was recovered, some fragments of the leather lining were found in the holders: but a comparison with horned helmets of the Italic (fig. 54)[132] and Greek world suggests that metal *cornicula* were more likely. On the helmet's bowl two small figurines of sea dragons held the horsehair crest (*lophos*) in place. This feature[133] is visible on another very decorative Negau helmet, of Etruscan origin, found in Livorno but nowadays kept in Pisa (fig. 33) and on the above-mentioned helmet from Lombardia (fig. 34). Both the helmets from Lombardia and Pisa are dated to the turn of the sixth and fifth century BC. The helmet from Lanuvium, the only Roman one found until now, shows how as early as in the fifth century the Romans used the feathered diadem described by Polybius 250 years later:[134] the three black or purple feathers, however, were replaced here by the side horns. In our case it would be a variation for officers with a central horsehair crest. A rather similar crest can be on a middle-Republican coin of the Aquilia family, where the horns are instead replaced by two feathers: the two horns or the side feathers or *geminae pinnae* were sacred to Mars/Mamers, since according to the ancient religious beliefs, this god would have appeared with such ornaments on his helmet;[135] during the Late Consular Age such side-feathers were considered as military decorations and the soldiers who bore them were called *insigniti milites*.[136] According to an allusion in the *Aeneid*,[137] perhaps such *milites* fought under the protection of Mars. For the period of the Punic Wars, Silius Italicus gives a gilded crest to the consuls[138] (Plates 6 and 7) and to the God of the War himself.[139] We can still find such in use in the accounts of Arrian (a Roman officer and historian of the second century AD) of the yellow crests of the cavalry described as *xanthai* or blond. It has been claimed that the horsehair and the feathers would have been hard to dye, but Plutarch notes how in the Greek world of the third century BC it was a matter of routine for the women to dye their husbands' crests.[140]

Some fragments of leather still remain stitched to the holes of on the outer rim of the Lanuvium specimen. The inner lining of Roman helmets is a component that was little studied: it was vitally important in keeping the helmet in the right position on the head, particularly with huge crests.[141] For this reason the wide strap was tied under the chin: the Romans called it a *vinculum*.[142] The exact shape of such a lining can be gathered from contemporary pictorial representations: a famous first-century AD fresco from Pompeii, copied from earlier paintings, shows a coif with a chinstrap;[143] a Greek cup of the fifth century BC, depicting Achilles assisting Patroclus, shows a quilted version.[144] Aristoteles[145] recalled how sponge was used as an alternative, as attested by some Etruscan helmets of the fourth–third century BC which came to light at Vetulonia in the nineteenth century. The lining was also usually extended to the cheek pieces.[146]

Besides the splendid helmet the grave revealed a precious cuirass of the type probably prescribed by the Servian regulation for the first class. Such expensive armour was restricted to the wealthier soldiers or *milites*: other classes would have used other protective items or breastplates.[147] The Lanuvium armour is a later evolution of the types of body armour composed of front and back plates, possibly conceived by the Greek armourers from the 'bell-shaped' example from Argos. The two plates, representing in detail the muscles of the human torso and back, were fixed by narrow shoulder pieces (*humeralia*) 6cm wide, by means of very modern hinges which left the arms free; similar hinges were attached on both sides (fig. 5).[148] The corselet protected the groin as well as allowing the wearer to sit on horseback. A helpful lining (existing still today) was stitched inside the rims of the shoulder-guards whilst on the whole perimeter of the cuirass it was fixed by rivets on a copper strip.[149] This strip was also a form of decoration. The cuirass too was covered with gold leaf: it was probably intended in the Roman conception as a symbol of splendour since such plated body armour shone brightly and did not oxidize; as noted by Pliny the Elder, the gold was believed to be an element which did not suffer from fire or bad weather.[150]

In the Lanuvium panoply the belt curiously also acted as an element of protection, evoking the *mitra-Zosteres* of the archaic Greek panoply. Almost all the warriors of the Latium were equipped with a sword-belt which, beyond its practical purpose, signified military service or *militia*.[151] The Romans also had a such belt, but the specimen from Lanuvium was further fitted with a bronze mail 'apron' acting as protection for the genitals.[152]

MILITARY DECORATIONS

These awards (*dona militaria*), were the result of the Romans' high regard for military valour.[153] The poems tell how from the early times a sword belt decorated with golden studs or *bullae* was awarded.[154] Armlets or *armillae* were also known.[155] In the legend of Tarpeia there is an early mention of the Sabines,[156] who wore golden armlets on their left arm.

The whole ritual custom of the *dona militaria* was connected to religious practice.[157] The equipment and weapons taken from an enemy in battle, might have had profound significance if they were *spolia opima* or rich spoils. This Roman tradition dates back to such spoils taken by Romulus and divided into three classes: *prima, secunda* and *tertia*, which according to Festus were also classified by the laws of Numa Pompilius.[158] The *spolia opima prima* or first, was taken by a commander from an opponent of the same rank and dedicated to *Juppiter Feretrius*;[159] the *spolia secunda* was captured from an officer of lower rank and devoted to Mars; the *tertia* was taken from a private soldier and were sacred to the god Quirinus.

THE FIRST VICTORIES OF ROME AND THE ORIGIN OF THE TRIUMPHAL PROCESSION

We need to look at the primitive age of Rome in order to understand the origins of the solemn triumphal processions that were at the basis of the successive parades, where the soldiers wore gleaming ornamented armour and displayed their military decorations.[160] At the same time, we should emphasise that the origin of Roman ornamented military equipment is linked with the decorated equipment of their Trojan forefathers, i.e. with that of the Late Bronze Age.

Most sources describing the Roman triumphs and parades in the Age of the Kings belong to the post-Consular period.[161] This does not mean that these sources are unreliable, because authors like Livy or Plutarch may well have had access to iconograpnic and literary sources which are now no longer available. However, to reconstruct the triumph and the appearance of the *pompa* equipment in a such remote age in the history of Rome, we need to use the narrative sources[162] together with archaeological ones.[163]

The triumph had Etruscan roots and many Roman authors linked its details with Etruscan precedents. According to Plutarch, the first Roman triumph was celebrated on 1 March 753 BC over Acron, King of Cenina, who Romulus himself had killed in a regular duel between champions.[164] This ceremony had clear religious connections. Before the duel Romulus had promised the weapons of his enemy to *Juppiter Feretrius*[165] and the arms of Acron were displayed on the holy oak, where later the Romans built the first temple to *Juppiter Capitolinus* (fig. 6).[166] However, the description left by Plutarch[167] shows that already these earlier triumphs had elements of lavish dress and solemnity:

> Romulus, that he might perform his vow in the most acceptable manner to Jupiter and withal make the pomp of it delightful to the eye of the city, cut down a tall oak which he saw growing in the camp, which he trimmed to the shape of a trophy and fastened on it Acron's whole suit of armour disposed in proper form; then he himself, girding his clothes about him and crowning his head with a laurel garland, his hair gracefully flowing, carried the trophy resting erect upon his right shoulder and so marched on, singing songs of triumph and his whole army following after, the citizens all receiving him with acclamations of joy and wonder. The procession of this day was the origin and model of all after triumphs. This trophy was styled an offering to Jupiter Feretrius, from ferire, which in Latin is to smite; for Romulus prayed he might smite and overthrow his enemy; and the spoils were called *opima*, or royal spoils, says Varro, from their richness, which the word *opes* signifies.

Both Plutarch and Dionysius mention that Romulus brought to Rome as war booty from Cameria a precious chariot, dedicated to the God Vulcanus;[168] for the first time in the Roman history, according to Livy, the triumph was celebrated on a bronze four-horse-chariot,[169] although Plutarch ascribes the first triumph with a chariot to Tarquinius Priscus.[170]

What we can say with certainty is that, since the earliest days of Rome, a triumphal cortege was instituted where the Sovereign – the *triumphator* – passed through the Capitoline Hill wearing military trophies and dedicating the captured weaponry to the Temple of *Juppiter Feretrius*. If this was still performed on foot by the early Kings, by the time of the Etruscan Kings the winner went to the Capitoline Hill in a *quadriga* and performed sacrifices to Jupiter.[171]

FIG. 6. Romulus with *spolia*. Fresco from Pompeii, first century BC, Rome, copy of the Museum of the Civiltà Romana. (Photo by R. D'Amato)

It is interesting to link this event to the discovery, in the Esquiline grave 94, of the remains of a two-horse bronze war chariot, including the iron tyres and nails from the wheels. Most probably this chariot was very similar to the Vulci specimen, dated between 680 and 670 BC.[172] This chariot was built using elm and yew wood, lined with and covered by bronze sheets, fixed by means of iron rivets. The wheels of the Esquiline chariots were instead of wood covered by iron tyres and also the shaft and the sides were covered by a nailed-on iron structure.[173] At that age, the employment in war of these chariots from the aristocratic warriors, like the one to which the Esquiline grave belonged, was still possible.

A leather collar directly attached two horses to the shaft (*jugales* or shaft-horses) while the other two side-horses (*funales*) drew the chariot just by straps attached to the cab.[174] The wooden frame had a semicircular cab (*diphros* in Greek). A luxurious appearance was added sometimes by bronze plates of Eastern influence:[175] the painted plaque from Praeneste shows triumphal chariots painted light blue which would emphasise their sacred nature, indeed the Romans considered everything coloured light blue, or *caeruleus*, as synonymous with heavenly deities.[176] The wheels, rather big, gave greater height to the crew; the wheels were provided with iron rims and Lucretius Carus still remembers in the first century BC the noise the iron-shod wheels made on the roads.[177]

The cab was furnished with handles, because the wheels were attached to a rigid axle without any suspension.[178] The height of the horses found beside the sixth-century BC Etruscan chariot at Statonia (modern-day Castro) measured just 1.23m! The horses of the Vulci chariot probably measured only 1.20m.[179] The Romans called such small horses *mannuli.*

A true Roman chariot of the archaic age was found on the Appia Antica.[180] The chariot, found by archaeologists in the second half of the nineteenth century, was reconstructed again in modern times according to scientific techniques. The final result was a chariot very similar to the other specimen from Monteleone of Spoleto, which belonged to a Sabine warrior chief of 550 BC.[181] Probably also the Roman chariot originally had a rich bronze decoration on its surface, but sadly this is mainly lost. However, the covering of the cab was humbler than the luxurious Etruscan specimens and the leather covering the three-part framed railing was left visible and not covered by bronze sheets.[182]

RELIGIOUS AND MAGICAL ELEMENTS OF ARMS AND ARMOUR DECORATION: THE *SALII* AND THEIR CEREMONIAL ARMOUR

A particular panoply which evoked that of the ancient aristocratic warbands was that of the *Salii*. According to Livy, the college of priests dedicated to Mars was created by Numa Pompilius:[183] they wore a fine embroidered tunic (*tunica picta et insigne*), a bronze breastplate (*aeneum pectoris tegumentum*), conical headgear or *apex*, a purple cloak with scarlet bands and brooches (*tebenna hemporpemenos periporphyros*), a spear (*logché*) – or a staff (*rabdon*) – and a sword (*xiphos*).

The equipment described by Livy is largely that of a very rich aristocratic Villanovian warrior.[184] Dyonisius and Plutarch mention the *Salii* having conical

FIG. 7. Pectoral in copper and gold found in the Regolini-Galassi Tomb from Caere, Città del Vaticano, Museo Gregoriano. (Photo by R. D'Amato)

headgear or *apex* (possibly a *pilos* helmet of Greek type): Dr Sekunda has recently pointed out a specimen recovered in a late Republican context,[185] made of silver, presumably preserving the shape of the archaic helmet, which would have been in bronze or in leather with metal fittings and bosses. It is also possible that the original helmets of the *Salii* warriors were identical to the Villanovan Age bronze

19

FIG. 7a. Narce pectoral, last quarter of the eighth century BC, Etruscan Gallery of the University of Pennsylvania Museum. (Museum photo)

helmets furnished with knobs (*apex*), like the specimens found in Populonia, Tarquinii and Mantua.[186]

Under the helmet, to reduce the weight of it, or sometimes in substitution for the metal one, the *pilleus*[187] (from the Greek *Pilos*), a conical cap of felt, leather or wool, was worn. Helbig had proposed it among the attributes of the warbands of the *Salii*,[188] on the basis of the Corneto warrior grave.[189] Here, beside the bronze weapons, were found the fragments of a leather cap reinforced by bronze bosses.[190] The cap could be used both as military headgear and as a religious symbol, considering the evolution of the institution of the *Salii* from the original warbands devoted to Mar.[191] For the *Salii*, this kind of under-helmet was particularly colourful, as shown in later paintings.

The bronze breastplate could also be something different from the squared Villanovan pectoral: a breastplate in fine gold and copper from Narce (fig. 7a),[192] could be the possible answer (Plate 1). The armour is shaped like a 'poncho' and is composed of a front and back plate made in one piece, held by straps joining the plates under the arms. A similar armour in copper and gold was found in the Regolini-Galassi tomb from Caere[193] (fig. 7). Possibly such types derived from the gorgets worn by the arcaic Macedonian and Thracian warriors. A possible linen version of this type, maybe reinforced with metal elements, can be seen on the famous 'Warrior cup' of Mycenae.[194]

The most peculiar part of the equipment of the first *Salii* warrior bands, as well as of the priests who kept this name, was without any doubt the bronze[195] figure-eight shield, the *ancile*,[196] derived from Aegean types. Roman tradition, according to Plutarch and Dyonisios, said that such shields were first fashioned by the mythical craftsman Mamurius Veturius reproducing twelve mysterious objects which fell from the sky during the reign of Numa Pompilius.[197] Cornelian intaglios[198] and the account of Festus[199] give us the possible configuration of these shields: it was made of bronze and decorated with relief work on its surface. The sides of the shields were indented.[200]

These kind of shields belonged to a very old tradition of Roman and ancient Latium armament. Since the eleventh century BC the Latial period is marked by the appearance of miniature grave goods showing the military accoutrements of leading tribal figures.[201] A grave from Caesar's forum, dated to this period, has revealed a statuette of warrior with the attributes of his power: the sword, also in miniature and two pairs of double-shields or *ancile*, later symbol of the *Salii*. The political status of these leaders united religious and military symbols.[202] The miniature representing the shield shows it as two round embossed bronze shields connected together with a central fitting, i.e. the composite *ancile*. The original should have looked very impressive, covering all the warrior in shining bronze (pl. 1) and very similar to the figure-eight shields of the Achaeans.[203] We can link these shields with the presence of refugees from the Aegeum Sea, which can confirm the legend of the arrival of the Trojans.[204]

2

DECORATED ROMAN ARMOUR IN THE AGE OF THE CONSULS

(509–27 BC)

ETRUSCAN AND GREEK LUXURIOUS ARMOUR AND ITS INFLUENCE ON THE ROMAN ARMOUR TRADITION

Rome expanded its influence throughout Italy in the fourth century BC. This resulted in a change in the nature of warfare in the peninsula. Conflicts became larger and more protracted. Livy wrote: 'The history will now be occupied with wars greater than any previously recorded; greater whether we consider the forces engaged in them or the length of time they lasted, or the extent of country over which they were waged'.[1] The wars of the second half of the fourth century in fact involved large coalitions, thereby increasing the number of military units, which began to undertake expeditions at greater distances than ever before. For example, at the Battle of Sentinum in 295 BC, the size of the Roman army, including the allied troops, was 40,000 men. Their enemies (Samnites and Gauls) had 50,000 troops.[2] Never before in Italy had such numbers been brought together for a single battle.

In terms of ethnic and cultural influences, it should be noted that virtually all the enemies of Rome had an effect upon the development of Roman armament in this period. But the greatest impact was made by the Greek colonies in the southern tip of the Apennine peninsula, the Etruscans and the Celts of Central Europe. It was in that period that the standardisation of armament took place as a result of several causes acting at the same time. The most important of these were: the consolidation of the Italic tribes under the hegemony of Rome and the need to simplify arms and armour, which had to be produced in ever-increasing quantities as the number of troops increased. Changes in tactics also had an effect: the shift away from using the phalanx in battle to the maniple caused changes in panoply (*panoplia*). It was now necessary to supply all soldiers with nearly identical weapons.

Far less decorated armour has been found dating from the Republican era than from the Imperial era. This is for a number of reasons. Firstly, it was a result of the change in panoply mentioned above, when it became necessary to equip troops

FIG. 8. Romano-Etruscan warriors on cinerary urns, from Volterra, second century BC. (Photo by R. D'Amato)

with near-identical arms and armour. It had to be relatively cheap, as the soldiers purchased it at their own expense. This to a large extent is why the number of helmet types decreases in the Republican period compared to the previous period. In this period, the most common helmet was the Montefortino type, which was simpler to manufacture. In general, this type of helmet was free from any decoration. Although its earliest examples still had some engraved decoration, this kind of helmet became increasingly simpler and cheaper over time, which allowed it to be produced in large numbers.[3] After the reforms of Marius authorised recruitment of the poorest citizens into the army, the mass production of cheap equipment began, so decoration disappears completely from most helmets.

Secondly, Roman literary sources idealised Roman simplicity when describing the weaponry of the Republican era. At the same time, the simplicity of Roman soldiers' armour was often contrasted with the expensive equipment of the enemies of Rome. Here are just a few examples of the numerous statements by ancient writers. Diodorus Siculus mentioned the golden armour of the Gauls.[4] Livy also wrote about golden Gallic armours and the gorgeous armament of the Samnites.[5] Describing the Battle of Chaeronea between Sulla and the Pontic army

FIG. 9. (Above) Roman Equites on cinerary urn, from Volterra, second century BC. (Photo by R. D'Amato)

FIG. 10. (Above right) Roman-Etruscan warriors from cinerary urns, Turin, Museo Archeologico, third century BC. (Photo by R. D'Amato)

FIG. 11. (Below) Etrusco-Roman cavalryman fighting a Celtic warrior, on cinerary urn, third century BC, Volterra Museo Archeologico. (Photo by R. D'Amato)

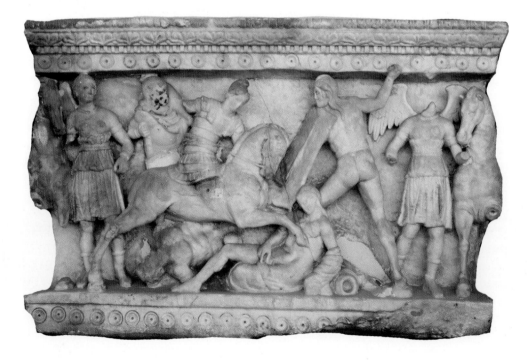

FIG. 12. (Above) Roman-Etruscan warrior on cinerary urn, third century BC, Florence, Museo Archeologico. (Photo by R. D'Amato)

FIG. 13. (Right) Detail of aspis of Roman-Etruscan warrior on cinerary urn, third century BC, Florence, Museo Archeologico. (Photo by R. D'Amato)

FIG. 14. (Left) Roman-Etruscan warrior on cinerary urn, third century BC, Florence, Museo Archeologico. (Photo by R. D'Amato)

FIG. 15. (Below) Roman-Etruscan warrior on cinerary urn, third century BC, Chiusi, Tomba della Pellerina. (Photo by R. D'Amato)

FIG. 16. (Opposite page) Roman-Etruscan centurion on cinerary urn, third century BC, Florence, Museo Archeologico. (Photo by R. D'Amato)

FIG. 17. Roman-Etruscan centurion on cinerary urn, third century BC, Florence, Museo Archeologico (Photo by R. D'Amato)

FIG. 18. Roman-Etruscan centurions on cinerary urn, third century BC, Florence, Museo Archeologico. (Photo by R. D'Amato)

of Mithridates VI Eupator, Plutarch mentions the splendour of the enemy's precious equipment which dazzled the Roman soldiers.[6] Aemilius Paulus was no less impressed by the gilded armour of the Macedonians at the Battle of Pydna.[7]

The Roman writers mentioned such impressions to emphasise the contrast between the Romans and the non-Roman peoples and barbarians. Emphasising their passion for luxury and ornamentation of weapons, they pointed to the lower combat effectiveness of barbarians who boasted of their exotic equipment. By highlighting the relative modesty of the Romans' weapons, ancient historians

FIG. 19. Roman Etruscan Centurions on cinerary urn, third century BC, Florence, Museo Archeologico (Photo by R. D'Amato)

brought Roman superior military prowess to the fore.[8] For example, in his account of the Samnite wars, Livy repeatedly contrasted the Romans with their valour to the Samnites with their luxurious weapons intended to cause psychological impact.[9] And Roman generals told their troops that warriors should not rely on gold and silver decorations, but on the iron of their swords and their own courage (fig. 23).[10]

However, we should not forget that in many cases, these accounts of Roman simplicity were written by authors living at the time of the Principate who were nostalgic for the 'good old days'. K. Gilliver[11] rightly notes that the Roman military paid the same attention to their appearance and its use as a means of psychological

FIG. 20. Roman Centurion on cinerary urn, first century BC, Florence, Museo Archeologico (Photo by R. D'Amato)

impact on the enemy as other peoples: moreover, they did not look like plain, rough soldiers. Plutarch reported that cavalrymen of Pompey the Great had boasted of their martial skills, shining armour and the beauty of their horses before the Battle of Pharsalus.[12] Describing the Battle of Philippi, Plutarch noted that almost all the soldiers of Brutus had had armament decorated with gold and silver, as Brutus believed that valuable weaponry was taken especial care of and that it had added to the bravery of ambitious soldiers in battle.[13] Caesar also ensured that his soldiers had had expensive armament decorated with gold and silver, both to make them look powerful and for them to hold onto them in battle for fear of losing such expensive items.[14]

This primarily pertains to the armour of the military officers. The Roman nobility was able to acquire expensive armament by ordering magnificent armour, a few examples of which have survived to the present day. These are what we are going to discuss.

FIG. 21. Ivory plaques with Roman legionaries and a standard-bearer, fourth century BC, Palestrina, Museo Archeologico Nazionale. (Photo by R. D'Amato)

FIG. 22. (Above left) Fragments of fresco from the Tomb of the Scipios, second century BC, *in situ*, Rome. (Photo by R. D'Amato) FIG. 23. (Above right) Roman general in sacrificial costume, from a situla of Praeneste, fourth century BC, Berlin, Staatliche Museum. (Drawing after Sekunda, Northwood, 1995, p. 45)

FIG. 24. (Below left) Capitol relief, clipeus with Genii and Aquila, circa 100–80 BC, Rome, Musei Capitolini, Centrale Montemartini. (Photo by R. D'Amato) FIG. 25. (Below right) Capitol relief, *clipeus* with Dioscuri, circa 100–80 BC, Rome, Musei Capitolini, Centrale Montemartini. (Photo by R. D'Amato)

SHIELDS

No decorated Roman shields of the Republican era have been found. Therefore, the main sources confirming their existence are images and written sources. For example, ancient authors mention what happened to Scipio Africanus. One day he noticed that a ceratin soldier's shield was rather elaborately decorated and reproached him, saying he did not wonder the man had treated it with such care, seeing that he put more trust in it than in his sword.[15] Silius Italicus relates that Scipio's shield was decorated with the images of his father and uncle.[16] Pliny the Elder also mentioned copper shields with silver faces.[17] However, he said these had been mainly votive shields depicting the face of their owners.[18]

FIG. 26. Capitol relief, *clipeus*, circa 100–80 BC, Rome, Musei Capitolini, Centrale Montemartini. (Photo by R. D'Amato)

FIG. 27. (Above) Capitol relief, Numidian shield with dragon device, circa 100–80 BC, Rome, Musei Capitolini, Centrale Montemartini. (Photo by R. D'Amato)

FIG. 28. (Below)Arms trophaeum from Alife, first century BC, *in situ*, Alife. (Photo courtesy of Alife Archeoclub)

FIG. 29. Trophies of arms and armour: Dyrrachium, first century BC - first century AD (armours, shields, helmets, etc). (Photo by Aleksandra Sojic)

FIG. 30. (Above) Trophies of arms and armour, first century BC, Narbonne, Musée Lapidaire (armours, shields, helmets, etc, of Caesar). (Photo by R. D'Amato)

FIG. 31. (Below) Trophies of arms and armour, first century BC, Narbonne, Musée Lapidaire. (Photo by R. D'Amato)

Roman reliefs show a greater variety of ornamental motifs on shields.[19] These shields are either painted or have embossed decoration, including images of animals and sacred beings capable of warding off the evil eye. There are pieces covered with embossed scales, with a medallion-*gorgoneion* in the centre. Shields also can sometimes depict gods: Roma, Victoria (fig. 24), and the Dioscuri (fig. 25). Roman reliefs dating from the end of the Republican era depict shields with lush floral ornament, the lightning of Jupiter, the signs of the Zodiac and mythical creatures.

HELMETS

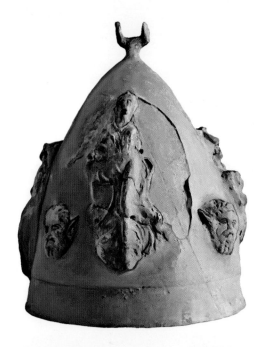

There are relatively few finds of ornate helmets dating from the Republican period, mainly incidental finds and pieces placed in burials. Some elements of decoration can be seen on Greek helmets used in Italy. Pilos-type helmets[20] sometimes have decoration in the form of an embossed wreath attached to the bowl (the helmet from the Louvre[21]) (fig. 32) and the helmet could be provided with horns cut from a metal sheet (Bari, Karlsruhe, the Louvre, the British Museum).[22] Bronze or gold wreaths attached to helmets can be interpreted as rewards for valour,[23] which were used not only as senior officers' insignia, but also as cult objects (as votive offerings, cult attributes or some grave goods).

Italic specimens, for example of the Negau type, dating to the early Republican period are distinguished by rich decor. There are several such pieces. Their bowls are decorated with

FIG. 32. (Above) Votive decorated terracotta pilos helmet from Tarentum, 350–325 BC, Louvre, Collection Piot, 1879. (Drawing by A. E. Negin)

FIG. 33. (Opposite top left) Decorated Negau-type helmet from Pisa, fifth century BC. (Drawing by A. E. Negin)

FIG. 34. (Opposite top right) Parade Negau-type helmet from Lombardia, fifth century BC. (Drawing by A. E. Negin)

FIG. 35. (Opposite bottom) Conversano-type helmets: (a) Conversano, fourth century BC; (b) Cortona, Ceccanti Collection, fourth century BC. (Drawing by A. E. Negin)

a

b

FIG. 36. (Left) Phrygian-type helmet from Herculaneum, fourth century BC, still in use in the first century AD, Paris, Louvre. (Drawing by A. E. Negin)

FIG. 37. (Below) Decorated Attic and Phrygian-type helmets of the fourth century BC: (a) Vatican museum; (b) from Sigliano (Castiglione del Lago) (the so-called helmet of Hannibal), Perugia, Museo Archeologico Nazionale dell'Umbria. (Photo by R. D'Amato)

a

b

relief volutes. A notch in the bottom of the bowl usually broadens out in the front, which results in an arrow-shaped (helmets from Pisa[24] (fig. 33) and Lombardy[25] (fig. 34)) or arc-shaped bowl (Lanuvium[26] (fig. 5), San Bernardino di Briona[27]). It has embossed eyebrows and sometimes eyes inlaid with blue glass (Lanuvium, Lombardy) and human faces (mascarons) (Pisa, Lombardy). The crest holder is in the shape of animals: lions (Pisa), hippocampi (Lanuvium) and swans' heads (Lombardy). Curly hair (Lombardy) or a feather pattern (Pisa, Lanuvium) is depicted on the brim. Such helmets appeared at the end of the Roman Kingdom and were used during the fifth century BC.[28]

Sometimes, embossed decoration can be seen on the so-called 'Samnite Attic'[29] or 'Italic variations of Chalcidian helmets'.[30] A distinctive feature of these helmets,[31] which are also known as Lucanian, is a high wall of the back of the bowl and deep ear cutouts into which the curved forward wall of the neckguard is slid. The extant pieces, mainly from burials, have holders attached for a central crest-shaped plume, as well as small tubes on the sides for feather-shaped decorations. The piece from Lavello[32] has a hair crest and feathers made from bronze sheet, which clearly demonstrates how the helmets looked like with real hair and feather decoration. In some cases, a pair of bronze wings, which came in several shapes, was fastened to the sides of the helmet.

The Italic variant of the Phrygian-type helmet became common in the late fifth century BC. It was a rare kind of helmet developed by Italic armourers, which combined elements both of the Phrygian helmet and the Chalcidian-Lucan variation. The most famous helmets of this type include a piece with wings, a crest and curls on the front found in the military burial at Conversano,[33] near Bari, which dates from the last quarter of the fourth century BC (fig. 35a). Almost all the known pieces originate from southern Italy. The shape of the bowl of this group of helmets corresponds to the Chalcidian helmet. Its distinctive feature is its more-or-less rich decoration, for example, depicting hair on the forehead, wings attached to the sides of the bowl, and figurative and floral ornament. The helmet from Herculaneum[34] (fig. 36) is an imitation of a real phrygian cap with its forward-curving top, folds of material and a marked longitudinal seam. However, this group also includes helmets with a round hemispherical bowl (helmets from the Vatican Museum[35] (fig. 37a) and Tiriolo[36] (Catanzaro Museum) (fig. 38). Both pieces depict satyrs peeking out from behind hair and in this case, perhaps, it refers to the role of the god in the cult of the dead. Decoration varies from designs well-known in the classical tradition in the shape of mascarons and wings to unambiguously cultic symbols. In the latter case, along with combat pieces (for example, as part of the complete panoply of the burial in Conversano) there were also helmets that had never been part of defensive armour, but only grave goods.

The widespread use and low cost of the Montefortino helmet has been mentioned earlier. However, there were also richly decorated examples. One of them was found in the Samnite sanctuary in Pietrabbondante[37] (fig. 39). It is supposed to be Roman as it may be a trophy (*spolia hostium*) captured in battle with Rome. This piece is provided with embossed cheek-pieces, depicting Tethys with her son Achilles' armour.

FIG. 38. (Left) Decorated Attic helmet from Catanzaro, fourth century BC, Catanzaro, Museo Provinciale. (Drawing by A. E. Negin)

FIG. 39. (Below) Fragments of Roman decorated helmets from a Samnite sanctuary at Pietrabbondante, fourth century BC, Napoli, Museo Archeologico Nazionale. (Drawing by A. E. Negin)

BODY ARMOUR

Graphic sources allow us to see what Roman armour of the early Republican period was like. The ivory plaques from Palestrina,[38] which date from the fourth century BC, depict warrior-hoplites (fig. 21). They have the armour and clothing usual for Latin heavy infantrymen at that time. They wear Attic helmets with a longitudinal crest. They are holding large round shields and their bodies are protected by an anatomical cuirass and greaves. This is undoubtedly ordinary combat equipment, as it has absolutely no decoration. But both the bronze cuirass and greaves could have magnificent engraved or even embossed ornamentation.

The armour of Roman legionaries during the Punic Wars and the late Republic are mainly known from iconography and the descriptions of ancient authors. It was usually inexpensive and consisted of a small square chest plate about 20cm x 20cm, which was called a breastplate[39] and one greave for the right leg. Wealthier legionaries had mail body armour.[40] Those who could spend a considerable sum on their equipment could acquire fine weaponry.

Unfortunately, there are very few real pieces of expensive Roman armour dating from the Republican period available to researchers. Although armours can be found in burials as a part of grave goods, but this became less common in the later period and researchers have to be satisfied with only a few graphic sources and even rarer artefacts.

Barbarian weapons captured in battle, even expensive silver-plated or gold-plated ones, interested a Roman soldier mainly as a trophy taken from the defeated enemy until the time of the developed Principate. Such trophies were not intended to be re-used by a Roman citizen. Enemy military equipment not burnt on the battlefield was thought to carry hostile and potentially destructive energy; they were captured *sacra*, as the weapons were believed to have a sacred essence. Their sacred status resulted in a ban on restoring or altering them.[41] This ban is mentioned by Plutarch as the explanation why the Romans left such trophies to perish over time.[42]

The armour of the Italic peoples is better studied than Roman armour. There are numerous extant pieces of armour from the early Republican period manufactured by the Etruscans and Greeks, as well as armour from the Samnite necropolises and sanctuaries. We can, however, consider the armour of the enemies of Rome as potential prototypes of proper Roman armament, as the Romans borrowed a lot from them. Moreover, these examples can be attributed to the arming of Roman allies (*socii*).

Despite the descriptions of Italic warriors' armour decorated with silver and gold, archaeologists have only a few pieces on which such ornamentation survives. One bronze belt kept in the British Museum has a silver clasp.[43] Silver clasps were also found on the Pontecagnano specimen.[44] There are several fully or partially silvered helmets extant. A Samnite Attic helmet found in burial 37 in Eboli has a small amount of silvering surviving on the edges.[45] Also, traces of silvering can be found on the Chalcidian helmets from Todi,[46] Perugia[47] and Vulci[48] (the National

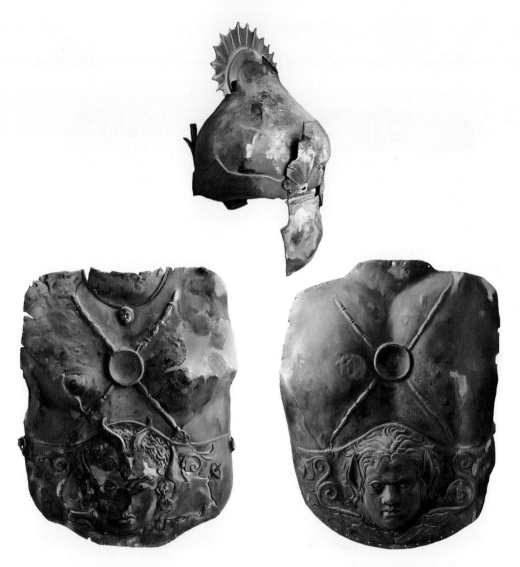

FIG. 40. (Above) Armour from Laos (Marcellina), circa 300 BC. (Drawing by A. E. Negin)

FIG. 41. (Opposite page) Triple-disc cuirasses, third century BC: (a) Ksour-es-Saf; (b) Ruvo; (c) Vulci; (d) Swiss private collection. (Drawing by A. E. Negin)

Library in Paris, Inv. 2013, 5650). The armour from Laos (Marcellina), more precisely its protective bronze belt, was decorated with silver figures of Scylla[49] (fig. 40).

Bronze breastplates (pectorals) of many Italic peoples, including the Etruscans and Romans, were decorated with embossed or engraved geometric or zoomorphic ornamentation. The most impressive decoration can be seen in triple-disc cuirasses common in the south of the peninsula. These are pieces from Ruvo[50] (Naples) (fig.

a

b

c   d

FIG. 42. (Left) This fragment of the cuirass with the head of Medusa was sold in 2011 at Hirsch-München Auktion 274, lot 1182. (Drawing by A. E. Negin)

FIG. 43. (Below) Fragments of bronze anatomical cuirass from Siris, 390–340 BC, London, British Museum. (After Bröndsted 1836, pl. V)

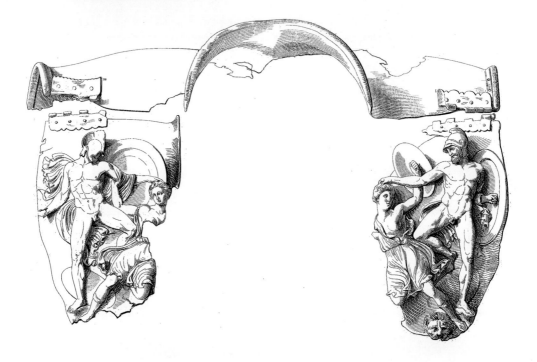

41b), Vulci (Boston, Museum of Art, inv. 64.727)[51] (fig. 41c), Ksour-es-Saf[52] (fig. 41a), Senise,[53] a Swiss private collection[54] (fig. 41d) and Ruvo (Karlsruhe).[55]

All of them are richly decorated with Greek-style motifs. The cuirass from Carthage (Ksour-es-Saf)[56] (fig. 41a) bears the face of Athena/Minerva on the lower disc. Her image can also be seen on another cuirass from Ruvo (now in the Archaeological Museum in Naples) (fig. 41b). The bottom disc of the cuirass from a private Swiss collection depicts the head of the Gorgon Medusa (fig. 41d). The piece from Vulci, purchased by the Boston Museum of Fine Arts, probably depicts Hercules (a head in a lion's skin) and, supposedly, Helios and Selene (fig. 41c).

Many neighbouring peoples had Greek-designed anatomical cuirasses common on the Italian peninsula but there are no real finds to confirm the Romans used them. Very close to Rome, in ancient Lanuvium, the previously-described 'Tomb of the Warrior' was excavated, in which was found a magnificent gilded helmet

FIG. 44. Bronze cuirass from Cueva del Jarro (Cave of Jars) in Almuñécar, first century BC. (Photo by R. D'Amato)

and muscle cuirass dating to the turn of the fifth–sixth centuries BC, i.e. the beginning of the Republican period.[57] The quality of the armour suggests that it was manufactured by Etruscan armourers.

In Italy the oldest example of the muscle cuirass with embossed decoration was found in a burial in Laos-Santa Maria del Cedro-Marcellina dated from 325–300 BC[58] (fig. 40). The cuirass realistically depicts a human torso with a bronze belt on. This belt is lavishly decorated with floral ornamentation and images of satyrs' heads. A fragment of a similar cuirass, but bearing the head of Medusa, was sold in 2011 at Hirsch-München Auktion 274, lot 1182 (fig. 42). Two embossed bronze reliefs probably formed part of the decoration of the shoulder straps of a cuirass found in the river Sinni (Siris) and there is also part of a muscle cuirass dating back to 390–340 BC[59] (fig. 43). This pieces depict a fight between a Greek warrior and an Amazon where he has won and is dragging her by her hair.

Undoubtedly, muscle cuirasses, widely used by the Greek and in Hellenistic states, were used in the Roman Republican Army, too, as Polybius[60] mentioned that weaponry had been borrowed from Hellenic designs. Moreover, in the fifth–first centuries BC muscle cuirasses were common over a vast area, from the Iberian Peninsula to the Urals.[61] They are even found in Sarmatian burials in Russia. If even nomadic Sarmatians had them, if only as spoils, then the Romans must have had them not only as symbols, according to the Hellenistic tradition, but as real armour for the commanders of legions. Unfortunately, no real pieces of muscle cuirasses dating to the time after the conquest of the whole Italian peninsula by Rome have been found. Based on the structural similarity[62] with the cuirass on the equestrian statues thought to be images of Marcus Nonius Balbus (the second half of the first century BC), we can assume that Cueva del Jarro (Cave of Jars) piece in Almuñécar[63] dates from the late Republican period (fig. 44). One similar cuirass was allegedly found in the Volga River (now kept in the museum of the Polish Army, Inv. 24067).[64] Unfortunately, the circumstances of the discovery of this item are unknown, which complicates its attribution and dating. We can only assume that if the cuirass was really found near the Volga River, it may be connected with the Sarmatian.

EQUIPMENT OF OFFICERS AND COMMANDERS

Commanders of different ranks in the Roman army had great opportunities to show their individual taste in the selection and acquisition of armour and personal military equipment differing in workmanship and individual parts, for example, use of precious metals and artistic elements in their decoration and, thus, in their cost.[65]

Obviously, the Roman commanders were no different in the splendour of their armour from Pyrrhus, who, according to Plutarch,[66] could be clearly seen from everywhere in battle due to the beauty of his weapons and the gleam of his luxurious armour. For example, Tiberius Gracchus had a magnificently ornate helmet which he wore in all his battles.[67]

There are several extant images that can help us to imagine what Roman generals and commanders of the Republican period looked like. We can visualise a

---

FIG. 45. (Opposite page left) Panoply of a Roman or Hellenistic general from Rhodes, second century BC, Rome, Museo della civiltà Romana, cast. (Photo by R. D'Amato)

FIG. 46. (Opposite page top right) Knee-protection from a greave with engraved Gorgon's head, first century BC, Museo delle Navi di Nemi. (Photo by R. D'Amato)

FIG. 47. (Opposite page bottom right) Scale armour now kept in the Royal Ontario Museum and presumably originating from Lake Trasimeno. (Drawing by A. E. Negin)

commander in expensive Hellenistic armour (fig. 45). It could be either a variation of the Greek *linothorax* or a muscle cuirass with *pteryges* (a leather or metal fringe). In addition, his panoply included a superbly-decorated silver or gilded helmet and greaves[68] (fig. 46). It is in this way that Silius Italicus describes the consul Flaminius in a helmet with a triple crest and an embossed image of Scylla, with a shield depicting the Capitoline wolf and wearing an ornate cuirass.[69] On the other hand, fragments of mail armour were found in the so-called 'Tomb of the Scipios'[70] on the Via Appia, which was used for burials from the third century BC to the first century AD and this may indicate that a mail shirt could be part of the panoply of Roman commanders. The scale armour now kept in the Royal Ontario Museum[71] and presumably originating from Lake Trasimeno could have belonged to some Roman officer (fig. 47), although it is quite possible that this armour could have been assembled out of fragments of several armours dating from different times and even partially complemented with contemporary details.

RELIGIOUS AND MAGICAL ELEMENTS OF ARMS AND ARMOUR DECORATION

Images of various deities, mythological characters and scenes prevailed in various forms of decoration and gave armours not only a symbolic value, but also a magnificent and sometimes terrifying appearance, for example, helmets having a terrifying bird of prey mounted on the bowl. Romans transformed an ancient tradition of depicting birds on helmets (for example, a Celtic helmet from Ciumeşti[72]) into a beautiful and heroic legend recounted by Livy[73] and Lucius Ampelius.[74] According to Livy, when Marcus Valerius, later surnamed Corvus, was fighting with a Gaul, a crow suddenly settled on Valerius' helmet facing the enemy. 'Not only did the bird keep its place on the helmet, but every time they clashed it rose on its wings and attacked the Gaul's face

FIG. 48. Capitol relief, panoply of a centurion, circa 100–80 BC, Rome, Musei Capitolini, Centrale Montemartini. (Photo by R. D'Amato)

 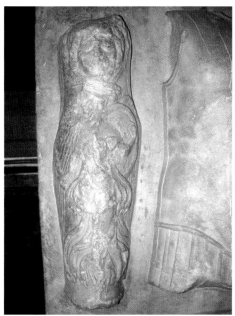

FIG. 49. (Above left) Capitol relief, horse *prometopion*, circa 100–80 BC, Rome, Musei Capitolini, Centrale Montemartini. (Photo by R. D'Amato) FIG. 50. (Above right) Capitol relief, greave, circa 100–80 BC, Rome, Musei Capitolini, Centrale Montemartini. (Photo by R. D'Amato) FIG. 51. (Below left) Capitol relief, *thorax stadios*, circa 100–80 BC, Rome, Musei Capitolini, Centrale Montemartini. (Photo by R. D'Amato) FIG. 52. (Below right) Capitol relief, *thorax stadios*, circa 100–80 BC, Rome, Musei Capitolini, Centrale Montemartini. (Photo by R. D'Amato)

FIG. 53. Bronze peytral (chest armour for a cavalry horse), Archaeological Museum of Naples. (Drawing by A. E. Negin)

and eyes with beak and talon, until, terrified at the sight of so dire a portent and bewildered in eyes and mind alike, he was slain by Valerius. Then, soaring away eastwards, the crow passed out of sight.'[75] A bronze model of Valerius Corvus's helmet depicting a crow and a laurel wreath on the bowl is in the Roman-Germanic Museum in Cologne.[76] Later on, the depicture of the intervention of divine will appeared in the shape of a stylised head of a bird of prey facing the enemy on other helmets. The head of a griffin on the helmet from Lake Nemi[77] and the crests having images of birds' heads on helmets of the third century AD (Heddernheim[78] and Worthing[79]) had the same significance.

Images of Athena/Minerva appeared as early as on Italic cuirasses (the triple-disc cuirasses from Ruvo and Ksour-es-Saf) (fig. 41a) as the embodiment of a holy war. Iconographic sources indicate that the image of the goddess Roma appears on shields as a symbol of the state and, in a narrower sense, the city of Rome. In addition, armour decoration can include images of Hercules (a cheek piece from Pietrabbondante)[80] (fig. 39) and Victoria (a cheek piece from Pietrabbondante[81]) (fig. 39).

In the late Republican period, weapons could already bear political symbols. It appears on the reliefs of Sant'Omobono[82] as a depiction of Sulla's victories (the image of the goddess Victoria can be connected with the agnomen Felix ['Lucky'], which could imply the special protection of the goddess) (fig. 48–50).

The image of Medusa's head (*gorgoneion*) can be considered as one of the magic elements of armour decoration. The *gorgoneion* is the most famous type of the *apotropaion* (from Greek αροτροπαιον, 'image warding off evil influences'), a ugly caricature that causes both laughter and fear. Plutarch said that such a talisman attracted an ill-wisher's evil eye by distracting him from the victim. The *gorgoneion* depicted on armour was to frighten the enemy, like the legendary Medusa[83] (fig. 51). The Greeks portrayed a *gorgoneion* on their shields and on the chest of the cuirasses (for example, the cuirass of the Elizavetinsky burial mound[84]), but, as can be seen on Roman sculptures, this element was still found on muscle cuirasses not only under the Republic (the relief of Sant'Omobono) (fig. 52), the portrait of a Roman general from Tivoli,[85] but also in the Imperial period. The head of Medusa is also on a bronze peytral (chest armour for a cavalry horse) kept in the Archaeological Museum of Naples[86] (fig. 53).

Another impressive helmet decoration was bronze horns attached to the bowls of some examples. In ancient societies (especially pastoral), the horns of bulls, cows, rams, goats and buffaloes were symbols of male morale, phallic power and of fertility and prosperity. Therefore, the meaning of horned combat helmets in the ancient world can be interpreted as a sign of strength, courage and masculinity (if the owner demonstrated heroism on the battlefield). It is known from written sources that Roman soldiers who distinguished themselves in action could receive silver horns to be mounted on their helmets.[87] In this case, it is obvious that the horns were placed on Montefortino-type helmets, especially as there are several images and similar finds from Italy. The painting of the tomb in Nola[88] depicts a cavalryman in a bronze Montefortino helmet with large bronze horns. An actual example from Fosdinovo[89] has horns identical to those on the painting in the tomb (fig. 54). It is difficult to say who influenced the Italic tradition of attaching decorative horns to helmets more, the Greeks or the Celts. Dionysius of Halicarnassus[90] mentioned that Gauls sometimes had horns on their helmets attached so that they seemed to be integral with the helmet. Based on the horned Montefortino helmets found on the north of the peninsula, we can state that the second wave of the fashion for such decoration comes from the south of the peninsula under the influence of the Celts in the late fourth century BC, subsequent to the examples of Greek horned helmets of the seventh–sixth centuries BC.

Such religious and magical elements of armour decoration were quite common and intended to magically protect the owner of the item from the

FIG. 54. Horned Montefortino helmet from Pulica, fourth–third centuries BC, Florence, Museo Archeologico Nazionale. (Drawing by A. E. Negin)

evil eye and enemy weapons. This semantic meaning of armament decoration still prevailed in the Republican period over scenes reflecting political and dynastic propaganda, which became widespread only in the era of the Principate.

3

DECORATED ARMOUR OF THE PRINCIPATE
(27 BC–284 AD)

When considering the richly-decorated Roman arms of the Principate, we should also remember that the Romans had to secure their borders at that time. This resulted in the strategy of building *limes* and stationing standing armies on them. This territorial dispersion of forces made it necessary to organise armament production in different parts of the empire; as a result, the equipment was manufactured according to different local features, which reflected the tastes of the soldiers of a certain unit and ethnicity. In fact, armament presented both in real examples and images is striking in its diversity. While Roman authors who wrote about the Republican period talked mostly about the modesty of the soldiers displayed in their military equipment,[1] in the Imperial period the brightness and richness of weapons was more often reported.[2] Apparently, this was due not only to the personal views of the authors of the texts, but also to the creation of a professional army and the relatively high incomes of the troops, who could therefore afford expensive items. Moreover, the expensive armour was not only used by elite units of the Roman army, such as the Imperial Guard (the Praetorian cohorts), but even by the *auxilia*. Most of the ornate armour discovered by archaeologists and linked to the times of the Principate was used by auxiliary cavalry. In historical studies, they are referred to as either 'parade'[3] or 'cavalry sport'[4] armour. However, some examples seem to clearly demonstrate their ceremonial purposes which was not limited to parades or cavalry competitions.

THE ROMAN ARMY IN TRIUMPHS AND PARADES

The function of ornate armour in the Roman army of the Imperial Period was, first and foremost, to display the status of the soldier. Under the Principate, Roman soldiers willingly wore the parade 'uniform'[5] and battle honours (*dona militaria*) at various solemn ceremonies, such as state events and traditional military ceremonies (payment of salaries and presentation of awards, ceremonial reviews after exercises, training and cavalry tournaments).[6] In this case, wearing

FIG. 55. Lawrence Alma-Tadema. *Triumph of Titus* (1885), Baltimore, the Walters Art Museum (Photo courtesy of the Museum)

magnificent and expensive armour that gleamed in the sunlight was seen as a transition from the routine of everyday military life to a solemn performance (fig. 55). It was no less important to impress the viewer with luxurious equipment at cavalry tournaments (*hippika gymnasia*) for which beautifully decorated and expensive armour and horse equipment were also manufactured as well. Such competitions, at which the cavalry soldiers displayed their skills, were organised due to the need to exercise not only individually, but also as units.

If it had not been for the various holidays, the routine of the Roman soldiers would have been even more harsh and joyless that it already was. As it can be seen from a Roman military calendar found at Dura-Europos,[7] many solemn ceremonies were held during religious festivals: parades, payment of salaries, decoration of distinguished troops and even the annual oath sworn by recruits. Typically, these events were held with unusual pomp and solemnity. All these events brightened the lives of soldiers, but it sometimes happened that the life of various garrisons was so filled with various holidays that rumours of their laziness and effeminacy spread far across the Empire.

On the other hand, expensive public ceremonies were intended to demonstrate the power of Rome to the citizens and non-citizens (*peregrini*). Based on the account written by Flavius Josephus describing the impression a military parade had on the besieged Jews in Jerusalem,[8] we must conclude that the Romans managed to achieve this aim.

TRIUMPHS AND PARADES

The majority of sources describing the Roman triumph date from the late Republican period. So, we can only present what later triumphs were like in general terms, using not only narrative sources, but also iconographic ones.

The ceremony of the triumph had Etruscan origins,[9] but we do not know what these solemnities held to celebrate a victory originally looked like. Undoubtedly, the Romans introduced a lot of changes into the conduct of triumphal processions, as evidenced by the evolution of the Roman triumph itself, some features of which had been formed by Hellenistic influences.[10] Originally, as we have seen, it was a pedestrian procession, as evidenced by Plutarch who described the very first legendary Roman triumph which took place on 1 March 753 BC.[11] At this early stage, the triumphal procession circled the Palatine on foot, the *spolia* being carried and captured weapons consecrated in the temple of Jupiter Feretrius. Then, a new form of the ceremony was introduced, in which the *triumphator* rode to the Capitol in a quadriga and made a sacrifice to Jupiter. In all likelihood, this type of triumph was created during the reign of Lucius Tarquinius Superbus (Tarquin the Proud) in Rome.[12] At the beginning of the imperial period, the triumph was adapted for the victorious emperor. The content of the ceremony itself did not change, but it was included into a broader context of imperial feasts.

Festive entries of emperors into Rome (*adventus*) were equal in status to large triumphal processions, even if they were not formally such processions.[13] Neither Constantine nor Constantius II celebrated a triumph, but their entries into Rome

FIG. 56. Soldiers with shields in a triumphal procession from a relief on the Arch of Titus, first century AD. (Photo by A. E. Negin)

were on as large a scale and as spectacular as any classical triumphal procession. It is in such bright colours that Ammianus Marcellinus depicts the entry of Constantius II into Rome, mentioning the participation of men-at-arms (*clibanarii*) in shining armour in the procession.[14]

With data from different sources combined, we can give a satisfactory description of the ceremony of the triumph under the late Republic and during the Imperial period. The figure of the *triumphator* was at the centre of the celebration. He was standing in a triumphal chariot (*currus triumphalis*) passing before the people of Rome. He went to the Capitoline Hill towards the temple of the highest god of Rome, Jupiter (*Iuppiter Optimus Maximus Capitolinus*).[15] The triumphal chariot was decorated with gold, jewels or ivory.[16] It was a quadriga and all four horses had gilded trappings.[17]

The *triumphator* was clothed in purple garments embroidered with gold, consisting of a tunic and a toga (*tunica palmata, toga picta*).[18] He had a laurel wreath on his head, and held a laurel branch in his right hand and an ivory eagle-tipped sceptre in his left one. Around his neck, he wore a gold amulet in the form of a capsule (*bulla*). A public slave (*servus publicus*) held a large and heavy golden crown over the *triumphator*'s head, named in sources as the *corona triumphalis* or *corona Etrusca*,[19] which must suggest a hypothetical Etruscan origin for the triumph. This heavy golden crown consisted of oak leaves with ribbons and jewels. The task of the public slave was to remind to the *triumphator* again and again, whispering in his ear: 'Look behind you! Remember that you are a man!' (*'respice post te, hominem te esse memento'*) (Tert. Apol. 33.4: 'hominem se esse etiam triumphans in illo sublimissimo curru admonetur, suggeritur enim ei a tergo: Respice post re! Hominem re memento!'). It was not a moral admonition, but a special sacred act, or, probably, a spell to ward off misfortune. This ritual was introduced as the level of personal exaltation of the *triumphator* in the ceremony increased in contrast to the original Etruscan ritual. He entered Rome at the head of the army with such a huge amount of gold and glory that it became necessary to protect the victorious general from the evil eye, Jupiter's jealousy and envy of the gods. Therefore, a number of rites came into being, among them the soldiers' songs making fun of the triumphator and a slave whispering into the general's ear to remind him of his human nature, as the *triumphator* tried to be like Jupiter Optimus Maximus, to this end even painting his face with bright red lead.[20]

The *triumphator* was preceded by lictors in scarlet military cloaks (*paludamentum*), who carried bundles of wooden rods entwined with laurel branches (*fasces*).[21] It is assumed that in the early period, lictors used to carry axes along with the fascia,[22] which might be used for the execution of prisoners. In the Imperial period this practice came to an end and prisoners were suffocated in a prison (*carcer*) after the triumphal procession was over.[23] The *triumphator* was accompanied by the consuls, praetors, quaestors, aediles and senators. The triumphal chariot was followed by prisoners or pardoned exiled Roman citizens. After them, the soldiers paraded wearing laurel wreaths and their military decorations.[24] Unfortunately, the written sources barely mention the equipment of the soldiers who participated in the triumph. We have to fill this gap relying on rare iconographic data.

A triumphal procession was the only occasion where a general had military power (*imperium*) within the city of Rome for one day. It was the highest military honour possible in the Roman army. Therefore, soldiers in the triumphal procession marched in military formation. They had laurel wreaths on their heads and wore their military decorations which can be seen on several reliefs. Such images can be seen on the famous relief of the Arch of Titus, which depicts a procession carrying the spolia captured in Judea. The soldier immediately behind the Menorah has a strap across his tunic, to which military decorations (*phalerae*) are attached. Furthermore, there is another relief on the Arch depicting a row of soldiers taking part in the procession (fig. 56). They are dressed in tunics, but equipped with ornate round shields. The relief has been badly damaged over time and it is unclear what material these shields were made of: either they were entirely of bronze with embossed decor, or they are ordinary shields decorated with portrait-shaped bosses. In any case, according to the sources, this implies that a number of soldiers could carry ornate ceremonial shields in a triumph.

There is at least one more iconographic source which may depict armed men participating in a triumphal procession. This is the mural paintings of the so-called

FIG. 57. Sculptural relief of the centurion Timokles from Epidaurus, first–second centuries AD. (Drawing by A. E. Negin)

Arieti Tomb on the Esquiline, which were destroyed during later building work.[25] These second-century BC images survive only as drawings made in the late nineteenth century. They depict soldiers who are marching in procession with oval shields and in helmets, while other fragments of the murals show lictors and a quadriga.[26] However, only hypothetically can one interpret this painting as depicting a triumphal procession.

Most sources show that soldiers involved in the triumph were not wearing armour. Based on this, we should conclude that no armour was worn during the ceremony and this was reserved exclusively for the parades which were the main type of military ceremony in the Roman army.

The ceremony of a general's solemn entry into Rome (*adventus*) was not formally a triumph and was practically a military parade, in which the soldiers wore ceremonial equipment and armour.[27] This conclusion is supported by Tacitus's account of Vitellius's entry into Rome. According to the historian, Vitellius retracted his decision to enter the city with the army as a victor and changed his military cloak to a toga, entering the capital city at the head of his army marching in close parade formation.[28]

The parade accompanied every solemn event in the life of any military unit: national holidays, the taking of the oath, payment of salaries, issuing *donativa* (imperial gifts of money), and the presentation of military awards and insignia of distinction. In getting ready for the parade, soldiers would polish their weapons and clean their equipment. However, only officers, including centurions, had a specific parade uniform: ceremonial armour, helmets and a scarlet cloak (*paludamentum*),[29] as opposed to the soldier's cloak (*sagum*). Other soldiers arrived at the parade with ordinary equipment, but they put their decorations on their coats of mail, attached plumes to their helmet and removed the usual covers from their shields (fig. 57).

Flavius Josephus left us the description of a military parade dedicated to the payment of salaries, which he had seen during the siege of Jerusalem.[30] This evidence shows that a military parade had a crucial importance as one of the rites in the Roman army. It is no wonder, therefore, that there was special ceremonial equipment serving as a kind of indicator of the owner's status and income, helping to demonstrate them to his colleagues and comrades in the context of mutual celebration.

THE IMPERIAL GUARD AND ITS LUXURIOUS EQUIPMENT

The figure of the emperor participating in a military parade or marching at the head of the army at the ceremonial entry into Rome usually suggests the presence of his guard. The guardsmen are known to be the most privileged military personnel. Their status was confirmed by the fact that they had a much shorter term of service than other soldiers. They were supposed to serve for sixteen years (instead of twenty-five years for legionaries). In addition, the Praetorians were paid three times more than the soldiers of the legions. Therefore, they could afford to buy expensive armour in which they could flaunt at parades and various ceremonies in which the emperor participated. As it can be seen from the reliefs of Trajan's Column, Praetorian armour worn on campaign differed little from legionaries' or cavalrymen's armour, although written sources record do some differences.[31] But the Praetorians also had to have a ceremonial set of armour, as they had to be suitably equipped when participating in magnificent ceremonies.

Images are our main source for studying the arms of the Imperial Guard. But it is logical to wonder how reliable these visual sources are. Do all the images available to us reflect the examples that existed in reality and if not, which of them reflect reality most closely? To understand this, we must understand what function a particular artefact performed, what attitude the artist performing the work had and what his objectives and the requirements of his customer were. In some cases, some of these questions are very difficult to answer, but in general, the answers help to build conceptual models for interpretation of the armament depicted.

Roman propaganda monuments are known best of all and they are still often cited, especially in Hollywood blockbusters. Despite the many doubts expressed by modern researchers, they continue in many respects to be valuable sources, as these monuments, mostly located in the capital, show how military weapons were perceived by the inhabitants of the capital, including the sculptors who were working on these monuments. Evidently, these artists primarily considered the weapons of the metropolitan garrisons, as well as examples from Greek and Hellenistic art, from which they learnt their craft. Apparently, they found it important to display the structural type, for example, of the so-called Attic helmet, which was fixed in the common person's mind; Romans saw it as consecrated by tradition and relating to a different, deep and slow-changing sphere of existence.

Some reliefs survive which are interpreted as depicting Praetorians (fig. 58). Their armament can be seen on the fragments of the 'Great Trajanic Frieze'[32] in Rome and on the so-called 'Praetorian relief' in the Louvre.[33] All the soldiers depicted on them have ornate Attic helmets with crests and plumes which are different from normal military equipment. However, the discovery of several fragments of helmets of this 'Attic' shape suggesting that they existed not only in images, but also in reality.

FIG. 58. Relief from Rome featuring Praetorians (Cancelleria), first century AD, Rome, Vatican Museum. (Photo by R. D'Amato)

There are many images of Attic helmets on Roman monuments dated back to the first two centuries AD. They are depicted on Trajan's Column, Trajan's triumphal relief, parts of which were subsequently embedded into the Arch of Constantine, on the famous 'Praetorian relief' in the Louvre and on other monuments. As a rule, all of them are richly decorated with embossed floral ornamentation, have a browband with volutes at the temples and are fitted with longitudinal crests with gorgeous plumes. But there are also actual surviving examples of such helmets, although it should be noted that in some cases they are unlikely to be authentic, for example the helmets topped with a ring from Homs (now in the Toledo Museum, Ohio, USA)[34] and a bronze piece from the Museum für Künst und Gewerbe in Hamburg.[35] Both of these pieces seem to be the products of antique dealers or, at least, are pastiches, i.e., they were created by combining parts of different helmets with missing parts restored according to modern concepts. Furthermore, nothing is known about the circumstances of the find of a bronze helmet with volutes and floral ornaments at the Ponte Sisto in Rome (fig.59).[36] This piece is similar to the helmet found in Pergamum (Bergamo, Turkey) (von Lipperheide collection)[37] and to the helmet from the burial which was destroyed during the construction of the Vladikavkaz fortress (State Hermitage).[38] Unlike the find in Rome, the latter pieces are not decorated and, apparently, are earlier, dating back to the Hellenistic era. Unfortunately, it does not seem possible to reliably date this interesting piece. But if this helmet really dates back to the ancient period, then this proves clearly that imitations of the Attic helmet existed in the Rome of the Imperial period.

There is other evidence that helmets with a browband shaped as a vertical fronton with volutes did exist. Their later modification is shown in by finds from Guisborough[39] (fig. 60a), Theilenhofen[40] (fig. 61), Chalon-sur-Saône[41] (fig. 60b), and Cetate-Războieni[42] (fig. 60c). The pieces from the first century AD – early second century AD are Weiler-type helmets with a decorated riveted browband. They are the helmets from Nijmegen[43] and Brza Palanka[44] (fig. 62d). A similar helmet is in a private collection. There are also some preserved browbands that were attached to helmets of this kind. Pieces of this type were found in Nijmegen[45] (fig. 63), Leidsche Rijn[46] (fig. 64) and in the Pamuk mogila near Plovdiv[47] (fig. 62c). The National Museum of Antiquities (Rijksmuseum van Oudheden) in Leiden has an embossed helmet browband which bears a bust of the emperor (?) in the centre and two male heads on the sides[48] (fig. 65). This find dates from around the early second century AD. The pieces from Butzbach[49] (fig. 62a) and Hallaton[50] (fig.

FIG. 59. Decorative Attic helmet from Rome (Ponte Sisto). (After Dehn 1911, S. 252)

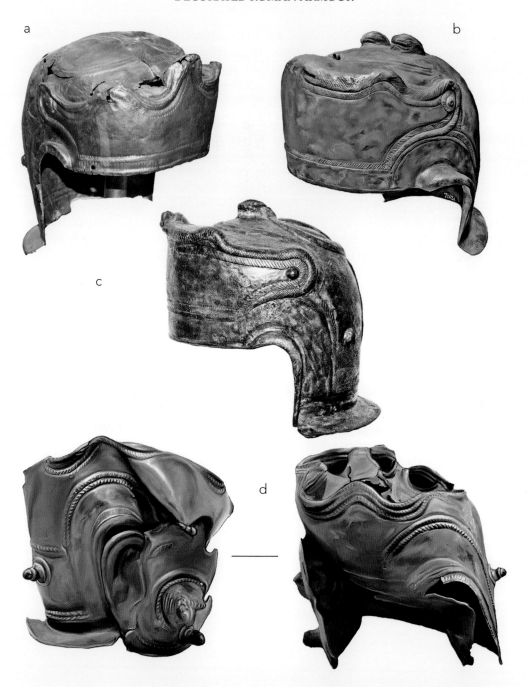

FIG. 60. Helmets of Guisborough type: (a) Guisborough, first half of the third century AD, London, British Museum; (b) Chalon-sur-Saône, first half of the third century AD, Saint-Germain-en-Laye, Musée archéologie nationale; (c) Cetate-Războieni, first half of the third century AD, Aiud, Muzeul de Istorie; (d) Gerulata, second half of the second century AD, Rusovce, Antická Gerulata. ((a), (c) Photo by R. D'Amato; (b), (d) drawing by A. E. Negin)

FIG. 61. Helmet from Theilenhofen, second half of second century AD, München, Archäologische Staatssammlung. (Drawing by A. E. Negin)

FIG. 62. Cavalry helmets with vertical fronton: (a) Butzbach, second century AD, Darmstadt, Hessisches Landesmuseum; (b) Koblenz-Bubenheim, end of the first – early second century AD, Koblenz, Mittelrhein Museum; (c) Pamuk mogila, end of the first – early second century AD, Plovdiv, Archaeological Museum; (d) Brza Palanka, end of the first – early second century AD, Kladovo, Iron Gates Museum. ((a)–(c) drawing by A. E. Negin; (d) Photo by R. D'Amato)

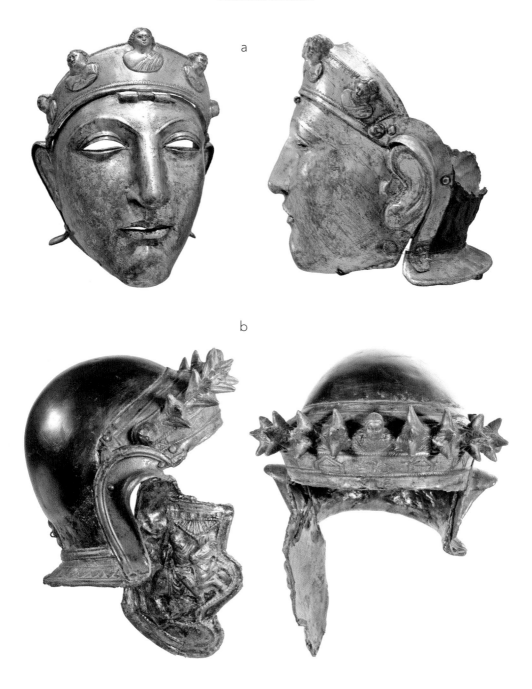

FIG. 63. Helmets with vertical fronton from Nijmegen, end of the first – early second century AD, Leiden, Rijksmuseum van Oudheden. ((a) Photo by R. D'Amato; (b) photo courtesy of Rijksmuseum van Oudheden, Leiden)

FIG. 64. Fragment of helmet from Leidsche rijn, end of the second – beginning of the third century AD, Utrecht, Museum. (Drawing by A. E. Negin)

FIG. 65. Embossed helmet browband with bust of the emperor (?) in the centre and two male heads on the sides, early second century AD, Leiden, Rijksmuseum van Oudheden. (Photo courtesy of Rijksmuseum van Oudheden, Leiden)

FIG. 66. Helmet from Hallaton, mid-first century AD. (Photo courtesy of Leicestershire County Council; reconstruction drawing by A. E. Negin)

Junkelmann) can be considered as a transitional design between early and later helmet modifications with a vertical fronton. Thus, all of the above finds suggest that Attic helmets with browbands, which are often depicted on Roman propaganda monuments, are not the sculptors' invention, but helmets that were actually common in the Roman imperial army, imitating the models from the earlier period (fig. 67–71).

It can be assumed that the helmets of the Imperial Guard soldiers had more archaic shapes, imitating Greek models. For example, a piece from the collection of Franz von Lipperheide, which was reported to have been found in the Lake Nemi, could be considered one of these[51] (fig. 72). The shape of this piece is very similar to the goddess Roma's headpiece topped with the Griffin's head, in which she was portrayed on coins of the third–second centuries BC.[52] The helmet is cast in bronze and gilded.

FIG. 67. Sculpture of pseudo-Attic helm from a private house in Rome. (Photo by R. D'Amato)

FIG. 68. Battle frieze, second century AD, Chiusi, Museo Arcivescovile. (Photo by R. D'Amato)

FIG. 69. Soldiers and officers of the Flavian Age, from the Templum Gentis Flaviae, last quarter of first century AD. (Photo by R. D'Amato)

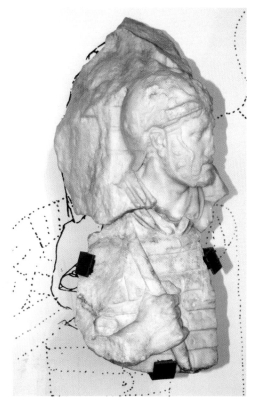

FIG. 70 (Above). Soldiers and officers of the Flavian Age, from the Templum Gentis Flaviae, first quarter of first century AD. (Photo by R. D'Amato)

FIG. 71 (Above right). Soldiers and Officers of Flavian Age, from the Templum Gentis Flaviae, last quarter of first century AD. (Photo by R. D'Amato)

FIG. 72 (Right). Attic helmet from Lake Nemi, 41 AD, Berlin, Antikensammlungen (copy in the Lake Nemi Museum) (Photo courtesy of Lake Nemi Museum)

FIG. 73 a–d. Trophies of arms and armour: Trasacco, oratory, first century BC – first century AD. (Photo by R. D'Amato)

In some places, the metal is as much as 7mm thick, which is unnecessary for the protective properties of a combat helmet. The helmet is 54cm high, which would have made it too uncomfortable to wear. The largest and heaviest gladiatorial helmets, which had the same high crest and were intended only for short combats, were only 40cm high.[53] Therefore, the helmet from Lake Nemi, if it had been made one of Caligula's guards,[54] would have significantly limited the mobility of the wearer's head due to its size and weight. For that reason, it seems more likely that this piece was part of a monumental frieze depicting armament, or part of some statue.[55]

Praetorians' equipment is depicted on the relief from the Villa Albani (now the Villa Torlonia in north-eastern Rome), which depicts the *spolia*.[56] Among them, we can see both helmets with longitudinal plumes and a muscle cuirass with a *gorgoneion* on the breast and *pteryges*[57] and ornate shields in different shapes. One of the shields bears the image of a scorpion,[58] which may indicate that this relief shows the armament of either the Praetorian Guard, or soldiers of the imperial horseguards (*equites singularis augusti*). Almost the same set of weapons is depicted in the relief from Trasacco (fig. 73a–d). But it shows scale armour instead of a muscle cuirass. This cannot be regular armour, but may be a gilded one, for example, similar to a fragment of scale armour made of gilded bone or ivory scales found during excavations at Pompeii.[59] According to the reports of ancient authors,[60] a gilded armour was not uncommon in the Praetorian Guard.

THE CAVALRY TOURNAMENTS (*HIPPIKA GYMNASIA*)

A cavalry tournament (*hippika gymnasia*) resembled gladiatorial games in terms of the participants' luxurious equipment, but differed from them in resulting in no casualties, since it was intended to perform a completely different task, i.e. to display military skills, the competition being in the form of a spectacular event. That is why a *hippika gymnasia* resembles a medieval tournament and may be considered to be the prototype of the latter. These cavalry competitions were not training exercises, because there was no room to perfect skills and the cavalrymen of the opposing team were the targets. It is appropriate to recall the words of Josephus Flavius who called such military performances 'bloodless battles'[61] due to the fact that special training weapons were used to fight, such as dummy javelins and darts. The art of swordsmanship required lengthy training and there is no doubt that even in the most distant past military techniques were perfected in mock battles. In this context, we can say that the tournament is no less ancient than war itself. However, only in Rome did it acquired a sort of cult status and visual appeal, due to which it gained particular popularity, as evidenced by the numerous finds of 'sporting' armament.

The earliest known cavalry tournament in Antiquity took place in the sixth century BC and was probably of Etruscan origin. It was called the *Lusus Troiae*.[62] This name, similar to the legendary city of Troy, previously led to misinterpretation, which has been refuted in later works, though it is impossible to prove it has nothing whatsoever to do with the legends of Troy.[63] These *Lusus Troiae* described by Publius Vergilius Maro[64] were performed by Roman boys of 6 to 17 years of age under the guidance of experienced coaches (*magistri*). They consisted in the entry onto the playing field, with subsequent changes in direction from circular rides to straight-line ones. Presumably, the patterns of the rides at those horse manoeuvres reproduced the layout of the Cretan labyrinth.[65] Special attention was paid to those games under Octavian Augustus. At that time this not only concerned the training of Roman youth, but also enabled the sons of aristocratic families to do justice to themselves before the Roman public, which could not but strengthen the status of the imperial dynasty and the prestige of traditional Roman values. These performances were held on different occasions: at funeral, at triumphal procession and the consecration of temples, as well as at the annual calendar holidays and, of course, at the Games.[66]

As early as under Augustus, the form of this ancient Roman cavalry tournaments was modified, but it was not until the reign of Hadrian that great importance began to be given to training horsemen to ride and fight in the Eastern manner, the better to confront the cavalry of the Empire's eastern enemies. *Hippika gymnasia*, of course, had little to do with the previous *Lusus Troiae*.[67] Arrian describes them as having a different origin. According to Arrian, *hippika gymnasia* were based on the cavalry games of various ethnicities who served in the Roman auxiliary cavalry. Along with the ancient Roman tradition, although Arrian did not directly mention *Lusus Troiae*, he highlights the influence of the Celtic cavalry which dominated the composition of the early Imperial cavalry units.[68] He also mentions Iberian, Scythian (Sarmatian), Parthian and Armenian influences.[69] Thus, Arrian describes an artificial product of Hadrian's era, which was newly created on the basis of many, more ancient formats.

Exercises to gain combat skills were extremely important in the Roman army, which can be seen from the lines written by a bystander, a former opponent of Rome: 'Their military exercises differ not at all from the real use of their arms, but every soldier is every day exercised and that with great diligence, as if it were in time of war ... nor would he be mistaken that should call those their exercises unbloody battles and their battles bloody exercises.' This is what Josephus wrote in 'The Wars of the Jews'.[70]

HIPPIKA GYMNASIA BY ARRIAN

On the appointed day, the audience and the rival teams of cavalrymen took their places on a specially constructed parade ground. The latter were in the field and the former on the spectators' tribune (*tribunal*). Arrian describes the venue of the cavalry tournament as a fenced square ground (Tact. 34.1). Unfortunately, Arrian does not tell us the size of this area, but the levelled grounds and earth-filled grandstand could be located near the fortresses. The best-known venues include similar grounds at Roman military camps in Great Britain: Hardknot – 160m x 90m, Maryport – 87m x 85m and Netherhall – 94m x 92m (all in Cumbria, a county in Northern England), and an unfinished ground at the castellum Tomen-y-Mur (North Wales) – 133m x 106m.[71] Their area is a little bit larger than a modern football field. For that reason, A. Hyland reasonably noted that these relatively small areas are unsuitable for simultaneous manoeuvres by several squadrons (*turmae*) and that such a limited space meant that the participants could only trot or canter.[72] Therefore, the parade grounds described by Arrian were intended exclusively for displays with a well-rehearsed choreography. Actual combat training of cavalrymen was held on different, more remote grounds, which, in addition, were larger and probably were not lacking in terrain obstacles.[73]

The tournament began with a spectacular circular ride of the squadrons,[74] during which the horsemen showed their formations in all their glory. The horsemen wore gilded iron or bronze helmets with anthropomorphic masks decorated with yellow plumes.[75] They carried brightly-coloured lightweight shields.[76] Instead of cuirasses, they wore special clothing for parades and equestrian exercises – multi-coloured 'Cimmerian' chitons[77] and narrow, tight-fitting trousers (*anaxirides*) of a design different to the wide trousers of the Parthian and Armenian style.[78]

According to Arrian, after the ride, a half of the riders remained on the left of the grandstand creating a formation the Romans called a 'tortoise' (*testudo*). They stood facing away from the opposing group, their backs being protected with shields.[79] The author explained that it was a defensive formation imitating an infantry 'tortoise'. In front of the right wing, two riders took up a position at some distance from the main formation, which would allow them to protect this wing while it reformed for a counter-attack.[80] It is still unclear what the formation of the opposing side on the right of the grandstand looked like. Arrian reports that the cavalrymen of this team attacked the enemy one after another.[81] At first, they attacked them as targets and threw blunt darts into them.[82] Then they turned to the right and rode back along an arc of a circle, apparently, to join their squadron.[83]

Then, the opposing team made a counter-attack, so that the attacking cavalrymen of both teams received all the darts thrown by both teams at each other. In this case, the most difficult task was to ensure that at the time of the throw the shields of the riders of both teams were opposite the shields of the opponents, i.e. on the right side of every fighter.[84] After that, the groups drew up in the original formation.

After the first attack, the teams repeated the whole procedure again, but in reverse: the attackers became defenders and vice versa.[85] This role reversal occurred twice, but the positions of the teams on the parade ground were changed for the third and fourth rounds.[86] This sequence is not mentioned in the text, but on the basis of the whole description, it appears that each group attacked once from the right and once from the left. According to Arrian,[87] the team that had been the first to attack was once again on the right of the grandstand in the last round.[88]

At the end of the first part of the exercise, the most skilled participants were still circling past the grandstand and throwing darts.[89] Then, a so-called 'Cantabrian attack' was arranged, whose origin Arrian links to the Iberian tribe of that name.[90] Both groups took again took up position opposite each other. The riders of both teams rode in turn, turned first to the left and then rode in a large circle in a clockwise direction. Where the two circles were almost touching, the riders threw by turns heavy darts into their opponents' shields. Since both opponents made their horses go faster and used heavy darts, the shields could sometimes be broken through, despite the fact that the darts did not have pointed heads. Therefore, the participants were instructed not to aim at the opponent's head or at his horse.

After the 'Cantabrian attack' the team exercises were over and they moved on to displays to demonstrate individual cavalrymen's skills in horsemanship and weapons-handling. Most of them were quite uncomplicated and are described in detail by Arrian, but the riders used regular combat equipment.[91]

MODERN RECONSTRUCTIONS OF CAVALRY TOURNAMENTS

At first sight, Arrian's description seems to be clear and understandable, but nowadays it is interpreted in different ways and different researchers propose their own versions for the reconstruction of the manoeuvres conducted by the cavalry teams, based either on theoretical considerations,[92] or from of practical

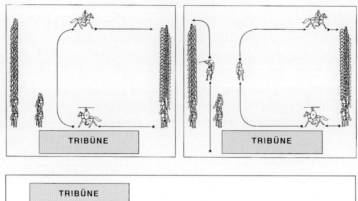

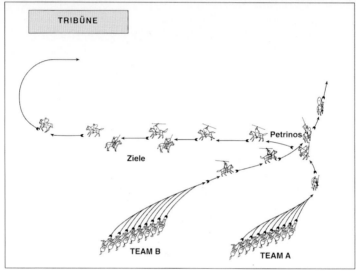

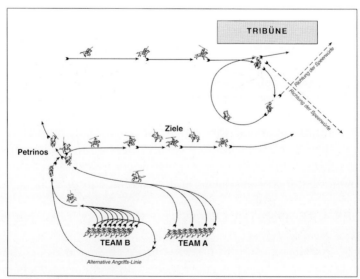

FIG. 74. Reconstruction of the manoeuvres of the opposing teams in *hippika gymnasia*. (After Lawson, 1980)

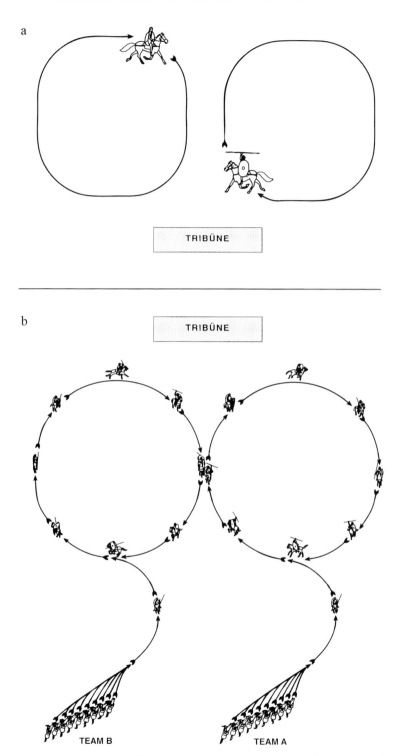

FIG. 75. Reconstruction of the Cantabrian attack during *hippika gymnasia*. ((a) after Lawson, 1980; (b) after Hyland, 1993)

experiments.[93] The first painting reconstructing these manoeuvres was by P. Connolly in his book about the Roman army.[94] In his artwork, a group of horsemen is galloping in a circle to the left and the riders throw spears to the right, without protecting themselves with their shields. Such a reconstruction contradicts the description given by Arrian and Connolly later corrected himself by making another reconstruction of a cavalry tournament for the illustrated biography of Tiberius Claudius Maximus.[95]

At first, A. Lawson[96] and then (after Connolly's accurate interpretation) A. Hyland[97] attempted to make a different reconstruction of the 'tortoise'. According to Lawson's interpretation, the horsemen of the defending team stand with their left side to the opponent, with their faces turned to the grandstand (fig. 74). The horses' heads are turned to the right to protect them from spears thrown and the shield just cover the left side of the horse and the rider. But in this case, Arrian's description is ignored, where he pointed out that the cavalry men were facing away from opposing group, protecting their backs with their shields.[98] The attacking group attacked in such a manner that the action took place just in front of the grandstand and such an arrangement might suggest that the defending team was more numerous, a fact which Arrian does not mention. (fig. 75)

FIG. 76. Reconstruction of the manoeuvres of the opposing teams in *hippika gymnasia*. (After Junkelmann, 1996)

An even greater discrepancy from the text of the source can be seen in the reconstruction made by A. Hyland.[99] The defending team ('Team B') stand facing the attacking group ('Team A'). Not only individual horses, but the whole front is at an angle to the line of attack, while the right wing is rather far advanced rather far and the horse on the left is at a distance of about one-third body length. In this case, the formation is so dense that those on the left could hardly have prevented their horses' heads hitting their neighbours' shields if they had turned their heads to the right. Furthermore, Hyland places both groups not on the left and right of the tribune opposite each other, but facing the tribune in parallel lines. In this case, in individual attempts she places both of them sometimes on the left-hand side of the parade ground and sometimes on the right. It is clear that for any manoeuvre it is the cavalry of the defensive 'Team B' who experience more difficulties, even in a counter-attack. This reconstruction received fair criticism from M. Junkelmann who tried to follow Arrian's text as close as possible (fig. 76). According to his interpretation, the men of the attacking team move out of the formation (also, perhaps, from the column) on the left and take up position in front of the defending team, standing with their backs to them in a 'tortoise' formation and the attackers throw blunt-headed spears at them. At the same time, the defending team sends out counter-attacking horsemen. This manoeuvre continues until each of the participants in the tournament has thrown his spear. The groups then switch roles.[100]

4

DECORATED ARMOUR OF THE PRINCIPATE IN ARCHAEOLOGICAL CONTEXT

PARADE, TOURNAMENT AND CEREMONIAL ARMAMENT: THE PROBLEM OF IDENTIFICATION OF 'PARADE' ARMOUR

Unfortunately, the written sources do not provide detailed descriptions of parade and tournament armour, so we have to restore the overall picture literally piece by piece and in some cases just theoretically. With this sort of problem, archaeological and iconographic sources are helpful. First of all, it is necessary to identify the main types of armour, helmets and other equipment, which could

be used during parades, triumphs and cavalry tournaments, from the iconographic sources showing various military ceremonies. As for the tournaments themselves, we have no surviving iconographic sources. The various military parades, triumphs and the emperor's solemn addresses to the army are a different matter; a sufficient number of different images depicting them survive. From these, we can learn the way emperors, commanders and soldiers were dressed at these ceremonies.

FIG. 77a–g (Right and opposite page). Roman decorated armour. Portonaccio sarcophagus, 190–200 AD, Rome, Museo Nazionale Romano (Palazzo Massimo) (Photo by A. E. Negin)

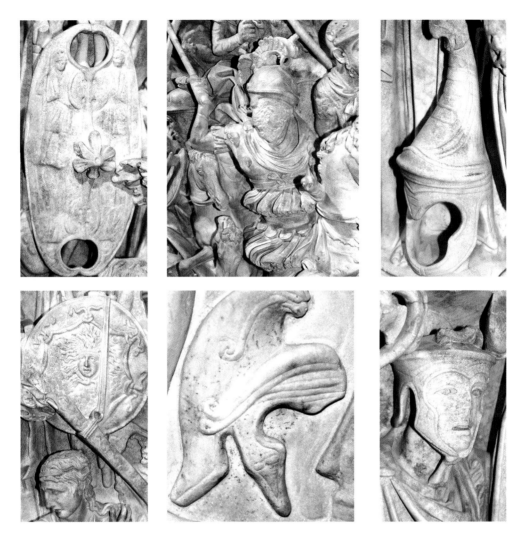

Most controversial is the classification of a particular richly-decorated item of weaponry as either parade or combat equipment. Many items of protective equipment, even decorated ones, have damage from the impacts of weapons, indicating that these items were directly used in combat. So, therefore, what are the basic criteria for determining what is parade armament? These may include the artistic look, profuse decoration and precious materials used in its manufacture or decoration, as well as its unusual shape. However, if the item has unquestionable protective properties besides all the above features, we should take into account its possible use for the protection of a fighting soldier in actual battle. Sometimes, some researchers refuse to believe that decorated armament would used in battle, as they think that it would be too expensive to repair damage to it.[1] We could accept this argument but we have some images of certain types of helmets, usually classified as ceremonial ones, which appear on reliefs depicting battles. So, fighting soldiers on the Portonaccio sarcophagus are shown wearing pseudo-Attic helmets (Heddernheim type)[2] (fig. 77a–g) and a Ribchester type helmet is clearly visible on the tombstone of the cavalryman Sextus Valerius Genialis, who shown attacking his enemies[3] (fig. 78).

If the rich decoration of an item is to be considered as the main feature of parade weapons, then it is hard to escape the conclusion that there was not only defensive parade armament, but also parade offensive weapons. For example, Herodian mentioned 'short swords used for processions'.[4] However, to date there have been no archaeological finds that would confirm the existence of special Roman parade swords. As for the so-called 'Sword of Tiberius', the scabbard of which is gilded and richly decorated with embossed ornamentation, it is most probably just a example of a ordinary combat weapon.[5] It reflects the trend for the elaborate decoration of weapons which was typical of the early Imperial period and the poor taste underlying this trend. From the reign of Octavian Augustus and Tiberius, the decor of sword scabbards bears the impression of a particular political ideology to ensure a dynastic succession.[6]

In contrast to the protective armament, a sword, a dagger and a military belt are items that were used not only in combat, as evidenced by the different iconographic sources. Therefore, great importance was attached to the decoration of these

FIG. 78. Gravestone of Sextus Valerius Genialis of Ala I Thracum, mid-first century AD, Cirencester, Omnium Museum, (Drawing by A. E. Negin)

items. However, careful analysis shows that even luxurious items of offensive arms, such as the 'Sword of Tiberius' or daggers and parts of the belt, were mass produced. Here, of course, it is difficult to draw the line between ordinary and ceremonial equipment, but the presence of these items in the majority of famous iconographic sources proves that they were used in everyday life.

Much more dispute arises as to the classification of items of panoply as ceremonial armament. Here, discussions concern face-mask helmets, richly-

FIG. 79. Cavalry helmet with tinning and embossed bronze sheet decoration (eagle) on iron base – former Axel Guttmann collection (AG 461), second century AD, Musée d'Art Classique de Mougins. (Photo courtesy of Musée d'Art Classique de Mougins)

---

decorated breastplates (and backplates) and shield bosses (medallions). All of them, even if they were richly decorated, could be used in combat as well. So, Guisborough/Theilenhofen-type helmets, which were the most widespread in the third century AD, are frequently classified as 'parade helmets' due their great weight.[7] (figs 60–61). However, researchers are currently inclined to believe that they were ordinary combat helmets.[8]

The basic shape of the Guisborough/Theilenhofen-type helmet[9] is substantially

FIG. 80a–b. (opposite and above) Helmet from Bryastovets, second century AD, Sofia, National Historical Museum. (Photo by R. D'Amato)

that of the Weiler/Koblenz-Bubenheim type-helmet[10] (fig. 62b), but in the first one the browband diadem is replaced with a vertical fronton with volutes and the crown is no longer decorated with curly hair and bears the image of figures, such as snakes, or several crests that imitate a plume of feathers. The cheek-pieces cover the ears, but the soldier's face remains exposed. The decorative design of the helmets resembles pseudo-Attic helmets existing at that time.[11]

Currently, several helmets, or fragments of them, have been found, which are transitional between the Weiler/Koblenz-Bubenheim type and the Guisborough/Theilenhofen type. The most complete piece was in the Guttmann collection (AG 461)[12] (fig. 79). Despite the rich decoration of these helmets, currently, there are no reasons to classify them as purely parade items.

It is also rather difficult to classify as cavalry 'sport' equipment the solid-forged sphero-conical helmets which are associated either with Sarmatian warriors of auxiliary units or Levantine archers.[13] These are pieces from Bryastovets (fig. 80a–b), Djakovo (fig. 81), Bumbeşti and Intercisa[14] The shape of these pieces resembles at the same time ancient 'bell-shaped' helmets from the territory of the Danube, sphero-conical helmets of the eastern Mediterranean world of the age of the Assyrians, Celtic helmets of the Berru type and even Montefortino-type helmets.[15] And half of the known examples have rich 'parade-styled' decoration.

The relief decoration of the Bryastovets helmet depicts a temple with the statues of Mercury, Apollo, Minerva, Victoria and Mars, and Neptune is depicted on the cheek-piece.[16] The Djakovo helmet is decorated with figures of Victoria, Jupiter

FIG. 81. Helmet from Djakovo, second century AD, Zagreb, Archaeological Museum. (Photo by R. D'Amato).

and Mars.[17] No images of the Greco-Roman gods, such as Apollo, Neptune, Venus and Bacchus, have been found on Roman parade armour. At the same time, Mars, Victoria and Minerva are quite common.[18] Such helmets were too expensive for an average infantryman who served in auxiliary units. It is more logical to assume they were used in the auxiliary Sarmatian cavalry (although iconographic monuments show segmental Sarmatian helmets), especially as there is an indirect indication of this. Lettering containing a double 'T' can be seen on the helmet from Intercisa, which was found during dredging operations in the Danube in the area where once there was a military camp of *cohors I milliaria Hemesenorum sagittaria equitata civium Romanorum*; the letters are thought to be a contraction of the word *turma*.[19] If that is true, then this group of helmets have no relation to infantry. But these helmets also have no relation to the Roman tournament helmets. It could be assumed that they had a purely ceremonial purpose, but these examples have good protective properties (the thickness of the material and additional protective parts in the form of cheek-pieces and scale aventails). At the same time, one of the reliefs in Adamclissi depicts Roman legionaries in very similar helmets, despite serious damages and cleavages on them. In this case, we can assume that a certain design of helmet was developed in a particular area under the influence of some purely local traditions, although we cannot exclude the influence of simultaneously-existing Eastern patterns as yet unknown to us that had been brought in by Syrian archers. In this case, the widespread hypothesis assuming that all these pieces belonged to soldiers of auxiliary troops of the Roman army is true. In this context, we can definitely assume that the helmets described were subjected to the influence of then-obsolete Montefortino and Coolus-type helmets. Not only is the shape of the crown similar, but in some cases, also the shape and parts of the pommels are similar. For example, the pommel of the Montefortino helmet from the Veselaya Dolina (Russia)[20] (where the button of the pommel was attached to the bowl with grooves and spikes) and that of the helmet from Djakovo are similar. The earliest of these helmets dates from the late first century AD, which also may indicate the influence of infantry helmets which had once been very popular, but by then were no longer in use. On the other hand, Eastern designs must have had a certain influence, particularly in terms of the decoration and various items for additional protection. But in any case, these helmets have no relation to the Roman cavalry sport helmets.

Medallions (20–30cm in diameter) are also related to the equipment used in *hippika gymnasia*, although their exact function remains to be discovered. Some authors consider them to be shield bosses,[21] while others, including P. Connolly, think that if they were oval, then they were decorative horse chest pieces.[22] Some of these medallions, those having holes for rivets, might be attached to the shields, but other ones were probably intended for other purposes. In any case, their aesthetic appeal was more important than their practical use. This observation can be extended to most of the equipment used in these shows. However, some of the medallions that have been found are damaged and the kind of damage indicates that in some cases it was inflicted with sharpened weapons, so therefore these items were not just used for tournaments.[23]

FIG. 82. Textile cover of Nijmegen helmet, Nijmegen, Valkhof-Kam Museum. (Photo by A. Pangerl)

Determining the purpose of face-mask helmets is the hardest problem. It is quite easy to identify the precursors of the Roman pieces, as well as their relationship with the Roman cavalry helmets. Among face-masks helmets

FIG. 83a–g. (opposite page) Details from the Sarcophagus Ludovisi, circa 251 AD, Rome, Museo of Palazzo Altems. (Photo by A. E. Negin)

FIG. 84. (Right) Roman statue of 'officer' in parade armour from Tyras, second century AD, Odessa, Archaeological Museum. (Drawing by A .E. Negin)

which became widely used under Augustus, there were examples the design of which was very similar to then existing helmets of cavalry units, that is, helmets which had an image of curly hair on the bowl. Moreover, helmets have recently been found that were covered by a wig of real horsehair. These wigs were on both combat helmets and face-mask helmets. Hellenistic pieces, as well as iconographic images of Alexander the Great, which were reflected in Roman art, could be the model for such helmets.[24] Most probably, a helmet with rendered curly hair became popular in the army as it copied the image of Alexander's helmet. Roman generals were depicted wearing similar helmets (see, for example, a bust of Germanicus from Erbach (Odenwald)[25]), which resemble, although in a somewhat modified shape, the image of Alexander appearing on a coin of Seleucus I.[26] Organic wigs of face-mask helmets from Nijmegen[27] and Vindonissa[28] (also used as a cover to protect the helmet from moisture) imitated the relief images of hairstyles on helmets (fig. 82). Even if the latter were equipped with masks, they also reproduced the iconographic image of Alexander the Great.[29]

Imitation curls on the crown can also be seen on Weiler/Koblenz-

FIG. 85. Decorated armour on the so-called Marius trophy, first century AD (?), Rome, Piazza del Campidoglio. (Photo by R. D'Amato)

Bubenheim-type helmets used by cavalrymen.[30] Some examples of this type are also richly decorated, due to which some researchers declare them to be ceremonial. However, M. Feugère places them between combat and parade pieces, which is more logical, as they have a number of features of both parade and combat helmets.[31]

Iconographic analysis of the face-mask helmets and the consideration of parallels from other cultural and historical periods lead to uncertain assumptions and associations. Reading the 'Tactics' of Arrian makes one believe that face-mask helmets were intended exclusively for use in cavalry tournaments. Arrian makes no mention of any religious or symbolic value they may have had, but he definitely distinguishes them from combat helmets. If we abandon these obvious conclusions from Arrian's text, the focus should be on two properties of these items, which are usually used to classify them as a tournament (sport) or parade armament, namely the richness of the decoration and the strength or weakness of the metal.

As we have seen, there is no precise definition for the criteria of parade armour, which means the classification of an item of armament as parade or tournament (sport) is difficult and there is no guarantee that it is reliable. There is only one criterion that can help to accurately determine parade armament, that is, the fact that decoration is made to the detriment of the protective properties of the armour. All other features do not allow precise classification and can often lead to misinterpretation, creating unnecessary confusion. It is, therefore, more appropriate to consider the majority of the items described herein as having diverse functions. Some of them could be used both at cavalry tournaments, in parades and at some ceremonies and even in battle. Therefore, some of the examples presented are classified as purely parade armament rather conditionally, based on the tradition of the European school of arms and armour studies.

ARMOUR

BREAST AND BACK PLATES

Since when describing the Cimmerian clothing of horsemen participating in the cavalry tournaments, Arrian says it was different from the ordinary cuirasss,[32] we can assume that a particularly lightweight type of scale or linen cuirass was used in tournaments. This was reinforced by a two-piece plate on the breast and a one-piece plate on the back which are well known to archaeologists. Due to the luxurious decoration on them, these plates were associated with the elements that classify these as parade or tournament cuirasses. This classification is also supported by the thinness of the plates, which rules out any practical protective role.

The typology given by J. Garbsch still continues to be the basis for classifying these breastplates.[33] New finds are also described according to his classification which considered two-piece breastplates almost exclusively[34] (figs 86–93). Such

FIG. 86. (Opposite top) Breastplates from Samum, second century AD. (Drawing by A. E. Negin after Isac, Barbulescu, 2008, Abb. 5)

FIG. 87. (Opposite bottom) Breasplates from Mušov-Burgstall and Orgovany, second half of the second century AD, Prague, Národní Muzeum, Kecskemét, Bâcs-Kiskun megyei müzeum. (Drawing by A. E. Negin)

FIG. 88. (Above) Breastplates from Manching, early third century AD, München, Archäologische Staatssammlung. (Drawing by A. E. Negin)

---

breastplates consisted of a pair of high rectangular plates, the narrow upper sides of which were cut, repeating the neck shape. When interconnected, they circled the neck. The lock which connected them consisted of rotary latches which were inserted into the cuts of the counter-fastener, rotated at an angle of 90° and fastened with a pin or a splint. A fastener with a splint located directly on the plates is less common. This rarer type of fastener is found on items from Pfünz and Künzing.[35] The outer edges of the plates have holes for rivets to attach the plates to the breast part of the armour shirt. Punched round holes for such rivets can be seen on the central part of the scales of the armour from Hrušica[36] (fig. 94). Older examples have vertically-arranged pairs of holes with surviving pieces of wire. They were used for linking in a similar way to the horizontal strapping of armour scales.

Trapezoidal one-piece back plates can be distinguished in all the materials published to date. These included pieces from Ritopek[37] (fig. 88), Carnuntum,[38]

Fig. 89: Breastplate of the second–third centuries AD from private collection, courtesy of the owner. (Photo by R. D'Amato)

FIG. 90. (Opposite) Part of decorated breastplate from Shumen, second century AD, Bulgaria, private collection, courtesy of the owner. (Photo by R. D'Amato)

Aquincum[39] (fig. 86a), Gherla,[40] Enns (Lauriacum)[41] (fig. 86b), Zalalevo[42] and the Romisch-Germanisch Zentralmuseum in Mainz[43] (fig. 86d) (figs 95–98). The plate from Ritopek (Tricornium) (Belgrade, National Museum Inv. 4180 / III) bears the images of seven busts of gods, a battle scene, two cohort standards, two eagles and also has some inscriptions (fig. 88). The seven busts seem to be the images of the seven gods of the days of the week. On the bottom left, there is a bust of Saturn (Saturday), whose attributes are a coverlet, a sickle and a bull; above him is Sol (Sunday; a wreath of rays and whip can be seen) and above them is the Moon (Monday), with the end of the lunar sickle behind her right shoulder. Mercury (Wednesday) with two wings in his hair is on the top right. The bust of a man wearing a helmet with a spear, in a cuirass and cloak is in the centre of the plate; he is Mars (Tuesday). The bust of Jupiter (Thursday) recognisable by a cluster of lightning bolts, is in the centre to the right. The bust of a woman with a stylised mirror is beneath him; she is Venus (Friday).[44]

The breastplate from Ritopek is unique in the iconography of parade armament. But if we analyse the statistics of the scenes depicted on Roman parade armament, we will have a somewhat different view. Preference is given to a standard set of characters: Mars, Victoria and the eagle of Jupiter (but Jupiter himself was depicted

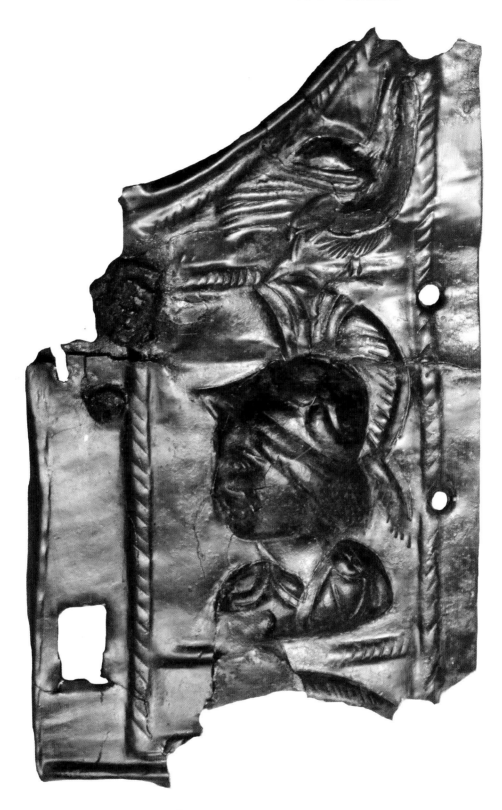

FIG. 91. Breastplate from Potaissa, second century AD, Turda, Muzeul de Istorie Turda. (After Isac, Barbulescu, 2008, Abb. 22)

---

only a few times). Older items dating from the beginning of the first–second centuries AD still depicted quite a wide range of gods, while at the end of the second century AD a fairly stereotypical iconographic combination was worked out, in which the busts of Mars and Minerva (or Virtus), and rarely Jupiter and Hercules, were depicted facing each other in an inversed manner on two-piece items. The eagle of Jupiter was usually placed on the wedge-shaped protrusion on the top of the plates.[45]

Although these plates are still directly linked to the parade/tournament armour due to their lavish decor, at the same time they are rarely found in the well-known buried hoards of specific parade/tournament armament. Breast or back plates have been found in three of the thirteen known hoards of parade and tournament armament dated from the first half of to the mid-third century AD. These hoards contain mostly ornate helmets, chamfrons, horse eye-guards and greaves, as these items were expensive and, in addition, were purely parade or tournament ones and were not widely used.[46] The situation was somewhat different for breastplates. They could be used in a wider range of applications, as there are strong reasons to assume that they were part of combat equipment. There are plates with inscriptions proving they were used by the legions (LEG X, LEG XIIII).[47] Hence, perhaps, they were used not only in the cavalry, as previously thought, but in the legionary infantry, as well. As suggested by M. Bishop, such plates could be used not only together with a mail or scale armour, but with segmental armour. The

FIG. 92. Breastplates of the second–third centuries AD from various private collections, courtesy of the owners. (Photos and drawings by R. D'Amato and A. E. Negin)

researcher came to this hypothesis due to the sculpture of Alba Iulia (Romania), which depicts a scale shoulder doubling, or gorget, with a double-wing breastplate embedded into it, which is put over a *lorica segmentata*.[48] According to the author of this interpretation, these plates enabled the neck opening of the armour to be

98

FIG. 94. (Above) Decorated breastplate from Hrusica, third–fourth century AD, Ljubljana, Narodni Muzej. (Photo by R. D'Amato)

FIG. 93. (Opposite) Roman decorated breastplates, second–third centuries AD: (a)–(d) Carnuntum (Brigetio) ((a) Vienna, Kunsthistorisches Museum. Antikensammlung; (b)–(d) Bad Deutsch Altenburg, Museum Carnuntinum); (e) Pernik, Pernik, Regionalen istoricheski Muzej; (f) Adana, Adana, Museum; (g) Alba Iulia, Muzeul National al Unirii Alba Iulia; (h) Lauriacum (Enns),Enns, Museum (i) Saalburg, Bad Homburg, Saalburg-Museum; (j) Mundelsheim, Stuttgart, Württembergisches Landesmuseum. (Drawing by A. E. Negin)

FIG. 95. Roman decorated breastplates, second–third centuries AD: (a) Aquincum, Budapest, Aquincumi Múzeum; (b) Lauriacum (Enns), Enns, Museum; (c) Heerlen, Heerlen, Gemeentelijk Oudheidkundig Museum; (d) RGZM; (e) Brigetio (Szöny), Budapest, Magyar Nemzeti Mûzeum ((a) Photo by R. D'Amato; (d) Photo by E. Künzl; (b), (c), (e) Drawing by A. E. Negin)

FIG. 96. Breastplate from Bertoldsheim; after and before restoration, second–third centuries AD, Neuburg an der Donau, Museum. (Drawing by A. E. Negin)

enlarged when it was being put on and after that, the armour was fastened, adjusting for the required neck diameter. Thus, decorated breastplates began to perform the function of the previous shaped flare hooks fastening the neckpieces of mail or scale armour at the end of the Republican period and in the Early Imperial period.[49] M. Bishop draws an analogy with the locks of the breastplates of *loricae segmentatae*, therefore linking the decorated breastplates and battle armour.[50]

M. Junkelmann offered a different interpretation of the plates in terms of their use in *hippika gymnasia*. Arrian does not mention any mail or scale armour, but describes the multi-coloured 'Cimmerian' chitons of the participants in these

FIG. 97. (Above left) Breastplate from Ritopek, early third century AD, Belgrade, National Museum. (Photo courtesy of National Museum Belgrade)

FIG. 98. (Above right) Breastplate fragment, late third century, Italian private collection. (Photo by R. D'Amato)

FIG. 98b. (Below) Armour plaques of *Squama*, third century AD, Italian private collection. (Photo by F. Casprini)

FIG. 98c. Armour plaque, third century AD, Italian private collection. (Photo F. Casprini)

events.[51] Therefore, Junkelmann assumed that a plate was sewn directly onto the linen armour.[52] In this case, it was more probably a decorative item, like other elements of tournament equipment, especially since a horseman who was protected by a shield could not be serious injured by a blunt spearhead. As to the classification of the plates as part of purely parade armament, any protective function is basically excluded in this case.

In light of the above, it is logical to assume that the breastplates were versatile and were used both in parade and tournament equipment and in combat, but in any case the plates served as cuirass buckles and, in addition to that, they acted as additional decoration of the armour.

MUSCLE CUIRASS (*STATOS* OR *THORAX STADIOS*)

Quite often, statues and other images (on coins, reliefs, murals) of emperors show them dressed in anatomical cuirass with pteryges (a leather or metal fringe) (*lorica musculata*). For the most part, we see emperors speaking to the army (*adlocutio*). Typically, such addresses were made during military assemblies (*contiones*), parades and other ceremonial events in the Roman army. So, richly-decorated anatomical cuirasses can also be classified as parade equipment.

The use of such cuirasses by Roman generals had quite a long tradition: they were worn from the Republican period up to the fourth or even the fifth century AD. However, some soldiers also sometimes wore similar armour as can be seen from graphic sources. The famous relief dated from the second century in the Louvre shows a group of Praetorians, or at least officers.[53] This image shows a wide range of items of military equipment, including a muscle cuirass worn by a soldier. On the reliefs located on the base of the column of Antoninus Pius, one of the centurions also wears a similar cuirass and Trajan's Column depicts almost all the officers in anatomical cuirasses. The officers' cuirasses shown on the columns of Trajan and of Marcus Aurelius are shortened versions of the ordinary anatomical cuirass.[54]

Most of the scenes depicting soldiers in such cuirasses also show various military marches, parades and meetings. Therefore, we can assume that again they are not combat equipment. All these cuirasses reveal natural simplicity and, at the same time, the armourer's workmanship. Obviously, such armour was very expensive and was most probably unaffordable by most soldiers, especially if it was made of bronze or iron. Bronze cuirasses were common in the Italic peninsula long before the Christian era. They are found, in particular, among the finds of Etruscan and Greek artefacts and the existence of iron pieces is supported by the fact that some sculptures of anatomical cuirasses have traces of blue paint.[55]

We can distinguish two kinds of cuirasses from the body of iconographic material. One has no marked waist, while other models are anatomically waisted. A soldier in armour with no marked waist is depicted on the relief shown a group of Praetorians from the Louvre. Designs with no marked waist apparently had disappeared by the time of the Nerva–Antonine dynasty. Iconography presents

FIG. 99. Roman cuirassed statues from Susa, first century AD, Turin, Museo Archeologico. (Photo by A. E. Negin)

FIG. 100. Statue of Titus in full armour, first century AD, Naples, National Archaeological Museum. (Photo by R. D'Amato)

various combinations of scenes, but some of them are more common than others and some can only be found during short periods of time.

The most typical style of decoration was that with an underlying propaganda message. There were also religious motifs to illustrate myths. For example, a griffin with its wings spread is one of the most common images that can be found on the anatomical cuirasses of the Imperial period. Cuirasses also depicted items of religious faith (chandeliers, skulls of sacrificial animals and garlands in the form of large bundles of flowers and fruit).[56] This rich decoration adorned not only the cuirass, but sometimes *pteryges* strips, which could depict cornucopias, birds (especially eagles, cockerels and pigeons), bears, badgers, wolves, griffins, the

FIG. 101. 101. Statue of Roman general or Mars, from the Forum of Nerva, end of first century AD, Rome, Musei Capitolini (Photo by A. E. Negin)

FIG. 102. Statue *loricata* of the governor of Asia, second century AD, Istanbul, Archaeological Museum. (Photo by R. D'Amato)

Capitoline wolf (*Lupa Capitolina*) with Romulus and Remus, the Dioscuri, rosettes, garlands, metal circles (discs) and river gods, Nereids, Mater Matuta and many others.

The cuirasses themselves bear far fewer images. Most frequently we see an apotropaic image in the form of the head of Medusa (*gorgoneion*) which is placed on the breast of the cuirass and sometimes on *pteryges* strips. The images of the goddess Nike (Victoria) who was the personification of victory, as well as an eagle (the symbol of the power of the Roman state) prove that the decoration of some cuirasses had propaganda value. The theme of victory over the enemy is rendered

FIG. 103. Cuirassed Hadrian from Tell Shalem (Scythopolis), second century AD, Jerusalem, National Museum. (Photo by M. Reuveni)

FIG. 104. Statue of Hadrian from Hierapetra, second century AD, Istanbul, Archaeological Museum (Photo by R. D'Amato)

FIG. 105 (a)–(b). Fragments of Lorica from statue, from Industria, first–second century AD, Turin, Museo Archeologico. (Photos by A. E. Negin and R. D'Amato)

FIG. 106. Emperor Caracalla in muscle armour, sacrificial scene, early third century AD, Warsaw, National Archaeological Museum. (Photo by R. D'Amato)

in the decoration of Roman weapons through the images of the military deities: Jupiter, Minerva, Mars, Victoria, Virtus and Bellona.[57] The Dioscuri and Heracles can also be included in the ranks of these deities. However, in addition to the deities listed above, victory was also symbolised by the figure of the victorious emperor.

Scenes with *spolia* and, in general with the captured arms and armour are allegoric presentations of the conquest of countries and provinces, as the idea of victory was impossible for the Romans without the consecrated seizure of enemy weapons after a victorious battle, which implied the taking of armour from dead enemies by the winners.[58] Without this, a victory seemed incomplete, as a general deserved honours only if he had in hand the actual proof of his victory over a strong and well-armed enemy. Lightning bolts, often placed on the shoulder doublings of cuirasses, are a fairly common military symbol, although the example is taken from the Greeks and obviously has a link to Jupiter the Thunderer.

FIG. 107. Trophies of arms and armour: Oberbayern, Prutting Church, AD 310–311 (mask helmets and other weapons). (Photo courtesy of Dr. Kreuzmer Theresia)

Most cuirasses had to be made of bronze or iron similarly to their Hellenistic prototypes, but it is probable that some could be made of leather. It is possible that some ceremonial muscle cuirasses were also painted like the cuirass of Augustus from Prima Porta. However, it is very doubtful that they were worn at various ceremonies and military parades. The lustre and shine of a metal cuirasses, which was polished and plated with gold and silver, was preferred for solemn events.

The most famous representation of a cuirass, which can be seen on the statue of Augustus from the Villa of Livia in Prima Porta, has a unique iconography that deserves special attention[59] (fig. 108). The figures shown on this cuirass represent the *Pax Romana* (Roman peace) established by Caesar Augustus. This is indicated

FIG. 108. (Opposite) Prima Porta Augustus statue. (After L. Fenger, 1886, courtesy of Staatliche Antike Sammlung and glyptotheke Anschrift, Munich)

by an allegorical figure supporting the heavens depicted on top of the cuirass. One of the diplomatic successes of Caesar Augustus is shown in the central part of the breastplate. After the Romans suffered a humiliating defeat at the hands of the Parthians at Carrhae (53 BC) and lost their standards and regalia, Caesar Augustus negotiated their return. The return of the standards was depicted in the decoration of the cuirass. Here, we can see the ideological message in action.[60]

During its long history, the Roman anatomical cuirass evolved from ordinary combat armour to the symbol of Roman military ranks. Every general, legate and emperor, wishing to emphasise their military merits and valour, had himself depicted in such a cuirass, which served as a symbolic embodiment of the idea of power. In a similar fashion, we can consider the statue of Augustus from the Villa of Livia in Prima Porta and the statue of Hadrian from Hierapytna[61] and many other images of emperors, as in the period of the Principate the victories of Roman arms were inextricably linked with the ruling emperor as a carrier of the highest *imperium* and the auspices.[62] Moreover, this propaganda was targeted at all parts of the Roman society and not just the Roman one. Conquered nations also had to experience the heavy hand of the emperor who had conquered them. The sculptures of emperors in armour (*loricati*)[63] having been set up in large numbers throughout the Roman Empire served as a constant reminder to such nations. It is absolutely no coincidence that the cuirasses of many statues depicted scenes with the conquered and defeated opponents of the Roman power. These were to hold in awe and inspire devotion in all enemies of the Roman state and all the conquered nations. According to K. Ando, these images of Roman triumph over and humiliation of the defeated enemy were originally seen in the newly-annexed territories as an insult and mockery and provoked resentment, which, however, eventually gave way to a realisation that Rome was ruling by the right of the strongest.[64] Simultaneously, such messages expressed in artistic images could serve as a warning to anyone who intended to threaten Roman power.[65] According to Gregory of Nazianzus, these images of emperors were intended for popular contemplation.[66]

However, it is quite reasonable to consider anatomical cuirasses of the Roman emperors and generals as parade items, as their ideological function was a necessary constituent part of the visual imagery of splendid military processions and other military ceremonies. As there is an insufficient number of real cuirasses available to archaeologists, the questions are of how reliable the iconographic sources are and to what extent they corresponded to the actual items, none of which have survived whole and undamaged to the present.

Until recently, the images were the only source of knowledge about Roman items. Earlier anatomical cuirasses manufactured under the Greek and Hellenistic influence are frequently found in graves in the territory of Greater Greece and Etruria. It is only by accident that pure Roman samples can survive until now as there was no tradition of putting armour into Roman graves under the late Republic and Empire, and because they were costly (especially those adorned with rich decoration and owned by the generals).

It is exactly these accidental finds that private collections receive. Although the dating of these fragments is often questionable, these finds do deserve the

FIG. 109. Late-antique muscled armour in bronze, ridge-helmet and spangenhelm check-guard, fourth century AD? – sixth century AD, Guttman collection. (Photo courtesy of Christie's)

attention of researchers. The former Guttmann collection contained the breast part of an anatomical cuirass,[67] which bore absolutely no additional decoration (fig. 109). This example has been given a wide range of dates in the auction catalogues:

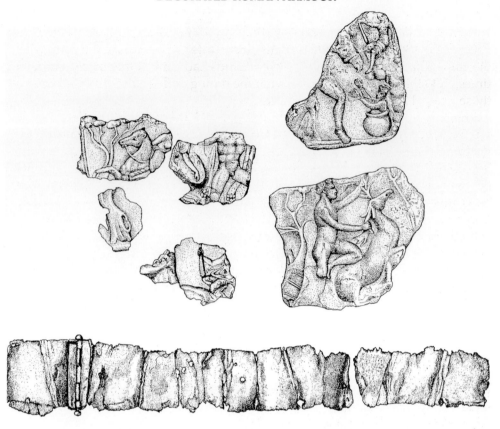

FIG. 110. Fragments of muscle cuirass from Kemnitz, first century AD, Wünsdorf, Brandenburgisches Landesamt für Denmalpflege und Arch. Landesmuseum (after Fischer, 2004)

from the first century BC to the first century AD. However, since this was an accidental find, the dating was made by analogy with the Roman images; as a result, its accurate attribution to a specific period is unreliable.

It should be noted that interpretation of such fragments can be complicated. It is difficult to distinguish fragments of real cuirasses from fragments of cuirasses from bronze statues or their imitations on the reliefs depicting *spolia*, as both were often manufactured life-size. However, in archaeological literature, some fragments are presumed to be associated with real cuirasses. A bronze relief depicting two Victories that are building a trophy, under which captive barbarians are sitting, can be classified as such. Possibly, this item was part of a cuirass, as suggested by the authors of the catalogue of the bronzes stored in the National Library in Paris.[68]

Some researchers believe that the bronze cuirass found in the so-called 'Cave of Jars' (Cueva del Jarro) near Almuñécar (Granada, Spain) is Imperial Roman in origin.[69] This armour was associated with Dressel 20 and 38 type amphorae found in the same place. However, the article published in 1974 reported that the cuirass was transferred to the museum without any amphorae. It is also noted that fishermen used to bring up items dated from different periods in the place where the cuirass had been found, since several ships had sunk at that place at different times.[70] On this basis, it is doubtful that the dating of this cuirass can be based on those Dressel 20 and 38 type amphorae.[71]

The only fragments, presumably being part of a Roman cuirass made of gilded bronze, are the finds in the grave of a German chieftain in Kemnitz, Brandenburg, Potsdam (Germany)[72] (fig. 110). In the grave were placed six fragments which depict the Labours of Hercules (the capture of the Ceryneian Hind, the capture of the wild Erymanthian boar and the battle with the Queen of the Amazons). It can be assumed that they were part of a captured Roman cuirass. The context of this find supports the idea that such decorated cuirasses were the very expensive equipment of senior officers of the Roman army and were coveted *spolia* for the enemies of Rome, who had something to boast about when they happened to take such symbolic embodiments of the power and might of Rome, as well as the symbol of the highest Roman military ranks.

GREAVES

Greaves were known as protective equipment as early as in the epics by Homer,[73] with archaeological finds coming from the Mycenaean warrior graves.[74] There were Greek and Etruscan pieces which protected the whole lower leg, but at the same time there were greaves of simple design, which were made of a bronze plate that was laced to the front of the leg only.[75]

FIG. 111. Straubing hoard: greaves, early third century AD, Straubing, Gäubodenmuseum. (Photo by R. D'Amato)

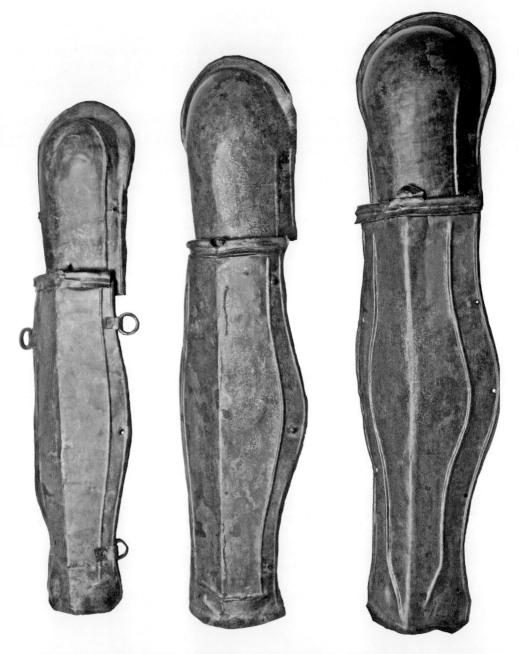

FIG. 112. (Above) Greaves from Eining, beginning of the third century AD, München, Archäologische Staatssammlung. (Photo by A. Lemeshko)

FIG. 113. (Opposite) Undecorated greaves: (a), (e) from lower Italy, second century AD, Brussels, Musée du Cinquantenaire; (b) Hebron hoard, early second century AD, Jerusalem, National Museum; (c) unknown provenance; (d) Oberstimm, second century AD, Ingolstadt, Museum. (Drawing by A. E. Negin)

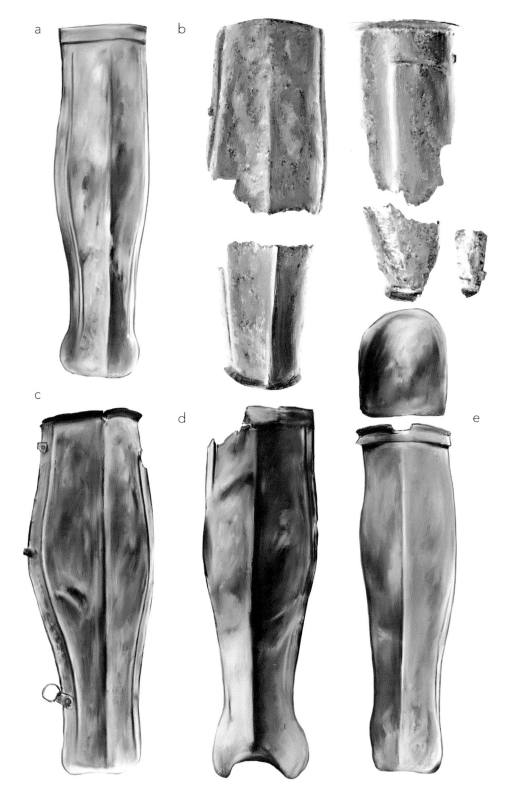

FIG. 114. Medallion and greave from Welzheim hoard, second century AD, Stuttgart, Württembergisches Landesmuseum. (Drawing by A. E. Negin)

Based on the iconographic sources, centurions in the Roman Imperial army wore decorated greaves.[76] Based on the images on the metopes of the memorial in Adamclissi, short, plain unadorned greaves evidently came to be used by the legionaries at the beginning of the second century AD in order to protect their right leg which was not covered by the shield.[77] Probably at the end of the third century AD or at the beginning of the fourth century AD, pairs of greaves came to be used by heavy infantry, as shown, for example, by the image of a pair of greaves on the

FIG. 115. (Opposite) Roman decorated greaves of the second–third centuries AD: (a) Aquincum, Museum; (b) Regensburg, Regensburg, Museum der Stadt; (c) Bad Deutsch-Altenburg, Bad Deutsch-Altenburg, Museum Carnuntinum; (d) Slavonski Brod, Slavonski Brod, Muzej Brodskog Posavlja; (e) Fort Louis, Haguenau, Musée de la ville. (Drawing by A. E. Negin)

FIG. 116. (Above) Knee pads for fixing scheme of greaves. (Drawing by A. E. Negin)

FIG. 117. (Below) Knee pads from Carnuntum, second–third centuries AD, Archäologische Staatssammlung München. (Drawing by A. E. Negin)

tombstone of the legionary Severus Acceptus of the Legio VIII Augusta.[78] All these cases concern infantry. Due to numerous finds in the buried hoards in Straubing[79] (fig. 111) and Eining[80] (fig. 112), decorated greaves were classified as being parade armour of auxiliary cavalrymen.

Undecorated bronze or iron examples found elsewhere have a vertical ridge along their whole length in the middle and a more-or-less tight bend copying the outline of the calf (figs 113–114). On both sides, there are two or three bronze rings riveted to them to insert leather straps to attach them to the leg. Since these greaves have a straight edge at top and bottom, they do not protect the knee or ankle, and due to this we can classify this design as an infantry version.[81] This seems logical, as the infantryman's knee would have been covered by his

FIG. 118. Greave from Merida, first century AD, Merida, Museo de Arte Romano. (Drawing by A. E. Negin)

FIG. 119. Greave fragment from Arbeia, early fourth century AD, Arbeia Roman Fort and Museum. (Photo by R. D'Amato)

FIG. 120. Greaves from private European collections, second–third centuries AD, courtesy of the owners. (Drawings and photos by A. E. Negin and R. D'Amato)

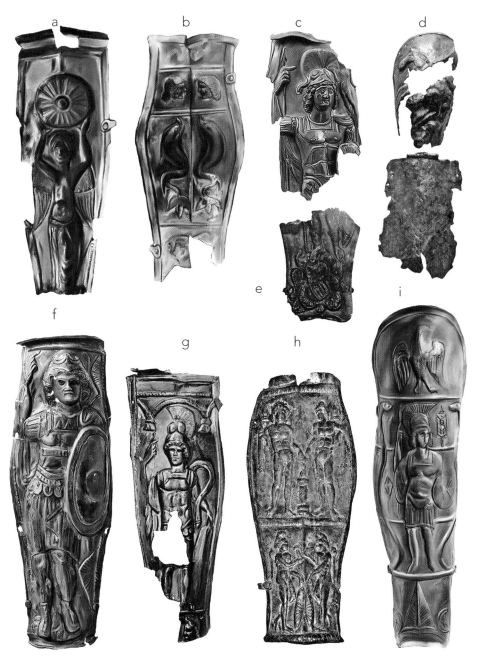

FIG. 121. Roman decorated greaves, second–third centuries AD: (a) Topči, Razgrad, Museum; (b) Giulesti, Bucharest, Muzeul National de Istorie a României; (c) Athens, Benaki Museum; (d) Augsburg, Augsburg, Römermuseum; (e) Novae, Novae, Archeological Museum; (f) Speyer, Speyer, Historisches Museum der Pfalz; (g) former Axel Guttmann collection (AG 807); (h) RGZM O.42646; (i) Munchen Kunsthandel, Gerhard Hirsch. (Drawing by A. E. Negin; (e) Photo by S. Dimitrov; (h) Photo by M. Greenhalgh)

fairly large shield and on the basis of images showing similar pieces on infantrymen.

A more complex shape, such as, for example, from the greave from Eining.[82] has a curved bottom edge or protruding side parts to protect the ankles. In addition, in such examples there is a hinged knee part with side loops for attaching a strap. According to J. Garbsch, protection of the knee and ankle proves that it is a cavalry version.[83]

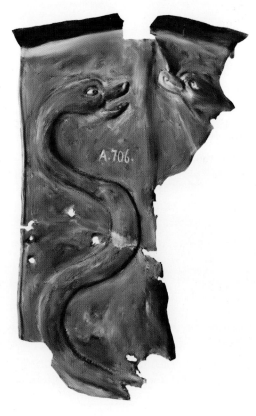

FIG. 122. (Left) Greave with representation of the god Mars, ex Guttman collection, second–third centuries AD.

FIG. 123. (Below) Decorated greave from Italy, second–third centuries AD, Brussels, Musée du Cinquantenaire. (Drawing by A. E. Negin)

FIG. 124. (Above) Fragments of greave from Enns, second–third centuries AD, Enns, Museum. (Drawing by A. E. Negin)

FIG. 125.(Right) Plane greave found on the site of the battle of Abrittus near Razgrad. (Photo courtesy of Prof. Valeri Yotov)

On decorated greaves (figs 115–125), the knee part also has some decoration, often in the form of busts or heads of Minerva (Virtus or Bellona?), Fortune and Mars.[84] The fastening of the knee part to the greave plate was in the same way as in the undecorated pieces, namely, by mean of an ordinary hinge. Generally, the greaves were tied to the leg with leather straps, but on the greaves from Fort-Louis thin chains were used instead.[85]

SHIELDS

According to Arrian, richly-painted shields with decorated bosses, lighter than military versions, were used at cavalry tournaments.[86] If the existence of special shields for *hippika gymnasia* is supported by what Arrian wrote, the manufacture of special shields for parades remains questionable, as Josephus Flavius wrote that ordinary uncovered shields were used at solemn processions.[87] Unfortunately, it

FIG. 126. Shields from Dura-Europos, early third century AD. (Top: drawing by A. E. Negin; bottom: drawing by Andrea Cipolla)

FIG. 127. Engraved and decorated umbos of first–second centuries AD: (a) Kirkham, London, British Museum; (b) umbo depicting scenes of the Dacian wars, private English collection; (c) Roshava Dragana, Stara Zagora Regional Historical Museum; (d) former Axel Guttmann collection (AG 598), Musée d'Art Classique de Mougins; (e) Syria (?) private collection; (f) Halmeag, Sibiu, Muzeul Național Brukenthal. ((a), (e) Drawing by A .E. Negin; (b) After Negin 2010, fig. 27; (c) Photo courtesy of Stara Zagora Regional Historical Museum; (d) Photo courtesy of Musée d'Art Classique de Mougins; (f) photo courtesy of Sibiu, Muzeul Național Brukenthal)

FIG. 128. Medallions (horse *falerae* and shield bosses), second–third centuries AD: (a) Miltenberg, Kopenhagen, Nationalmuseum; (b) Tabriz, Archäologische Staatssammlung München; (c) Bad Deutsch-Altenburg, Bad Deutsch-Altenburg, Museum Carnuntinum; (d) Schwarzenacker, Speyer, Historisches Museum der Pfalz; (e) Lauriacum, Enns, Museum; (f) Köln, Köln, Römisch-Germanisches Museum; (g) Bonn, Bonn, Rheinisches Landesmuseum; (h) München, Archäologische Staatssammlung, Inv. no. 1996, 2087 ((a) – Photo by Kopenhagen, Nationalmuseum; (c) Photo by RGZM; (g) Photo by Dr Michael Greenhalgh; (b), (d), (e), (f), (h) Drawing by A. E. Negin)

FIG. 129. (Above left) Medallion or shield boss from Blerik, second century AD, Nijmegen, Valkhof-Kam Museum. (Photo by R. D'Amato)

FIG. 130. Above right) Decorated shield boss from Bali Bunar, second–third centuries AD, Sofia, National Historical Museum. (Drawing by A. E. Negin)

is absolutely impossible to formulate criteria to describe parade shields, except for the assumption that they were lavishly painted.

In this connection, three oval shields of the third century AD from Dura-Europos, made of poplar boards1cm thick, are referred to as parade shields (fig. 126). They were not covered with leather or other material and the painting was applied directly to the wood. One depicts a battle with Amazons (Amazonomachy) and the other a scene of the Trojan War. The names of the main characters in Greek are preserved on both paintings. The third shield shows a huge soldier with a shield and a spear, which is thought to be the image of the warrior god Yaribol.[88] However, what is the definition of lavish painting, which allows an item to be characterised as a costly one for parades? Numerous shields depicted on Trajan's Column and other Roman monuments allow an insight into the variety of decorative painting of shields, from simple ones to the most intricate. On the other hand, the pieces of Dura-Europos were made using the standard palette of colours available to Roman artists: white, black, sienna and red ochre. More expensive paints were provided to the artist by the customer.[89] Therefore, we can judge whether the painting of these shields was costly only in terms of the whole range of work produced by the artist.

If the parade and tournament shields were splendidly painted, they would probably have been provided with no less beautiful engraved, embossed and relief bosses. Similarly to the bosses of combat shields, bronze or iron parade bosses were usually made flat at the edges, with four holes for rivets and a convex hemisphere in the middle, to put the hand when holding the shield. Several so-called

FIG. 131. (Above) Decorated shield boss, second century AD, Sofia, National Historical Museum. (Photo by R. D'Amato)

FIG. 132. (Opposite page) Rectangular shield boss with bust/head of Dionysos surrounded by foliate scrollwork, end of the second – beginning of the third century AD, private collection.

'medallions' have been found, which are interpreted either as shield bosses or as horse chest guards. Researchers who oppose the theory that these medallions were bosses claim that if they were indeed a part of a shield, then they could only be used for the purposes of parade armament, as prominent reliefs of heads and busts would inevitably have been damaged in combat and would have been much more difficult to repair than ordinary bosses.[90] But what is most important, according to supporters

of this theory, is that in most cases, they could not accommodate a fist holding the shield, due to the fact that they are not convex enough. In general, they agree that this group of large medallions made of sheet bronze with artistic decoration belongs, in terms of style, to parade items, but, however, they classify them as horse equipment, especially the oval ones, which are not typical for the Roman bosses of battle shields. However, to date there is no definitive argument that can support this conclusion. In fact, it is almost safe to say that if these medallions have a rectangular plate with punched holes at the edges, there is no doubt that they are shield bosses similar to heavier versions of the second century AD, with engraved and embossed decor.

FIG. 133. (Above) Square shield boss, second century AD, Archäologische Staatssammlung München. (Drawing by A. E. Negin)

FIG. 134. (Below left) Decorated shield boss with lion's head, second century AD, from the former Axel Guttmann collection(?).

FIG. 135. (Below right) Parade shield boss from Budaörs, mid-second century AD. (Drawing by A. E. Negin)

FIG. 136.(Opposite) Decorated shield boss with Hercules wrestling with the Nemean lion, late second–first half of third century AD, private European collection. (Courtesy of the owner)

MILITARY DECORATIONS (*DONA MILITARIA*)

From the time of the Republic, the Romans would reward soldiers who had displayed bravery in battle. There were the following incentives: a gift of money, a larger amount of loot, *spolia* in the form of weapons and jewellery taken from defeated enemies, and *dona militaria* – special military decorations.[91]

These various marks of honour awarded as *dona militaria* were very important in a legionary's movement up through the ranks. According to V. Maxfield, between 13 and 25 per cent of legionaries who had them reached the rank of centurion. At the same time, of the centurions who had such decorations, more than half reached the rank of primus pilus or higher.[92] *Dona militaria* themselves did not give any benefits other than honour and prestige, but they could increase the chances of promotion and were an important element of in a military career.[93]

Besides wreaths (*coronae civica, navalis, aurea, muralis, vallaris*), other items could be used as *dona militaria*, such as spears (*hasta purae*), which were given to senior centurions only, and flags (*vexilla*), necklaces (*torques*), bracelets (*armillae*) and phalera (*phalerae*), a kind of medal of varying size and degree of decoration. Necklaces and bracelets were military decorations and symbols of nobility in some Indo-European cultures: the Scythians, Celts, etc. Most probably, the Romans introduced them as a result of wars with the Gauls, originally as war booty. However, in contrast to their opponents who wore necklaces around their necks and bracelets on their wrists, the Roman soldiers attached them with special leather loops to the front of the cuirass.[94] Necklaces and bracelets were given to distinguished soldiers, from privates to the centurions, usually in pairs and often at the same time: both necklaces and bracelets. They were made of different metals and plated with silver and gold.

There were smooth, flat medals (*phalerae*) and also those with a knob at the centre and with concentric circles radiating from it. Medals also depicted the heads of the gods, spirits of the underworld, birds and lions. Medusa was the most popular. Real sets of *phalerae* similar to those shown on the monuments to Marcus Caelius, Quintus Sertorius Festus and Celer Allius, were found in Neuss,[95] Lauersfort[96] and Newstead.[97] Usually, in the period of the Principate, *phalerae* were bestowed together with other awards. According to the iconographic sources, sets of *phalerae* usually consisted of nine discs, but only seven are depicted on the tombstone of Quintus Sertorius Festus and only five on the tombstone of Marcus Caelius. They often came in different sizes and patterns and were attached in different ways to leather straps, which, in turn, were tied together in the form of a sword knot and were put over the head to be worn over the armour. The straps of this ensemble were put on the shoulders with enough left free to be held together with clasps at the back. The way *phalerae* were attached to the straps can be seen from the Lauersfort set (fig. 137). The inner side of each plate had three small metal tabs, apparently, to be inserted into a cut on the strap and to be secured with pins. In addition, the discs might be sewn to the straps.

In the Imperial period, military awards were divided into those for officers and enlisted men. With few exceptions, wreaths, flags and spears became awards for officers. The range of awards for soldiers was limited to necklaces, bracelets and medals.[98] These awards were given to legionaries most frequently on behalf of the emperors, less often on behalf of the generals belonging to the imperial family, and rarely cases on behalf of generals who had been awarded a triumph.[99] Awards were usually given on the occasion of victorious campaign for which a triumph was granted. Roman soldiers wore their decorations for valour not only on parade, but also in combat. However, the priority was the observance of the ancient custom of wearing rewards for valour at ceremonial processions and triumphs,[100] as well as at various parades.[101]

FIG. 137. Lauersfort *phalerae*, first century AD, Krefeld, Museumszentrum Burg Linn. (Photo by M. Greemhalgh)

In the second century AD, *dona militaria* were gradually supplanted by more material means to provide incentives to distinguished soldiers: gifts of money, increased food rations, additional leave, etc. *Dona militaria* completely disappeared under the Severan dynasty.

Horse Eye-guards, Chamfrons and Chest Pieces

FIG. 138. Horse eye-guard: (a) Pompeii, first century AD, Pompeii, Antiquarium; (b) Carnuntum, first century AD, private collection; (c) Dalj, first century AD, Zagreb, Arheoloski Muzej; (d) Regensburg, second century AD, Regensburg, Museum der Stadt; (e)–(f) Eining, beginning of the third century AD, Archäologische Staatssammlung München ((a) Photo by R. D'Amato; (b)–(d) Drawing by A. E. Negin; (e)–(f) Photo by A. Lemeshko)

Defensive chamfrons for horses have been known since ancient times, being used in Italy from the fifth century BC.[102] In contrast to the horse armour (cataphract) that was used in battle, in Imperial times horse eye-guards and chamfrons were apparently only used in *hippika gymnasia*.

At the beginning of the first century AD horse eye-guards in the shape of rounded bronze grilles were widespread in the Roman army. Obviously, the main purpose of these was the protection of the animal's eyes, but they would also have acted as blinkers, helping prevent the horse being startled. Two-part eyecups could be connected by leather straps and three-piece examples with bronze central flaps were connected by hinges. Both of these modifications appear simultaneously in the early first century AD.[103] One example of a two-part eyecup connected by leather straps was found in Pompeii[104] (fig. 138a) and one three-piece examples with a bronze central flap connected by a hinge was found in the village of Dalj (Croatia) and is held in the Archaeological Museum in Zagreb[105] (fig. 138c).

Chamfrons of the Principate differed in design, form and material. Leather chamfrons with built-in round or oval latticed eyecups were found at Newstead[106] (fig. 150), Vindolanda[107] (151a–c) and Carlisle.[108] Similar lattice eyecups are among the finds from Neuss[109] and Carnuntum,[110] suggesting widespread use of leather

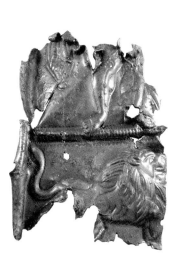

FIG. 139. (Above) Horse eye-guards, second century AD, Italian private collection. (Photo by R. D'Amato)

FIG. 140. (Left) Horse eye-guards from Herrera de Pisuerga, early first century AD, Madrid, Museo Arqueológico Nacional. (Drawing by A. E. Negin)

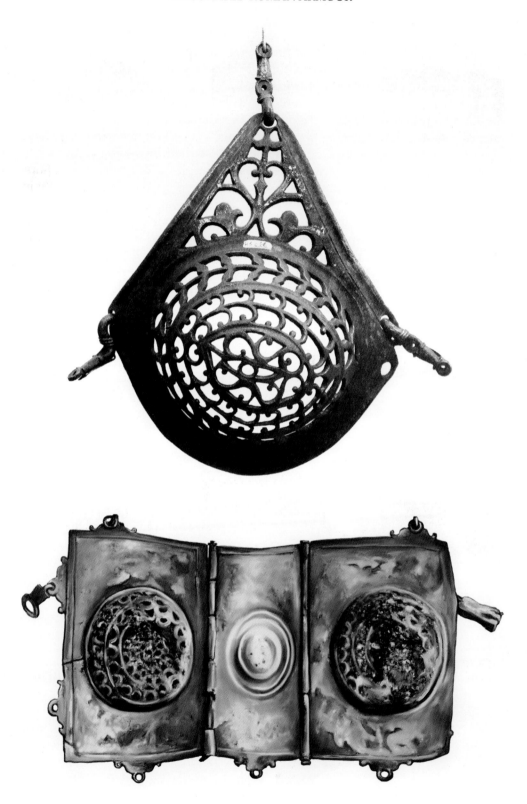

FIG. 141. Horse eye-guard, second century AD, Split Museum, place of discovery unknown. (Photo by R. D'Amato)

FIG. 142. Nawa horse eye-guards, second century AD, Damascus, National Museum. (Drawing by A. E. Negin)

FIG. 143. Fragments of chamfrons and eye-guards of the third century AD: (a) Künzing, Archäologische Staatssammlung München; (b) Cinquantenaire, Brussels, Musée du Cinquantenaire; (c) Lower Danube, Mainz, Römisch-Germanisches Zentralmuseum; (d) Weißenburg, Weißenburg, Museum; (e) Gilau. (Drawing by A. E. Negin)

FIG. 144. (Above) Fragments of horse equipment, Volubilis, second–third century AD, Rabat, Musée Archéologique. (After Boube-Piccot, 1994)

FIG. 145. (Below) Chamfron and eye-guards from various private collections.

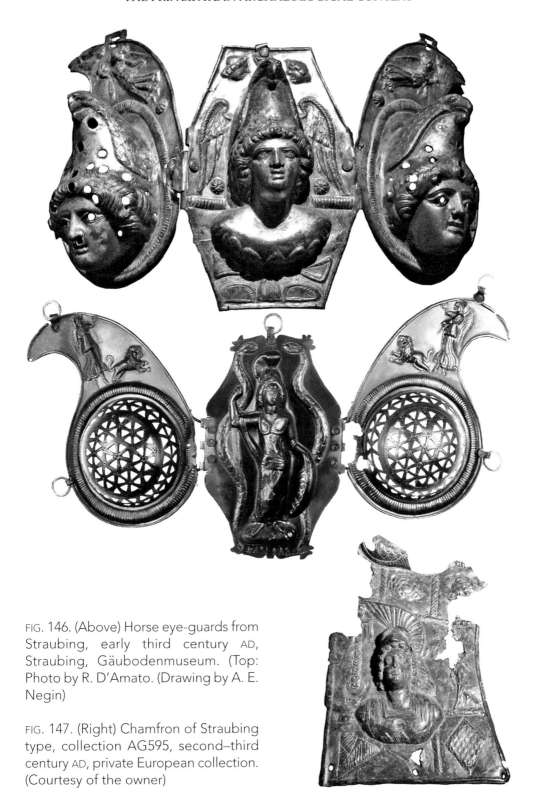

FIG. 146. (Above) Horse eye-guards from Straubing, early third century AD, Straubing, Gäubodenmuseum. (Top: Photo by R. D'Amato. (Drawing by A. E. Negin)

FIG. 147. (Right) Chamfron of Straubing type, collection AG595, second–third century AD, private European collection. (Courtesy of the owner)

FIG. 148. (Above) Chamfron in Hellenistic style from Nijmegen, first century AD, Nijmegen, Valkhof-Kam museum (Photo by R. D'Amato)

FIG. 149. (Right) Chamfron from Neuss (Novaesium, first century AD, Bonn, Rheinisches Landesmuseum. (Photo by M. Greenhalgh)

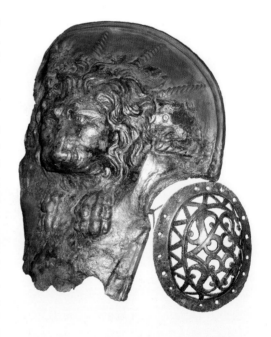

chamfrons. (figs 150–151a–c). In the second–third centuries AD bronze three-part chamfrons, consisting of centre and side plates, were used. Long specimens have tapering down central panel. The eyecups were punched with small triangular holes, but were sometimes made in the form of conventional lattice bulges. The longest such chamfrons are 40–45cm.[111] Small and medium-sized specimens have an octagonal (sometimes rectangular) central plate. The side plates are made in the form of decorative ring around the round eye-holes. On the small examples this plate is almost triangular in shape. But on the larger examples these side plates could be kite-shaped with thin upper portion curving outwards. Obviously, along with these ornate specimens, simpler two-part sets consisting of two baskets connected by straps were used. One bronze chamfron depicting a lion's head was found in Neuss[112] (fig. 149). It is made of a single embossed plate and is stylistically different from other Roman chamfrons, referring to Hellenistic models.

FIG. 150. Leather chamfron from Newstead, first century AD, Edinburgh, National Museum of Scotland. (Drawing by A. E. Negin)

Horse chest-guards for *hippika gymnasia* in the first–second centuries AD would probably have been made from leather, like chamfrons. Arrian in his 'Tactica' confirms that chest-guards were part of the *hippika gymnasia* equipment. Unfortunately, he does not mention the material from which they were made. O. Gamber suggested that leather specimens were decorated with a pattern of bronze studs.[113]

FIG. 151(a)–(c). (Left and below) Leather chamfron from Vindolanda, first century AD, Hexham, Vindolanda Museum. (Photo by R. D'Amato)

FIG. 152. (Bottom) Chamfron from Gherla), second–early third century AD, Bucharest, Muzeul Naţional de Istorie a României. (Drawing by A. E. Negin)

FIG. 153. (Above and below) Chamfrons from Eining, beginning of the third century AD, Archäologische Staatssammlung München. (Top: Photo by A. Lemeshko; bottom: drawing by A. E. Negin)

FIG. 154. (Above) Gherla fragment of chamfron (?), second–third century AD, Bucharest, Muzeul Naţional de Istorie a României. (Photo by Bucharest, Muzeul Naţional de Istorie a României).

FIG. 155. (Opposite page) Straubing hoard: chamfrons, early third century AD, Straubing, Gäubodenmuseum. (Drawing by A. E. Negin)

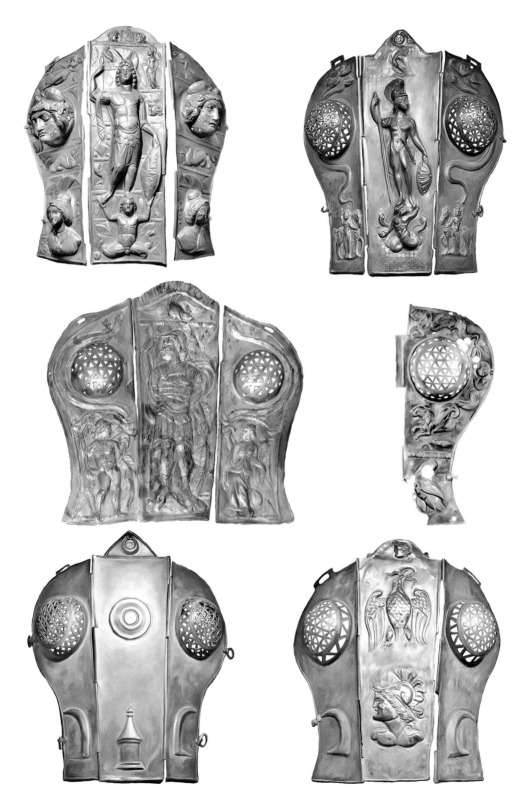

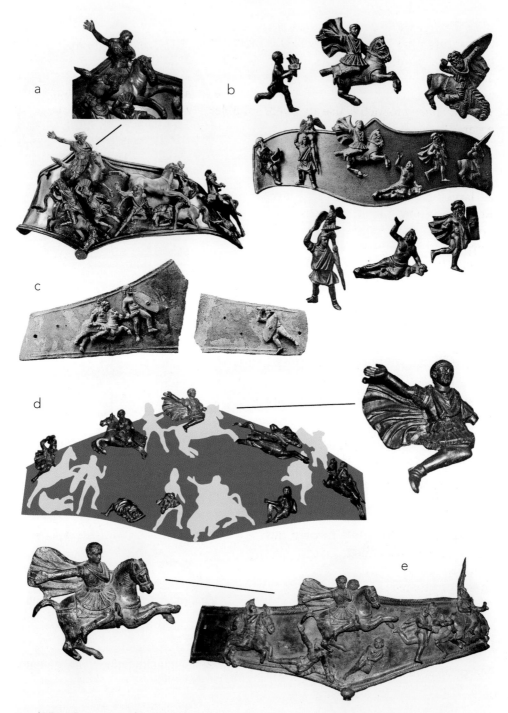

FIG. 156. Decorated peytrals of the first–second centuries AD: (a) Aosta; (b) Kunsthistorischen Sammlungen, Vienna; (c) Arcalia; (d) Industria; (e) Brescia. ((a), (d), (e) Photo by R. D'Amato; (b) After Sacken, 1883, Taf. IV; (c) After Domaszewski, 1888)

Bronze ceremonial peytrals are known in several museum collections, although apparently they are preserved specimens that once belonged to imperial equestrian statues[114] (fig. 156). Peytrals from Aosta[115] (fig. 156a), Brescia[116] (fig. 156e), Arcalia, com. Şieu-Măgheruş[117] (fig. 156c) and Kunsthistorischen Sammlungen, Vienna[118] (fig. 156b) had massive toreutic decoration. Perhaps they were too heavy for active use and were suitable only for a horse moving slowly in a parade.

FACE-MASK HELMETS

A large group of finds of ancient Roman armament is helmets with anthropomorphic masks. Their purpose has been disputed for a long time. This dispute began with the founder of Roman military archaeology, L. Lindenschmidt, who thought them to be combat equipment.[119] His opponent in this matter, O. Benndorf, held an opposing view, classified them as a part of funerary gifts.[120] According to him, the masks could be funerary ones as some of them were found in graves. As a result, the researcher drew an analogy with other masks whose funeral purpose was undoubted. However, the majority of Roman face-mask helmets found to date are not associated with burials, but as part of votive offerings (buried in the ground or thrown into water), as well as in the military camps of the legions and auxiliary troops.[121] In these case, there is no link to funerals at all. So, what was their purpose?

Unlike the face-mask helmets of Parthian and Sassanid cataphracts, which are mentioned by Ammianus Marcellinus and Julian the Apostate in

FIG. 157. Gravestone of Quintus Luccius Faustus, second half of the first century AD, Mainz, Landesmuseum. (Drawing by A. E. Negin)

the context of battle, the Roman face-mask helmets were mentioned by those authors only in their descriptions of military parades,[122] so we can consider face-mask helmets as part of parade or tournament equipment.[123] In fact, Arrian leads us to believe that face-mask helmets were intended exclusively for use in the cavalry tournaments, as he mentions neither any religious nor symbolic meaning, but definitely distinguishes them from military helmets.[124] Real examples of face-mask helmets in burials at Tell Oum Hauran[125] and in Ain Grimidi,[126] which contained ordinary combat helmets along as well, also suggest their ceremonial or presentational nature, as those decorated helmets and masks could be part of *dona militaria*.[127]

Graphic sources predominantly depict face-mask helmets among captured armament.[128] This should come as no surprise, as the loss of the colour from the depictions makes it impossible to distinguish the masks, which were extremely realistic, from the soldiers' faces in many Roman reliefs. However, there are images definitely showing face-mask helmets worn by soldiers. For example, the tombstone of the signifer Quintus Luccius Faustus shows a face-mask helmet covered with hide, which is slung on his left shoulder[129] (fig. 157). We can assume that the soldier is shown not in parade dress but in ordinary equipment suited for combat. Another tombstone depicts the cavalryman Sextus Valerius Genialis riding down the enemy in a Ribchester-type helmet[130] (fig. 78). Most probably, in this case, we have here the iconographic canon for depicting the glorious military exploits of the

FIG. 158. (Above) Gravestone of Flavinus from Ala Gallorum Petriana, end of the first century AD, Hexham Abbey. (Drawing by A. E. Negin)

FIG. 159. (Opposite page) Face-mask helmets on iconographic representations: (a) Pergam relief; (b) Orange arch; (c) Teramo relief; (d) Cologne column; (e) Vesunna column; (f) relief from Museo Atestino, Este; (g) Porte Noire in Besançon. (Drawing by A. E. Negin)

deceased. But here, it seems strange that the parade/sports helmet is depicted on the cavalryman's head but not separately, as, for example, in the stele of Quintus Luccius Faustus mentioned above, or on those reliefs, where the parade and presentational equipment is shown separately from the outfit worn by the soldier.[131] In addition, Sextus Valerius Genialis' horse is depicted without a chamfron which was an indispensable attribute of horse equipment for cavalry tournaments, according to Arrian.[132] Therefore, it is logical to assume that the tombstone does not show specific armament for *hippika gymnasia*. Despite the 'iconographic canon' where depicting face-mask helmets is not typical, we can however see the same Ribchester type helmet on the tombstone. If the use of such a helmet in combat was completely excluded, then, probably we would not have such a depiction at our disposal. These individual examples of face-mask helmets depicted in battle scenes support the fact that they could be worn in combat.

Considering the possible use of ceremonial masks in combat, we should note that one mask was found on the battlefield at Kalkriese,[133] although it is still impossible to prove that masks were actually worn in battle and it is quite possible that it was from the looted baggage train. The most compelling evidence for the use of masks in combat is the particular type of damage seen on some of them.

FIG. 160. Detail of trophy with a possible mask helmet from the sarcophagus of the Amazon from Kuthaya, second century AD, Khutaya, Archaeological Museum. (Photo by R. D'Amato)

FIG. 161. Trophies of arms and armour: Arles, Arc admirable, third century AD (armours, shields, mask helmets, etc) (Photo by Agostino Carcione)

FIG. 162 (a)–(k). (This page and opposite) Trophies of arms and armour, first century AD, Turin, Museo Archeologico. (Photo by A. E. Negin)

The mask of Mainz has a trace of a weapon blow on the left.[134] The mask of Thorsberg moor has similar damage.[135] On both of these examples, we have marks from an edged weapon, which makes it impossible for them to be damaged at a cavalry tournament where, as reported by Arrian, only dummy weapons were used.[136]

The possibility of masks being worn in battle has also been examined by modern researchers through experimental archaeology. This approach allows empirical analysis of the objections to the use of masks in combat. It is known that the masks fitted tightly to the face and had small openings for the eyes. This supports the assumption that the masks significantly restricted both visibility and breathing: a soldier in a mask would be very hot and could hardly see the enemy, both problems in combat.

In a large portion of the Roman masks found, the material is too thin to withstand the impact of weapons. But this is only true for the examples from the second– third centuries AD. Face-mask helmets of the first century AD were usually made of thick sheet iron and were perfectly suitable for combat. For example, an iron mask from the military burial at Chassenard (Allier, France)[137] is 4mm thick and the mask from Mainz is 2–3mm thick[138] and we should take into account that it was originally covered with a sheet of bronze.[139] Thus, the metal thickness of the mask of the first century AD is comparable to that of helmets of the same period and often exceeds it.[140] Since such helmets were considered sufficient protection in combat, it can be concluded that the masks met the same requirements. Compared to these pieces, the subsequent ones seem to be purely decorative and not all of them were suitable for battle. Even in the second–third centuries, the helmet bowl was often made of sheet iron of a thickness (usually about 1mm) sufficient to attenuate the force of a moderate blow. Moreover, it often had some embossed decoration which cushioned blows even more due to numerous planes projecting at different angles.[141] For comparison, we can refer to the corrugated or ribbed armour of the fifteenth–sixteenth centuries. Its surface is six times stronger than a smooth one.[142] Bronze masks were 0.2mm to 2mm thick.[143] The thickness of items of ancient armour to be used in battle also did not exceed 2mm,[144] which clearly suggests that the face-mask helmets could be used in combat, especially as experiments have shown that these pieces offered fairly good protection. In tests, M. Junkelmann shot models of armour with arrows from a range of 2m, flung a spear (*hasta*) at them from the same distance and stabbed them with a cavalry sword (*spatha*). First, the experiment was made on a 0.5mm thick flat sheet of plain brass which an arrow pierced through to a depth of 35cm. The spear pierced the same sheet to the depth of 12cm and the sword blow resulted in a dent with a depth of about 2cm, but the sheet was not cut through. Then the experiment was repeated with a 1mm-thick brass sheet. An arrow penetrated to a depth of 2cm, the spear to a depth of 3cm and the sword blow resulted in a dent with a depth of about 0.7cm. However, the protective properties of the helmets and masks were even higher, since in the experiment the impact was made at a direct angle to the flat surface. If the blow fell on the curved surface of the helmet, then in general it glanced off. It should also be remembered that in some places on decorated helmets and other parts of ceremonial armament the thickness was actually higher due to clumps of material formed during the manufacture of the item, and the use of leather or felt as a lining further enhanced its resistance to blows. In subsequent experiments carried out with a 1.2mm-thick convex and relief-embossed plate imitating a helmet bowl fashioned as a curly hairstyle, it was found that most of the blows glanced off and left scratches only. Direct arrow hits pierced the sheet to a depth of only 1.5cm. When flung, the spear bounced off several times, but in one successful direct hit the spearhead penetrated the plate to the depth of 4mm. Sword blows resulted in dents with a depth of up to 2mm.[145] Furthermore, as shown by microscopic examination of the metal sample of an original iron Nijmegen-type mask, the sheet metal used for masks of this type could be multi-layered, which improved its hardness and strength.[146] In addition to this, a group of scholars from the Netherlands and Germany held a series of experiments using a reconstruction of a Roman bolt-shooting torsion catapult of the first century, the frame of which had been found in Xanten-Wardt.[147] The ballista (*scorpio*), placed

FIG. 163. Trophies of arms and armour, early first century AD, Teramo, cathedral. (Photo by Dr Antonio di Michele)

at a distance of 7m from the target, fired at three metal plates: 1) a 1.5mm-thick low-carbon iron plate, 2) a 2.5mm-thick eight-layer iron plate manufactured according to Roman techniques by hammer welding and subsequent cold forging, 3) a 2.5mm thick bronze plate (94 per cent copper and 6 per cent tin).[148] None of the plates was pierced through. A bolt fired at the first plate left a 6mm deep dent.[149] Bolts fired at the second and third plates resulted in no damage except for light scratches on the surface. It turns out that the helmets and masks of this thickness gave quite good protection from most ancient weapons. Serious danger was only in the case of a direct hit by an arrow. However, in this case, they penetrated chain mail and scale armour as well, so no type of armour could guarantee absolute protection.

Thus, the protective properties of Roman face-masks were quite sufficient; consequently, the benefits of using them in combat are beyond doubt. However, we still have to consider how functional they were in battle in terms of how easy they were to wear and how they affected the wearer's vision. Observations based on wearing different types of masks in different conditions follow.

A reconstruction of the Kalkriese-type mask[150] was tested in a dismounted formation.[151] Face-masks of this type were attached to the centre of the bottom edge of the front of the helmet bowl frontal part with a hinge. Additionally, they were securely fixed to the face with the helmet cheek pieces, which, in turn, were tied with leather laces to secure the helmet to the soldier's head.[152] The original masks of this type had no fittings for additional fasteners. As shown by wearing the reconstruction, they are not required at all. It should be noted that this method of attaching a mask to an ordinary infantry helmet allows it to be removed easily, when it is wanted to wear the helmet without it.

A reconstruction of a mask and a Nijmegen-type helmet was tested in a mounted formation.[153] This reconstruction was based on an iron original of the mid-first century AD.[154] This type of mask was also attached to the helmet with a hinge. In addition, the mask is secured by a leather strap, extending from one cheek of the mask to the other over the helmet neck-guard, attached to wide headed rivets on the sides of the mask. This type of mask covers not only the front of the face, but also the horseman's cheekbones and ears. In other words, this mask forms an integrated whole with the helmet, fully protecting the wearer's head. Due to its design and method of attachment, such a helmet, unlike the version used with Kalkriese-type masks, is not designed to be worn without the mask.

Wearing any of the masks causes some discomfort. Experience shows that the air flow through the nose and mouth openings is adequate for normal respiration. During an experimental two hours of intense running, specially carried out by M. Junkelmann, it was found out that the air flow is sufficient even for heavy exertion, but in hot weather sweat accumulates on the mask's inner surface and on the face, trickling down the face onto the chin and causing discomfort. However, by force of habit, this discomfort can be ignored quite quickly. In addition, it should be noted that some masks of the first century AD have additional air holes.[155]

Limitations on vision and hearing are more significant in determining the suitability of masks for actual combat. Thus, masks completely block peripheral vision.[156] On the other hand, due to the fact that the mask is secured close to the face, the eye holes are large enough to provide an acceptable frontal view. Nijmegen-type masks covered the ears and thus limited hearing.[157] Besides, the rider's breathing and the whistling of the wind through the eye and mouth holes when riding fast also adverse affect hearing. However, due to the fact that the ear shapes of this type of mask have holes of 4mm diameter,[158] a horseman in a such mask can hear reasonably well.

Those who say that these disadvantages meant that masks could not be worn in battle should be asked to recall examples from other periods. Troops would rarely refuse any additional protection, that might save their lives, despite the discomfort wearing it might cause. Here, we may recall that the First World War saw the invention of gas masks to be used in cavalry units, including those designed for horses. Perhaps, the comparison may seem inappropriate, because gas masks absolutely had to be worn in a chemical warfare environment as the soldier's life depended on them. In the Roman army, helmet masks did not play such an important function; i.e. in most cases, a soldier's life did not depend on the protection of his face with a masked helmet. At the same time, it is known that facial injuries are always more painful than other wounds and can throw the wounded man into confusion and cause him to quit the battle. It is worth noting that a soldier worries less about the parts of his body protected by his armour than about the unprotected ones. So, in some cases, it was actually reasonable to protect

FIG. 164. Mask from Kalkriese, early first century AD, Osnabrück, Museum und Park Kalkriese. (Drawing by A. E. Negin)

FIG. 165. Unfinished mask from Haltern, early first century AD. (After Kropatscheck 1911, Taf. 39, 2)

the face with a face-mask despite the fact that this obviously limited vision and hearing. Not all soldiers needed to have a clear view of the whole of the battlefield to see the enemy attacking them, and neither did they all have to wield a sword themselves, being protected by their brothers-in-arms around them. Standard-bearers were among such soldiers. Their immediate task was to monitor the transfer of commands and instructions from the centurion or decurion. In this case, it was enough for them to always keep a wary eye on the commander, which was possible even with a fairly limited general view. Furthermore, as a standard-bearer's hands were full, he would find it difficult to dodge or parry blows, in which case, additional protection for the face was not superfluous at all. As well as this, masks could have been worn in combat to intimidate the enemy.[159] In fact, an infantryman always saw a cavalryman as a more powerful enemy, more dangerous and less vulnerable due to his speed. The more he was protected by his armour, the less vulnerable and, therefore, more terrible he seemed to be. It is no coincidence that Ammianus Marcellinus compared a *clibanarius* who was encased in armour from head to foot, to a statue by the famous Greek sculptor Praxiteles, as such a heavily-armoured horseman seemed more like a statue than a living man.[160]

All the above makes it possible to conclude that the inconveniences due to wearing a mask were not critical and entirely permit masks to have been in combat. It should be noted that the Roman face-mask helmets provided a better view than some of the gladiatorial or later medieval helmets.[161] That is, even a significant restriction of vision did not mean that face-masks could not be used in combat. The main argument supporting the use of masks in battle is undoubtedly their protective qualities. A soldier's unprotected face is very vulnerable and even minor facial injuries could put a soldier out of action due to shock or bleeding. Almost complete facial protection was a big advantage. Thus, it is quite probable that face-mask helmets (especially those of the first century AD) were used in combat along with other protective equipment and especially by those soldiers for whom it was difficult or impossible to use a shield to protect the face, e.g. cavalry or standard-bearers.

According to the archaeological data, face-mask helmets became widespread in the Roman army under Augustus. The oldest example of the silver-plated iron mask was found in 1991 on the site of the alleged defeat of Quinctilius Varus's legions in the Teutoburg Forest[162] (fig. 164). An earlier unfinished iron mask found in the legionary camp at Haltern[163] (fig. 165) was lost during the Second World War; however, both pieces unequivocally confirm that iron masks were used in the Roman army as early as at the end of the reign of Augustus. The next decades are represented by a number of finds originating mainly from Lower Germany, Gaul, Thrace and Syria. Helmets from the newly-conquered province of Britannia should be dated to the late first century AD. Face-mask helmets are found in the burials of Roman auxiliaries among the votive offerings. Some of them were recovered from rivers, which apparently can indicate not only that some pieces were accidentally lost, but also the practice of votive offerings.

The period of the second and third centuries AD is mainly represented by finds made in the Danubian provinces. Especially rich material related to face-mask helmets and other components of 'parade armament' was found in the region of Raetia which comprises modern southern Bavaria, as well as parts of Wurttemberg, Switzerland, Vorarlberg and the Tyrol. Approximately 40 per cent of all the material found to date is from this province alone, where the Alamanni spread terror in the middle – second half of the third century AD. Almost all of these finds are concentrated around fortresses on the Roman border line where they originally must have been stored in the arsenals (*armamentaria*). However, only two of the hoards were found actually within the boundaries of fortresses (Künzing and Pfünz). The others were buried outside the fortifications: in the *vicus* (a settlement near a military camp) (Künzing, Pförring, Eining and Weißenburg) or a nearby Roman villa (Straubing and Sittling).[164] The composition of the hoards suggests that richly-decorated helmets were the type buried most often.

No find of the fourth century AD made in the Danubian provinces or anywhere else within the Roman Empire contains a single item of parade/tournament equipment. This is surprising, as Ammianus Marcellinus mentioned face-mask helmets already being used by opponents of Rome, the Sassanian cataphracts,[165] and these protective headpieces were depicted among the parade arms in the nonextant column of Emperor Arcadius (395–408 AD).[166] Only one face-mask found in the River Kupa at Sisak in Croatia probably dates to this time[167] (fig. 166).

There are quite a few extant graphic sources depicting Roman face-mask helmets. However, it is necessary to take into account the fact that after the original painting of the sculptures has worn off, masks can hardly be distinguished from the actual faces of legionaries. Friezes depicting weapons and spoils offer better chances to identify face-mask helmets. A column of the early Imperial period, which is now in the museum of Perigueux (Dordogne, France) (fig. 159e), show an image of a Weiler/Koblenz-Bubenheim type helmet with a mask in the form of a young beardless face among shields, armour and other weapons.[168]

L. Lindenschmit finds several disputable images on the tombstones of the second half of the first century AD. In particular, the monument to the signifer of Legion XIV, Quintus Luccius Faustus (fig. 157) shows a mask in a strange helmet-like item which can be seen above the standard-bearer's shoulder.[169] In opposition to this interpretation, O. Benndorf saw just the 'usual headwear of standard-bearers' in the depiction.[170]

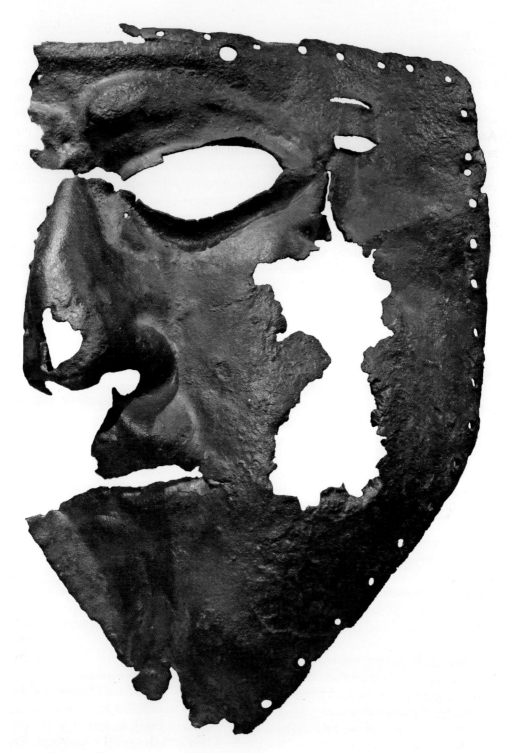

FIG. 166. Mask from River Kupa (Sisak), third–fourth centuries AD, Sisak, Arheoloski Muzej. (Photo by R. D'Amato)

It is possible that face-mask helmets are depicted on two more tombstones of Roman cavalry standard-bearers. The tombstone of the signifer Flavinus from Ala Gallorum Petriana (fig. 158) shows a splendid helmet decoration made of horsehair and feathers.[171] Until now, face-mask helmets are the only cavalry helmets of the early Imperial period on which we can find the remains of attachments for plumes and feathers. This fact coincides with the description by Arrian who mentioned plumes of yellow hair that had no practical value and served only as decoration. Another tombstone shows Sextus Valerius Genialis from Ala I Thracum[172] (fig. 78), whose helmet has a raised pointed peak similar to those on Ribchester-type helmets. If all of these tombstones really depict face-mask helmets, this can mean they could belong to, at least, the parade equipment of both infantry and cavalry signifers. A different interpretation would be difficult because not only the purpose of masks attached to the helmet remains disputable, but also how and from where they appeared in the Roman army. Sources, as already mentioned, are extremely scarce and do not answer these questions, so the researchers suggest several hypotheses related to the appearance of face-mask helmets in the Roman army. Among the most interesting and noteworthy are the oriental, Hellenistic, Thracian and Italian theories.

Proponents of the oriental theory believe that the tradition of using face-mask helmets had grown upin the East. At least, ancient sources starting from the second century AD describe the cataphract cavalry of the Parthians and then the Sassanids, which was equipped with face-mask helmets.[173] It is another matter that the only evidence that face-mask helmets had been used in these areas before the Christian era are the images of the relief in the temple of Athena in Pergamon[174] (fig. 159a) and a statuette of a soldier from Syria,[175] although they certainly have the features of the Hellenistic tradition.

In recent decades most attention has been given to the thesis of the Thracian origin of face-mask helmets which were later borrowed by the Romans. This hypothesis was first put forward by F. Drexel[176] and later supported by the Bulgarian researcher I. Venedikov who pointed to some anthropomorphic cheek-pieces of some Phrygian-type helmets from the territory of Thrace as the obvious prototype of the anthropomorphic mask.[177] However, the transition stage from the bearded cheek-pieces to the anthropomorphic mask in this area has not yet been identified. More evidence for the Thracian theory lies in the fact that lots of early face-mask helmets are found in military burials in Thrace itself, as well as in Gaul. In Gaul, face-mask helmets could be have brought as spoils by Gallic cavalrymen who took part in the suppression of Thracian rebellions in the AD 20s.[178]

Another theory says that the Romans borrowed face-mask helmets from the Etruscans who had used them in their religious and cultic ceremonies or in cavalry games. According to Livy, the Romans learned to hold equestrian games from the Etruscans.[179] H. von Petrikovits tries to link the use of face-mask helmets with the equestrian events for patrician youths (*Lusus Troiae*), as well as with the ancient Roman custom of making masks of their ancestors.[180] M. Kolert supported this hypothesis by noting that Augustus, whose reign the archaeological finds of the earliest Roman face-mask helmets date from, revived many ancient customs

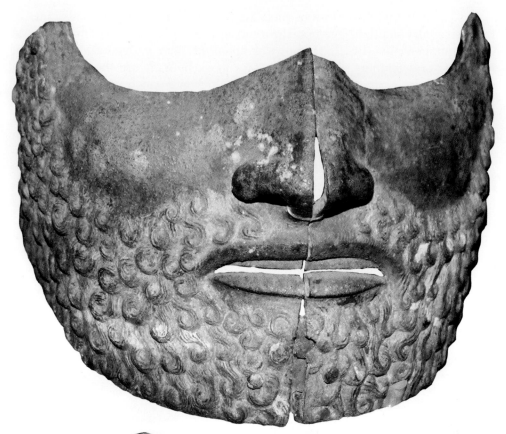

FIG. 167. (Above) Etruscan anthropomorphic cheek-pieces, fourth century BC, Vatican, Gregorian Museum. (Photo by R. D'Amato)

FIG. 168. (Left) Attic helmet-mask type from San Marino, Milan, private collection. (Drawing by A. E. Negin)

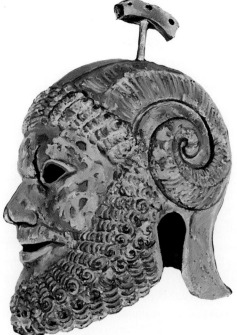

(including ancient equestrian games), but also re-designed them.[181]

As to the Etruscans, two finds indicate they did use helmets with certain elements imitating facial features. The Museo Gregoriano Egizio in the Vatican has a Negau-type Etruscan helmet which was believed to have been found together with cheek-pieces covering almost the entire face

PLATE 1

PLATE 1

SALII PRIEST IN CEREMONIAL ARMOUR, EIGHTH CENTURY BC

The *Salii* or warrior-priests accompanied public processions with war-dances like the *tripudium* that was danced by beating the feet on the ground and clashing the spear on the shield three times. Some chants were also intoned in such an ancient Latin language that it was not understood in Cicero's day!

The *Salii* were created by Numa Pompilius and had the attire described by Livy (I, 20): a fine embroidered tunic (*tunica picta et insigne*) and a breastplate (*aeneum pectoris tegumentum*). Dyonisius and Plutarch mention also conical headgear or *apex* (possibly a *pilos* helmet), a purple cloak with scarlet bands and broaches (*tebenna hemporpemenos periporphyros*), a spear (*logché*) – or a staff (*rabdon*) – and a sword (*xiphos*). The waist was covered by wide bronze belts or *chalkais mitrais* (Plut., II, 70; Numa XIII).

PLATE 2

ROMAN CHAMPION 'ORATIUS', SEVENTH CENTURY BC

The description of the mythical duel between the *Oratii* and *Curiatii*, for the predominance of Rome and Alba Longa in central Latium is rich in details related to the archaic Roman equipment. According to Livy (I, 25) and Dyonisius (III, 18) the champions were armed with glittering swords (*arma*) in their right hands, and shields. The whole body of each warrior was protected by the choicest armour, according to Dyonisius, i.e. helmet, breastplate and greaves ('all of them armed in the most splendid fashion and withal dressed like men about to die'). Here the Roman champion has been given the proto-Corinthian helmet of Lake Nemi, the breastplate of the Regolini-Galassi grave and a precious shield made of bronze sheets. According to the archaic fighting style of the *devotio* he is dressed in the *cinctus gabinus*, i.e. the *toga*, worn at that time as combat dress.

PLATE 3

FIRST-CLASS (*CLASSIS PREIMA*) HOPLITE, ROMANO-ETRUSCAN ARISTOCRAT IN BATTLE ARMOUR, AGE OF TARQUINIUS THE BOLD

The man is reconstructed from the fragments of a fictional duel between a Greek and an Amazon from the pediment of a temple on the Esquiline. The Corinthian type of helmet (*galea*) has been copied from the Civitavecchia's specimen. The colours of the horsehair crest (*lophoi*) have been based on those from a Palestrina fragment representing a warrior procession, where all the hoplites are shown with blonde horsehair crests with the upper part dyed red on their helmets. The linen armour (*linothorax*) shows wide trapezoidal shoulder-guards (*epomides*) fastened with red laces across the breast, and by means of a bronze boss on the centre of the armour. The original armour from which the fictitious sculpture was copied was lavishly decorated: the central boss is surrounded by a blue indigo floral motif, only just visible on the

PLATE 2

PLATE 3

PLATE 4

original sculpture. The decoration of the armour presents, on the shoulder guards, a star in blue, indigo and red. Under the blue indigo floral motif surrounding the central boss there is a wide belt (painted in red) inside which there is a solar motif of interlaced swastikas, painted red and blue/indigo. Under the lower edge are attached two rows of rectangular lambrequins (*pteryges*). They were also made of linen and were directly sewn to the lower border of the armour. The legs are protected by bronze greaves (*ocraeae*) and thigh protectors, here copied from the *Falerii Vetere* sculpture. The main offensive armament of the first-class hoplite was the spear and the sword (*gladius*), here a Greek-type *xiphos*.

PLATE 4

ROMAN *MAGISTER EQUITUM* – BATTLE ORDER 500 BC

In a warrior burial from Lanuvium (nearby Rome), dated to the first half of the fifth century, a complete panoply was found with its weapons. The recovered bronze horse-bit ('ring shaped') shows that the grave was of an élite cavalryman, maybe a patrician officer. Some authors claims it to be the grave of a *Magister Equitum* (Chiarucci, 2003, p. 14). The panoply and weapons appear rather similar to those of the first Servian class: bronze helmet, plate armour, spear and javelin, sword. In the Lanuvium grave two javelin points were found, measuring 15cm and 19cm. Their pyramidal shapes were very common, as being easier to make from an iron rod. The points were fixed with small rivets and thus each javelin would be about 90cm long. No butt had been found in the Lanuvium grave.

The sword's curved blade, of *Màchaira* type, measured around 81 cm. in length (Chiarucci, 2003, p. 14, fig. 7c). Its upper edge was a rib and the lower one was sharpened. The wider part of the blade measured 7cm and was inclined forward to strengthen the blow. The hilt, fused with the blade when recovered, retained small wooden fragments of the handle. Some fragments of leather were still fixed to the blade, probably the remains of a scabbard.

In the Lanuvium panoply, no metallic traces of a shield have come into light: this would possibly indicate it was of non-metallic construction. Livy describes such cavalry-shield around 509 BC and gives its latin name as *parma equestris* (Liv. II. 6): the cavalrymen are often described as *Cohors parmata*.

The Lanuvium helmet (belonging to the Negau type of the Vetulonia category, see Antike Helme, 1988, pp. 249–50 and 252) lacked check-guards. The skull, pushed forward, was about 16cm in height and had charming eyes of gold and enamel, encircled in silver and surmounted by stylised eyebrows (fig. 5). Such a precious helmet was suitable for high-ranking officers: a similar Etruscan helmet of Negau class, adds a fine bearded mask (Robinson, 1975, fig. 128).

The Lanuvium helmet shows that in the fifth century the Romans were already using their distinctive crest as described by Polybius 250 years later, composed of a feather diadem (*lophos*) probably of the blonde colour described by the Imperial Age sources for the Roman cavalry. The central horsehair crest would be a variation for officers. Beside it, the new study of Lanuvium helmet here proposed shows the missing part of it like *cornicula* or horn-shaped ornaments, as can be understood from the

VI

remains on the helmets, in a change from their previous interpretation as holders for side-feathers. During the third Samnitic War such *cornicula*, symbolising power and fertility, are mentioned on the helmet of some *equites* (Liv. X. 44. 5).

The Praenestine *cistae* of the fourth–third centuries BC, depict some rare examples of such *cornicula*, shaped like wings, also on some Conversano-type helmets (Antike Helme, 1988, p. 147 fig. 14).

The precious Lanuvium cuirass is composed of two plates fixed with narrow shoulder pieces (*humeralia*) by means of very modern hinges which left the arms free; similar hinges were attached on both sides.

No metallic leg-guards were used by the cavalry, but a pair of leather boots was worn protecting the shins (*calcei repandi*). Their use seems quite probable in the early Roman period: in around 100 BC Cicero has them as part of the ceremonial attire of the statue of Juno Sospita, dressed according to the early fashion (Cicero. *De Divin*. I. 29; *De Natura Deor*. I. 28). Their characteristic pointed shape would possibly suggest an Eastern origin.

PLATE 5

Italic *Socius* warrior in Marcellina armour, fourth century BC

The Marcellina warrior was found, in his grave, with a gold *diadema* (which was not, however, associated with the helmet), the panoply, the horse equipment (bit and spur), spear and javelin, bronze belts, knives, strigils and some ceramics.

He is armed with an iron spear and an iron javelin. Due to the absence of a shield in the grave, in combat possibly more javelins could be carried. The javelin is leant on the shoulder, and while he is wearing a belt, another belt found in the grave is worn like a military trophy or standard, as seen on many Lucanian sources. The point pierced a bronze belt as a trophy taken from an enemy. Although in battle it could have been a kind of sign: indeed Livy casually quotes the Decurion S. Tempanius calling his men to follow his spear as a standard (Volscian War). The shiniest parts of his equipment are the helmet and the cuirass. The bronze helmet, with a hemispherical bowl, is Phrygian in shape. Note the articulated cheek-guards with their rounded back profile and stepped at the front. The frontal is decorated by an embossed area, with a sinuous upper edge and central apex. Aligned with each cheek-guard, on the bowl, is a cylinder for the insertion of plumes. On the top of the bowl, a double sheet with crested profile, decorated with embossed rays on the top, is fixed by two rivets in the back part. The anatomical armour, made of two sheets, has embossed decoration. Here only the frontal part is visible: the lower edge is sinuous and slightly rounded, the top edge is flat, with oblique area to protect the neck, the armpits fuller light. Along all the edges, a series of holes (between 1cm and 1.8cm apart) were for the sewing holding the padding. The junction was effected by four rings: two at the height of the hip, two behind. The embossed decoration presents, under the oblique area of the neck, a mask of Medusa. On the chest are diagonally intersecting two rows of oblong elements, interspersed with crushed biconical elements. At the crossing of the two rows, slightly over the pectorals, a circular *phalera* whose concave surface is over-posed. At the extremity of the work is inserted an eyelet, to which is fastened a ring attached to a

PLATE 5

PLATE 6

second ring, this last fixed to one eyelet which ends in an ivy leaf shape. This one held to both the rows a simulated belt, of which is evidenced only the sinuous upper edge: at the centre of the embossed belt there is a horned head of god Pan, with floral elements on the side. The footwear or *crepidae* are of Greek type and followed the Roman style, having spurs. The bronze anklets or *periskelides* were probably amulets. The spurs, of iron, are of arched shape, triangular point and rhomboid section.

PLATE 6

CONSUL CAIUS FLAMINIUS NEPOS, BATTLE ORDER, 217 BC

The armour of Flaminius, described in detail by Silius Italicus in the *Punica* VI, 132 ff., is confirmed on the Etruscan urns of the Period, an important source for the Punic Wars: 'His tough helmet was made of bronze and the tawny hide of a sea-calf; and above it rose a triple crest, with hair of the Suevi hanging down like a mane; and on the top stood a Scylla, brandishing a heavy broken oar and opening wide the savage jaws of her dogs. When Flaminius conquered and slew Gargenus, king of the Boii, he had fitted to his own head this famous trophy that no hand could mutilate, and proudly he bore it in all his battles. Then he put on his breastplate; its twisted hooks were embossed with plates wrought of hard steel mingled with gold. Next he took up his shield, formerly drenched with the slaughter of Gauls and adorned with their blood; and on it the She-wolf, in a dripping grotto, was licking the limbs of a child … Lastly he fitted the sword to his side and the spear to his right hand. His war-horse stood by, proudly champing the foaming bit; for saddle he bore the striped skin of a Caucasian tiger.' The brass and bronze helmet is coated with yellow sealskin, with a triple plume. The helmet is decorated with the figure of Scylla breaking the oars with her canine heads leaned forward. As a basis for the reconstruction of this helmet we have employed a precious Celtic helmet on which we have put the bronze engraving of Scylla. On the back is located a triple-crest holder, one of them running from a bronze button, the other two tubes closer, from which the yellow horsehair crest of Suebian type hangs, that is, in three large 'ponytails'. The cheek-pieces have five curvilinear lobes of superimposed iron plates, one of which is decorated with knurled circles and cantilever leaves. On this latter are arranged three bronze discs attached to two sheets headed with round nails in turn encrusted with red glass opaque. The cheek-pieces were connected to the base of the dome by means of a hinge. The entire lower part of the skull and the edge around the cheek pieces is lined with yellow sealskin, as well as the chinstrap.

The armour is a mixture of iron rings and gilded iron scales woven together. The source for the reconstruction of this armour is from an Etruscan *urna* in the Florence museum, showing a Roman commander fighting with Celts. The armour is formed of a corselet complete with mail shoulder pieces, fastened by means of bronze buttons on the front. The chest, however, is covered with golden scales. A strap structure in crimson red leather divides the two parts of the armour. Also the lower part of the corselet and the upper edges show red and white leather *cymation* and a single row of *pteryges* in linen.

The shield is embossed with the image of the she-wolf, inside the cave, affectionately licking one of the twins. The shield consist of several overlapping sheets of bronze.

PLATE 7

Consul in Rhodian Armour, second century bc

This reconstruction of the Roman consul Lucius Aemilius Paulus is based on the statue of an armour from Rhodes.

The helmet is of brass and bronze, a transitional type from the Attic to the Corinthian patterns, richly embossed on the skull with two almost-naked warriors fighting. It has a diadem-shaped brow and the cheek-pieces decorated with a Gorgon's head. The crest holder is a crouched sphinx supporting the very imposing horsehair plume, which is dyed yellow as according to Silius Italicus. The armour protection is a bronze *thorax statos* with a long, curvilinear protection for the abdomen, so probably more suitable for fighting on foot than on horseback. The shoulder guards are of leather but painted the same colour. It is modelled on the human body and worn over a padded doublet provided with *pteryges*.

These last are very fine textured in strengthened linen, bleached or probably dyed (two rows – one short and one long – under the waist; one coming out from the shoulders). The fastening system of the armour is realised in two different ways: on the shoulders and on the sides.

The two halves were fastened, on both sides, by side seams. On the opposite side, under the left arm there are strap hinges that pull the seams together. These hinges are made from a flexible material, most likely leather or yellow fabric, like in the famous Prima Porta armour. At least five hinges are clearly visible in the detail under the right arm of the statue. The second hinge from the bottom actually closes the seam of the cuirass at the narrowest point on the torso where the ribcage meets the abdomen. Since the hinge second from the bottom bends right at this point, it must also be made of leather or a similar flexible material, coloured yellow. The main fastener is under the armpit. The hinges appear to be straps threaded through the backplate and breastplate.

The fastening on the shoulder is by means of a scarlet tie or thong, to the ring on the breastplate. The harness curves smoothly over the shoulder, hugging it tightly until it reaches a similar fastener on the back. The fact that the harness follows the curve of the shoulder so closely shows that this is a flexible material (i.e. leather).

The bronze armour is decorated with a strong embossing, with the representation on the upper breast of two lions killing a bull, and on the lower part by the usual war of the Greek Heroes (or Arimaspians) against the Griffins. Also the shoulder guards are embossed with the image of a thunderbolt.

The sculpture shows the employment of a double baldric, of woven cloth usually of scarlet colour, closed by clasps and decorated by pendants, for the suspension of the *Parazonium* sword of Hellenic type. The massive pommel was fixed to a spiral hilt, presumably of ivory, while the pommel was gilded. The scabbard, fastened with the baldric passing on the right side of the body, ends in a *pelta* shape. The wooden scabbard was also ivory-coloured, either covered with ivory plates or white leather.

The cloak or *paludamentum* is a quadrangular mantle in wool, usually, for senior commanders, dyed in red vermillion or carmine purple, fastened on the left shoulder by a crossbow-shaped brooch draped on the left arm.

PLATE 7

PLATE 7

PLATE 8

The white linen tunic shows the senatorial mark, the wide purple central stripe called *laticlavius*, dyed red-purple. The pair of boots or *calcei lunati*, are black, having four thongs for closing. He wears on them the peculiar badge of the little half-moon, made of bone or bronze, sewn on the footwear.

PLATE 8

CAESARIAN *CENTURIO*, GALLIC WARS, 58–52 BC

The *centurio* is reconstructed here with the equipment represented on the monument of Saint Remy, representing a battle of the Civil Wars, integrated with the details of the monument from Narbonne, celebrating Caesar's victories.

The *coolus* helmet is of polished bronze, fitted with a wide flat neck-guard and crest holder. The cheek-guards are attached to the bowl with riveted hooks. The crest consists of a central plume, mounted on a wooden support painted silver and nailed to the bowl. The plume is made of eagle feathers rounded at the top and inserted like a peacock tail. They were silver painted with a red border at the top.

The mail armour (*gallica*) has shoulder guards with a double-button fastening system. The armour has a crimson leather lining sewn all round, and it is worn over a second cuirass of linen, formed of a linen body fitted with double ranks of *pteryges* at the shoulders and under the waist.

Over the armour the *centurio* wears an array of military decorations (*phalerae*) mounted on a 'webbing' of natural leather.

Three silver *phalerae* are inserted in the upper and lower row. The *phalerae* are simple embossed discs with concentric circles inside. On the sides are three big *phalerae* (including those of the upper and lower rows already mentioned) but between the two larger ones smaller *phalerae*, decorated with small faces, are also mounted. In the same way also four smaller *phalerae* are mounted on the cross-belts, while on the central vertical strap are visible – from the bottom to the top – two bigger discs, followed by a *phalera* with a human image and one shaped like a small armour trophy.

These decorations are copied from the *phalerae* represented on a gravestone found in Narbonne. He is armed with the *gladius hispaniensis* found in Osuna, a Caesarian-period sword dating to about 50 BC. Note his round gilded shield (*clipeus*) embossed with the *Sidus Julium*, the symbol of Caesar's family.

PLATE 9

THRACIAN ARISTOCRATIC AUXILIARY CAVALRYMAN FROM VIZE, 45 AD

In 1938, near the town of Vize, the archaeologist Arif Müfid Mansel excavated tumulus A in a large group of burial mounds. Gold items having been found in the tomb chamber prove that this is the tomb of an aristocrat. There is a supposition that the ashes of the Thracian king Rhoimetalkes III, son of Kotys III, a Roman by inclination and views, who was brought up with the Emperor Caligula, were buried in this barrow. He was killed in a conspiracy in AD 46, and Thrace was declared a Roman province. The burial is really very rich. The sarcophagus contained a laurel wreath of

PLATE 9

gold leaf and silver cups with exquisite reliefs. Weapons were also placed in the sarcophagus: a sword, four iron daggers, spearheads, a coat of mail and a silvered bronze face-mask helmet.

Hybrid feathered armour is chain mail with small bronze or iron scales intertwined over it. It is made up of a mail backing of alternating rows of riveted and solid rings; the outer diameter of the links measuring no more than a few millimetres. The Vize example is the only surviving piece in which the textile lining is preserved.

Its design is reminiscent of a *linothorax*, i.e. the shoulders are protected with two 18cm wide pieces extending from the back. The upper part of the chest is protected by a square section on which there were two pairs of buttons for attaching the hook fastenings that held the shoulder pieces. These fastenings are made of silver-plated bronze. The scales are made of bronze and silver-plated iron. The Iron scales are arranged to create a diamond pattern on the shoulder pieces and the hem.

According to the study, the surviving lining was originally purple. Jürgen Driehaus, who investigated the armours of Vize and Augsburg, concluded that both of these examples were so similar that they could have been made in the same workshop, and even by the same armourer (Driehaus, 1968, pp. 15–16). In addition, he observed that the *lorica* from Vize had not been finished by the armourer, as the person whom it was being made for died suddenly. However, the Turkish researcher Somay Onurkan, who had also studied this specimen, refrained from such a conclusion.

The attribution of the barrow as that of King Rhoimetalkes III is rather questionable, but, without doubt, it is the burial of a very rich man. This archaeological find made it possible to get an insight as to how a rich Thracian warrior in Roman service would be equipped.

PLATE 10

QUINTUS LUCIUS FAUSTUS – *MILES LEGIO XIIII GEMINAE MARTIAE VICTRICIS*

The *Signifer*, copied from his famous stela, wears a mask-helmet with a Weiler-type bowl and an Attic diadem. It shows that these masked helmets were of composite construction, with a stylised human face mask of iron, silver or copper-alloy attached separately, having narrow eye-slits, and pierced nostrils and mouth. The attachment to the skull was by means of holes and rivets at each side and a hinge on the brow.

Different from the usual interpretation, we have reconstructed the armour of Quintus as a leather corselet, well fitted to the body, with a thick collar, wide shoulder-guards, and short cut sleeves. On the shoulders, on the breast and on the sides the leather was thicker.

The shoulder pieces were wide, made of more rigid and strong leather. They have small opening like lappets, followed by three ranges of very thick *pteryges*; they are hinged down on the shoulders, by means of small bronze hinges in bronze. Around the neck and on the upper breast a collar was disposed around the front and the back part of the body, made of beef leather, slightly softer than that of the shoulder-guards. On the front the symbol of the cohort, an half-moon, is visible towards the right side of the body. The other pieces of the armour were sewn around, forming a decorated pattern visible on the leather.

PLATE 10

PLATE 11

The armour was worn over a leather *subarmale* visible only by the triple row of thick *pteryges* on the shoulders. Indeed, it is not clear if these *pteryges* were part of an undercuirass garment or of the leather armour itself.

He wears two simple but wide *cingula* around his waist, metal plated and furnished with aprons (*balteoli*). One is used for the sword (on the right side of the body) and the other one for the dagger (on the left). The reconstruction of the *Signum* follows the original stela.

PLATE 11

BATAVIAN AUXILIARY CAVALRY, MARCIANUS, FROM NOVIOMAGUS, SECOND HALF OF THE FIRST CENTURY AD

The auxiliary camp of Noviomagus (Njimegen) has been a goldmine of highly-decorated military equipment to modern archaeologists, especially in terms of masked helmets. This cavalryman, equipped for battle, wears the precious specimen of the mask with fronton found there, combined with a real wig with ribbons which required a lot of work to manufacture.

The Batavian cloak is just as important a aspect of his accoutrements, and shows that already in the first century AD the mixture of Roman equipment with barbarian dress could produce a mixed panoply of barbaric splendour. The woven woollen cloak (*sagum*), lined with fur, is approximately 5ft wide, rectangular-shaped and measures 236cm x 168cm. It is woven in light and dark blue, chequered and hemmed by a wide band with lighter blue bars and long fringes, that formed a kind of plush. We can see two different kinds of weaving: a herringbone weave for the fabric and a tablet weave for the hems. However, the cloak could present different shades of colour: it could be a cross-coloured striped cloak called *gunna* or *gonella*, which in the Carolingian Age was still known as a 'Frisian cloak'. It took two weavers a whole working year to make such a cloak. The blue colour indicated royal or noble rank. As a matter of fact, the god Wotan still appeared in the latest Germanic legends with a cloak of such colour.

The horse is no less adorned: in Noviomagus various remains of leather horse armour were found, and so we have equipped our man with the horse-chamfron found at Vindolanda. The high quality of the leather employed and its decoration is a further proof of the employment of organic protective equipment by the Romans.

PLATE 12

ROMAN *MAGISTER EQUITUM*, AD 117 (NAWA GRAVE)

A high-ranking Roman officer was laid to rest this Syrian grave. The man who found it considered him to have been a Roman commander from Trajan's war against the Parthians.

His highly-decorated mask helmet presents Eastern features, perhaps the portrait of the man himself. The skull, made of a single piece of bronze, is oval. On the front, over the border, a floral embossing is visible, beside two further embossed parallel lines. A three-dimensional armed figure is shown at the centre of the brow, flanked by eagles, and surmounted by a sunburst. Under this is represented the bust of a victory,

Plate 12

raising her arm. At either side, on the back, a pair of *quadrigae* are shown, with naked male figures driving them with a spear in hand. The helmet has a very large neckguard. The ear-guards are one with the skull.

An edge 1cm wide was fitted with some holes on the front to allow the attachment of the lining, intended to absorb the weight of the mask. On the front a clasp for attaching the mask is also visible. The mask, covered in silver, carries an embossed and engraved moustache and long curled Eastern-style sideburns.

The armour consists of bronze scales no longer than 4cm. The description of the scale armour found in the grave fits well with several scales found in Israel. They were found very close to each other and attached to each other with large nails. Some of them were furnished with a metallic hinge for the attachment between them.

The finder of the grave speaks about the presence of now-disappeared shoulder-guards, which were attached with rings to the body of the armour. The scales were attached to a linen backing through which laces of leather were sewn and a leather edging was fixed. It is extremely interesting that – unique in Roman finds – the decorative pieces of the waist *cymation* were preserved: they are five bronze discs and three lobate elements, all covered with silver.

The *subarmalis* worn under it is a thick woollen felt garment visible only in the lower sleeves and under the groin, appearing from the sleeves of the *squama*. These *pteryges* are reinforced on their surface with bronze quadrangular scales, copied by the image of the warrior engraved on the other helmet found in the grave (fig. 198).

The breast and the muzzle of the horse are covered by straps embossed with roundels. In the grave big *phalerae* were also found. These five big bronze and silver *phalerae* are arranged as fastening elements, with squared or round rings for the fitting of the leather straps. They are decorated with the usual decorative scheme provided for them, ivy leaves and acanthus leaf decoration. Only one of them, however, is prolonged with an oval piece towards the bottom, ending with a gilded acanthus leaf between two gilded triangular geometric motifs. The second part forms a sort of border to the first one. They are decorated by floral images and mythological figures of Satyrs. They are positioned at the intersections of the *antilena* and *postilina* straps.

In the grave were found also five discs and forty-one silver and bronze buttons ending with acanthus leaves, positioned on rectangular pieces. Immediately interpreted as belt, they are most probably roundels for the leather straps.

The head of the horse is protected by a bronze frontal. It is composed of three quadrangular articulated plates, linked by clasps extended along their longer side. The two side plates are identical, and each have a gilded eye-guard embossed like a half-sphere, decorated with a geometric design. The central plate is decorated by a half-sphere, but not gilded. The horse's breast, at the intersection of the straps, was decorated by a bronze disc with a bust of Minerva.

PLATE 13

ROMAN OFFICER OF OSROENE CAVALRY, REIGN OF ALEXANDER SEVERUS, AD 235

At the beginning of the third century AD, the Emperor Alexander Severus gathered numerous troops for a punitive campaign against the Alemanni. Among those many

XXI

PLATE 13

Easterners, and especially Parthians, were recruited (Herodian, *Historiae*, VII). The Emperor had employed looted weapons captured in the war against the Sassanians who had come to power in Persia at the beginning of AD 227 to fit out his own cavalry. The man, maybe an Easterner in the service of Rome, is dressed with the most splendid equipment: a new mask helmet of *mater castrorum* type, worn with a Brigetio-type bowl, leaves only his face visible. A splendid example of a metallic *thorax stadios* provided for the cavalry is worn over a *subarmalis*, richly decorated with bronze and silver fittings on the *cymation*, and furnished with thick linen *pteryges* protecting the shoulders and the groin. The sword with the eagle pommel marks his belonging to the Imperial Guard, while his decorated shield, copied from the Dura Europos specimen, denotes his oriental origins. The shield I of Dura Europos represented here is the so called 'Trojan Shield', the one with lavishly paintings of scenes from the Fall of Troy. The central umbo of the shield is the head of the Gorgon.

On the red surface of shield I from Dura were represented scenes from the *Iliad*. This decoration is not only important for the shield decoration by itself, but also because it represents the rich range of clothing used on the Euphrate frontier by Roman soldiers and *auxilia*. In the scene of the sack of Troy the forearms of the soldiers are left uncovered, but the figures show the sleeves of the blue tunic rolled up above the elbow. This element suggests a firm grasp of military reality, where the warriors who finished off fleeing enemies or massacred captives rolled up their sleeves to stop them getting stained with blood. On the other hand the same Greeks, with their short tunics, their *paludamenta* and anatomical cuirasses are nothing more than a reflection of the Roman soldiers contemporary with the painter. A shield is even shown from the back, showing the strap for the forearm and the handgrip, noteworthy for the reconstruction of how shields were carried.

PLATE 14

CAVALRYMAN IN *HIPPIKA GYMNASIA* ARMOUR, SECOND – THIRD CENTURY AD

The image of Alexander the Great inspired the rich equipment of the *Hyppika Gymnasia*. The mask, of the Herzogenburg type, is from Straubing, and it is nothing other than the portrait of the great Macedonian. Atop the helmet, for which the Straubing bowl has been used, are the tall yellow plumes described by Arrian. The most precious item is his linen armour, again an imitation of that of Alexander as shown on the mosaic from Pompeii representing the battle of Gaugamela: at the centre of it is sewn, according to Junkelmann's interpretation, a plate with the polished image of Medusa, with precious stones inserted in the eyes. The terrific aspect of this kind of armour was intended to provoke fear and terror in the enemy, as can be seen in the similar armour worn by Sextus Valerius Genialis (fig. 78) which proves the employment of such armours on the battlefield. The greaves are those from Straubing, decorated with images of Hercules and Mars. The horse's chamfron is also copied from that found at Straubing. The central medallion of the horse's *antilina* is from Bad Deutsch-Altenburg. The shield's *umbos*, however, are taken from the Tabriz (Archäologische Staatssammlung München) specimen. Note the Cimmerian tunic, with long sleeves and the long *anaxyrida*. The purple colour is associated with the imperial one, considering that the cavalryman is thought to represent Alexander.

XXIII

PLATE 14

PLATE 15

PLATE 16

PLATE 15

DRACONARIUS IN HIPPIKA GYMNASIA ARMOUR, THIRD CENTURY AD

The splendid equipment of the standard-bearer is based on Arrian's descriptions and actual examples from the Paul Getty collection (the female mask helmet), Niederbieber (the *draco* standard), the Mithraeum of Capua (the Cimmerian tunic), Vimose (the decorated baldric), and Samum (the breastplate). With the *Hippika Gymnasia* we have the first written reference to the Roman use of the 'windsock' standard, called a *draco*, and composed of a multicoloured cloth body to which the bronze head of a serpent (*draco* or oriental *senmurvu*) was attached, hissing in the wind when the air rushed through it. The windsock tubular body of the Draco standard follows Arrian's description: 'sewing pieces of dyed material together'. The different pieces are silk covered. The awesome sight of such cavalrymen left a vivid impression on contemporaries. Maybe the first description of the *Hippika Gymnasia* equipment can be found in the Apolcalypse of Saint John (John. Ap. IX. 7ff; see also D'Amato–Sumner, 2009, pp. 197–8).

PLATE 16

STRAUBING 'AMAZON' WARRIOR ON HORSEBACK, THIRD CENTURY AD

The military equipment from the fort at Straubing, the ancient Serviodurum on the Raetian *Limes*, has revealed one of the richest hoard of equipment designed (also) for the *Hippika Gymnasia*, all belonging to the late second or the early third century AD. The German archaeologists have found six greaves, a complete set of horse eye-guards, six examples of tripartite horse chamfrons, various fragments of helmet bowls, four specimens of male masks (Alexander), three Amazon masks, a complete helmet bowl, a female mask of the *Mater Castrorum* type, and various other parts of armour. The 'Amazon' warrior reconstructed here is covered by scale armour, fastened on the breast through a decorated breastplate and worn over a linen *subarmalis*. The greaves are decorated with the bust of *Virtus*, under which Mars in full armour is standing over two tritons. The decorated Cimmerian tunic, from the Capua's Mithraeum, and the related trousers or *anaxyrida* correspond to Arrian's descriptions.

PLATE 17

DRACONARIUS OF THE DOMESTICI EQUITUM CATAPHRACTARII, AD 356

This shows one of the elite cavalrymen paraded by Constantius II during his triumphal entrance into Rome, described in a famous passage in Ammian Marcellinus's *Res Gestae* (XVI,10,8): among the waving standards and the shining of the gilded and purple *dracones*, encrusted with precious stones and with the waving body covered by precious silk, between two ranks of infantrymen of the *Cornuti*, rode the *Cataphracti Equites*: '… the so-called *Clibanarii* of the Persians, protected by armoured coverings and tightened in belts of steel, that you could reckon them statues chiselled by the hand of Praxiteles, not men; thin circular plates fitted to the curves of the body entirely covered their limbs

PLATE 17

PLATE 18

in so cunningly articulated way that it adapted itself to any movement the wearer needed to make.' Constantius's predilection for such troops is attested by the numerous regiments raised by him and mentioned in Julian's funerary oration for him. This reconstruction is partially based on the Dura Europos material, where a complete suit of armour and graffiti representing armoured cavalrymen were found by the archaeologists; noteworthy is the helmet which represents transition between the 'ridge' Roman helmets of the fourth–fifth centuries and their Sassanian prototypes. The bowl of the helmet, reconstructed in gilded iron, is of composite construction, formed by two halves meeting on a longitudinal axis and joined by an external central ridge, to which they are riveted independently. The ridge runs from the neck to the brow.

PLATE 18

CATAPHRACTARIUS OF SCHOLA SCUTARIORUM SECUNDA, SCHOLAE PALATINAE, FROM THE COLUMN OF ARCADIUS, EARLY FIFTH CENTURY AD

The column of Arcadius, raised in Costantinople in AD 402 AD, recorded in its images the main events of the campaign against the Goths of Gainas. The fragments and the drawings of its sculptures by artists and travellers through the ages, compared to archaeological finds of the fourth–fifth centuries, allow us to reconstruct the splendid equipment of the Imperial Roman Guard Cavalry. Shield blazons engraved on the column pedestal confirm the presence of the *Scholae Palatinae* and *Domestici Protectores* on the battlefield, armoured in elegant body-hugging muscle *thoraces* of iron or painted leather. Masked helmets with human faces (*personati*) were still employed by cavalryman, often covered in decorated red leather: the column shows the use of both male and female types. This is the last example, in Roman art, of the use of the traditional masked helmet on the battlefield.

Claudian, in his panegirics, describes the distinctive signs of the armoured cavalrymen of the Imperial retinue: sashes around the waist, peacock feathers on the helmet and gold and silver armour and shoulder-guards: 'When she sees the mail-clad knights and brazen armoured horses she would fain know whence that iron race of men is sprung and what land it is gives birth to steeds of bronze. Has the god of Lemnos, she would ask, "bestowed on metal the power to neigh, and forged living statues for the fight?" Joy and fear fill her mind; she points with her finger how Juno's bird decks the gay crests upon their helmets (*picturatas galeae Iunionis cristas ornet avis*), or how, beneath the golden armour on their horses' backs, the red silk waves and ripples over the strong shoulders.'

A regiment of such *clibanarii*, attached to the person of the Emperor, should have been under the command of the *Magister Officiorum*, commander of the Imperial Guard. Interestingly, the column shows the employment of the old *pelta* : the shield is reconstructed here covered in sheep or goat skin, the unusual type is evidenced by the column reliefs and should be still used by the cavalry. We can imagine a leather shield, anticipating the roundels of the cataphracts fixed on the left arm. It was held by two internal leather straps. The *deigmaton* of the *Schola* is painted, from *Notitia Dignitatum*, completely in red except for the central part with the golden star and centre in dark green, with the *umbo* either painted yellow or gilded. The double axe the cavalryman carries, copied from a specimen found in Constantinople, is also visible on the Column among the weaponry of the heavy cavalry.

PLATE 19

PLATE 19

JUSTINIAN IN THE TRIUMPHAL COSTUME OF ACHILLES

In his book *De Aedificiis* (Buildings) Procopius (I, ii, 5, 12) describes in the following words the Equestrian Statue of Justinian in the *Augusteum* of Constantinople: '… And on the summit of the Column stands a gigantic bronze horse …upon this horse is mounted a colossal bronze figure of the Emperor. And the figure is habited like Achilles, that is, the costume he wears is known by that name. He wears half-boots and his legs are not covered by greaves. Also he wears a breastplate in the heroic fashion, and a helmet covers his head and gives the impression that it moves up and down… in his left hand he holds a globe…yet he had neither sword nor spear nor any other weapon, but a cross stands upon the globe which he carries, the emblem by which alone he has obtained both his Empire and his victory in war … ' From this it is clear that the costume described did exist and that it was one of the Imperial costumes, as is further confirmed by the medallions and coins (Grabar, 1971, pl. XXVIII, n. 4; Evangelatou, Papastavrou, Skotti, 2001, p. 14; Lusuardi, Perassi, Facchinetti, Bianchi, 2002, p. 35, n. 12) of the Emperor representing him in such attire. The statue has been preserved in a drawing by Cyriacus of Ancona when the monument still existed in early fifteenth century (Evangelatou, Papastavrou, Skotti, 2001, p. 27), which allows us a complete knowledge of this attire (fig. 317). The costume of Achilles (σχῆμα Ἀχιλλεῖον) consisted of a gold muscled armour (*thorakion heroikôn*), red or purple imperial half-boots (*arbulai*, i.e. *cothurni*) and, in the case of the statue, in the crown-helmet known as a *toupha*, or at other times the jewelled crown-helmet derived from the Persian helmets and decorated, on the top, by a crest made of peacock feathers (Ravegnani, 1988, pl. 2; Bianchi, Munzi, 2006, p. 300, fig. 4,5). This imperial warlike attire could be completed, as visible on the coins, by the spear symbolising *Imperium* (military power). That this imperial attire was known as the costume of Achilles is clear from the fact that it is the costume usually worn by Achilles in late Roman iconography (fig. 316).

The costume was not only the triumphal military costume of the Emperor, but also – according to Rodenwaldt – the interest in the antique conception of the Empire which is clear in the opera of Justinian. The doubts about the existence of such a costume have been overcome by the evidence of it being worn in imperial triumphal processions before Justinian.

The Emperor Basiliscus (AD 475–6) was persuaded by his wife Zenonis to appoint to a high office the young Armatus, an Emperor's nephew and the lover of the Augusta (Bury, 1923, I, p. 392). According to Suidas he rode around the city in the costume of Achilles. Suidas, s.v. Armatiòs, probably a fragment from Candidus the Isaurian, reported thus: '… and this elated him beyond any measure, so much that he dressed the costume of Achilles (σκευὴν Ἀχιλλέως) and went with it on horseback…'. See on the topic also Dewing, 1940 (1996), pp. 395–8). The incident certainly indicated that the costume was thought to be especially appropriate for a brave commander, and that probably was, at that time, the one of the Emperor triumphing like a victorious *Imperator*.

and having a relief image of a nose, lips, a moustache and a beard[182] (fig. 167). These cheek-pieces seem to be an improved version of the bearded cheek-pieces of the Phrygian-type helmets from Thrace and Southern Greece (Kovachevitsa, Asenovgrad, Pletena, etc.).[183] Another allegedly Etruscan helmet is a modification of the Attic type, the faceplate and bowl of which are made from one piece and realistically imitates a bearded face (fig. 168). The facial features are well worked out and framed with detailed curls of the fringe and beard. The sides of the bowl have embossed steeply-curved ram's horns embossed on them, images of which are found both on the Greek helmets and Italic ones. In the ancient world, ram's horns were primarily associated with combat helmets and later, probably, they were ceremonial helmets. The meaning of horned combat helmets in the ancient world, apparently, was a sign of strength, courage and masculinity (if the owner displayed heroism on the battlefield). As reported by Livy, Roman soldiers who distinguished themselves in action could receive silver horns to be worn on their helmets.[184] In addition, the horns symbolised protection from evil spirits, demons and the evil eye; they were also believed to be able to attract the genii of victory in battle. The helmet described has a holder for a large crest and could easily be used as an element of parade panoply.[185] Nowadays, however, this helmet is considered to be a skilful fake, as it is completely non-functional and similar in style to the fakes made by Italian antique dealers of the late nineteenth or early twentieth centuries.[186] Italic finds are limited to these pieces and, therefore, it is currently impossible to trace the development of face-mask helmets in Italy. None of the above hypotheses have yet received any substantial supporting evidence in the form of continuous archaeologically-proven lines of development of helmets with anthropomorphic visors in any of these areas. Thus, questions related to the origin and development of Roman face-mask helmets up to the beginning of the Christian era remain unresolved.

There are several classifications of face-mask helmets, which differ in some details, but area still well-developed and quite acceptable at this stage of the study of the archaeological material. The most important classifications have been developed over the last three decades. The first one is the typology by the British expert in Roman armour H. R. Robinson. He arranged face-mask helmets and ornate ceremonial helmets in a group of nine types which he named 'Cavalry Sport helmets' and related them to *hippika gymnasia*.[187]

Type A consists of only one example found in 1854 near the village of Kostol (Kladovo) (fig. 169). The helmet is fashioned as a bearded head and has an elegant portrait mask. It is distinguished by the fact that the mask is fixed. The dating of this item raised great controversy. O. Benndorf dated it from the beginning of Anno Domini,[188] while the Belgrade Museum catalogue shows a later date – the beginning of the second century AD.[189] H. R. Robinson dated this specimen to the first century BC. According to him, the helmet originates from Hellenistic Greece and can be included in the same group as the face-mask helmet on the relief of Attalus I of Pergamum[190] (fig. 159a). Actually, we might want to associate the helmet from Kostol with the group of helmet, one of which is depicted on the relief in the Pergamon sanctuary of Athena. However, it should be remembered that the frieze was erected by Eumenes II (197–159 BC) to commemorate the victory of his father Attalus I over the Galatian tribes and possibly depicts the captured weapons of the defeated enemy.[191] The similarity between the masks is obvious, but the helmets are quite different. The shape of the helmet on the relief is closer to a sphero-conical one and has no decoration except volutes. The Kostol helmet is hemispherical and imitates abundant curly hair made in a pretty realistic fashion. In addition, the helmet is unusual due to the fact that its design and appearance demonstrate a combination of several traditions in manufacturing military headgear. The bottom edge of the helmet is bent in the form of a hem and has a lot of holes intended either to attach the lining or to suspend some sort neck protection in the form of a lamellar or scale aventail, which is not typical of Roman helmets and worn in the Roman army only by soldiers of Eastern auxiliary units.[192]

Type B: Helmets with a rather large projecting forehead peak which was primarily designed to enhance their protective properties. This peak is similar to the small projecting peak on infantry and cavalry helmets of the same time, though larger in size. All the archaeological finds of this type date from the late first – early second centuries AD.

Type C: Helmets of this type date from a rather wide timespan (the late first to the early third centuries AD). H. R. Robinson considers their distinctive feature to be the skilfully-worked image of a youthful face framed by locks of curly hair.

Type D: Masks included in this group and dated back to the first century AD, are characterised by horizontal hinges that are mounted low down, almost over the eyebrows.

Type E: A number of bronze masks dating from the late first–third centuries AD, which depict faces with feminine features.

Type F: Three-part examples. They consist of a two-part helmet having a back and face piece with a removable central area of the mask that covers the eyes, nose and mouth.

Type G: Three-part helmets varying from the previous examples by having a high curved crest and an front face part imitating that of the Apulian-Corinthian helmet.

Types H and I: Another kind of three-part helmet of pseudo-Attic shape. Found examples suggest that a mask was not always used to protect the face; this could sometimes be achieved by the framed face part of the helmet.

We can see from the above classification by H. R. Robinson that he based it on the structural features of helmets and masks. However, a large role is also played by the decorative design of items, which take into account the ideals of Roman portraiture of the first–third centuries AD, although we must be aware that masks are not portraits. They have their own specific character and development, so they are only partially coincident with the Roman portraiture. They have highly generalised features and belong to the military and religious spheres. The art historian M. Kolert developed her own classification of Roman parade helmets and masks for the catalogue under the general editorship of J. Garbsch.[193] When defining the typological groups she singled out the technical properties of masks

FIG. 169. Helmet with mask from Kostol, mid-first – early second century AD, Belgrade, National Museum. (Photo courtesy of National Museum Belgrade)

FIG. 170 (a)–(b). (Opposite top left and right) Helmet from Pfrondorf, second half of the second century AD, Stuttgart, Württembergisches Landesmuseum. (Photo by A. Pangerl)

FIG. 171. (Opposite bottom) Masks from Pfrondorf-type helmets: second–third centuries AD: (a) Weißenburg, Ansbach, Kreis- u. Stadtmuseum; (b) Mainz, Mainz, Mittelrheinisches Landesmuseum; (c) Osijek, Osijek, Muzej Slavonije; (d) Sotin, Zagreb, Arheoloski Muzej. (Drawing by A. E. Negin)

FIG. 172. (Below) Helmets of Pfrondorf type, end of the second century AD: (a) Former collection of A. Guttman (AG 804); (b) Vechten, private collection; (c) Ober-Florshtadt, ((a) Photo courtesy of Musée d'Art Classique de Mougins; (b) Photo courtesy of Rijksmuseum van Oudheiden; (c) After Robinson 1975, p. 129)

(the location of the hinge, material) and their morphological features (hair, face shape). This resulted in six types indicated by Roman numerals.

Type I: Masks are male, mostly beardless faces, usually with generalised features, the hinge securing the mask to the helmet is located low in the centre of the forehead. In general, the group corresponds to H. R. Robinson's Type D.

Type II: In contrast to the previous type, the hinge connecting the mask and helmet is in the middle of the helmet bowl, i.e. in the highest point on the top of the head. The ornamental hair image remains a constant feature of this type too, but along with that there are also versions with a diadem-fronton on the forehead, which is decorated with figures (masks of Hellange[194] and Ribchester[195]), although its prototype can already be observed on the Type I mask from Nijmegen.[196] Masks of this type are, in most cases, mixed types in which male facial features are combined with women's hairstyles. These classic, ideal types probably originated in late Hellenistic centres (Asia Minor, Alexandria and Antioch). This coincides with Robinson's Type B.

Type III. includes rather heterogeneous items. Robinson's Types F, G, H and I are included in it. According to M. Kolert, the main feature of all these helmets is their three-part design and cheek-pieces or a replacing face part with a cut and a mask that is sometimes inserted into it.

Type IV. Similar to Robinson's Type A.

Type V. Similar to Robinson's Type C.

Type VI. Similar to Robinson's Type E.

A further classification was offered by the German military historian M. Junkelmann.[197] It is based on the design features of helmets and on their decoration. All this has led to quite a fractional division of the material: fourteen types were defined based on the decoration and seven types based on design features.

Type I. Helmets with masks having a headpiece hinge low down. It includes three subtypes: Kalkriese, Nijmegen and Vize.

Type II. Masks with a high-mounted parietal hinge. It includes three subtypes: Ribchester, Silistra and Herzogenburg (Alexander type).

Type III. Helmets where masks have parietal hinges and are designed as feminine faces. Subtypes: Resca and Straubing.

Type IV. Helmets with a face cutout (with and without mask). Subtypes: Pfrondorf, Heddernheim and Worthing.

Type V. Pseudo-Attic parade helmets with Guisborough/Theilenhofen-type face-guards.

FIG. 173. (Opposite top) The three-part helmet (Pfrondorf type) from Ostrov, second half of the second century AD, Muzeul de Istorie Naţională şi Arheologie Constanţa. (Photo by R. D'Amato)

FIG. 174. (Opposite bottom left and right)Helmet from Vechten, second–third centuries AD, private collection. (Drawing by A. E. Negin)

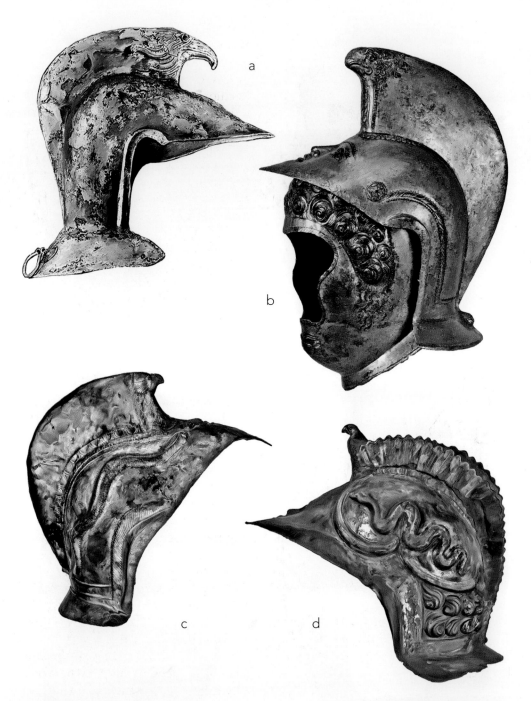

FIG. 175. Heddernheim-type helmets, end of the second–beginning of the third century AD: (a) Woerden,Stadsmuseum Woerden; (b) Frankfurt-Heddernheim, Frankfurt, Museum für Vor- und Frühgeschichte; (c) Brigetio, Budapest, Magyar Nemzeti Mûzeum; (d) Iron Gate, Budapest, Magyar Nemzeti Mûzeum. (Drawing by A. E. Negin)

FIG. 176. Helmet from Zeugma, mid-third century AD. (Drawing by A. E. Negin after Excavations at Zeugma, 189, fig. 1–2)

Type VI. Helmets with masks fixed to a Kostol-type helmet bowl.

Type VII. Helmets with masks (?) and a Phrygian-shaped crest. Type Vechten.

Junkelmann's classification seems to be the most complete and corresponds to the current volume of archaeological material. However, the researcher was unable to avoid an excessive fractionality. For example, helmets with masks having hinges mounted low on forehead were divided into three subtypes: Kalkriese, Nijmegen and Vize. The primary difference of the Vize type from the Nijmegen type was established to be a relief image of the cheek-pieces on the sides of the mask. In fact, it is as much an element of decoration as the image of curly whiskers and moustache. There is no other significant difference between these two types. Thus, there is no need to define them as two types instead of one. The same may be true for the Vechten type distinguished by M. Junkelmann based on a fragment of a high crest ending with the head of a bird of prey. However, this fragment seems to be one of the modifications of the crest on Heddernheim-type helmets.

Within the scope of this book, it would be redundant to provide a detailed description for each of the above types defined based on the geography of finds. So, we group face-mask helmets into two large groups with some transitional versions sharing some features of both groups. These are helmets with masks depicting male faces and helmets with masks with feminine features. The material of the first group corresponds to the Kalkriese, Nijmegen, Ribchester, Herzogenburg and Kostol types as defined by Junkelmann.

FIG. 177. Facial masks of 't'-shape, first half of the third century AD: (a) Doboj, Sarajevo, Historijski muzej Bosne i Hercegovine; (b) Rodez, Rodez, Musée Fenaille; (c) Aschberg, Dillingen Museum; (d) Worthing, Norwich, Castle Museum. (Drawing by A. E. Negin)

FIG. 178. Helmet from the former Axel Guttmann collection(AG 451), end of the second–beginning of the third century AD. (Drawing by A. E. Negin)

The second group includes the Reşca and Straubing types respectively. However, unlike M. Junkelman, we will define types in the group of helmets with feminine masks not based on their geography but on their intended function.

Helmets with a facial cutout (Pfrondorf, Heddernheim and Worthing) and pseudo-Attic Guisborough/Theilenhofen type ceremonial helmets with cheek-pieces are somewhat different. But anthropomorphic visors were only made for three-part helmets with a facial cutout and not even on all of them.

Masks depicting male faces appear at the turn of the eras. The earliest finds originate from a legionary camp at Haltern[198] (fig. 165) and from the alleged defeat of the legions of Varus in Kalkriese[199] (fig. 164). Several later examples dating back to the first quarter of the first century AD were found in Vechten[200] (fig. 182) and Nijmegen[201] (fig. 183). A badly-damaged mask, possibly of the same type, originates from Cologne[202] (fig. 184). Some more pieces of unknown origin

FIG. 179. (Opposite) Parade helmet from Durostorum, end of the second century AD, Sofia, National Museum of History. (Photo by R. D'Amato)

FIG. 180. (Above) Face-mask of Pfrondorf type, end of the second century AD, from private European collection. (Photo courtesy of the owner)

FIG. 181. Helmet from Vetren, first half of the third century AD, Silistra, Local Historical Museum. (Photo by R. D'Amato, drawing after Georgiev, Bacharov, 1987)

FIG. 182. (Above left) Mask from Vechten (Fectio), early first century AD, Leiden, Rijksmuseum van Oudheden. (Drawing by A. E. Negin)

FIG. 183. (Above right) Mask from Nijmegen, first century AD, private collection. (Drawing by A. E. Negin)

FIG. 184. (Below left) Mask from Cologne, early first century AD, Berlin, Pergamon Museum. (Drawing by A. E. Negin)

FIG. 185. (Below right) Mask, early first century AD, from private collection of Vassil Bozhkov, Bulgaria. (Drawing by A. E. Negin)

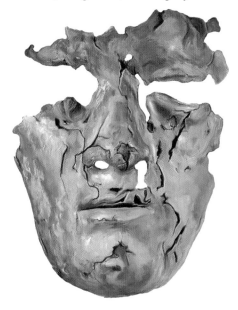

FIG. 186. (Above) Mask early first century AD, former Axel Guttmann collection (AG 812), Musée d'Art Classique de Mougins. (Photo courtesy of Musée d'Art Classique de Mougins)

FIG. 187. (Opposite top) Cavalry helmet (Weiler/Koblenz Bubenheim type) with mask (Kalkriese type), early first century AD, former collection of Axel Guttmann (AG 599), European Private Collection. (Drawing by A. E. Negin)

FIG. 188. (Opposite middle) Reconstruction of the helmet with Kalkriese-type mask. (Drawing by A. E. Negin)

FIG. 189. (Opposite bottom left) Fragment of a mask from Neuss, first half of the first century AD, Bonn, Rheinisches Landesmuseum. (Photo by Michael Greenhalgh)

FIG. 190. (Opposite bottom right) Kalkriese type mask, early first century AD, private European collection (Photo courtesy of the owner).

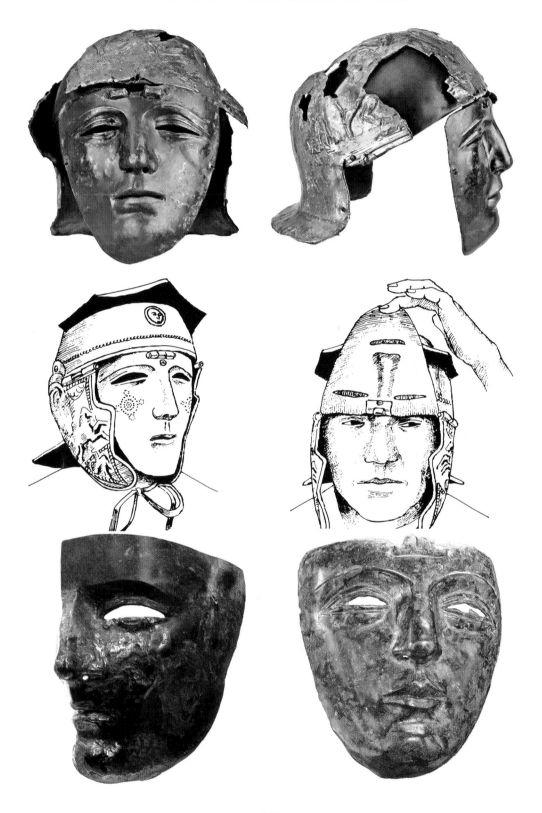

were sold at antique auctions. These masks are still very different from those common to the second–third centuries as they have no imitation ears and cover only the front of the face. However, there are helmet cheek-pieces between which the mask was held and which rigidly fixed it in place. We can also assume that it was secured by a chin strap inserted through the mounting ring on the inner side at the lower edge of the mask. Masks of this type were used with Weisenau-type helmets (an example from the Shelby White and Leon Levy collections)[203] (fig. 192 (top left)) or Weiler/ Koblenz-Bubenheim helmets (Guttmann collection, No. AG 599)[204] (fig. 187). Nijmegen type masks appeared as early as in the middle of the second quarter of the first century. M. Junkelmann was the first to distinguish these two types. Earlier they were taken together and the fact that the first kind of masks had no cheek part with a relief image of ears was not taken into account.

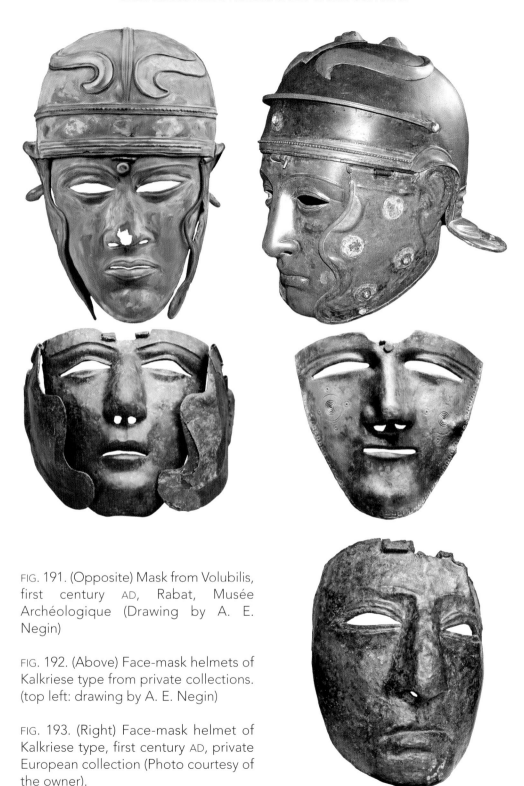

FIG. 191. (Opposite) Mask from Volubilis, first century AD, Rabat, Musée Archéologique (Drawing by A. E. Negin)

FIG. 192. (Above) Face-mask helmets of Kalkriese type from private collections. (top left: drawing by A. E. Negin)

FIG. 193. (Right) Face-mask helmet of Kalkriese type, first century AD, private European collection (Photo courtesy of the owner).

FIG. 194. (Opposite) Helmets and masks from Nijmegen hoard, mid-first century AD, Nijmegen, Valkhof-Kam Museum. (Photo by R. D'Amato)

FIG. 195. (Above) Mask from Nijmegen (Noviomagus), first century AD, Nijmegen, Valkhof-Kam Museum. (Photo courtesy of Nijmegen, Valkhof-Kam Museum)

FIG. 196. (Right) Mask from Nijmegen (Noviomagus), mid-first century AD, Leiden, Rijksmuseum van Oudheden. (Photo by Leiden, Rijksmuseum van Oudheden).

FIG. 197 (a), (b). (This page and opposite) Armour from Vize, first half of the first century AD, Istanbul Archaeological Museum. ((a) Photo by R. D'Amato; (b) Reconstruction by M. Wijnhoven, drawing by A. E. Negin

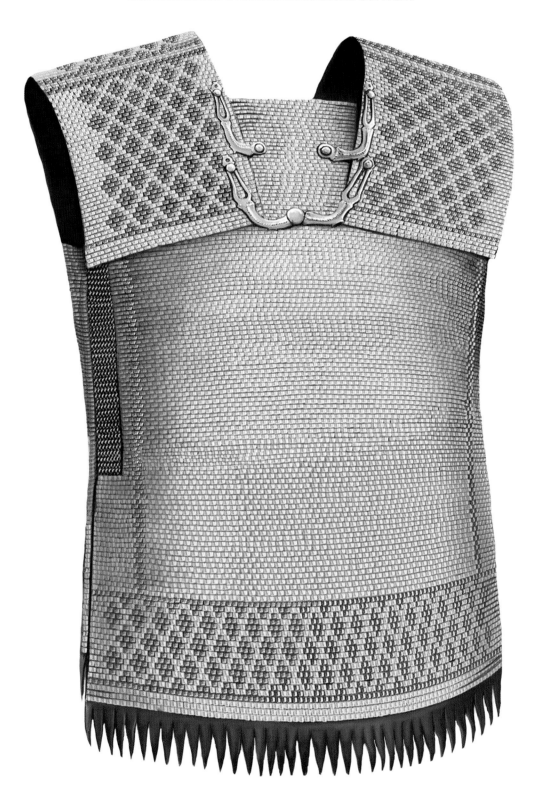

FIG. 198. Helmets from Nawa, first–second century AD, Damascus, National Museum. (Drawing by A. E. Negin; decoration drawing after Abdul-Hak 1954–1955)

FIG. 199. (Top left) Helmet with a mask from Plovdiv (Philippopolis), mid-first century AD, Plovdiv, Archaeological Museum.(Drawing by A. E. Negin)

FIG. 200. (Top right) Helmet with a mask from Homs, first half of the first century AD, Damascus, National Museum. (Drawing by A. E. Negin)

FIG. 201. (Above left) Mask from Chassenard, first half of the first century AD, Saint-Germain-en-Laye, Musée d'Archéologie nationale. (Drawing by A. E. Negin)

FIG. 202. (Above right) Mask found in Turkey, mid-first century AD, former collection of Axel Guttmann (AG 339). (Photo courtesy of Hermann Historica München)

FIG. 203. (Above left) Helmet from Sheik Ibada (Antinopolis), first–second century AD, Berlin, Antikensammlung. (Drawing by A. E. Negin)

FIG. 204. (Above right) Helmet from Jordan, mid-first century AD, Berlin, Pergamon Museum. (Drawing by A. E. Negin)

FIG. 205. Below left) Mask from Belene, mid-first century AD, Pleven, Archaeological Museum. (Drawing by A. E. Negin)

FIG. 206. (Below right) Mask from Mainz (Mogontiacum), second half of the first century AD, Vienna, Kunsthistorisches Museum. (Drawing by A. E. Negin)

FIG. 207. Fragments of the two masks from Neuvy-Pailloux, early second century AD, Paris, Louvre. (Drawing by A. E. Negin)

FIG. 208. (Below left) Fragments of mask from Brecon Gaer, end of the first century AD, Cardiff, National Museum (Drawing by A. E. Negin)

FIG. 209. (Below right) Mask from Reinheim, mid-first century AD, Museum für Vor- und Frühgeschichte Saarbrücken (Drawing by A. E. Negin)

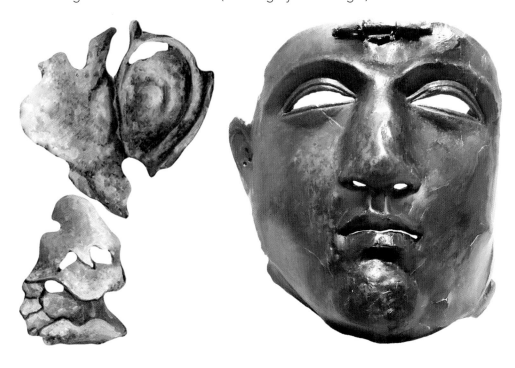

The Nijmegen type was named after a legionary camp at Nijmegen (the Netherlands) where five masks and helmets were found at different times[205] (figs 194–196). The design of the Nijmegen type differs from the Kalkriese type not only because of the different shape of the mask, but also due to the way it was attached to the helmet bowl. Riveted pins for leather straps to attach the mask after the helmet had been put on were placed at the sides of the mask directly under the ears. The straps were attached to the mask by inserting them through a small slot on a large-headed nail (the Nijmegen masks), or by a ring (the Plovdiv helmet[206]) (fig. 199). Both straps were fastened with a buckle directly over the neck-guard. The earliest example of this group originates from Homs (Emesa; Syria)[207] (fig. 200). The helmet from the Thracian burial at Vize[208] in Turkey dates approximately from the same time (fig. 197a).

FIG. 210. Mask from Rome (from the river Tiber), mid-first century AD, Copenhagen, Nationalmuseum. (Photo courtesy of National Museum of Denmark)

FIG. 211. (Above left) Mask from Gorny & Mosch collection, first century AD. (Drawing by A. E. Negin)

FIG. 212. (Above right) Face-mask of Nijmegen type, first century AD, private European collection (Photo courtesy of the owner)

As suggested by H. R. Robinson, the distinctive feature of the Ribchester type face-mask helmet is considered to be the highly prominent raised triangular projecting peak of the helmet bowl.[209] The mask forehead became higher and, thus, the leading edge of the helmet bowl was moved back, which resulted in the loss of some of its protective qualities. The large hinges used to attach masks to helmet bowls in the early Imperial period became less common and they were gradually replaced by a simpler fixture in the form of a hook and a loop or a flat pin and a cut. Lifting up the mask was no longer possible and would result in a helmet broken down into two pieces.[210] These modifications were made not due to any functional problems but only for aesthetic considerations. Large mask hinges mounted low on the forehead prevented the facial features from being ideal and the height of the forehead was increased to make the mask compositionally perfect and its decorative design more impressive. The increased forehead area was filled with representations of decorative diadems framed with embossed curls. But no diadem was made on some masks and luxurious curls were depicted instead of it, which made these examples look similar to the Silistra-type pieces that appeared at the end of the Flavian dynasty. The diadem or curly hair, besides being decorative, was also designed to cover a simpler and less reliable design of hinge.[211] It would be logical to assume that due to their extremely poor defensive qualities, Ribchester-type helmets were a transitional link between combat face-mask helmets and what were purely ceremonial modifications. However, we can notice a more protective than decorative purpose of the projecting peak, which

FIG. 213(a)–(b). (Top left and right) (a) Helmet from Ribchester, end of the first century AD, London, British Museum; (b) Modern reconstruction of the Ribchester helmet, Mainz, Römisch-Germanisches Zentralmuseum. ((a) Photo by P. Hudson; (b) Photo by M. Greenhalgh)

served the same function that the visor of combat helmets performed. It was intended to cushion the impact of cutting weapon, as to cut a greatly projected surface was difficult and the strength and direction of impact in most cases could change when the weapons simply slid down the low-sloped edge of peak. Combat use of the Ribchester type helmet is confirmed by the thickness of the masks, averaging 1mm and in some cases reaching up to 2mm.[212]

Some of the characteristics inherent in the Herzogenburg type appear as early as in the first century. They can be seen on the Newstead helmet (fig. 218), although there are only some components of the set of features (e.g. locks) depicted.[213] The development of the type took place under Hadrian. The earliest example having the features of this type originates from a cave in Hebron where it was hidden, most likely during the Bar Kochba revolt[214] (fig. 219). There was neither modelling of the face and especially the forehead as found in later pieces nor prominent eyebrows, though the head was provided with a Hellenistic hairstyle in the manner of the sculptural tradition of depicting Alexander the Great. The final formation of the type can be seen in an example from Herzogenburg in Lower Austria[215] (fig. 220). The second name (the Alexander type) was given to these face-mask helmets due to their similarity to the image of Alexander the Great which was very common in ancient times.[216] The Herzogenburg type is represented by numerous finds that often show a remarkable uniformity in design when compared to other types of face-mask helmets.

FIG. 214. (Above left) Helmet from Nikyup (Nicopolis ad Istrum), circa 100 AD, Vienna, Kunsthistorisches Museum. (Drawing by A. E. Negin)

FIG. 215. (Above right) Mask from Hellange, second half of the first century AD, Luxembourg, Musée National d'Histoire et d'Art. (Drawing by A. E. Negin)

FIG. 216. (Below left) Face-mask helmet of Ribchester/Silistra type, second half of the first century AD, private European collection (Photo courtesy of the owner)

FIG. 217. (Below right) Bronze helmet from Newstead, end of the first century AD, Edinburgh, National Museum of Scotland. (Photo by A. Pangerl)

FIG. 218. (Above left) Newstead face-mask helmet, end of the first century AD, Edinburgh, National Museum of Scotland. (Drawing by A. E. Negin)

FIG. 219. (Above right) Face-mask helmet from Hebron, early second century AD, Jerusalem, National Museum. (Drawing by A. E. Negin)

FIG. 220. (Below) Face-mask helmet from Herzogenburg, mid-second century AD, Herzogenburg, Augustiner Chorherrenstift. (Drawing by A. E. Negin)

FIG. 221. Helmet from Chatalka, second half of the first century AD, Stara Zagora, Regional Historical Museum. (Photo by S. Dimitrov)

The body of archaeological finds of Roman face-mask helmets includes a number of examples, subdivided by researchers into several types, which are fashioned as beautiful female faces and have lush hairstyles. These pieces are very different from other known Roman face-mask helmets with typical masculine faces, whiskers and a hairstyle sometimes topped with a military wreath (figs 239–

FIG. 222. Helmet and mask from Ain Grimidi, end of the second–early third century AD, Alger, Musée National des Antiquités. (Drawing by A. E. Negin)

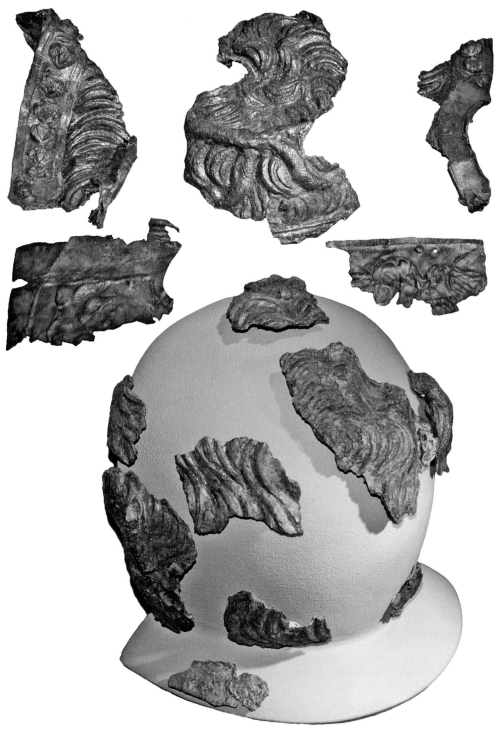

FIG. 223. Various Straubing finds, early third century AD, Straubing, Gäubodenmuseum. (Photo by D. Bullard)

FIG. 224. Straubing hoard: helmets and masks, early third century AD, Straubing, Gäubodenmuseum. (Drawing by A. E. Negin)

248). Some pieces are a kind of transitional link from masks with purely masculine features. There, we can see coarse, seemingly, non-feminine facial features and whiskers and, at the same time, luxurious hairstyles with curly locks and, obviously, curls waved in neat rows. Despite the fact that their decoration contains a number of specific details typical of feminine masks, these examples cannot be

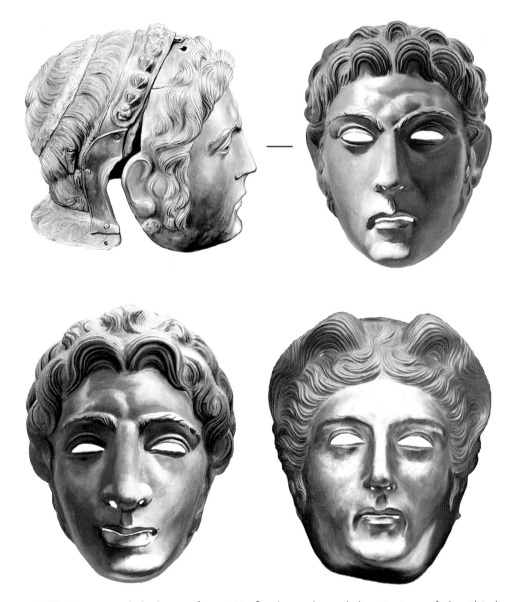

FIG. 225. Face-mask helmets from Weißenburg hoard, beginning of the third century AD, Archäologische Staatssammlung München. (Drawing by A. E. Negin)

classified as representations of women. Silistra-type masks,[217] named after the Bulgarian town[218] where a helmet was found, are of this kind (fig. 242). The range of this type is rather heterogeneous, as there are pieces of transitional Ribchester/Silistra and Silistra/Reşca types. A mixture of features of different mask types can also be seen in the examples from Rapolano[219] and Weißenburg[220]

FIG. 226. (Above left) Mask (Herzogenburg type) from Ubbergen, mid-second century AD, Nijmegen, Valkhof-Kam museum. (Drawing by A. E. Negin)

FIG. 227. (Above right) Mask from Stokstadt, mid-second century AD, Aschaffenburg, Schlossmuseum. (Drawing by A. E. Negin)

FIG. 228. (Below left) Mask (Herzogenburg type) from Strass Moos, second half of second century AD, Archäologische Staatssammlung München. (Photo by R. D'Amato)

FIG. 229. (Below right) Mask from Foktorok, second half of second century AD, Tata, Kuny Domokos Museum. (Drawing by A. E. Negin)

FIG. 230. (Above left) Helmet from Ruit, second–third centuries AD, Stuttgart, Württembergisches Landesmuseum. (Drawing by A. E. Negin)

FIG. 231. (Above right) Mask from Stuttgart Bad Cannstatt, second half of the second century AD, Stuttgart, Württembergisches Landesmuseum. (Drawing by A. E. Negin)

FIG. 232. (Below left) Face-mask helmet from Aalen, second century AD, Aalen, Limesmuseum. (photo A. Pangerl)

FIG. 233. (Below right) Mask from Welzheim, second–third century AD, Stuttgart, Württembergisches Landesmuseum. (Drawing by A. E. Negin)

FIG. 234. (Above) Mask from Gaziantep, circa 100 AD, London, British Museum. (Photo by R. D'Amato)

FIG. 235. (Left) Mask from Ehzell, mid-second century AD, Saalburg, Bad Homburg, Saalburg-Museum. (Drawing by A. E. Negin)

FIG. 236. (Opposite) Fragment of face-mask helmet from Vieux, second century AD, Vieux, Musée de Vieux-la-Romaine. (Photo by P. Vipard)

FIG. 237. (Above) Masks from Ilısu Höyük, second–third century AD, Mardin Museum. (Photos by Hatice Deniz and Umut Özgür Özel)

FIG. 238. (Below left) Mask from Urspring, second half of the second century AD. (Reconstruction drawing by A. E. Negin)

FIG. 238a. (Below right) Mask helmet of Alexander type, second century AD, Plovdiv, Vatev collection. (Museum photo)

FIG. 239. Mask from Dormagen (Durnomagus), second half of the second century AD, Bonn, Landesmuseum. (Photo by M. Greenhalgh)

FIG. 240. (Above left) Mask from Conflans, first century AD, present location unknown. (Drawing by A. E. Negin)

FIG. 241. (Above right) Mask from Hirshova (Carsium), second half of the first century AD, Bucharest, Muzeul Național de Istorie a României. (Drawing by A. E. Negin)

FIG. 242. (Below) Helmet from Silistra (Durostorum), second century AD, Sofia, National Museum of History. (Photo by R. D'Amato)

FIG. 243. (Above) Mask from Smederevo (Vinceia), second century AD, Belgrade, National Museum. (Photo courtesy of National Museum Belgrade)

FIG. 244. (Below left) Face-mask from the former Axel Guttmann collection (AG 813), first half of the second century AD. (Photo courtesy of Christie's)

FIG. 245. (Below right) Mask from Roomburg (Matilo), end of the first beginning of the second century AD, Leiden, Rijksmuseum van Oudheden. (Photo courtesy of Rijksmuseum van Oudheden, Leiden)

FIG. 246. Face-mask helmet fragments: (a) Dalkingen, second century AD, Stuttgart, Württembergisches Landesmuseum; (b) Longthorpe, mid-first century AD, Peterborough, Museum; (c) Zwammerdam, mid-first century AD, Rotterdam, Bureau Oudheidkundig Onderzoek. (Drawing by A. E. Negin)

where coarse facial features are complemented with a long-haired mane which looked more like a female hairstyle than a male one.

Early pieces of the currently-known female-mask helmets date to the late first century AD. There is a brass mask with a portion of the helmet bowl from Rapolano,[221] Tuscany (fig. 249) and a mask made of bronze or brass from Newstead,[222] Scotland. The further development of the feminine helmets in the early second century AD is represented by the androgynous Silistra type. Along with the Reşca type prevailing at that time, a strictly stylised type appeared in the early second century AD which transforms, finally, into the 'Oriental' Straubing type. In the beginning, the boundaries between the Reşca and Straubing types are

FIG. 247. Fragments of helm of Herzogenburg type, from Balkans, third century AD, private Italian collection, (Photo by R. D'Amato)

quite vague, which can be seen in the mask from Visegrad,[223] Hungary. The fragmented mask from Grafenhausen[224] has completely non-classical features, although it already has a high cone-shaped hairstyle typical of the Straubing type. A little later, we see a transition to that classical type, which is represented by three 'Oriental' masks from the Straubing hoard and a very similar mask from Eining in Lower Bavaria.[225]

If we disregard the fractional geographical typology and bring together all the decorative elements of the masks and helmet bowls of the female type currently known, we can analyse available pieces by means of iconographic analysis and by comparing them with the canons of Roman portraiture. In this case, we can define three groups of masks based on the images embedded by armourers when creating them. The proposed typology of female masks is based on their functional purpose, which is determined based on sets of features forming certain images. Due to these, the full range of finds can be divided into three conditional types.

FIG. 248. (Right) Face-mask from Leon Levy and Shelby White collection, first century AD, (Drawing by A. E. Negin)

FIG. 249. (Below) Helmets and masks from Rapolano, second half of the first century AD, Florence, Museo Archeologico Nazionale, (Photo by R. D'Amato)

1. Helmets with 'Amazon' masks

The first group includes masks bearing female faces with oriental features and a high, conical hairstyle made of many small waved curls. On the forehead of some masks there is a septal inlay-work with coloured glass, which apparently is a kind of apotropaion. Three masks of this kind came from the hoard found in Straubing[226] (fig. 250). The hoard contained masks representing both female and male faces.[227] This suggested that the buried hoard contained items of arms and equipment of the two opposing teams which performed at theatrical cavalry tournaments.[228] And all the three female masks had the same high conical hairstyle that resembles the Phrygian cap and Amazons' hairstyles appearing in some iconographic sources. Based on this, we can assume that female face-mask helmets found in Straubing could be used in a theatrical Amazonomachy. This scene was popular among Roman soldiers as evidenced by the fact that it is depicted on one of the three supposed oval parade shields of the third century AD from Dura-Europos.[229]

The representation of an Amazonomachy scene was not only a tribute to mythological tradition. In warfare, time after time the Romans encountered women fighting against them.[230] Flavius Vopiscus wrote that women dressed in male attire (apparently, Sarmatian women) used to fight against the Romans on the side of the Goths even in the late second century AD.[231] Therefore, the imitation of confrontation with these militant women might be quite popular for theatrical cavalry tournaments, as well as for the visualisation of mythological scenes. No wonder that even the Emperor Commodus entered the arena of Rome dressed as an Amazon.[232]

The Phrygian cap actually was depicted in art of the Greek and Roman periods representing the Amazons. But this shape of headwear is known as an attribute of the followers of Mithraism.

The Mithraic cap, similar to the Phrygian cap, appears in numerous images of the scene 'Mithras Tauroktonos'. Such a shape is also used in helmets the masks of which cannot be unambiguously classified as imitating female faces. For example, a helmet with a bowl in the shape of a Phrygian cap (or a Mithraic cap) recently found in Crosby Garrett,[233] Cumbria (Britain), can be interpreted as a depiction of the god Mithras, which would be suitable for the Mithraic Mysteries rather than for *hippika gymnasia*[234] (fig. 252).

In the context of the find in Straubing, there is no doubt that the presence of identical masks proves that an entire team of cavalrymen was equipped with them and it is absolutely impossible to think that several soldiers could represent Mithras at the same time.

Thus, it was indeed a team of 'Amazons'. The presence of the Herzogenburg-type masks which, according to one version, reproduced the image of Alexander the Great[235] also supports the fact that the masquerade, for which the Straubing pieces were made, was intended to represent a struggle between the Greeks and the Amazons.

FIG. 250. Straubing hoard: helmets and masks, early third century AD, Straubing, Gäubodenmuseum, (Drawing by A. E. Negin)

FIG.251. Female face-mask helmets of the 'Amazon' type and fragments of unspecified type. (a) Grafenhausen, second century AD, Stuttgart, Württembergisches Landesmuseum; (b) Eining, beginning of the third century AD, Archäologische Staatssammlung München; (c) Rudna, beginning of the third century AD, Ljubljana, Narodni Muzej; (d) Pfünz, beginning of the third century AD, Eichstätt, Museum; (e) Bad Deutsch-Altenburg, beginning of the third century AD, Bad Deutsch-Altenburg, Museum Carnuntinum; (f) Thamusida, beginning of the third century AD, Rabat, Musée Archéologique; (g) Pfünz, beginning of the third century AD, Eichstätt, Museum; (h) Künzing, beginning of the third century AD, Archäologische Staatssammlung München. ((a)–(h) Drawings by A. E. Negin; (c) Photo by R. D'Amato)

FIG. 252. Face-mask helmet from Crosby Garrett, late second or early third century AD, private collection. (Photo courtesy of Christie's)

2. Helmets with '*Mater castrorum*' masks

The second group includes helmets with masks that do not have the high conical hairstyles of the first group, the hair being dressed in 'waves'.

Sometimes the masks are topped with a tall hairstyle – the *tutulus* which adorned the ancient Roman *mater familias*.[236] And hairstyles of only few masks of this group are dressed in the shape of small curls. In some cases the hair is adorned with diadems, garlands and other jewellery and on the back of the head the hair is often shaped into a bun. Faces do not have any distinctive oriental features and a crescent (*lunula*)[237] is depicted on the forehead of some masks. The mask face and hair contrasted with each other as the hair, covered with gold or being of untinned bronze, was golden while the face, which was tin-plated or painted, was white. Such masks with lofty golden hairstyles evidently represent popular blond wigs or bleached hair.[238] [fig. 253–260]

A prime example of this type is a mask of the late second century AD from the Olt river, Romania, recovered from the water near Reşca[239] (fig. 255b). On this piece, we can see brushed-back hair retained with a strap knotted on the forehead. A wreath is on the hair; a beaded pendant in the shape of a small crescent (*lunula*) is twisted in the headband. Similar jewelled hairstyles are shown on the masks from Nola[240] (British Museum) (fig.255e), in the J. Paul Getty Museum's collection[241] (fig. 255d), on the mask from Ostrov[242] (fig. 173) extant in parts and re-made according to the new fashion (a T-shaped face cut was made), as well as on the pieces from Newsted[243] (fig. 255c), Visegrad,[244] (fig. 255a) Petronell-Carnuntum[245] (fig. 254f)), Krivnja[246] (fig. 254g), Madara[247] (fig. 261b), Cincşor[248] (fig. 255f), Gilău[249] (fig. 254h), Aquincum[250] (fig. 261a), Pfünz[251] (fig. 251g) and Thorsberg,[252] (fig. 255h) and in private collections (sold at Christie's and Galerie Puhze)[253] (fig. 255g).

Sometimes these masks are named 'Oriental' due to their similarity with the image of female faces on funeral steles of Palmyra.[254] E. Bartman believes that if the masks portrayed Oriental women the latter were not ordinary ones but those of noble blood and those ones who had lead the opponents of Rome and had been directly involved in the persistent and violent opposition, displaying military prowess.[255]

This suggests, again, a recalling of the image of an Amazon as a worthy and dangerous opponent. However, if this theory is true, then the purpose of these masks can easily be found.

How effective was wearing helmets with masks depicting a heroine probably unknown to most enemy barbarian soldiers in battle? Also, as narrative sources throw no light, it is difficult to imagine in which public ceremonies images of barbarian queens could be necessary. Could they be objects of worship or veneration for the Roman soldiers, if even the author of the theory agrees that it is difficult to imagine a Roman cavalry soldier who was familiar with the works of classical rhetoric, praising the courage and bravery of such characters as Artemisia of Halicarnassus, Tomiris or Zenobia.[256]

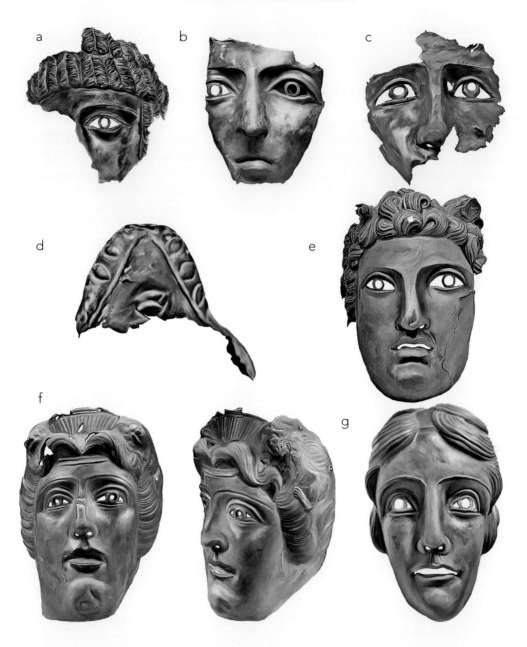

FIG. 253. Female face-mask helmets of 'Mater castrorum' and mixed types. (a) From Germany, third century AD; (b) former Axel Guttmann collection, (AG 709), third century AD, private collection; (c) Sostra, third century AD; Sostra museum; (d) Sittling, beginning of the third century AD, Archäologische Staatssammlung München; (e) Varna, mid-second century AD, Varna, Archaeological Museum; (f) private collection (Christies. 11 December 2003. Sale 1314, Lot 2341), beginning of the third century AD; (g) – private collection (Metropolitan Museum), beginning of the third century AD. (Drawing by A. E. Negin)

FIG. 254. Female face-mask helmets of 'Mater castrorum' and mixed types. (a) Former Axel Guttmann collection (AG 449), beginning of the third century AD; (b) Former Axel Guttmann collection (AG 450), beginning of the third century AD; (c) ex-C. Levett collection, beginning of the third century AD, Musée d'Art Classique de Mougins; (d) Straubing, beginning of the third century AD, Straubing, Gäubodenmuseum; e) Bad Deutsch-Altenburg (Carnuntum), beginning of the third century AD, Vienna, Österreichisches Archäologisches Institut; (f) Carnuntum-Petronell, beginning of the third century AD, Bad Deutsch-Altenburg, Museum Carnuntinum; (g) Krivnja (near Razgrad), second half of the second century AD, Razgrad, Museum,; (h) Gilău, end of the second century AD, Cluj-Napoca, Muzeul Naţional de Istorie a Transilvaniei. ((a)–(b) – Photos courtesy of Christie's; (c) Photo courtesy of Musée d'Art Classique de Mougins; (f) Photo by R. D'Amato; (d), (e), (g), (h) Drawing by A. E. Negin)

FIG. 255. Female face-mask helmets of 'Mater castrorum' type, second–third centuries AD: (a) – Visegrad, Visegrad Matyas Kiräly Müzeum; (b) Resca, Vienna, Kunsthistorisches Museum; (c) Newstead, end of the first century AD, Edinburgh, National Museum of Scotland; (d) Paul Getty collection; (e) Nola, London, British Museum; (f) Cincşor, Muzeul Ţării Făgăraşului; (g) private collection (Galerie Puhze. Kat. 12, 1997, Nr. 79); (h) Thorsberg, Schleswig, Schleswig-Holsteinisches Landesmuseum für Vorgeschichte. (Drawing by A. E. Negin)

FIG. 256. Female face-mask helmet, end of the second century, private collection. (Photo by A. Pangerl)

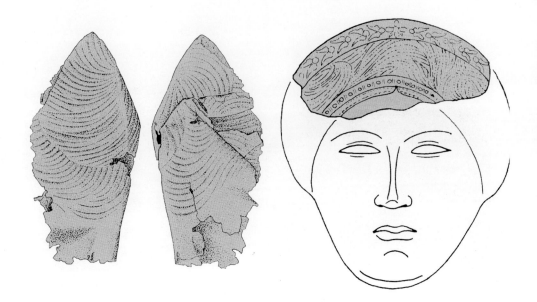

FIG. 257. (Above) Fragments of two helmets from Herten, second–third centuries AD, Freiburg im Breisgau, Museum für Ur- und Frühgeschichte. (After Reuter, 1999)

FIG. 258. (Opposite) Helmets from Eining, beginning of the third century AD, Archäologische Staatssammlung München. (Photo by A. Lemeshko)

But such masks could be an object of worship if they depicted not an abstract and little-known image of an oriental female ruler but the image of the 'mother of the camp' which was much dearer to any soldier of Rome.[257] E. Künzl noted the similarity of some masks with images of soldiers' empresses of the third century AD and suggested their relationship with the cult of *mater castrorum* (mother of the camp).[258] It is commonly known that, besides civilian titles, an empress receive this honorary title for her participation in military campaigns. Faustina the Younger was the first to receive this title as she had accompanied Marcus Aurelius 'in all the campaigns, so he called her "the Mother of the Camp"'.[259] However, Julia Domna got this title after the invasion of Adiabene and, seemingly, partly due to the reason that she was a prominent figure among people around her husband while he was on campaign.[260]

All the examples in this group of masks date from the second half of the second to the first half of the third centuries AD. It was not necessary to make an exact copy of the portrait of a woman of the imperial family. It was sufficient to have a few distinguishing features on an item and achieve a general resemblance.[261]

According to J. Oliver, celebrations in the calends of January (*Kalendae Ianuariae*), as marked in the military calendar from Dura-Europos (*Feriale Duranum*), namely 1 January, were intended to honour and bring sacrifices to the mother patroness

FIG. 259. (Above) Fragments of decorated helmets from Thamusida, second–third centuries AD, Rabat, Musée Archéologique. (After Boube-Piccot, 1994)

FIG. 260. (Below) Fragments of decorated helmets from Volubilis, second–third centuries AD, Rabat, Musée Archéologique. (After Boube-Piccot, 1994)

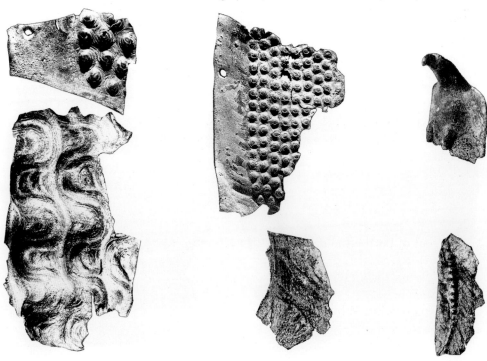

of the military camp (*mater castrorum*).[262] We can assume that during the solemn and theatrical ceremonies the masks of this type could be worn by the celebrant representing the divine patroness of military camps.

The relationship, at least, of a number of female masks to the cult of *mater castrorum* partly explains the fact that Arrian in his treatise on cavalry tournaments mentioned nothing about masks depicting female faces, as Faustina the Younger was awarded this title forty years after this source had been written.

3 HELMETS WITH 'MEDUSA' MASKS.

In the catalogue edited by J. Garbsch, the mask from Weißenburg (Biriciana), Germany, is defined as depicting a beardless male face.[263] However, wings and snakes in the hair are depicted on it. We could assume that the armourer wanted to show a scene of a struggle between an eagle with a snake, i.e. opposing symbols which were popular in ancient stories. This scene embodied the struggle between two principles and the eagle with the snake defeated was a symbol of forthcoming victory. However, the mask does not even hint at the death of the snake in the eagle's claws. The snake is depicted to crawling out of the curls, which suggests a different interpretation of the mask's decoration as representing the face of the Gorgon Medusa.[264] Wings flying over the head of hair, as well as snakes crawling out of the hair, are often seen on Roman images of Medusa.[265]

Two more very similar masks with feminine features, one from Kalenik,[266] Bulgaria (fig. 261e) and the other of unknown origin, which was sold at Christie's[267] (fig. 261f), also have images of snakes crawling out of the hair and they can also be interpreted as the image of the Gorgon Medusa.

The best extant example of the helmet depicting Medusa is that from Pfrondorf[268] (fig. 270a, b). This is a three-part helmet consisting of a back part (helmet bowl), a face part with a cutout for eyes, nose and mouth into which the anthropomorphic visor was inserted. It was found in 1868 in an abandoned stone quarry. The mask is made of silver-plated copper sheet by means of embossing. An eagle with its wings spread is on the forehead. Snakes entwine the eagle's wings and go down the cheeks in the form of curls. Two snakes entwine around the back of the head to the parting. A wreath tied back with a ribbon is on the head.

A removable mask capable of being taken off at any time proves that this type of helmet could be used not only during parades and other ceremonies but also in combat. It is in battle that the use of masks depicting Medusa is most probable. It is difficult to imagine in what ceremonies soldiers could wear these helmets while in the heat of battle this image performed both of its functions – to protect the owner and to intimidate the enemy. However, intimidating the enemy using the image of a mythical character who had malicious powers could be effective only so long as there was a mythological consciousness that believed in it and did not call it into question. When faith in the myths was lost, this function was no longer relevant. So, now, it hard to imagine how strong the faith in the apotropaion was and how widely it was used in real combat, rather than in costumed pageants.

FIG. 261. (Opposite) Female face-mask helmets of '*Mater castrorum*' type and masks with representations of the head of Medusa, second–third centuries AD: (a) Aquincum, Aquincum, Museum; (b) Madara, Shumen, Local Historical Museum; (c) Krefeld-Gellep, Krefeld, Museumszentrum Burg Linn; (d) Weißenburg, Weißenburg, Museum; (e) Kalenik, Lovec, Istoritcheski Muzej; (f) private collection (Christies. 8 June 2005. Sale 1531. Lot. 177) ((a) After Kocsis, pl. 7; (b) Photo courtesy of Shumen, Local Historical Museum; (c)–(f) Drawings by A. E. Negin)

FIG. 262. (Above) Face-mask helmet from second–third centuries AD, private collection, Plymouth, Providence Academy. (Photo courtesy of Providence Academy)

Ancient sources throw no light on the purpose of masks depicting female faces. Because of this, they were even interpreted as burial masks[269] as they sometimes have decorative motifs which are closely related to the world of the dead and belief in the afterlife, such as snakes which are considered to be chthonic creatures symbolising the world of underground dwellers and also being a symbol of the soul. However, in general, burial masks had no eye, nose and mouth holes as the deceased did not need to hear, see and talk.[270] On the contrary, people who wore masks at a masquerade certainly needed all this.

It should be noted that it is difficult to include some of the found masks with feminine facial features in any of the above types. These include the masks from Rapolano[271] (fig. 249), Weißenburg[272] (fig. 261d), Krefeld-Gellep[273] (fig. 261c) and

Varna[274] (fig. 253e). Furthermore, small fragments of masks and helmets from Künzing[275] (fig. 251h), Gnotzheim,[276] Pförring[277] and Thamusida[278] (fig. 259) can be defined as female ones only due to the long, wavy strands of hair in their decoration. Consequently, it is rather difficult to interpret the purpose of each specific mask and, moreover, a badly fragmented item. However, in general, it is possible to discuss their basic functions if we associate them with various ceremonial practices.

It should be specified that we must refute right away the supposition that they could be used to mislead enemy soldiers. Although ruses can be found in the ancient tradition when male soldiers disguised themselves as women,[279] there is no hint of honouring the courage and valour of women in those episodes. In addition, the ancient sources do not mention this practice being widespread in the Roman army. But a striking resemblance of some masks to female facial features and clay theatrical masks vividly recalls that male actors traditionally disguised themselves in theatrical performances and other ritual acts where it was necessary to re-create some event or action in the form of a theatrical performance.

The addiction of the Romans to theatrical productions explains the popularity of Amazonomachy performances as ritual battles between two groups of figurative players; some of them had to disguise themselves to portray a legendary image. Oriental women, certainly, were famous in the ancient world for their ferocity and bellicosity[280] but it is impossible to assume that women (who could have used the masks) served in the Roman army, even in the auxiliary and irregular units consisting of foreigners, as there are no sources to suggest this. Sometimes, though, based on some unconfirmed data, sensational statements are made about the presence of some 'Amazons' in Roman irregular units, for example, a recent statement made on the basis of the study and publication of the data of burial excavations in the vicinity of the Roman fort at Brougham, Cumbria, Britain, where a unit of the Roman army (*Numerus equitum Stratonicianorum*) was located.[281] Two burials were found there, preceded by a cremation ceremony and containing, presumably, the remains of women. Burnt remains of animals were placed in them, too. Bone plates were found, which had been used to decorate caskets, as well as parts of a sword scabbard and fragments of pottery. In the burial of another woman aged, presumably, 21 to 45 years old, a silver cup, a sword scabbard with bone inlays, horse skeletons and items suggesting the Danubian origin of the deceased were found.[282] However, H. Cool who studied the materials of these burials is not very enthusiastic about the classification of the remains as female ones in her monograph on the excavations in Brougham.[283] Although the theory of 'Amazons' in the Roman army could be supported by the two previously-mentioned masks found in the female graves in Nola and Varna, no other arms are reported to have been found in these burials, therefore, there is no reason to suppose that female warriors were buried in those graves.

Putting on the attributes of a different gender identity, male soldiers impersonated women both in theatrical performances of Amazonomachy and in ceremonies honouring the 'mother of the camp'. Such an impersonation could be comparable, for example, to the way an emperor honoured in a triumph temporarily took on a divine persona. But when the triumph was over, he became again the man he was. In the same way, a male soldier performing a female warrior possessed this new ludic identity only for a short period of time. In this case he was not an actor by profession and it follows that he did not become an actor even for the time of the performance. And such a temporary change of identity did not lead to a change in his colleagues' attitude towards him because they were well aware that the main cause of the 'cross-gender acting' in this theatrical performance was not a need for identity, but the simple lack of members of the opposite sex. At the same time, the participants and spectators had no cognitive dissonance, as in this case, the gender identity was only casual. Moreover, the mythical image implemented by means of a female mask had a special power, as it created a new identity sparking not only interest but also the respect of the Romans. In the context of *hippika gymnasia*, such a helmet represents a quasi-ritual form of disguise. Similarly to the military initiation rite of the earliest times the masks enabled the suspension one's own identity for a short period of time and, paradoxically, even intensified the masculinity of a man disguised in a women's costume. This was achieved by displaying a lack of fear of losing masculinity for some time. On the other hand, a helmet with a mask depicting a female face was nothing more than the image of a barbarian warrioress in this context. A man disguised as an Amazon represented a legendary exotic character of foreign origin, disengaging himself for a while from traditional Roman values, according to which the woman was subordinate and dependent on the man. In this case, the gender identity was ignored and the character was represented as an opponent equal in strength and courage to a Roman soldier. In this case a male soldier did not find it shameful to wear a female mask.[284] The same psychological and religious connotation operated where the empress venerated by the soldiers was represented.

The group of helmets with masks depicting female faces described also includes mask from Nola. But the female facial features are complemented with a stylised image of a helmet put on the head. In this connection it can be assumed that mask from Nola depicts the goddess Minerva or Victoria. This goddess is well suited to being depicted on protective arms since, unlike Mars, who loved blood, war and violence in any form, Minerva represented sacred defensive war and was the goddess of defence. Being depicted on armour, the goddess symbolised the protection and patronage granted to the soldier.

In the imitation of the Corinthian helmet, Minerva is depicted in the decoration on breastplates from Nimes, Manching and Pfünz;[285] on greaves from Straubing[286] and large medallions from Tabriz and Miltenberg,[287] which are believed to be horse phalerae or the bosses of parade shields;[288] busts of Minerva can also be seen even on *lorica squamata* scales.[288] An imitation of the Corinthian helmet as part of Roman helmet decoration can be seen on pieces from Heddernheim, Porţile de Fier (the Iron Gates),[290] Szőny[291] and on the example in the former Axel Guttmann collection (AG 451),[292] which also have mascarones on the forehead. Moreover, the example of the former Guttmann collection displays hippocampi on its bowl.

Images of these half-horses/half-fish are typical for another mask that is very similar to the mask of Nola. This piece is in the collection of the Roman Catholic Providence Academy in Plymouth, Minnesota, USA[293] (fig. 262). Unlike the Nola mask that has pieces missing from its top, the Providence Academy example is in good condition. Relief images of hippocampi are on this example where there are gaping holes in the Nola mask. In other respects, the decoration of the masks strongly resemble each other: even the embossed list of small archlets framing the edge of the helmet and tiaras is similar. Although fragments of characteristic tails surviving on the Nola mask also suggest that it too bore the images of hippocampi. Hippocampi are also shown on the breastplates depicting Minerva from the fortress of the auxiliary troops at Samum (Dacia), where *Cohors equitata* were based.[294] And in this context the hippocampus in this piece can hardly be taken for the legionary emblem. Most probably, the hippocampi depicted at Minerva's feet and, here, on Minerva's helmet embody her victory over Neptune, god of the sea, and are, ultimately, a symbol of victory and superiority.

Thus, female masks were the result of the ceremonial aspect of life in the Roman Imperial army and are a cultural phenomenon, the further study of which will allow the understanding of many nuances of religious and ceremonial performances involving Roman soldiers.

THE ICONOGRAPHY OF PARADE AND TOURNAMENT ARMOUR

DECORATION OF CEREMONIAL ARMAMENT

In contrast to the previous hypothetical reconstructions, new studies more often involve meticulous work on a full-scale reconstruction of the face-mask helmets using authentic materials and methods of manufacture. Such a combination of high technology and experimental archaeology opens up wider opportunities of the study of ancient technology (metallurgy and smithcraft). Research conducted jointly by experts of the Museum het Valkhof in Nijmegen and the Rheinische Landesmuseum in Bonn has shown how profound the knowledge of Roman armourers of the characteristics of the materials used in armament manufacture was and what levels of skill those manufacturing decorated armour possessed.[295]

The metal structure of one of the masks found in Nijmegen was examined under the microscope. Eight layers were found that had been formed by triple folding and welding iron during hammer forging. This technique was necessary due to the fact that the Roman iron was too soft (due to low carbon content). Therefore, armourers achieved the optimum strength by proper arranging the layers of a metal item and its subsequent hammering. Studies have shown that the masks under study were hammered from the inside after they had cooled down, in the last stage of forging.[296]

The examples studied were coated with silver, giving the helmets an amazing shine and also protecting the iron from rusting. Additional protection against moisture was provided by horsehair wigs with elements of the textile coating that used to be put on the bowls. Their structure could be taken using the remaining materials of three helmets from Nijmegen and one from Xanten-Wardt. Such wigs

FIG. 263. Helmet from Xanten-Wardt, mid-first century AD, Bonn, Rheinisches Landesmuseum. (Photo by M. Greenhalgh)

were reinforced with additional wide ribbons and, apparently, sewn down through the holes in the helmet bowl or stuck to it with glue. During the full scale reconstruction, the manufacture of wigs with their additional decoration in the form of woven ribbons and zigzag decorative knitting took no less than 150 hours of hard work: it is quite clear that the decoration of parade/tournament helmets was not easy and required particular skills. Attaching a wig to a helmet bowl took at least a further 50 hours[297] All this suggests that these items stood out from the normal range of products manufactured by armourers and cost much more in comparison with other ones.

The richness of weapons served to demonstrate status and prestige. In parades and other military ceremonies, a soldier inevitably boasted of his acquisitions and ultimately his financial situation and his rewards for

FIG. 264. (Above) Helmet from Weiler, mid-first century AD., Musée Archéologique d'Arlon (Drawing by A. E. Negin)

meritorious service. Such display of status could occur in combat, also. But, standing out by the richness of weapons and rewarding decorations, a soldier deliberately made himself a more desirable target for the enemy. However, these fears could be outweighed by the desire to stand out from the crowd of his comrades in arms due to a brighter outfit, as in this case, the soldier had more chance of his bravery in battle to be noticed and appreciated by his commanders and comrades. Lucius Annaeus Florus told of one soldier of this kind, the centurion Cornidius.[298] His desire to stand out and simultaneously instil fear in the enemy came true in a very shocking manner. He arrived at the battlefield carrying on the top of his helmet a pan of coals which were fanned by the movement of his body, and he scattered flames from his head, which had the appearance of being on fire. There is no doubt that his efforts were rewarded, as this case was described in the historical records. However, this case is an exception to the rule. A much more common way to draw everyone's attention was expensive armour with beautiful decoration.

The decoration of parade weapons included both popular religious motifs and quotations and other elements of embellishment, the most common of which was the imitated hair on the parade helmets as mentioned before and the floral ornament usual on helmet bowls (most often on the neckguard) although it can also be found on some of the parade shield bosses (Blerick[299] and from the former

FIG. 265. Cavalry helmet of bronze sheet over iron base. Decoration features a laurel wreath, sphinx on the two cheekpieces and martial/dionysiac attributes (bowl), second century AD, Musée d'Art Classique de Mougins. (Photo courtesy of Musée d'Art Classique de Mougins)

Guttmann collection[300]). Anatomical cuirasses also are often decorated with vegetal sprouts and leaves, including those of the acanthus.

Another popular decoration element of parade and tournament helmets and sometimes even combat ones was the image of such military decorations as the

FIG. 266. Helmet with vertical fronton, first century AD, private European collection. (Courtesy of the owner)

wreath and crown. The *corona civica* is depicted prominently on the helmet bowl from Vize,[301] in which the short wavy hair is topped with a realistically-fashioned wreath of oak leaves and acorns. Wreaths are depicted in two ways on face-mask helmets. Some of them are on the top or back of the helmet bowl, while others adorn the forehead like diadems. The first kind is characteristic of Herzogenburg/Alexander type face-mask helmets.[302] It is not known whether the depicted wreaths are directly connected with actual ones awarded to the owners of the helmets. As for *corona aurea*, they were awarded quite rarely and not to anyone below the rank of centurion or decurion.[303] Thus, only the outstanding commanders and soldiers could own such helmets. At the same time it is more logical to consider as the images of wreaths such forehead diadems as the *corona muralis* on the helmet from Ribchester,[304] or the *phalerae* on the mask diadem from Hellange. However, this design can be interpreted in both cases as a cult motif. M. Junkelmann believes that the *corona muralis* of the Ribchester helmet could symbolise a military genius and the *phalerae* on the mask of Hellange could indicate Bacchantic motifs.[305] Certainly, helmet masks should not be associated with specific religious ceremonies. This concerns mainly the decorative use of religious motifs, which, of course, could be connected in a particular case with the specific religious preferences of the owner and/or his unit (depending on who was the owner of the item).[306] It seems that in most cases, depicting *corona civica* on the parade armour has no connection with the helmet wearer, but is a common element of decoration and the owner of the helmet would not necessarily have been awarded such a wreath. The same applies to the *corona muralis* and to other types of wreaths, depicted in relief on the helmets from Rapolano,[307] Newstead,[308] Straubing[309] etc.[310] In the first–second centuries AD, helmets, muscle cuirasses and other items of protective equipment were decorated with battle scenes. Such scenes are present on the helmets from Ribchester and Nava.[311]

The masks functioning as an anatomical visor of a helmet can be classified as an element of decoration as well. Moreover, it should be remembered that the masks cannot be considered to be portraits. They are a special kind of portraiture and have their own specific character and development, so they are only partially coincident with Roman portraiture in general.[312] Formal elements, obviously, were borrowed from portraiture and ideal plastic arts, but they are redesigned as independent types. Furthermore, these types existed for a long time, undergoing only slight changes and responding very slowly to new influences. Local versions of the types deserve special attention. The fact that they were mixed with local forms and that they spread quickly and existed for quite a long time in some places can be explained by their fixation in local traditions. The finds suggest that the more distant local workshops were from the centres of Roman portraiture, the more significantly local traditional beliefs influenced their products.[313]

RELIGIOUS AND IDEOLOGICAL VALUES AND MAGICAL ELEMENTS OF DECORATION

The decoration of Roman arms sometimes contains themes that are directly related to state propaganda, as well as to the imperial cult. These scenes are most common on parade armour but can also be found on ordinary weapons. Their appearance is connected with the reign of Augustus and with proclaiming the idea of the imperial 'Augustan Peace'[314] and the 'Golden Age'.[315]

As the army and the emperor were the guarantors of 'Perpetual Peace' and the 'Golden Age' in official propaganda, their military successes were the main motif of the visual embodiment of propaganda messages in the decoration of weapons. For instance, the emperor appears in the decoration of Roman armament mainly in connection with the allegory concerning the conquest of countries and provinces. In this case, he is usually portrayed amidst spoils erected on the occasion of a victory. In addition, the emperor is represented as a lucky general. Only the helmets from Tell Oum Hauran (Nawa),[316] Newstead,[317] Ribchester[318] and Nikyup[319] have scenic compositions depicting battles, prisoners and the coronation of the Roman emperor by Victoria, as well as the rite of sacrifice, which also could somehow glorify the successful results of emperors' military campaigns.

Protective equipment, including parade equipment as well, has a dual function: to protect the owner and intimidate the enemy. Both of these functions were not usually combined in a single item but protective weapons can bear an anthropomorphic mask of Medusa and the eagle of Jupiter and Heracles with his club: all of them were intended both to protect and intimidate. The images of the gods are well suited to achieving this goal. It is not surprising that weapons began to bear images of the gods of war (Jupiter and Minerva, Mars and Victoria, Virtus and Bellona), among which we also can include the Dioskouri and Heracles. Jupiter, his wife Juno and Minerva form the Capitoline Triad of the supreme gods of Rome. Jupiter, the supreme god, the god of thunder, became the protector of

FIG. 267(a)–(b). Helmet from Autun, first century AD, Autun, Musée Rolin. (Photo by M. Greenhalgh)

FIG. 268. (Above) Helmet from The Morven Collection of Ancient Art, end of the second–beginning of the third century AD. (Drawing by A. E. Negin)

FIG. 269. (Below) Helmet AG 471, former Axel Guttmann collection, third century AD, Musée d'Art Classique de Mougins (photo courtesy of Musée d'Art Classique de Mougins)

the Roman state, the personification of Roman power and the army. The cult of the Capitoline Triad also had official status and was mandatory for all the Roman citizens wherever they might live. This triad played a primary role also in the hieratical practices of the Roman army, as evidenced by numerous dedications.

As the god-protector of the state and the army, Jupiter was the most esteemed. He was depicted with a bunch of lightning bolts. An eagle very often was his attribute. The combination of an eagle, Minerva and the bust of Mars also can be understood as an image of *dii militares*. Minerva is excellent to be depicted on the protective arms as, unlike Mars who loved blood, war and violence in any form, Minerva represented holy defensive war and was the goddess of defence. Being depicted on this element of armour, the goddess symbolised the defence and patronage granted to the soldier. Mars was also among the most

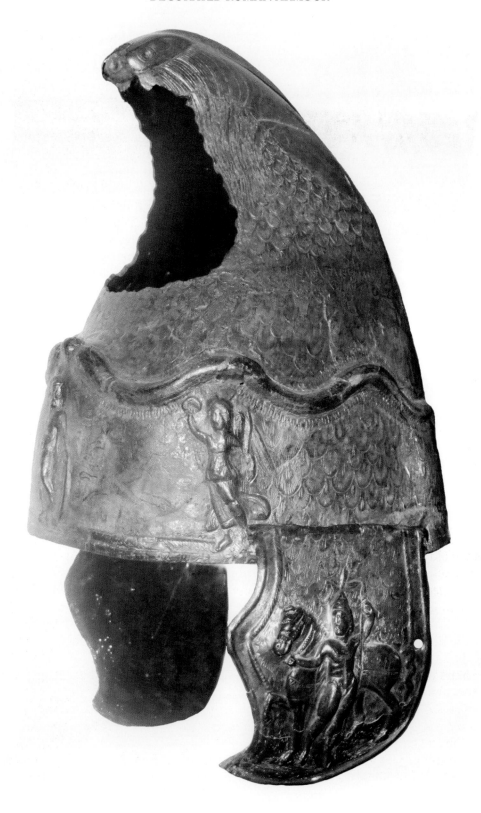

FIG. 271. (Above left) Decorated cheek-piece from Ijzendoorn, first century AD, Leiden, Rijksmuseum van Oudheden. (Photo courtesy of Rijksmuseum van Oudheden, Leiden)

FIG. 272. (Above right) Decorated cheek piece from Albertfalvá, end of the second–mid-third century AD, Budapest, Magyar Nemzeti Mûzeum. (Photo by R. D'Amato)

FIG. 270. (Opposite) Decorated helmet from Ostrov, mid-second century AD, Constanța, Muzeul de Istorie Națională şi Arheologie. (Photo by R. D'Amato)

---

revered deities in the imperial army. After Jupiter, he was the most aristocratic god of the old Italic religion. He was a master of armament, governed military service (*militiae potens*) and oversaw the drill ground, for which he was named *Campester*.[320] But for everybody he remained *Gradivus* ('the Marching God') – this ancient epithet emphasised his militant temper. The Emperor Augustus only named him *Ultor* ('Avenger') and dedicated to him a luxurious temple in the centre of the Forum in gratitude for his victory over the murderers of Caesar and, in addition, granted to him the privileges of the Capitoline Jupiter. However, the cult of Mars was particularly prevalent among the auxiliary troops. The iconography show him sometimes divinely nude, in a Corinthian helmet with a cloak hanging over his hand, armed with a spear and a round shield, sometimes also with a sword slung at his side. Mars was sometimes portrayed in full armour, in an anatomical cuirass, greaves and boots.

The cult of Victoria became widespread as early as about 300 BC. As Victoria of Augustus, she embodies the power of the emperor's and general's victory in the

FIG. 273. Decorated checkpieces of first–second centuries AD, private collections. (Photos and drawings by R. D'Amato and A. E. Negin)

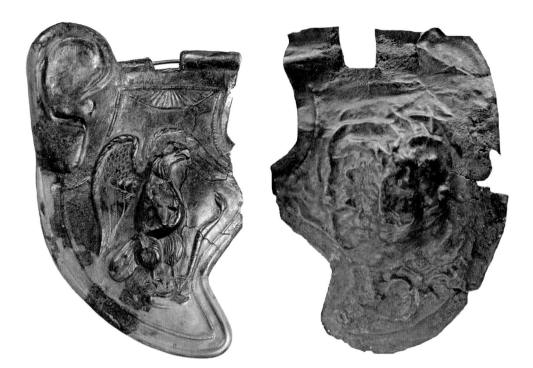

FIG. 274. (Above left) Helmet cheek piece from Gradistea Muncelului, early second century AD, Cluj-Napoca, Muzeul Național de Istorie a Transilvaniei,. (Photo courtesy of Prof. Radu Ardevan)

FIG. 274b. (Above right) Decorated unfinished *buccula*, first half of the second century AD, Gaziantep, Glass Museum. (Photo by R. D'Amato)

army of the Imperial period. She is often depicted to be winged or even floating in the air in a long flyaway dress, with a wreath of victory in her right hand and a palm-branch in her left one. Thus, the images of Mars and Victoria can be seen in the context of the 'ideology of victory' fostered in the Roman army and based on the 'Roman myth' and the idea of the 'Golden Age'.

Heracles, an ideal patron of soldiers, is linked with *dii militares*. In the images he is carrying a club and wearing a lion's skin as a reminder of the battles with the Nemean lion and the Hydra of Lerna. The divine twins Castor and Pollux (the Dioskouri) also number among the gods helping in combat. They are depicted as horsemen, which indirectly links them with the cavalry. Appearing before the audience as an inseparable pair, they represent the fraternal friendship that was fostered among soldiers (*commilitones*).

Other deities can also be found in the decoration of Roman ornate weapons. Medallions and shield bosses predominantly have the image of Ganymede being abducted by Jupiter's eagle, while Minerva is often portrayed as well. According to the legend, Ganymede was the son of the Trojan king Tros and was abducted because of his ethereal beauty by Zeus (Jupiter in Roman mythology) who had sent his eagle to bring him. The eagle brought Ganymede to heaven where he became the cupbearer of the gods and enjoyed eternal youth. Ganymede is depicted on parade weapons as the guarantor of the soul's ascension to heaven and the continuation of life after death.[321]

It is more difficult to interpret the images of sea creatures and other animals on parade and tournament armour. Perhaps the only character directly related to the 'Roman myth' is the Capitoline Wolf (the she-wolf who suckled the twins Romulus and Remus). The she-wolf was depicted on the parade equipment buckles and breastplates.[322] It is safe to classify a dolphin, a hippocampus, a sealion and other non-identifiable underwater monsters as apotropaions. They all are included in the retinue of the sea god Neptune and symbolise the journey to the otherworldly world of the ocean that bathes the world of the living.[323] Tritons as the gods of sea and satellites of Neptune are also members of this group.[324] Definitely, the head of Medusa with snakes and wings on her face and in her hair is an apotropaion.[325] This is what she looks like on the helmet masks, medallions and horse face-pieces. Due to her origin from the gods of the sea, Medusa is connected with numerous sea monsters that are depicted on the items of armament where they have the same value as an apotropaion.

Finally, the fantastic Griffin, a creature with the head of an eagle and the body of a lion, as it is shown on the helmet from Sheikh 'Ibada,[326] is an apotropaic symbol, too. Such animals as a Taurus or Capricorn (*Capricornus*) shown on several breastplates lead to another area. Here, we have the symbols of particular military units, mainly legions.[327] Thus, the owner of one of the breastplates found in Carnuntum could be assigned to one of the two Italic legions, as the Capitoline Wolf is depicted on the plate. The owner of the other breastplate from Carnuntum was a soldier of the Legio XIII Gemina.[328]

Roman parade equipment is abundantly decorated and at first sight has remarkably varied iconography. Actually, we can pinpoint a number of themes that can be found only once, twice or several times in the total range of items found. Apparently, this can be explained by the individual taste of the owners. According to E. Künzl, the iconography of Roman parade armament presents the following set of characters and themes.[329] The images of Mars, Minerva, the eagle, Victoria and a snake can be found most often. These are the main characters. Numerous images of a snake cannot be explained as a Mithraic element. The only allusion to Mithraic iconography can be seen on the greave from Regensburg[330] where two snakes are depicted facing a large vase (*krater*). However, the snakes, which are generally depicted in pairs, can be considered rather as an apotropaion since snakes in this function, always in pairs, are depicted on the frescoes of Pompeian *lararii*. Generally, scenes of mysteries did not play any role on parade armament. This fact amounts to very little for the statistical result, but it is important in terms of methodology, since the motifs of the parade armament decor are characterised by the lack of close connection with the actual mystery religions. The parade armour is characterised by a conservative artistic style with images of Greek classical art of the fifth–fourth centuries BC. The images on the armament used in *hippika gymnasia* were a part of a closed military community. Outsiders could rarely see these things, usually only at cavalry tournaments. Therefore, the iconography of items was directed inwards to this community of initiates and its symbolism was well understood among the military who served during the period from Augustus to Gallienus. In this period of time parade and tournament armour became the last conservative haven of ancient iconography in which the Olympian gods and their world dominated without restriction.

5

DECORATED ARMOUR OF THE DOMINATE

(284 BC–565 AD)

THE DECORATION OF WEAPONS IN THE LATE ROMAN ARMY

The lavish decoration of arms and armour did continue in the Late Empire, although in a different way and, progressively, with a greater degree of simplification. The symbols of the new Christian God, whose religion had been the official imperial one since Theodosius the Great (AD 380–395), required less work from the craftsmen of the Imperial *fabricae* and symbolic ideas could also be expressed with simplified signs and dots. Silvering and gilding were taking the place of elaborate helmet decoration. Notwithstanding this, the appearance of Late Roman elite warriors and commanders was no less impressive than that of their third-century predecessors: a combination of pearls, jewels, gold and silver, often enriched by the presence, in the accoutrement of warriors, of lavishly ornamented clothes and shoes, gave Roman soldiers a glittering appearance. Moreover the new kind of weaponry used in the fourth century, the product of an evolution which already begun in the third century, was often employed with the old forms, some of which, like the muscle armour or *Thorakion Herôikon*, survived until the end of the Eastern Roman Empire in AD 1453.

SHIELDS

The decoration of the shields was, particularly from the early fourth century, confined to the creation of precious *umbos* or shield fittings and to the lavish painting of the front of the shield. There are two main types of shield boss in this period: the Liebenau type and the Vermand type.[1] The first, characterised by a fluted pipe rising up over the bowl, appears in prototype form in the Roman army as a result of the Marcomannic wars. In these specimens the bowl is a little raised above the flange.[2] Similar highly decorated and gold-plated Germanic examples from the early fourth century were found in the Vandal Prince's grave at Herpály.[3] Grave 1 of Liebenau, from the mid-fourth century AD,[4] confirms that in this period this kind of *umbo* was definitely an integral part of Roman weaponry.[5]

The Vermand type, found in the famous grave of the Romano-Germanic officer probably belonging to a unit of the field army,[6] shows that the fluted pipe had now become a spiked point,[7] transforming the *umbo* in a deadly weapon (fig. 275a). The precious Vermand boss is covered by a sheet of gilded silver and the rivets on the flange are silvered and decorated with fake cabochons.[8] The diameter of the shield boss is 20cm, its height 16cm.[9] The grip was formed by a short bar – 36.4cm long – covered in silver and fastened to the shield by nine silvered rivets.[10] The shield itself was spectacular, covered with red purple leather with a layer of gold foil plates stretched over it.[11]

Of course the Vermand specimen was an exceptional object, made for a senior military commander:[12] specimens of these *umbones* were widespread in the Roman army of the late fourth century as a consequence of the revival of this typical Germanic shape,[13] not only in the Western army, but also in the Eastern army, especially in the Black Sea garrisons. From the regions of Aj-Todor (Harax) and Catyr-Dag, where groups of Gothic *Phoederati* had been stationed by Constantine the Great since the early fourth century, shield bosses of Germanic origin spread throughout the regular Roman army and became part of the regular equipment of the Late Roman soldier. The large numbers of Germans in the Late Roman army lead to the formation of a military Romano-Germanic sub-culture, destined to further influence the style the Roman weaponry and the form of the army itself.[14]

Mixed Romano-Germanic specimens from Crimea (Kertch, fig. 275b) and from the graves of the Abkhazia, on the eastern shore of the Black Sea, show gilded and silvered types with low conical or hemispherical bowls, large flanges,[15] or high conical pointed bowls, decorated with nails arranged as studded ornamentation. M. Kazanski has compared various different kinds of *umbones*, proving that, in the period of the fifth and sixth century, many reciprocal influences evidenced uniformity of equipment between East and West.[16] Faceted *umbones* or ones with vertical grooves, dated between the end of the fourth century and the beginning of the fifth century (Dobrodzien type), are represented on the Stilicho dyptich (certainly one gilded one, belonging to a *Magister Militum*) and have been found in great numbers in the Crimea and Black Sea region, Romania and the Balkans.[17] They were probably produced in the Western armouries of Noricum, but they have been found also among the Absilii' military aristocracy, who were in Roman service.[18]

In the Absilian graves of the fifth–seventh centuries, spiked *umbones* of the western Liebenau type,[19] and a very high conical specimen, identical to that found in the Vermand grave,[20] were discovered by archaeologists. Gilded and silvered specimens of these *umbones* are depicted on the shields of soldiers of Western units in the Santa Maria Maggiore Mosaics in Rome[21] and on those of Eastern soldiers, on the mosaics from Apamea in Syria and Urfa (Edessa) in Turkey, as well as on the mosaics from the Mount Nebo Basilica (Jordan).[22] These latter, dated to AD 530, in all probability[23] are representing warriors of the elite *Lycocranitai* Regiment. Archaeologically, the wider use of these bosses is attested in Gaul and Britain during the fourth and sixth centuries.[24] Domed bosses continued to be used alongside the pointed and conical ones and some of them were expensively silvered and chiselled. A specimen from Misery, made of silvered iron, presents four rivets for the attachment to the shield-board and an imperial figure stamped on the flange with the inscription MAR (TENSES SENIORES).[25] Two other types of domed *umbones*, discovered in a fifth-century Eastern context (Beth-Shan, Palestine) and represented on the Apamea mosaic, show a lot of parallels to Western equipment.[26]

Of course the most precious *umbones* were reserved for the Imperial guard and *comitatus*: two surviving examples from Rome, preserved in the Gregorian Museum in the Vatican, are gilded and embossed with the head of the Emperor Probus (third century) and with the image (fourth–fifth century) of a *Magister Militum* and his wife (fig. 275).[27] In both examples, the figures are surrounded by a laurel crown: a powerful image of the glory of Rome, still present in weapon decoration in this late period. A splendid mosaic of early fourth century, recently discovered in Alter do Chão (ancient Abelterium) in Portugal, show the precious shield of a warrior – representing the mythical hero Aeneas or maybe Alexander the Great dressed in late Roman accoutrements – decorated with a painted image of Medusa, around which a laurel crown is lavishly painted (fig. 275c).[28] This image shows that, at the beginning of the fourth century, Roman craftsmen were still skilled enough to create precious chiselled and painted weapons.

Late Roman shields were also decorated with bronze appliques and fittings, as well as embossed figures: the shield of Stilicho, on the Monza Dyptich, is ornamented with two bronze images of the Emperors Arcadius and Honorius, as befitted his role of *Defensor Augusti*.[29] An actual surviving fragment of a similar shield, representing the bust of the Emperor Honorius, measures 20cm in height and is made of bronze (fig. 322).[30] The Imperial shield, as represented on medallions and coins from the early fourth century until the end of the seventh century, was splendidly embossed: earlier with images of battles, celebrations of imperial victories and with the figure of the *Sol Invictus*,[31] and later mainly with the image of a cavalryman,[32] or with Christian symbols. This round shield is correctly called a *clypeus*, because this is the shape visible on all imperial coins and representations of the emperor's weaponry, often preciously chiselled and with gems and precious stones inlaid in it.

The very recent discovery in Egypt of fragmentary specimens of shields has provided better knowledge of the structure and composition of the Roman round shield in the fifth and sixth centuries and of their beautiful decoration (fig. 275d). It is clear that these shields recall the tradition of lavishly-painted shields, such as the Dura Europos shields: one of them represents Romans in combat with North African natives; a second one represents a hunting scene and a full-length military officer, painted below the boss, wearing a white tunic and a short cloak; the third is decorated in a purely geometric style.[33] The analysis of these three circular shields, all found in the Fayum region, and still preserved in Trier University, by Dr Klaus Peter Goethert revealed the following characteristics:[34]

1. The shields were made of cedar wood and covered with leather made from goat or sheep skin.

2. The wooden planks were 4–6cm wide and with a thickness of about 7cm; the stitching measured about 6cm: the planks were glued in a flat way, then slightly cut in wedge shape in an irregular way. The leather was fixed on the wooden surface with animal glue, which shield 1 (the one decorated with geometric patterns) still bore traces of;[35] then – a common characteristic of most Late-Roman shields – it was sewn all around the edge; the holes of the sewing about 4–8mm. from the outside edge and at intervals of 2–2.2cm. or about 3cm;

3. All the shields were lavishly decorated on their leather surface, with scene of hunting, battle scenes, floral and geometrical motives (a ten-rayed star[36]); in the geometrical decoration of the shield 1 the painter imitated pearl ornamentation around the rim.

4. The painter decorated the shields in the following way: first it was given the basic background colour (white, yellow and red *carminium* in our shields), then the decorative circles were painted, the floral and ornamented decorations, and finally the other figures; after it, the painter gave brilliancy to the colours.

5. In shield 1,[37] the centre was about 12cm in diameter, although there were no traces of a metallic *umbo*, which on the other hand was probably present on shield 2 (the one with the hunting scene);[38] a metallic handgrip was fixed inside the shield and this fits well with the metallic handgrips found in great numbers in the warrior graves of Abkhazia, Crimea and the Black Sea,[39] whose shape correspond also to that of the figures on the monuments.[40]

6. The diameter of the shields was: 103cm (shield 1); 108cm (shield 2); 98cm (shield 3); the shields' convexity varied from 5.5cm to 6cm.

The shields of the *Doukes* and senior officers[41] were often personalised in their *deigmata*: the officer's shield shown on shield 2 is divided in two halves, off-white and purple, and decorated with a gold lion over the *umbo*[42] (fig. 275d). This is identical to the fifth-century specimens from the Black Sea region,[43] typical of the Eastern Army between the last quarter of the fourth and the first quarter of the fifth century, derived from Gepid, Goth, Vandal and Suebian models. This underlines the very strong presence of Germanic troops in Egypt, here around AD 379–380.[44] This is also proved by an iron *umbo*, an actual circular specimen of circular shape found in Egypt,[45] with a plain short spike, probably belonging to a Frankish unit stationed in Thebais.[46] The shields have been dated to the sixth century (shield 1), the beginning of the fifth century (shield 2) and a period between AD 453 and the beginning of the sixth century (shield 3).[47]

The above-mentioned kind of decoration and ornamentation of shields was most impressive on those of the Imperial Guardsmen. The oval shields of the *Protectores Divini Lateris* are well represented on the Arch of Constantine and their shape and lavishly-coloured patterns can be seen on the mosaics of Piazza Armerina.[48] The same quartered shield of one of them is also visible on a funerary monument of a *Protector* from Aquileia. Identical big oval shields are held by the *Protectores* of Theodosius the Great, on his *Missorium*, although their shields are

FIG. 275. (Opposite top) Decorated shield *umbones*, third–fourth century AD, Musei Apostolici Vaticani. (Photo DAI, Rome, neg. 1937.581 and 1937.582)

FIG. 275a. (Opposite centre) Vermand's umbo and shield handle, late quarter of the fourth century AD, New York, Metropolitan Museum of Art. (Museum photos)

FIG. 275b. (Opposite bottom) Gilded Umbo' shield, Kerch, the Crimea, first half of the fifth century AD, iron, gold, St Petersburg, Hermitage. (Photo by R. D'Amato)

FIG. 275c. (Above) Mosaic from the Villa Romana de la Casa de la Medusa representing Aineias and Turnus or Alexander the Great at the Battle of Hydaspes, early fourth century AD, *in situ*, Abelterium. (Museum photo)

FIG. 275d. (Above) Painted shields from Fayoum, fifth–sixth centuries AD, RGZM. (After Goethert)

decorated with a different *deigmaton*.[49] The surface of the shields are decorated with rows of paired geometrical triangles which Racinet[50] and Hottenroth[51] showed as being alternately red and blue, although this may be a hypothetical reconstruction, because, according to Sinesius, this kind of *scuta* should have been completely gilded.[52]

Indeed, the old Roman tradition (fig. 58) of the gilded shield decorated with scales (gold foils)[53] survived in the Imperial shields and in those of the senior military commanders. The shield of Stilicho is the most striking example,[54] but a squared bronze stathmos (weight of two litres) from Constantinople shows the

FIG. 276. Fragment of the Column of Theodosius, AD 395–400, *in situ*, Istanbul, Beyazit Hamam. (Photo by R. D'Amato);

Emperor Arkadius and Honorius clad in muscled armour and bearing such shield.[55] The only difference is that the *umbo* is not a Dobrodzien specimen like on Stilicho's shield, but a lion's head virtually identical to the so-called Sassanian Lion *umbo* preserved in the British Museum,[56] a type used by the Romans since the third century[57] (fig. 134). In Imperial hands small chiselled shields are sometimes represented, called in the sources *cheiroskoutaria* (hand-shields).[58] The shields of the Imperial Guardsmen on Theodosius' column had the Christian monogram and various floral patterns[59] (fig. 276), similar to the later models seen on the Justinian mosaic in San Vitale, Ravenna.[60] Identical shields can also be seen on the base of the Arcadius Column (fig. 277). The Christian symbol, on these shields, was often embellished by the insertion of precious stones, cabochons and gems.[61] Some of them are round, very large and correspond in shape to the shields of the *Notitia*.[62] Other are large and oval, like the shields of Ravenna.[63] The patterns of the *Notitia* shields are mostly geometrical, except one with the image of a dragon, but one of them could have been very similar to the blazon of Justinian's *Primoscutarii* in Ravenna. The only difference between the two shields is that the sign **I** R. of the Greek letter *Rho* is only represented, on the *Notitia*, like a horizontal staff I without the small right arch of the **P** R.[64] Considering that on the *Notitia* the shield is that of the *Scutarii*, we can suggest the hypothesis that the author of the miniatures, in the *Notitia* Manuscript, had omitted to copy the whole Christian Symbol, or, most probably, that the *Chrismon* was added only later, on the shield of the *Scutarii*, in the time of Justinian or shortly before. Wide oval shields with different precious

FIG. 277a. (Opposite top left) Freshfield drawing of the base of the Column of Arcadius, AD 400–402, south side, *in situ*. (After Giglioli, 1952, fig.17)

FIG. 277b. (Opposite top right) Freshfield drawing of the base of the Column of Arcadius, AD 400–402, eastern side, *in situ*. (After Giglioli, 1952, fig.19)

FIG. 277c. (Opposite centre) Freshfield drawing of the base of the Column of Arcadius, AD 400–402, Western side, *in situ*. (After Giglioli, 1952, fig.15)

FIG. 277d. (Opposite bottom) Fragments of cavalry battle from the Column of Theodosius or Arcadius, early fifth century AD, Istanbul, Archaeological Museum. (Museum photo)

---

deigmata, some of them recalling the *Notitia Dignitatum* blazons, are visible in the hands of the guardsmen of Valentinian III as represented in the Gènève *Missorium*.[65]

HELMETS

In the later Empire the helmet was generally designated by the words *cassis*, *galea* or *kranos*.[66] A great number of types is visible in the figurative sources and confirmed by the archaeology, and each of them received its appropriate decoration.

1. HEDDERNEIM-STYLE HELMETS

The specimens of Rainau-Buch/Niederbieber, and evolution from the Niedermormter type, all enclosed around the face, introduce the new infantry and cavalry helmets of the late second and early third centuries AD.[67] This kind of helmet, commonly known as the Niederbieber[68] type,[69] are most attested archaeologically for the first half of the third century, but the artistic sources give evidence of their employment at least up until the first quarter of the fifth century.[70]

The helmets found in the fort at Heddernheim, from the beginning of the third century AD, since the time of Robinson's classification have been considered to be typical cavalry helmets.[71] However, today we can say that these helmets were used both by cavalry and infantry.

This is attested by various iconographic sources, among which there is a very interesting relief from *Intercisa-Dunapentele*, showing legionaries training or fighting with the typical equipment of the late third century.[72] The legionaries are protected by very heavy helmets identical to the masked bronze type with the eagle-headed crest[73] found in Heddernheim,[74] that represents a last evolution of the Pseudo-Corinthian type (fig. 175) with the adding of a mask protecting the whole face, leaving only the usual T-shaped opening. As we have seen this helmet, was embossed with stylised hair, a human face on the long visor and serpents on the sides.[75] On the carved relief the use of helmets with metal eagle's heads on the embossed feathered crest is also illustrated, similar to the Brigetio type (figs 175,178), with the face on the peak and snakes at each side of the skull.[76] Similar helmets are worn by the Maxentian defenders of Verona on the Arch of Constantine[77] and it is not a case of artistical convention that they are also represented on the heads of the *milites* of Constantine first's medallion, coined in 312 AD.[78] It is clear that such beautiful helmets were still in use in the early fourth century AD, reserved to elite units.

Further proof of it is the representations of such helmets in the splendid mosaic of Alter do Chão (ancient Abelterium), where most of the warriors have Heddernheim-type face-mask helmets, either splendidly gilded or ornamented with multicoloured plumes (fig. 275c).[79]

2. PSEUDO-ATTIC STYLE HELMETS

The Attic helmet is still well represented on the late Roman monuments (figs 276, 277, 278, 279), demonstrating the persistence and the evolution of a long Hellenic tradition, since the adoption of the Chalcidian helmets. The production of such helmets was probably never abandoned, especially in the Eastern workshops of the Empire.[80]

This type of helmet was furnished with an attached fronton or *diadema*, riveted at the sides and not removable, as it is also attested in the so-called pseudo-Attic type, well exemplified by splendid cavalry specimens from Worthing, Cetate Razboieni (Alba Julia), Chalon-sur-Saône and other parts of the Empire.[81] The *bucculae*, clasped at the level of the diadema's volutes, were long and wide at cheek height (figs. 60, 177, 181). On the Arch of Constantine arch the Roman legionaries on the pilasters of the arch, coming from a monument of the Tetrarchic age and the most part Constantine's warriors are wearing these Attic or pseudo-Attic helmets.[82]

This is not an artistic convention. In fact these helmets are well represented besides well known helmet types, like the Hedderneims with eagle peaks or the Intercisa Romano-Sassanian helmets (see *infra*, figs. 280, 281, 282). The artists represented in detail all the types of helmets in the Roman army of their day. It is clear that the artists of the great Constantinian frieze had helmets like these before their eyes when they represented them on the arch in the Roman Forum. Interestingly, the helmets visible on the heads of Maxentius' Praetorians and Maxentius himself are also all of pseudo-Attic type, recalling, as correctly pointed out by Künzl, the helmets of the Guisborough type (figs. 60, 61, 177,1 81).

The employment of elaborate types of pseudo-Attic helmets is still recorded in the late fourth century, worn by the *Protectores Domestici* of the Emperor Theodosius, on the fragments of the Column of Theodosius and Arcadius (figs. 276, 277, 278). These helmets are of the late Attic type or in any case a sort of intermediate form between the Attic type and the simpler ridge type, furnished with a diadema-fronton. This was probably a bronze helmet or a leather *galea* with

FIG. 278. (Above) Fragment of the Column of Theodosius, AD 395–400, Istanbul, Archaeological Museum. (Photo by R. D'Amato);

FIG. 279. (Right) Head of a statue of a general from Constantinople, sixth century AD, Istanbul, Archaeological Museum. (Photo by R. D'Amato).

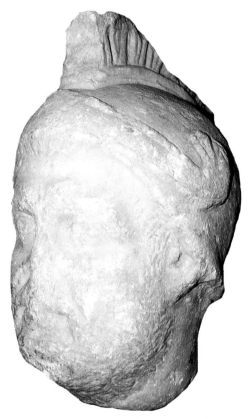

metal fittings, attested by the very fragmentary pieces found in Richborough.[83] The colours reconstructed by Hottenroth show these guardsmen wearing red-lacquered muscled armour and the helmets painted in yellow or gold with red-crimson crests and garments of the same colour. Cavalry are wearing gilded or yellow-brown leather armour, gilded pseudo-Attic bronze helmets[84] with white crests and dark purple trousers and *sagum*[85] and even face-mask helmets (fig. 277). The Freshfield drawings of the Renaissance, done when the columns were still in existence, show also for cavalrymen a kind of helmet very similar to the Hedderneim type with eagle-peak.[86] The existence of pseudo-Attic helmets with fronton is attested in the Eastern Empire until the sixth century (fig. 279) where, apart from the iconography, a fronton of a similar helmet was found in Egypt, splendidly embossed with Christian symbols.[87] After the sixth century the helmet disappeared from the iconographical records of Byzantium and, we can suppose, also from the Imperial arsenals.

3. THE RIDGE HELMETS AND THE SPLENDID HELMETS OF THE *BARBARICARII*

A further kind of helmet produced for the late Roman soldier was of Perso-Sassanian derivation.[88] Such helmets, made of two halves connected by a central longitudinal 'ridge' or 'comb', sometimes high and securely fastened on the lower riveted rim, were the prototypes of many helmets of the Middle Ages. They were sometimes fitted with movable nose-protection and cheek-guards and neck protection attached to the bowl's lining by stiching.[89] The Sassanian origin of this type of helmets has been already well explained by James and does not need to be gone through again here.[90] However, the Roman samples that have been found appear to be an amalgam of several barbarian, Roman and Persian features and show certain elements of improvement introduced by the Roman armourers, who created preciously-decorated and embossed specimens (figs 280–285).

A considerable number of infantry helmets usually dated to the fourth century AD have been discovered in Europe since the nineteenth century and recently new specimens have been restored and published. All these helmets share certain common features, most notably a skull or bowl of composite construction, with, attached to the two half-skulls, a continuous front-to-back strip.[91] They show a simpler and lighter form than the helmets of the same type used by officers and cavalry, having the skull halves made of single pieces of metal riveted to the ridge strip. The precious metal with which they were covered, i.e. a silver plate, decorated by a relief frame – as in the cavalry helmets – and sometimes gilded, like in the specimens of Augsburg-Pfersee,[92] shows that they were intended for elite troops.[93] Similar helmets were found in Worms,[94] Intercisa,[95] Augsburg-Pfersee, the Mosa Valley and in various other locations.

The precious specimens found in Augsburg-Pfersee (fig. 280), with an iron core and a cover of gilded silver were probably reserved for officers.[96] These specimens were half-way between the lighter examples and the heavier specimens, which Klumbach and James assigned to the cavalry and to the generals and emperors. They show that some of these helmets were fitted also with outlined, prominent and anatomical nose-guards.[97] Among the very important specimens from the fortified camp of Intercisa, one is also furnished with a metal crest.[98] The metal-crested helmet of the Intercisa type was also used by the troops in Britannia, as attested by a watercolour of a mosaic from Bramdean, probably from the age of Constantine II. The mosaic represents Mars, dressed like a Roman officer and wearing a similar silver helmet.[99] The helmet with metal crest may have been for the junior officers, or even of *Centenarii* or Centurions, if silvered.[100] A striking example can be seen on a painting from the Hypogeum of Villa Maria, in Siracusa, Sicily (fig. 285b), where Flavius Maximianus,[101] a soldier of an unknown *Numerus*, is represented in full uniform,[102] with *hasta* and *scutum*, wearing upon the head a gilded specimen of 'crested Ridge-helmet with frontal eyes' identical to the real specimen from Intercisa. The importance of the source is that it proves the existence of gilded or brass versions of these iron 'officers' helmets. Gilded and silvered specimens of ridge-helmets, furnished as well with metal crests, simpler

FIG. 280. Ridge helmets of the 'heavy' type. (a) Berkasovo II, fourth century AD, Novi Sad, Vojvodina Museum; (b) Berkasovo I, fourth century AD, Novi Sad, Vojvodina Museum; (c) Augsburg-Pfersee, mid-fourth century AD, Nurnberg, Deutsches National Museum; (d) Augsburg-Pfersee, mid-fourth century AD, Nurnberg, Deutsches National Museum. (Photos by R. D'Amato)

FIG. 281. Ridge helmets of the 'heavy' type. (a) Jarak, fourth century AD, Novi Sad, Vojvodina Museum; (b) Budapest-Aquincum, fourth century AD, Aquincum Museum; (c) Deurne, mid-fourth century AD, Leiden, Rejisk Museum; (d) San Giorgio al Nogaro, mid-fourth century AD, Aquileia, Museo Archeologico Nazionale ((a) Photo courtesy the museum; (b) drawing by A. E. Negin; (c) photo courtesy the museum; (d) Photo by R. D'Amato)

than the Intercisa find, have been confirmed recently by the archaeology[103] (fig. 109) and are illustrated in other pictorial sources.[104] Again a ridge helmet of Intercisa type, fitted with a metal crest,[105] is well represented on the funerary monument of an unknown *Protector* from Aquileia, dated to AD 352.[106]

The new helmet pattern of Romano-Sassanian origin found its way into the cavalry troops very soon. The heavier helmets of the ridge type are the most decorated and precious samples of this category (figs 280, 281, 282, 283).[107] They are usually considered to be cavalry helmets and they are marked by a band surrounding the head, to which are attached the nose-guard, the neck-guard and the wide cheek-guards, covering cheeks, ears and the side of the neck. The bowl is composed of two half-halves, each formed by a single piece or more pieces. In the best preserved specimens a side band covers the junction between the front band and the cheek-guards.[108]

Among the most important of these specimens are the two helmets found in Berkasovo (Serbia) and now preserved on the Novi Sad Museum. The most striking sample is Berkasovo I.[109] It probably belonged to an officer of the Licinius *Comitatus*. This helmet, lost during the Battle of Cibalae in October AD 314,[110] was found with its gilded silver sheathing preserved. It is divided up into four quarters and an additional band, riveted around the inside of the rim, is present on each bowl (fig. 280).[111] A T-shape nose-guard was riveted to the front as further protection. The cheek-pieces covered almost the whole side of the wearer's neck and head.[112] A pair of buckles for the attachment of straps were fixed on the neck-guard. A metal crest-band, visible also on the coins representing such helmets,[113] surmounted the helmet with golden studs doubled over, while each bowl was encrusted with precious stones.[114]

The second example (Berkasovo II) is similar in structure to the first, but it presents an open space over the ear, thanks to an arched cut in the upper parts of the cheek-guards and the doubling of the lateral band. It is not ornamented with gems or precious stones, but only with a single row of studs/pearls on the crest holder (fig. 280).[115] A third similar helmet, known as the Jarak helmet (fig. 281), can be included in this type, characterised by a somewhat simpler construction of the bowl than the Berkasovo I, made up of two segments fastened by a longitudinal crest. Certain details enabled the determining of a closer typological designation.[116] The shape of its crest, which is of the same height along its entire length, made the Jarak specimen similar to the Ausburg helmet (fig. 280) and to the helmets from Intercisa and Worms. As well as the Berkasovo II specimen, this type include also finds from Koblenz (fig. 284) and Heteny (fig. 282), as well as the helmet from Budapest-Aquincum,[117] that was more richly adorned with reliefs, ornaments and glass paste insertions. The Budapest specimen (fig. 281) shows gems not only on the bowl, as in the Berkasovo specimen, but also on the frontal band and once had a metallic crest on the top. The helmet should originally have been fitted with an organic crest, kept in place by the four silver buckles embossed on the bowl.

Other very striking specimens of this category are the magnificent gilded silver helmet covering which belonged to the *Equites Stablesiani* dated AD 319 and found

FIG. 282. (Left) Ridge helmet of the 'heavy' type, Alsóhetény, fourth – fifth century AD, Budapest, National Museum. (Drawing by A. E. Negin)

FIG. 283. (Below) Ridge helmet of the 'heavy' type, Concesti, fifth century AD, St Petersburg, Hermitage. (Photo by A. E. Negin);

in Deurne, Netherlands and the silver covering of San Giorgio of Nogara,[118] found in Northern Italy and only partially preserved (fig. 281). The precious helmet from Concesti presents a slightly different form of construction, with the intersection of two bands at right-angles to each other over the helmet's top.[119] The helmet was found in a Hunnic grave of the early fifth century, probably a valuable purchase by a Hunnic leader from Byzantium's

workshops. This is therefore the most recent example of the category found up to now and the structure of the bowl seems related to the structure of the *Spangen-helme* bowl made up of in four or six plates, which was very widespread from the second half of the fifth century.[120] However, the crest of this helmet is worn longitudinally, similarly to the other ridge-helmets and not according to the radial structure typical of the *Spangen-helme*. The Western Guardsmen of Valentinian III in the above-mentioned *missorium* wear ridge-helmets recalling the Berkasovo II specimen, as well the Deurne helmets and the other helmets of Sassanian derivation, furnished with nose-guard and having a high central crest which follows the ancient Roman tradition.

The silver (Intercisa and San Giorgio al Nogaro) and gilded helmets (Berkasovo, Budapest, Deurne, Augsburg Pfersee, Koblenz,Worms, Mosa Valley and partially Concesti) were probably used by imperial

FIG. 284. Ridge helmet of the 'heavy' type, Koblenz, fourth century AD, RGZM, Mainz. (Drawing by A. E. Negin);

bodyguards (for example, the *Protector* from Aquileia[121]), elite troops or officers. This was, for instance, the case of the Deurne helmet, whose unit (*Equites Stablesiani* – part of the Imperial *Comitatus*), is mentioned clearly in the inscription on it.[122] It has been proposed recently that the San Giorgio al Nogaro helmet also belonged to the *Stablesiani*, as it presents strong affinities with the Deurne and Berkasovo II helmets.[123] The cheek-guards of both helmets (San Giorgio and Deurne) have only embossed decoration and, differently from Berkasovo II, the dividing line between the *bucculae* and the lost bowl is straight, without opening for the ears. Nineteen fragments of helmet, included a nasal in gilded bronze, have allowed Hungarian archaeologists to reconstruction of a Roman 'ridge'-type helmet from Heteny (fig. 282).[124] As already mentioned the helmet, with its characteristic raindrop pattern points, belongs to the Berkasovo II category, decorated with pearls and a metal crest. The characteristic of the nasal was that the *Cristogramma*, i.e. Jesus Christ's initial, the Chi-Ro, was impressed upon it.[125]

The decoration of the Heteny helmet opens another window on the ornamentation of Late Roman helmets. The symbols of the new religion were now impressed on the bowls, or applied through fittings positioned over the front of the helmet, round and embossed with the Christian monogram.[126] This element is clearly visible in the artworks, as well as well documented in the archaeology.[127]

FIG. 285. (Above) Attempt at reconstruction of the helmet of Constantine the Great, AD 312. (After Lusuardi Siena, Perassi, Facchinetti, Bianchi, 2002, pl. II)

FIG. 285b. (Opposite page) Hypogeum Fresco from the Grave of Flavius Maximianus, soldier of an unknown *Numerus*, mid-fourth century AD, *in situ*, Syracuse. (Photo by R. D'Amato)

The many fittings found on the helmets (like the one of the Mosa Valley) has given concrete proof of the presence of such symbols on the helmets of the fourth century, exactly as described by the sources for Constantine's helmet.[128] The famous silver coin of Constantine I (AD 306–337), minted in AD 315, shows him clad in armour and with his head crowned by a precious specimen of ridge-helmet of the Berkasovo type, decorated with the Christian monogram.[129] The silver buckle on the front of the Budapest helmet was probably originally covered by a metal Christian *Chrismon*. Beside it, the winged victories still represented, in the Koblenz specimens (fig. 287), the last legacy of the embellishment of the cheek-guards following the ancient Roman tradition. But the time of the ancient gods was gone: the winged victory was soon transformed in the leader of the Heavenly Court, Saint Michael, destined to be one of the most visible emblems of the Christian Roman Empire.[130]

Coins of the fourth century represent emperors wearing crested and bejewelled four-part ridge helmets. These helmets were characteristic of all the late Roman Emperors, as can be seen in the coins and iconography from the fourth to the seventh century.[131] Constantine I wore a jewel-encrusted gold helmet of 'Persian' ridge type,[132] which he received as a gift from his future wife Fausta. The event was celebrated in a mosaic in the imperial Palace in Aquileia now lost, but described by the anonymous author of a Panegyric written in AD 307,[133] on the occasion of their marriage. Fausta presented him, as *sponsale munus*, with a splendid helmet shining with gold and precious stones, crowned by the plumes of a magnificent bird (*galeam auro gemmisque radiantem et pinnis pulchrae alitis eminentem*).

A second description of a similar helmet worn by Constantine (or perhaps the same helmet) is given by Nazarius in the Panegyric written in the Emperor's

FIG. 286. (Above left) Attempt at reconstruction of the Monza Corona Ferrea as the helmet of Theoderich the Great, fifth – sixth century AD. (After Lusuardi Siena, Perassi, Facchinetti, Bianchi, 2002, pl. I);

FIG. 287. (Above right) Cheek-piece of helmet from Koblenz with image of Victoria, fourth century AD. (Photo and drawing by A. E. Negin)

FIG. 288. (Below left) *Spangen-helm* of Baldenheim type from Vezeronce, second quarter of fifth century AD, Grenoble, Musée Dauphinois. (Drawing by A. E. Negin)

FIG. 289. (Below right) *Spangen-helm* of Baldenheim type from Krefeld-Gellep, first quarter of sixth century AD, Krefeld, Museum Burg Linn. (Drawing by A. E. Negin)

honour in AD 321. It describes the battle of the Milvian Bridge and how, during the fighting, the Imperial helmet was shining and the gems decorating it showing with their brightness the divine head of the Emperor.[134] This helmet, decorated with the Christian *Chrismon*, is clearly seen on his coins and medallions,[135] surmounted by a rich peacock plume (fig. 285) and corresponds to the type of the splendid specimens found in Berkasovo and Budapest-Aquincum.[136] The helmet of the Emperor, as represented on the Ticinum medallion, has a bowl decorated by gems arranged like a rose, separated by three *cabochons* arranged vertically. The middle part of the helmet is characterised by a row of precious stones (or precious nails) of globular shape. On it is attached the imposing crest of peacock feathers, formed by a double (or triple) row of plumes. On the front of the helmet is fixed a large jewel, decorated with the metallic application showing the Christian monogram, the *Chi-Ro*. Also, the narrow band of the helmet crown is encrusted with precious gems. Another helmet of Constantine, of the same type, is represented on a coin (*solidus*) from Ticinum[137] and it is similar to the first but it has a cut on the upper rim of the cheek-pieces, like the Berkasovo II helmet.

A similar helmet is mentioned for Valentinian I by Ammianus and was worn by his *Primicerius-Cubicularius*, who lost it in a marsh.[138] It was ornamented with gold and precious stones (*galeam auro lapillis distinctam*) and is well represented on a coin where the Emperor, wearing such a helmet, is seizing a captive barbarian by the hair.[139] The helmets of Theodosius I are described by Claudianus[140] as *Galeae redundantes hyacinthis*, i.e decorated from precious stones of Hyacinth, which Isydorus classified as a red-coloured Ethiopian stone.[141] The helmets described in the sources as having precious stones and gems, even on the *bucculae*, from the fourth century are confirmed by the coins as an imperial prerogative and show a perfect correspondence with the Berkasovo and Aquincum specimens. They were correctly identified as of Persian derivation by Alföldi,[142] for the morphologic similarity with the crown-helmets of the Sassanian Emperors. Maybe the triumph of Galerius in AD 298 over the Persian King Narseh, celebrated with great pomp by Diocletian in AD 303, in which the gemmed crowns of the King were paraded, introduced the taste for such Imperial helmets.[143] Before Constantine in fact, all the Imperial helmets shown on the third century coins are precious specimens of the Attic or Pseudo-Corinthian type,[144] akin to the Hedderneim and Brigetio types (fig. 175, 268). After the victory of Constantine, with few exceptions,[145] the Imperial helmets all belong to the Persian ridge type. The one represented on the coins of Constantius II is slightly different from the one of his father, because it seems be made of a single bowl on which the crown has been mounted.[146]

With Constantine the Great the jewelled helmet begins to be an Imperial symbol, copied from the Persian helmet-crowns of the Arsacid and Sassanian monarchs. In the Late Roman Empire – as shown by the much greater diffusion of the coinage showing the Emperors with the helmet – the *galea* ornamented with gems and precious stones was not only worn as armour but also as a symbol of power.[147] These bejewelled helmets of the Emperors were the origin of the crown-helmets of the Gothic Kings and of the Eastern Roman Emperors (*pilos, Kamelaukion*), for example the *corona ferrea* of Monza, what it is left of the precious helmet of

Teoderich the Great (fig. 286), which, as symbol of the imperial power, has been recently connected with the helmet of Constantine.[148] Under Justinian the Great the imperial *pendilia* with pearls was added to the helmet, thus making it exclusively a symbol of the Imperial power (Plate 19).[149]

These precious helmets were manufactured by a special category of Imperial workshops, each with their function, like the armourers, the *Barbaricarii* and the workers of textiles.[150] The various iron parts were worked by hammering by the armourers and at the same time – or maybe a short while later – the *Barbaricarii* prepared the precious silvered or gilded coatings, varying in thickness between 1 and 2mm, slightly smaller than the iron plates.[151] After a careful check by the *Verificatores* of the weight of the precious metal employed, the iron parts were plated, by placing the silver coating on the metal and fixing it with rivets. The joining of the two parts could be helped by using fish glue, as has been verified, for example, on the Augsburg helmet.[152] After that the parts of the bowl were further secured with nails, the leather lining inserted and the cheek-pieces and neck-parts attached.

3. The *Spangen-helme*

The literary sources attest to the existence of conical helmets topped with crests.[153] This is a clear reference to the conical *spangen-helm* (figs 288–311), whose centres of production have been recently identified in the workshops of the Eastern Empire,[154] although many specimens have been found in Germanic graves or in the territories of Germanic kingdoms.[155] The *spangen-helmen* are distinct from the other helmets in one major respect, namely that their skulls consist of several vertical strips of iron, attached to a central roundel.[156] This radial rather than bipartite construction is the source of their name. This helmet, of Near Eastern origin, in the Late Empire and especially during the fourth–fifth centuries, became one of the most employed typed and splendid gilded specimens, produced by the

---

FIG. 290. (Opposite top left) *Spangen-helm* of Baldenheim type from Morken, last quarter of sixth century AD, Bonn, Rheinisches Landesmuseum. (Drawing by A. E. Negin)

FIG. 291. (Opposite top right) *Spangen-helm* of Baldenheim type from Stössen, circa AD 500, Halle, Landesmuseum für Vorgeschichte. (Drawing by A. E. Negin)

FIG. 292. (Opposite bottom left) *Spangen-helm* of Baldenheim type from Planig, second half of fifth century AD, Mainz, Mittelrheinisches Landesmuseum. (Drawing by A. E. Negin)

FIG. 293. (Opposite bottom right) *Spangen-helm* of Baldenheim type from Gültlingen, first quarter of fifth century AD, Museum Hermagor (Drawing by A. E. Negin)

FIG. 294. *Spangen-helm* of Baldenheim type from Baldenheim, second quarter of sixth century AD, Strasbourg, Musée Archéologique. (Museum Photo)

Imperial '*Fabricae*' (so called '*Baldenheim*' type) have been found in the graves of Barbarian chieftains both allied with and also enemies of the Empire.[157]

This kind of *spangen-helme* could have round (fig. 293) or domed (fig. 288) bowls, made up of four[158] (figs 295, 299, 300) or six[159] bands. The segments forming the framework of the helmet were usually in a shape of an inversed T, riveted with round nails or hinged with small hooks[160] upon the alternating plaques that filled the empty spaces. These segments were often made of gilded bronze riveted over iron, copper-alloy or bronze plaques,[161] shaped like rhomboids or laurel-leaves (fig. 289), or sometimes simply oval (fig. 311). It was held together by a bronze disk or *apex* on the top and a bronze or copper-alloy band on the lower rim, often heavily embossed or punched with floral decoration, hunting scenes[162] or episodes recalling Christian motifs. In particular, the band-crown of some *spangen-helmen* (figs 289–292, 296) show that the tradition of the antique wreaths (the hero-wreath symbolism) had now been transferred to the metal helmets.[163] The purpose was to provide the warrior with a mark of honour, by acknowledging his heroic deeds with a wreath decorating his helmet.[164] Moreover the Christian symbols on the sixth–seventh century helmets[165] conferred on them divine protection on the battlefield and were symbols of what awaited the warrior after death as the reward for his heroism in defending the Christian faith.[166] These symbols of rank and

FIG. 295. *Spangen-helm* of Baldenheim type from Torricella Peligna, sixth century AD, Crecchio, Museo dell'alto Medioevo. (Museum Photo)

FIG. 296. *Spangen-helm* of Baldenheim type from Gammertingen, sixth century AD, Sigmaringen, Furstlich Hohenzollernsches Museum. (Drawing by A. E. Negin)

FIG. 297. *Spangen-helm* of Baldenheim type from Chalon sur Saône, fifth–sixth century AD, Berlin, Deutsches Historisches Museum. (Drawing by A. E. Negin)

FIG. 298. *Spangen-helm* of Baldenheim type from the Caucasus, seventh century AD, private European collection. (Photo courtesy Sotheby's)

FIG. 299. *Spangen-helm* of Baldenheim type from Saint Bernard sur Saône, sixth century AD, New York, Metropolitan Museum of Art (Museum Photo)

dignity of the Roman Christian Empire, since the fourth century, were the ideal successors of the laurel wreaths worn on the helmet by the pagan Roman soldiers as a sign of their heroic status.[167]

The *spangen-helm* seems to have been the most commonly-employed helmet between the end of the fifth century and the beginning of the sixth century, as various specimens have been found throughout the European territory.[168] The Roman versions were usually fitted with cheek-guards, chain-mail neck protections (*aventail*)[169] and were often furnished with a crest holder.[170] Bands and

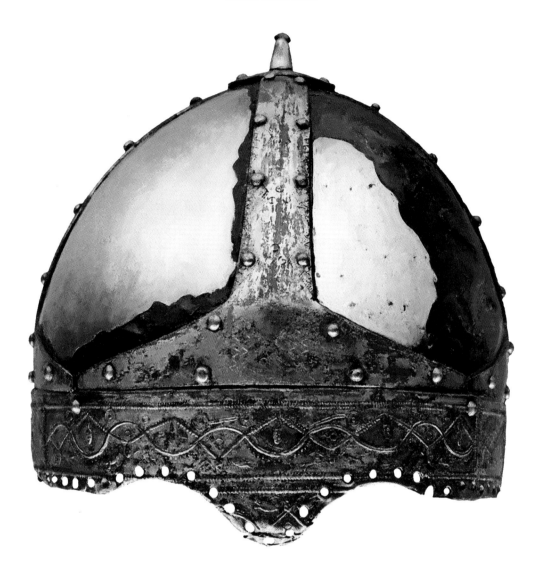

FIG. 300. *Spangen-helm* of Baldenheim type from Genfer See, sixth century AD, Zurich, Schweizerisches Nationalmuseum. (Drawing by A. E. Negin)

cheek-guards produced in the Imperial workshops were often decorated with punched and embossing triangular or fish-scale patterns (figs 290, 292, 303). Often the skilled Roman workshops gilded the surface of the bands and cheek-guards by the *encausto* technique.

Such helmets, which in sixth-century Italy were made by local workshops, combined ornamental elements of the typical classical tradition with new subjects introduced from the Germanic mythological tradition, often punched upon the bands and segments (fig. 298).[171]

271

FIG. 301. (Above left) *Spangen-helm* of Baldenheim type from Budapest, sixth century AD, Budapest, National Hungarian Museum. (Drawing by A. E. Negin)

FIG. 302. (Above right) *Spangen-helm* of Baldenheim type from Dolnie Semerovce (II), fifth–sixth century AD, Bratislava, Slovenské Národné Museum. (Drawing by A. E. Negin)

FIG. 303. (Below left) *Spangen-helm* of Baldenheim type from Dolnie Semerovce (I), fifth–sixth century AD, Bratislava, Slovenské Národné Museum. (Drawing by A. E. Negin)

FIG. 304. (Below right) *Spangen-helm* of Baldenheim type from Batajnica, first half of sixth century AD, Zagreb, Arheološki Muzej. (Drawing by A. E. Negin)

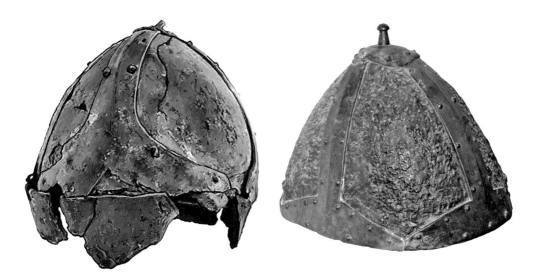

FIG. 305. (Above left) *Spangen-helm* of Baldenheim type from Leptis Magna, first half of sixth century AD, Sabratha, Archaeological Museum. (Drawing by A. E. Negin)

FIG. 306. (Above right) *Spangen-helm* of Baldenheim type from Solin, first half of sixth century AD, copy in the Archaeological Museum of Split. (Photo by R. D'Amato)

FIG. 307. (Below left) *Spangen-helm* of Baldenheim type from St. Vid I Narona, first half of sixth century AD, Copy in the Archaeological Museum of Split. (Photo by R. D'Amato)

FIG. 308. (Below right) *Spangen-helm* of Baldenheim type from St. Vid II Narona, first half of sixth century AD, copy in the Archaeological Museum of Split. (Photo by R. D'Amato)

FIG. 309. *Spangen-helm* of Baldenheim type from Heraclea Lyncestis, AD 610–615, Bitola, Narodni Muzej. (Photo courtesy Marina Persengieva)

Besides the *spangen-helm* the Late Roman Army also used the composite form called *banden-helmen* by modern scholars, where single or doubled bands composing the bowl of the helmet cross over it without a fastener at the top, on which was inserted the crest.[172]

At the moment only one highly-decorated specimen of this type has been found in the military camp of Iatrus-Voivoda, in Bulgaria (fig. 313).

FIG. 310. (Middle left) *Spangen-helm* of Baldenheim type from Steinbrunn, sixth–seventh century AD, Vienna, Kunsthistorisches Museum Waffensammlung. (Drawing by A. E. Negin)

FIG. 311. (Left) *Spangen-helm* of Baldenheim type from Hermitage, seventh century AD, St Petersburg, Hermitage. (Drawing by A. E. Negin)

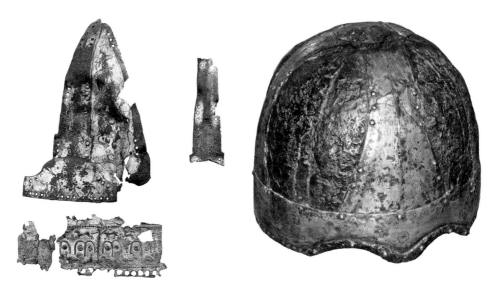

FIG. 312. *Spangen-helm* of Baldenheim type from Caricin Grad (Justiniana Prima), sixth–seventh century AD, Leskovac, Narodni Muzej. (Photos by R. D'Amato and V. Ivanisevic)

FIG. 313. *Banden-helm* of composite type from Voivoda, fifth century AD, Schumen, Historical Museum, (Photo by R. D'Amato)

GENERAL REFERENCES TO HELMET DECORATION

There are many references in the sources to gleaming helmets and to their brightness. Ammianus speaks of shining helmets (*cum essent visi corusci galeis*)[173] and Claudianus, speaking about the helmet of Stilicho, says 'Your head, who often shines for the helmet' (*solitas galea fulgere comas*).[174] Other expressions often used for shining helmets are *micans Galea, splendentes Galeae*.[175]

The sources also confirmed the use of crests on the top of the helmets: in Ammianus we have the expression *cristatis galeis corusci*, i.e. shining for the crested helmets (*cristatae galeae*).[176] There are three words in the Latin sources that refer to the plume of the helmet: *conus, crista* and *juba*. According to Isydorus the *conus* (in greek $\kappa\omega\nu o\varsigma$[177]) is more properly the arched profile protruding from the helmet, upon which is inserted the crest.[178] The prominent part of the helmet, to which the crest is attached, is called by Isydorus *apex*. With this word, the author more exactly means *quo in summa galea eminet, quod figitur crista*, i.e. what it is protruding from the top of the helmet, a kind of point to which the crest is fixed (fig. 302, 304, 306). Claudianus called this part *ferrata*, i.e. made of iron.[179] The plume is more properly the *juba* or *tufa*, mentioned by Vegetius to indicate the crest whose waving, during the battle, allows the *ductor* to indicate the direction towards which the soldiers who belong to a certain cohort should move.[180] The colour of the plume, in the

FIG. 314. (Above) *Spangen-helm* of Baldenheim type from Giulianova-Montepagano, sixth century AD, Berlin. Deutches Historisches Museum. (Museum photo)

FIG. 315. (Opposite) Graffito drawing on ancient brick representing a Roman cataphract with mask helmet from Bezmer, near Tervel, fourth century AD, Silistra, Historical Museum. (Photo and drawing by V. Yotov)

sources and iconography, is often associated with various shades of red: *ruber* (vermilion), *rubens* (scarlet red), *puniceus* (purple-red), and *fulvus* (reddish).

The helmets of the Imperial *Excubitores*, according to Corippus, were gilded and surmounted by a red plume.[181] The choosing of a bright colour like red (fig. 275c) was well suited to the function of the crest, with its double purpose of the

identification of the wearer and of psychological impact on the enemy.[182] Sometimes the plume is called *niveus*, i.e. white (fig. 275c). The Imperial helmet and those of the Imperial retinue were instead decorated with peacock feathers, as remembered from Claudianus[183] and as confirmed by the iconography (figs 285, 315).

The plumes were often worn, according to the Roman tradition, front-to-back or as a flowing 'mane' (*'juba equina'*).[184] The helmet's chinstraps were called *habenae* or *vincula*.[185] Internal linings in leather or other organic material were provided for the helmets, as shown by the holes on the rims of actual specimens (figs 289, 307, 310).[186] As visible in the artistic works, the colour of such a material was often red, yellow and light blue.

Body Armour

Between the third and fourth centuries AD, elite units, bodyguards[187] and emperors wore highly ornamented armour (figs 275c, 276, 277, 278, 318). The categories were those of the previous century, i.e. the muscled armour, scale armour and ring-mail, all of them undergoing a little progressive evolution.

The heavily-muscled cuirass, in hardened leather or in metal, seems to have undergone something of a revival at the beginning of the third century among the ordinary legionaries.[188] It is represented on the Arch of Septimius Severus Arch on groups of soldiers who are simple *milites Gregarii*.[189] A relief of legionaries engaged in training or battle from Intercisa/Dunapentele, dated to the end of the second – beginning of the third century AD,[190] gives a very clear idea of its shape, the same visible on the legionaries, standard-bearers, officers and guardsmen represented on the Arches of Galerius and Constantine.[191]

As already explained by Phil Barker, the muscle shapes and navel are so well detailed on the monuments, alongside other kinds of armour like mail and scale, that it is really hard to not believe that they are representations of real armour. This armour, both in the leather or metal versions, was furnished with separate round shoulder-guards, and was usually worn over an under-garment furnished with *pteryges* and lambrequins.[192] It is worn by the Roman infantrymen represented on the Arch of Galerius in Thessaloniki, on the Arch of Constantine by *auxilia Palatina*[193] and by the legionaries on the pilasters on the reliefs of the so-called *Arc Admirable* in Arles (fig.161), on Christian *sarcophagi* and many other monuments of the third – fifth centuries, coins and medaillons.[194] The last monument on which such kind of armour is worn *en masse* by guardsmen (probably *domestici protectores*), heavy cavalrymen and Palatine legionaries are the Columns of Theodosius and Arcadius (figs 276, 277, 278).[195] They were probably made of *cuir bouilli*, which permitted the leather to be moulded and shaped as well as hardened.[196] The leather was probably prepared in a manner similar to that of the modern blocking process which allows a piece of leather be set to a specific shape, probably in a mould. The efficacy of hardened leather as body protection has been proved also by recent Late Roman re-enactment groups.[197] Dan Shadrake has found, in the reconstruction of such armour, that thick, hardened leather or hide can turn the sharpest blades. Even so, many modern scholars still consider the representations of such armour on the monuments as an artistic convention! We should ask them why, on the same monuments, belt fittings, helmets, sword fittings, clothing and many other items correspond perfectly to actual specimens and their authenticity has never been doubted.[198]

These *loricae* were often made of tanned leather in various colours. The surviving colour depictions show often a leather corselet *tout court* in yellow-brown or brown, like in the fresco in the *Vibia Hypogeum* on the Appia Antica,[199] representing a late-Roman warrior wearing such armour, or the mosaics of Santa Maria Maggiore, where the muscled cuirasses are in brown, gold, silver and purple.[200] The *Historia Augusta* describes the armour of Maximinus as painted purple, so it was probably a leather or linen *lorica*. According to Hottenroth and Racinet, the cuirasses worn by the warriors of the Columns of Arcadius and Honorius were of painted leather (wired and gold).[201] As in previous centuries, the muscled cuirasses could be ornamented with metal fittings. Among the fittings and appliqués of this kind of armour, archaeology often reveals the head of Medusa (*Gorgoneion*):[202] the head of the Gorgon was believed to be able to turn anyone looking into its eyes to stone! So psychological warfare is not a modern invention! A small Gorgon is visible on the plated armour of Crispus, son of Constantine, in a *Cameus* preserved in Utrecht.[203] Also the head of Minerva was, at least until the fourth century, used in the same way.[204] A very clear specimen of it is visible on the Probus Dyptich, of AD 406, representing the Emperor Honorius wearing a decorated muscle cuirass clearly made of leather – as can be deduced from the attached shoulder guards and from the lappets of the *cymation*'s armours – decorated with the usual *Gorgoneion* applique on the upper chest.[205]

Many small decorations in gilded bronze and cloisonné enamel like small *phalerae* have been found in military contexts.[206] They have often been interpreted as horse-harness fittings, but their shapes and dimensions (pelta and round[207]) exactly correspond to the fittings attached to the *cymation* of many leather muscle armours in the statues of *loricati*. The *cymation*[208] was a scalloped border in leather or coarse linen attached to the lower edge of the armour and on the shoulder edges: it was composed, sometimes, of simple leaf-shaped tongues, or from more elaborate trapezoidal patterns[209] and often decorated with metal appliques. The fastening system of such armours was by shoulder-pieces (*humeralia*) fastened on the front by bronze buttons or bosses, or by simple laces, although sometimes these *humeralia* were merely decorative[210] and the main fastening system was left to side pins passing through clasps and buckles, or leather or linen laces on the sides. Metallic muscle armour was probably very rare, but a bronze specimen from the Axel Guttmann collection (fig. 109), 47cm high,[211] although dated to the first century AD, seems to be much more stylised in the representations of the muscles and navel, like Late-Antique specimen.[212] However, its heart-shaped umbelicus recalls very closley a Roman ivory of the eighth century AD.[213] So perhaps dating this specimen to the late third–early fourth century is not ruled out.[214]

Muscled body armour was obviously worn by senior officers and emperors, in both versions and coloured gold, silver and purple. The armour of Constantine II, represented over his statue in Rome, presents what it seems a metallic reinforcement around the side openings for the arms,[215] while the armour of the Barletta colossus (fig. 316a, Marcianus?[216]) clearly has metallic clasps on the sides and shoulders and the lower border is clearly of beaten bronze. Their structure and general aspect in both cases suggest metal armour, instead of the usual leather

FIG. 316. Mosaic representing Achilles and the weighing of Hector's body, fourth century AD, *in situ*, Villa Romana del Tellaro. (Photo courtesy Soprintendenza Archeologica per i Beni Culturali della Sicilia)

FIG. 316a. The colossus of Barletta, mid fifth century AD, *in situ*, Barletta, cathedral square. Clockwise from top left; general view, detail of armour, details of clasps, details of fastening system. (Photo by R. D'Amato)

FIG. 317. Virtual reconstruction of the statue of Justinian the Great in the costume of Achilles, Istanbul, Archaeological Museum. (Photo by R. D'Amato)

FIG. 318. (Top left) Torso of an armoured emperor, fifth century AD, from the decoration of the Golden Gate, Istanbul, Archaeological Museum. (Photo by R. D'Amato)

FIG. 319. (Above) Sarcophagus of a military commander from Sid, first half of the fourth century AD, *in situ*, Sid. (Photo by R.D'Amato)

worn by the Illyrian Emperors in their official portraits and by Justinian on the Barberini Diptych. They were frequently fastened by means of short shoulder pieces (*humeralia*) attached by rings and wide ivy-leaf shaped plaques to the breast[217] (fig. 316a). Sometimes the fastening system is only made of side and shoulder buckles and laces and the shoulder bands are not visible (fig. 277, where both types are represented; fig. 276). On some coins the imperial armour is bordered, along the edge, by a nailed metal band[218] which represents the *cymation* decorated in fact by holes, like in the Barberini Diptych.[219] This is the place in which – instead of small decorative heads typical of the armour's borders (fig. 316a) – there were inserted precious stones (Plate 19) so confirming the mention, by Claudianus, of Theodosius' armour decorated with green emeralds.[220] Generals and emperors still displayed on the breastplate the knotted *cinctorium* done in leather[221] and silk (fig. 316a).

The poets and the authors of the Dominate provide clear references to the nature of the cuirasses worn by the emperor and his generals in Late Antiquity.[222] One passage by Ammianus is of particular relevance because it refers to the employment by Valentinian I of an iron muscled *lorica*. A man in charge of a workshop (*praepositum fabricae*)[223] brought the Emperor Valentinian I, a man renowned for his irascible character,[224] an iron cuirass (*férrea*), for which he expected a reward.[225] But the emperor, upon finding out that the piece of armour weighed a little less (*pondus paulo minus*) than the *praepositum fabricae* had stipulated, ordered the unfortunate man to be put to death. Of interest to us is that *thorax* is found in the following ablative absolute construction: *oblato thorace polito faberrime*.[226] Literally, the cuirass was 'polished/embellished/wrought, etc. most skilfully'. The meaning of *politus* enable us to identify Valentinian's cuirass with great precision: *politus* here means 'polished', so it refers to a muscle cuirass.[227]

Nothwistanding Robinson's doubts,[228] the leather version of muscled armour still existed in the sixth century, as proved by the decorated shoulder-clasps of such an armour found in the Sutton Hoo treasure.[229] The imperial plated armour is also visible on the Justinian Medallion as the parade armour of the Emperor and on the general and the emperor of the Barberini Dyptich,[230] as well as on a fragmentary statue of Justinian from *Prima Justiniana* (Caricin Grad).[231] The name of this armour is recorded by Procopios: *thorakion Heroikon*, i.e. the 'heroic armour'. The continuation of the Greco-Roman tradition allowed the use of such armour for a long time, probably until the end of the Eastern Empire, and effective metal versions for the battlefield were used by *Doriphoroi* and *Buccellarii* in single combat.[232]

From the sources and from the iconography we can see that, besides the muscled armour, the *aurea* or *argentea lorica* of the Emperors could also be a scale or lamellar *squama*, chain mail or a simpler gold-lacquered leather corselet, like the armour of the Tetrarchs today in Venezia and once decorating the *Philadelphion* of Constantinople.

The Emperors also wore ring-mail armour, but unlike that of the ordinary soldiers this was a precious example, often gilded: the silver coin of Constantine I shows his breast protected by armour rendered in regular circles divided in parallel lines.[233] This can be only a representation of ring mail, here fitted with bossed shoulder-guards. A similar armour is represented on a rare coin of his son Constantine II (AD 337–40) found in the area of the old city of Cissa (today Novaljia in Croatia), where the ring-armour is worn over a *thoracomacus* with fringes and lappets visible on the shoulders.[234] Another one is visible on a very rare coin of Julian I (AD 361–3), which shows also him clad in an iron mail cuirass of simpler design: the rendering of the interlaces rings is excellent in this representation.[235] The imperial mail armour is expressly mentioned also by Sidonius Apollinaris with reference to the Emperor Anthemius, when he was still not Emperor. Anthemius, when he went riding in his youth, burdened his horse *'cum pondere conti indutas Chalybum ... catenas'*. The latter two words represent a clear reference to a coat of mail (or 'steel chain-armour'), i.e. a cuirass made of iron rings.[236]

Imperial scale armour is well recorded in the sources as well and it is the poet Claudianus[237] who provided a vivid description of the *squama* of Emperor Honorius (395–423 AD*): '*How fair art thou in shield and golden scale armour, with waving plumes and taller by the height of a helmet!'. Shining scale armours are furtherly mentioned by Sidonius Apollinaris for the Emperor Majorian (*thorax acerbat squamis*) [238] and for the Emperor Avitus[239] (*squameus*). The imperial *squama* of the fifth century can clearly be on the coins,[240] but also on a sculpture once decorating the Golden Gate of Constantinople, similar in structure to the image of the famous Tetrarchs,[241] but wearing scale armour (fig. 318).

The descriptions of the mail and scale imperial armours poses the question whether decorated versions of these two types of armour were still being worn by officers or elite soldiers. It is clear that at the beginning of the fourth century scale armours fitted with breastplates were still in use, as the specimen from Hrusica shows (fig. 94).[242] Corippus mentions for an officer of the African Army of the sixth century an armour (*thorax*) made with *Squamis Fulgentibus* (shining scales), while another officer, richly armed, seems to wear an armour made with in alternating silver and gold scales: '… taken up the shining arms has got in his hands high javelins. Himself sparkles in all his iron body: he marks the scales with gold ornaments ; blazing is worn over the gold helmet iron mixed ; then a horsehair embellishes the top and the plume'.[243]

Chain mail of silver and gilded iron is visible on the mosaics of Santa Maria Maggiore,[244] created in the first half of the fifth century[245] and representing in all probability Western elite troops and *Buccellarii*. The mosaics of Santa Maria Maggiore are also very informative by the use of multi-coloured armour and helmets, on which high plumes are waving, and on the wide use, still in the Late Empire, of evolved types of linen armour. They are lavishly painted and ornamented – in the case of the military commanders, in purple and with the *Gorgoneion* on the breast, in the best Roman tradition.[246]

The greaves (*ocreae*) are scarcely mentioned in the sources but they were widely used by heavy infantry and cavalry, officers and Emperors. One of the most interesting quotations is from Sidonius Apollinaris, who describes the battle gear of the Emperor Avitus. He[247] writes that '… At length he dashes forward, shouting again and again for his arms and they bring him his corselet, still clotted with gore, his lance blunted by wounds dealt upon the barbarians and his sword notched by unceasing slaughter. He cases his legs in greaves and puts upon his head a gleaming helmet, whereon a golden crest-base rises aloft, darting an angry flash from on high…' The beautiful mosaic of Abelterium (fig. 275c) shows on the warriors of such status greaves furnished with separate knee protection, similar to the third-century specimens (figs 112, 113, 114). One of the few specimens of embossed greaves (in this case bearing the image of a winged victory) came from the Constantinian layers of Arbeia, the Roman Fort at South Shields, maybe belonging to the *Quinta Cohors Gallorum*[248] (fig. 119).

HEAVY CAVALRY, FACE-MASKS AND HORSE ARMOUR

The above-mentioned description of Avitus by Sidonius make clear that the Roman elite fought as super-heavy cavalrymen (*clibanarii* or *cataphractarii*),[249] as shown by reference to the greaves and to the long cavalry spear (*contus*)[250] and from the description of his weapons as *sordentia* (heavy, burdensome). The arms and armour of these heavy cavalrymen could be often silvered and gilded and horses and men covered with splendid specimens of armour. From iconographical representation,[251] together with the descriptions in the sources,[252] we are able to have a quite good image of the luxuriously-equipped *Cataphractarii* and *Clibanarii*. Conical helmets were worn, developed from the conical helmets of the Sarmatians, consisting of multiple metal plates joined at the *apex* (*spangen-helm*), or of ridge

FIG. 320. *Prometopion* of a horse decorated with Auriga, from Rome, second half of fourth century AD, Berlin, Antikensammlung. (Museum Photo)

construction like the helmet of the dead Persian found in Dura (Plate 17). On the top of helmets were fastened fluttering ribbons, or crests and plumes made of peacock feathers, for the imperial guards sometimes painted (*picturatas cristas galeae*),[253] probably in purple (Plate 17, Plate 18). The helmet could be worn, following the tradition of the Thracian and Persian cataphracts, with a mask (*simulacra humanorum vultuum*[254] or *personati*[255]) or a scale or chain-mail visor. Prototypes of such masked helmets, still visible on the base of the Column of Arcadius (fig. 277),[256] were the mask visor helmets of the early centuries, both in the West and in the East.[257] The Prutting Altar shows a Hedderneim-style helmet complete with high crest, feathers and mask (fig. 107). A sample of an unusual mask, very similar to the ones of the base of the Column, has been found in Siscia (Sisak, fig. 166).

The body protection consisted of different parts, fitted to the body of the wearer: the sleeves were made of broad parallel metal plates (*manica*); the chest was covered by scale armour alone or together with oblong metal plates horizontally disposed, similar to the construction of *lorica segmentata* (*circuli lamminarum*). The protection of the lower body was by scale or mail (*catervae ferratae*), while legs and feet were covered with the same pliable armour as the breast and sleeves (*lamminis tectae, limbi ferrei*), i.e. broad parallel metal circles (Plate 17, Plate 18, fig. 277). The various parts of the armour were held together by clasps (*peratai*). Some *cataphractarii* represented in the frescoes of the Via Latina *catacombae* of Dino Compagni (fig. 321) are much more similar, in their appearance, to the description in the *Oratio* of Julian,[258] contemporaneous with the triumphal procession of Constantius II.[259] They show the use of old types of masked helmets with eagle protomes of the Hedderneim (fig. 175) or Vechten type (fig. 174) and the wearing of a metallic *stadios* (muscled armour), like the armour shown for the *cataphractarii* on the base of the Column of Arcadius (fig. 177). The use of this armour for *Clibanarii* was usual also amongst the Sassanian commanders, following their traditional links with Greco-Roman heritage.[260]

As previously, the cavalry armour was sometimes complete, protecting all parts of the horse's body, but sometimes it was only partial, protecting only certain vital areas.[261] The armament of the heavy armoured horse is well described in the Peri Strategias,[262] showing the great importance of the cataphracts in the sixth century: 'The horses of the soldiers in the front line should not be too young or unused to noise and confusion. They should be equipped with iron armour for their heads [*prometopida*], breast [*peristernia*] and necks [*peritrachelia*]. These will protect the parts of the horses most exposed in action, for if they become wounded they may easily get out of control and throw their riders. In like manner, the horses' hooves should be protected by iron plates [*sidera petala*], so they will not be injuried by caltrops and similar devices.' In the Late Empire the gravestones and the other representations of *cataphractarii* always show a horse without protection: this is the case for instance of the stelae of the *Equites Cataphractarii Pictavenses* and *Ambianses*.[263] Claudianus Ingenuus, *Ex Centenarius* of the *Numerus Equitum Cataphractorum Seniorum*, from *Lugdunum* (Lyon), is represented on his *stela* armed with a *contus* and a long coat of scale armour, a plumed helmet and boots, riding

FIG. 321. 'The army of the Pharaoh' and 'The passage of the Red Sea', frescoes from the Catacombs of Dino Compagni, Via Latina, Rome, second half of fourth century AD, *in situ*, Rome. (Photos of the Pontificia Accademia)

an unarmoured horse. Vegetius calls the cataphracts *Equites Loricati*[264] but he does not mention horse armours. Maybe the units of *cataphractarii* listed in the *Notitia*, unlike the *Clibanarii*, had no horse protection as a rule, what corresponds also with the representations of heavy cavalry in the Catacombs of the Via Latina (fig. 321) or in other biblical scenes[265] and with the limited number of armoured horses represented in the iconography (fig. 315).

Six types of horse armour are known from the sources: chamfrons for the head, crinets for the neck, peytrals for the chest, metal or leather trappers for the body, *knemides* for the legs, and iron plates for the hooves.[266] Complete cavalry equipment still consisted of eye-protectors,[267] sometimes worn in combination with horse-armour, while a metal mask (chamfron) was also worn,[268] often adorned with plumes, although only a few examples have been found up to now in the

FIG. 322. Shield's decorative plate, representing the Emperor Honorius, from Pannonia, early quarter of fifth century AD, ex Kaus. (Photos courtesy Institut für Byzantinistik und Neogräzistik der Universität Wien)

archaeological records (figs 155b, 320). We should remember here the previously-mentioned splendid specimens of eye-protectors, in bronze and iron (fig. 138c), found in Dalj (Serbia), where the *Notitia Dignitatum* mentions two regiments of cavalry,[269] that shows eyes protectors separate from the chamfrons. Metal full-face chamfrons of the third century AD, with eye-protectors incorporated, found in Gherla (Romania)[270] and Strasbourg (France), as well as in other places, consisted of a number of copper-alloy triple plates, intended to cover the front and the sides of the horse's head (figs 152–153). When available, a scale coat of armour covered the whole body, hanging down on both sides. The best evidence for scale armours used as the horse trappers comes from Dura Europos,[271] where three scale trappers were found, two of them complete: two of them had copper-alloy scales, the other iron. The scale armours covering the horse body were called *loricae plumatae*.[272]

Notes

CHAPTER 1
1. Plut. Rom. XXI–XXV; Diod. XXIII. 2. 1–2; Liv. I. 11. 7.
2. For the Roman shield of Plutarch's age see Ios. B. Iud. V. 5. 95; Tac. Ann. II. 21; D'Amato, Sumner, 2009, pp. 101ff.
3. Dion. Hal. IV. 16.
4. Like the small bronze of the warrior from the grave of the Circolo of the Tritone, Vetulonia, see Sekunda, Northwood, 1995, p. 6; Comis, Re, 2009, fig. 12C.
5. From Verrucchio, grave B/1971, see Stauffer, in Bentini et al. 2006, p. 14.
6. For the manufacture of such shields in Etruria and in Tarquinii, and their effective military employment, see Martinelli, 2004, pp. 47–49; Montanaro, 2009, p. 18; Kilian, 1977, pp. 70ff.
7. Fossati, 1987, pp. 11, 30–2 and 61; Martinelli, 2004, pp. 42–3.
8. Hencken, I, 1968, fig. 406; Saulnier, 1980, p. 51; Bedini, 1990, p. 64.
9. Saulnier, 1980, p. 30.
10. Fossati, 1987, pp. 32–3; Menichelli, Magno, Orsingher, 2008, p. 63; Martinelli, 2004, pp. 49–50.
11. Cerchiai, 1995, pp. 76 sq.; Bartoloni, 2003, pp. 168–71; Montanaro, 2009, p. 18.
12. Strøm, 1971, pp. 146–9; Guzzo, 2000, pp. 135–47 (graves of Cuma);Sabbatini, 2008, pp. 51–70 (grave of Matelica).
13. Fossati, 1987, p. 6; Bergonzi, 1992, p. 60 and note 3; Menichelli, Magno, Orsingher, 2008, p. 13.
14. Cherici, 2008, p. 219, on the Northern Etruria; ibid., 2009, p. 163, footnote 43 and p. 166; Nizzo, 2012, p. 86; Drago 2009, pp. 229–87; Aurino, Gobbi, 2012, p. 823.
15. Fulminante, 2003, pp. 22–3; Montanaro, 2009, p. 17; Nizzo, 2012, pp. 87–8.
16. Cherici, 2002, p. 191, on the Villanovian helmets.
17. Connolly, 2006, p. 91; Sekunda, Northwood, 1995, plate A, p. 42.
18. Tagliamonte, 2002–2003, p. 110; Martinelli, 2004, p. 49; D'Amato, 2009, XIV.
19. On the *Salii* and *ancilia* in general see Sekunda, Northwood, 1995, pp. 9–11; Martinelli, 2004, p. 24; Cherici, 2009, p. 162.
20. Coussin, 1926, p. 72; Saulnier, 1980, pp. 20, 31; Turfa, 2011, p. 112.
21. Verg. Aen. XII. 925.
22. Sekunda, Northwood, 1995, p. 5 (circles, shield from Esquiline grave 94); Chiarucci, 2003, p. 9 (spirals, circles, dots, half–moons, processions of animals, vegetal decoration, shield from Praeneste); Connolly, 2006, p. 94 (dots, circles, triangles, shield from Bisenzio).
23. Pinza, 1905, p. 148 fig. 62 (shield of Corneto); Sekunda, Northwood, 1995, plate A2; see the way to wear the shield on the back with straps on the statuette of warrior from Vetulonia, Montanaro, 2009, p. 15.

24. Fossati, 1987, pp. 30–3.
25. Grave 94 s. Pinza, 1905, pp. 144–5 and 148, fig. 62; Sekunda, Northwood, 1995, p. 5; grave 98, Cascarino, 2007, p. 22 fig. 1.13.
26. McCartney, 1917, p. 147; Aigner-Foresti, 1994, pp. 6–7.
27. Pinza, 1905, pp. 145–6.
28. Travis, 2014, pp. 20–1 wrongly attributes the diameter of 61cm to the shield of grave 94, because he based his opinion on the text of Sekunda, Northwood, 1995, p. 5; this is instead the diameter of the similar shield of grave 98, see Cascarino, 2007, p. 22.
29. Attempts of reconstruction from Coussin, 1926, planche 1; Sekunda, Northwood, 1995, p. 5 (back) and plate A1 (front); Sumner (with research of D'Amato) 2009, plate 1, but dimensions are again less than the real ones.
30. Similar decorations on the shields of Corneto–Tarquinia s. *Annali dell'Istituto di corrispondenza archeologica*, 1829, p. 97, plate B (warrior's grave with a complete armour and two shields found in 1826); the famous shield of the *Tomba del Guerriero* always from Corneto–Tarquinia, see Babbi, Peltz, 2013, cover; the shield from tomb A of Casale Marittimo, see Martinelli, Paolucci, 2006, p. 176.
31. Pinza, 1905, plate XI, nn. 20–1.
32. Like on the internal side of the shields from Bisenzio, see Paribeni, 1928, pp. 459ff. and figs. 40–41 (Olmo Bello grave 16); Geiger, 1994, plate 46 (Olmo Bello tomb 10); Martinelli, 2004, p. 28.
33. Pinza, 1905, plate XV, nn. 8, 9.
34. Pinza, 1905, plate XI, nn. 20–20a; v. similar pendants also in the shield of Tarquinia, Martinelli, 2004, pp. 48–49, 60.
35. Like in the Narce grave, see Turfa, 2011, p. 125, cat. 68; while there are five staples on the Bisenzio's shields: Connolly, 1981, p. 13; ibid., 2006, p. 94.
36. Other pendants, of anthropomorphic shape, were identified on the shield of the tumulus Lanciani of Decima (C tu), and in the Grave of the Warrior (O 600) from Osteria dell'Osa, see Bedini–Cordano, 1977, pp. 290–2; Nizzo, 2008, pp. 119–20, 135.
37. Connolly, 2006, p. 95; Martinelli, 2004, pp. 52–3.
38. Serv. In Eclogas. I. 58; II, 393; X, 381, 817.
39. Forestier, 1928, p. 39; Sekunda, Northwood, 1995, p. 16; D'Amato, 2011, plate A and p. 43.
40. Sekunda, Northwood, 1995, p. 14; reconstruction in plate C2; see also Salvetti, Sommella, 1994, fig. 15.
41. Isid. Or. XVIII. 14. 8.
42. Prop. El. IV. I. 29.
43. Varro L.L. V. 166.
44. Pinza, 1905, plate XI n. 11; Forestier, 1928, p. 37.
45. Coussin, 1926, p. 88, fig. 33; Sekunda, Northwood, 1995, p. 6, grave 94.
46. See: Connolly 1988, p. 102, figs. 2–2a; Antike Helme, 1988, p. 223, *Variante Vetulonia*.
47. Connolly, 2006, p. 102, figs. 2–2a, from Sesto Calende; see also the helmet from Picenum, Antike Helme, 1988, fig. 18 p. 240, and the Murlo and Trestina variants, ibid., p. 232 fig. 10 and p. 234 fig. 12.
48. Antike Helme, 1988, p. 452, plate 57; measurements: 17cm high; 28.4cm long.
49. Born, Hansen, 1992, fig. 1; Sekunda, Northwood, 1995, p. 42.
50. Fossati, 1987, p. 50, fig. 4; Antike Helme, 1988, pp. 223–4, fig. 3, p. 231 fig. 9.
51. Antike Helme, 1988, fig. 1 p. 223; reconstructions in Connolly, 2006, fig. 12; Sumner, 2009, col. fig. 1.
52. Hottenroth, 1888, I tav. 58 nr. 50; Antike Helme, 1988, p. 231.
53. Connolly, 2006, figs. 1 p. 102.
54. Martinelli, 2004, p. 17.
55. Sekunda, Northwood, 1995, plate D and p. 34; Martinelli, 2004, pp. 25–6; Connolly, 2006, p. 96.

56. Frazer, 1894, p. 51; Spineto, 1997, pp. 17–24.
57. D'Amato, 2011, plate A1 and p. 43; D'Amato, Salimbeti, 2014, plate A, pp. 6–7.
58. Connolly, 2006, pp. 95–9; D'Amato, 2011, pp. 34–5 and plate A.
59. Fossati, 1987, pp. 49ff.
60. Sekunda, Northwood 1995, p. 15; Pensabene, 2001, pp. 55–9; Touring Club, 1981, p. 92.
61. See Pallottino, 1952, pp. 30–1, painted scene of Achilles ambushing Troilus in the tomb of the Bulls; Achilles is dressed in a red loincloth, wearing a Corinthian helmet and a pair of greaves; see also the small statuette of armed Aphrodites from the Gravisca Sanctuary, in Torelli & others, 2000, p. 101.
62. Fossati, 1987, pp. 52–3; Connolly, 2006, pp. 61, 100, figs. 6, 7.
63. Antike Helme, 1988, pp. 108ff.; Torelli & others, 2000, pp. 510–11.
64. See the facing slab with departing warriors from the Piazza d'Armi sanctuary at Veii, early sixth century BC, preserved in the Museo Nazionale Etrusco of Villa Giulia, Rome; Martinelli–Paolucci, 2006, p. 182; Colonna in Emiliozzi, 2000, p. 17; Moretti Sgubini, 2001, p. 34.
65. Connolly, 2006, pp. 52, 58, 81, 88.
66. Antike Helme, 1988, pp. 107–36; fig. 19; Coussin, 1926, p. 150 fig. 43 and p. 152; following the classification of Bottini, the type E presents the mask completely closed under the eyes and the nose.
67. Kools, 2013, figs. 9–10 p. 14; fig. 12 p. 15; fig. 13 p. 16.
68. Kools, 2013, fig. 141 (Mars from Larino), pp. 60, 101; Tuck, 2015, p. 28 (Minerva from Lavinium).
69. Term, 1983, pp. 530ff.; Connolly, 2006, p. 97 figs 1 & 2; p. 98 fig. 14; p. 100 fig. 7.
70. Funerary stele of Avele Feluske, Fossati, 1987, p. 39 and plate D1 p. 24; reconstructions of crested helmets of the period in Connolly, 2006, p. 88.
71. Pericoli, Conde, 1976, pp. 25, 27; Fossati, 1987, pp. 54–5.
72. D'Amato, 2011, pp. 34–5, 43, 45, plate A1 and A3.
73. Sekunda, 1986, plate A1, pp. 3, 6; Connolly, 2006, pp. 41, 102.
74. Fossati, 1987, p. 48.
75. D'Amato, 2011, p. 4; for similar *antefissae* with helmets and transverse crest see Pandolfini Angeletti, 2006, pp. 176 n. 15, 179, fig. 4 (Apulo–Corinthian helmet of Minerva with the transverse *lophos* of the helmet and the crest–holder decorated with snakes).
76. Pandolfini Angeletti, 2006, pp. 67–9; Isler-Kerényi, 2009, fig. 1, 3 p. 58 and fig. 6 p. 62.
77. Negin, 2010a, pp. 82–5; D'Amato, 2011, p. 44; Travis & Travis, 2014, fig. 28.
78. Liv. I. 35. 9; Pericoli, Conde, 1976, pp. 18–19; Fossati, 1987, p. 40.
79. Petrikovits, 1952, p. 137.
80. Fossati,1987, pp. 20, 29, and plate A.
81. Graves pp. 14, 86, 87, 94, 98; v. Pinza, 1905, pp. 70, 72, 135–7, 157, plate XV n. 8, 9, 18; Sekunda, Northwood, 1995 p. 42; Chiarucci, 2003, p. 10.
82. Salvetti, Sommella, 1994, p. 11.
83. Polyb. VI. 23. 14; Connolly, 2006, pp. 93–4 and 131–2.
84. Pericoli, Conde,1976, pp. 20, 23; Connolly, 2006, p. 91.
85. Sekunda, Northwood, 1995, p. 8 and plate A; for the Etruscan specimens see Martinelli, 2004, p. 69; Tomedi, 2000, pp. 97, 108.
86. Martinelli, 2004, p. 68; for the Monterozzi pectorals see De Marinis,1976, types B n. 7 and A n. 1; Tomedi, 2000, pp. 2, 11, 29, fig. p. 24, 31.
87. The height measures 16cm. and the width 12cm in the middle of the sides.
88. Pinza, 1905, p. 71, fig. 24 e tav. XV, fig. 8.
89. De Marinis, 1976, type B n. 1, and La Rocca, 1976, p. 153 n. 3; Tomedi, 2000, pp. 24–6.
90. Tomedi, 2000, pp. 28, 30 (n.6); see a similar pectoral in the Gorga collection, in Sannibale, 1998, cat. 128, p. 113.
91. Gjerstad, 1956, pp. 203–4, fig. 181, n. 3; Müller Karpe, 1962, p. 86 plate 15; Sannibale, 1998,

p. 112.

92. Gjerstad,1956, pp. 225–6, fig. 223, n. 1; Müller Karpe, 1962, p. 86 plate 15A, 4; Tomedi, 2000, fig. p. 24.

93. Tomedi, 2000, pp. 27, 29 n. 1; De Marinis, 1976, type B2 n. 2.

94. Pinza, 1905, p. 157; Gjerstad,1956, pp. 234–5, fig. 210, n. 4; Müller Karpe, 1962 p. 86, plate 14, 16.

95. Coussin, 1926, p. 97; Schliemann, 1880 (1967), p. 301.

96. Sekunda, Northwood, 1995, pp. 9–11, 42, plate B.

97. Sekunda, Northwood, 1995, pp. 13ff.; Connolly, 2006, pp. 95ff.; Cherici, 2009, pp. 157–61.

98. So-called from the first prototype found in Argos, Greece; see Snodgrass, 1967 (1999), fig. 17; Martinelli, 2004, pp. 73–4; Connolly, 2006, p. 55, nn. 1–2.

99. The armour is also called *gutter* or *gouttière* shape by the scholars for this peculiarity; see DAGR (Daremberg–Saglio), 1887–1919, vol. III, col. 1304; Courbin, 1957, pp. 340–51, 355ff.

100. Coussin 1926, pp. 158ff.

101. See for instance the specimen from Olympia: in Connolly, 1988, p. 55 fig. 6.

102. DAGR (Daremberg–Saglio), col. 1304, quoting Pausanias X. 26. 6.

103. For the reconstruction of the fastening system see Connolly, 1988, p. 55, figs. 1–12.

104. Connolly, 1988, pp. 38–9.

105. DAGR (Daremberg–Saglio), col. 1305, fig. 4525.

106. Coussin, 1926, p. 159 and n. 1.

107. Velkov, 1928, fig. 78 (armour fragment from Thracian *tumulus*); DAGR (Daremberg-Saglio), 1887–1919, vol. III, col. 1311, fig. 4537.

108. Pellegrini, 1899–1901, pp. 87–118.

109. La Regina, 1992, p. 66, cat. 7; Holliday, 2002, p. 49.

110. Fossati, 1987, pp. 55–6; Martinelli, 2004, p. 78; Connolly, 2006, pp. 97–8.

111. Connolly, 2006, p. 59; Sannibale, 2008, p. 231, cat. 138–139, for the continuative use of such greaves still in the fourth century BC; Caccioli, 2009, p. 80 cat. 42; Stary, 1981, p. 73, 479, fig. 2.7.

112. Sacred to the God Hercules, see Fossati, 1987, p. 56.

113. Fossati, 1987, p. 54; Connolly, 2006, pp. 60–1; Caccioli, 2009, p. 80 cat. 42.

114. Mc Cartney, 1917, p. 122; Connolly, 2006, p. 93; Cherici, 2009, p. 165.

115. Plut. Numa 17.

116. Camporeale, 2001, pp. 85, 110, 223.

117. Coussin, 1926, p. 159 n. 2.

118. Torelli & others, 2000, p. 615 n. 249; also DAGR (Daremberg–Saglio) considered this gravestone like one of the first example of leather *lorica*, see col. 1313 and fig. 1834; the stela is dated to 560 BC, see Martinelli, Paolucci, 2006, p. 186.

119. Sekunda, Northwood, 1995, p. 43, plate C2.

120. For terracotta reliefs and bronze warrior figurines, see a list in Jarva, Rovaniemi, 1995, p. 46; see also Connolly, 2006, p. 57 n. 2, 4, and p. 97 fig. 1.

121. Brennan, 2000, pp. 34, 38, and especially pp. 43ff.

122. Galieti, 1938, II, pp. 281–7; Cialdea, 1940, II, pp. 91–6, spec. 93; Zevi, 1993, p. 409.

123. Di Mino and Bertinetti, 1990, pp. 166–70; Cristofani, 1990, pp. 264–9; Various, 1990, figs. 428–441.

124. Colonna, 1977, pp. 131–65; ibid., 1988, p. 493, fig. 488–90; Zevi, 1993, p. 417.

125. Fuss, 1840 (2013), p. 227; Zevi, 1993, fig. 6; Brennan, 2000, p. 46.

126. Zevi, 1993, p. 438; Scott, 2005, p. 104; Fulminante, 2003, p. 2 n. 12.

127. Paddock, 1993, pp. 174ff. figs. 36–75; Connolly, 2006, p. 98.

128. Fossati, 1987, pp. 48–9, 63.

129. Zevi, 1993, fig. 10, p. 433; Paddock, 1993, pp. 204ff.

130. Antike Helme, 1988, pp. 250–4, 485–90; Zevi, 1993, p. 431.

131. Robinson, 1975, fig. 128; Negin, 2010a, p. 83, fig. 80.

132. Salmon, 1967, p. 108, with references to the horned helmets of the Samnites; see also Cherici, 2008, figs. 55–56.
133. Details in Zevi, 1993, fig. 11.
134. Polyb. VI. 23.12; Colonna, 1987, pp. 7–42, especially 13ff. and note on p. 30; Zevi, 1993, p. 434.
135. Val. Max. I. 8. 6; Salmon, 1967, p. 108 and especially n. 3.
136. Varro V. 142.
137. Virg. Aen. VI. 777–780.
138. Sil. Ital. Pun. VI. 674.
139. Sil. Ital. Pun. IX. 450.
140. Plut. Phil. IX; on painted crests, see also Virg. Aen. IX. 49 and Potter, 1818, p. 26.
141. White, DeVries, Romano, Romano, Stolyarik, 1995, p. 15; Spence, 2002, p. 171.
142. Val. Flac. Argon. VII. 626.
143. Coarelli & others, 1975, p. 1417; Buzzi, 1976, p. 5.
144. DAGR (Daremberg-Saglio), col. 1110 s.v. *Chirurgia*; col. 1307 s.v. *lorica*; Moscati, 1976, p. 68.
145. Aristot. Hist. Anim. V. 16.
146. Term, 1983, vol I, pp. 234, 464, 524.
147. Fossati, 1987, p. 39; Cascarino, 2007, pp. 34, 50–1, 263 and plate II.
148. Details in Zevi, 1993, fig. 12; Cowan, 2013, fig. 39, 2 and pp. 747–9.
149. Zevi, 1993, p. 434; Fields, 2011, pp. 34–5; for the lining of the cuirasses see also Burns, 2006, p. 57.
150. La Regina, 2003, cat. N. 47; Colivicchi, 2009, p. 75; Plin. HN. XXXIII. 59.
151. DAGR (Daremberg, Saglio), 1873–1919, sub voce *Cingulum*, col. 1178, vol. I second part; Lipkin, 2014, pp. 50, 53–4.
152. Lipkin, 2014, p. 38.
153. Pericoli, Conde, 1976, p. 88; Feugère, 2002, pp. 52–7; Cascarino, 2007, pp. 198–201.
154. Virg. Aen. IX. 359–360.
155. Liv. I. 2; X, 44; Daremberg-Saglio, 1873–1919, sub voce *Armilla*, col. 438, vol. I first part.
156. Liv. I. 11. Plut. Rom. XVII; Prop. El. IV. 4. 91.
157. DAGR (Daremberg, Saglio), 1873–1919, sub voce *Dona Militaria*, col. 438, vol. II first part; Versnel, 1970, p. 305.
158. Fest. p. 204L; Mora, 1995, p. 210 n. 158; Woodard, 2006, p. 9.
159. To the category of *spolia opima prima* belonged the armour of Acron, taken by Romulus; following Livius the term was applied only when the commander-in-chief of a Roman army stripped it in a field of battle from the leader of the enemy (Liv. IV. 20).
160. For the early history of the Roman Triumph see Versnel, 1970, pp. 14ff. and 305ff.; Mora, 1995, p. 210.
161. See, for instance, Liv. XXVIII. 9–10; Aul.Gell. V. 6. 21; Val. Max. II. 8. 7.
162. Liv. I. 10. 6.
163. Cherici, 2008, p. 212 (*cista prenestina*); 2009, p. 163 (sarcophagus of the Sperandio).
164. Cairo, 2009, p. 27 n. 128, 162; Nizzo, 2012, pp. 88–89.
165. Cairo, 2009, p. 132; *feretrius* comes from *ferire* = kill, hit, or from the verb *fero* = to bear gifts.
166. Cairo, 2009, p. 159 esp. n. 701.
167. Plut. Rom. XVI. 5–8.
168. Plut. Rom. 24. 3; Dion. Hal. II. 54.
169. Prop. El. IV. 1. 32.
170. Plut. Rom. 16. 8; Flor. I. 5. 6.
171. Bonfante, Warren, 1970, pp. 49–66; Mastrocinque, 1993, p. 100; Cairo, 2009, p. 157 n. 684.
172. Torelli & others., 2000, p. 568; Emiliozzi, 1997, pp. 9–10; for a reconstruction see: Camerin, 2000, pp. 91–2.
173. Pinza, 1905, pp. 146–8; Junkelmann, 1991, p. 27; Sekunda, Northwood, 1995, p. 42.

174. Virg. Aen. VIII. 280; Suet. Tib. VI; DAGR (Daremberg Saglio), 1873–1919, vol. III, 1, p. 665, s.v. *Jugum*.
175. Emiliozzi, 2000, p. 26 fig. 1 (chariot from Pontecagnano); plate XIX, fig. 1 (chariot from Rome).
176. Luzzatto, Pompas 1988, pp. 130–45.
177. Lucret. De Rer. Nat. VI. 549.
178. Emiliozzi, 2000, pp. 85, 91 fig. 6, 96–7.
179. Emiliozzi, 2000, pp. 70–1; De Grossi Mazzorin, 1995, p. 19; Martinelli, 2004, pp. 166–8.
180. Dennis, 1848, p. 450; Colonna, 1996, pp. 346–50; Camerin, 2000, p. 87.
181. Furtwängler, 1905, pp. 315–30, plates 30–32; Richter, 1915, pp. 17–29, n. 40; De Puma, 2013, cat. 41, pp. 47ff.
182. Visconti, 1796, plate B, pp. 75, 84, 86; Helbig, 1912, pp. 374–5, n. 657; Emiliozzi, 2000, pp. 190ff.
183. Liv. I. 20. 4; Plut. Numa 13. 4–6: '… Now the Salii were so named, not … from a man of Samothrace or Mantinea, named Salius, who first taught the dance in armour; but rather from the leaping which characterised the dance itself. This dance they perform when they carry the sacred buckler through the streets of the city in the month of March, clad in purple tunics, girt with broad belts of bronze, wearing bronze helmets on their heads, and carrying small daggers with which they strike the shields … they move gracefully, and execute with vigour and agility certain shifting convolutions, in quick and oft–recurring rhythm. The bucklers themselves are called "ancilia", from their shape; for this is not round, nor yet completely oval, like that of the regular shield, but has a curving indentation, the arms of which are bent back and united with each other at the top and bottom; this makes the shape "ancylon", the Greek for curved …'
It is also worth mentioning the description of Dion. Hal. II. 70. 99–103; 71: 'The sixth division of his religious institutions was devoted to those the Romans call Salii, whom Numa himself appointed out of the patricians, choosing twelve young men of the most graceful appearance. These are the Salii whose holy things are deposited on the Palatine hill and who are themselves called the (Salii) Palatini; for the (Salii) Agonales, by some called the Salii Collini, the repository of whose holy things is on the Quirinal hill, were appointed after Numa's time by King Hostilius, in pursuance of a vow he had made in the war against the Sabines. All these Salii are a kind of dancers and singers of hymns in praise of the gods of war … They wear embroidered tunics girt about with wide girdles of bronze, and over these are fastened, with brooches, robes striped with scarlet and bordered with purple, which they call trabeae; this garment is peculiar to the Romans and a mark of the greatest honour. On their heads they wear apices, as they are called, that is, high caps contracted into the shape of a cone, which the Greeks call kyrbasiai. They have each of them a sword hanging at their girdle and in their right hand they hold a spear or a staff or something else of the sort, and on their left arm a Thracian buckler, which resembles a lozenge-shaped shield with its sides drawn in, such as those are said to carry who among the Greeks perform the sacred rites of the Curetes.'
184. Saulnier, 1980, p. 28; Martinelli, 2004, pp. 60, 343.
185. Sekunda, Northwood, 1995, pp. 10–12; but it could also be a *apex Dialis*, i.e. the *Tiara* worn by the High Priest of the cult of Jupiter.
186. Antike Helme 1988, pp. 182, 447; Martinelli, 2004, p. 24.
187. Liv. I. 34. 8.
188. Helbig, 1905, pp. 232ff.
189. McCartney, 1917, pp. 140, 147, 150, plate 51 fig. 2; plate 53 fig. 3.
190. Helbig. 1905, p. 3, fig. 16–18.
191. Helbig, 1905, pp. 265–6; McCartney, 1917, p. 160; Sekunda, Northwood, 1995, pp. 10, 42, plate B.
192. Connolly, 1988, pp. 93–4, fig. 6 and reconstruction in p. 92; Fossati, 1987, p. 29.

193. Naue, 1896, p. 98; Coarelli & others, 1975, p. 1192; the breastplate from Caere is oval with a straight side and a small gorget. It is richly embossed by a series of concentric rows in which are repeated theories of animals: sphinges, monsters, felines, griffins, chimera and the so-called motif of the *Despòtes Theron*, the Lord of the Animals, represented by a human figure flanked by animals.

194. Cassola, 1973, pp. 63ff.; plates XXXI,1; XXXII, 2; D'Amato, Salimbeti, 2011, pp. 33, 36–7.

195. Some authors, like Coussin, 1926, pp. 51–2, doubted the bronze composition of the *Ancile*, considering it made of perishable material, like its Achaean prototype. But the actual archaeological evidence shows different, see Martinelli, 2004, p. 50.

196. Liv. V. 52. 7.

197. Dion. Hal. II. 70: '… Numa … caused many other bucklers to be made resembling the one which fell from heaven, Mamurius, an artificer, having undertaken the work; so that, as a result of the perfect resemblance of the man–made imitations, the shape of the buckler sent by the gods was rendered inconspicuous and difficult to be distinguished by those who might plot to possess themselves of it. … For in all of them young men clad in handsome tunics, with helmets, swords and bucklers, march in file … '. Plut., Numa, 13, : '… The buckler came, he said, for the salvation of the city, and must be carefully preserved by making eleven others of like fashion, size, and shape, in order that the resemblance between them might make it difficult for a thief to distinguish the one that fell from heaven. He said further that the spot where it fell, and the adjacent meadows, where the Muses usually had converse with him, must be consecrated to them; and that the spring which watered the spot should be declared holy water for the use of the Vestal virgins, who should daily sprinkle and purify their temple with it. Moreover, they say that the truth of all this was attested by the immediate cessation of the pestilence. When Numa showed the buckler to the artificers and bade them do their best to make others like it, they all declined, except Veturius Mamurius, a most excellent workman, who was so happy in his imitation of it, and made all the eleven so exactly like it, that not even Numa himself could distinguish them. For the watch and care of these bucklers, then, he appointed the priesthood of the Salii… ' See also Cherici, 2009, p. 162 n. 41.

198. Sekunda, Northwood, 1995, p. 9; Torelli et al., 2000, p. 461; note the perfect correspondance of the intaglios with the words of Dyonisius: '… Among the vast number of bucklers which both the Salii themselves bear and some of their servants carry suspended from rods, they say there is one that fell from heaven and was found in the palace of Numa, though no one had brought it thither and no buckle road that shape had ever before been known among the Italics; and that for both these reasons the Romans concluded that this buckler had been sent by the gods …'

199. Fest. Ep. 31.

200. Sekunda, Northwood, 1995, p. 10, who publishes a very interesting miniature specimen from Bolsena, which he classifies as a figure-eight shield with rivets on the borders; in reality the specimen of Bolsena is a pectoral breastplate having the shape of an *ancile*, belonging to Type A of the pectorals according to the classification of the Marinis. But true samples of *Ancilia* are attested at Lavinium, Grottaferrata, Norchia and Veii. See Colonna, 1991, pp. 69ff.; Boitani, in Moretti Sgubini, 2001, p.112.

201. On the grave 21 of Pratica di Mare with samples of Ancilia see Sommella, 1973–1974, pp. 33–48; on the different kind of *ancilia* and the one of the *Salii* see Colonna, 1991, pp. 55–122; Borgna, 1993, pp. 9–42.

202. Cirilli, 1913, p. 147; Nizzo, 2012, p. 74; Borgna 1993, p. 23.

203. Martinelli, 2004, p. 54; Scubla, 2012–2013, pp. 11ff.

204. McCartney, 1917, pp. 126–7.

CHAPTER 2

1. Liv. VII. 29. 1.

2. About this campaign: Liv. X. 10–27.
3. Paddock, 1985, p. 143; Paddock, 1993, p. 45.
4. Diod. V. 27. 3–4.
5. Liv. VII. 15. 8; 23. 9; IX. 40. 2–5, 15; X. 40. 12; 46. 4.
6. Plut. Sulla. 16. 3–5.
7. Aem. Paul. 18. 3–4.
8. Liv. XXXVII. 39. 7; 40. 1 sqq.
9. Liv. X. 38.
10. Liv. IX. 39. 11–13; 40. 1–6.
11. Gilliver, 2007, p. 9.
12. Plut. Caes. 42.
13. Plut. Brut. 38. 5.
14. Suet. Div. Iul. 67; Polyaen. VIII. 23. 20.
15. Front. Strat. 4. 1. 5.
16. Sil.Ital. Pun. XVII. 395–398.
17. Plin. HN. XXXV. 2–4.
18. Plin. HN. XXXV. 4.
19. Polito, 1998, pp. 38–45.
20. Anderson, 1970, pp. 29–37.
22. Lipperheide, 1896, Abb. 362.
23. Lipperheide, 1896, Abb. 26, 362, 245; Waurick, 1988, S. 152, Abb. 1, 1.
24. Arr. An. VII. 5. 4.
25. Antike Helme, 1988, S. 485–486, K 85, Abb. K 85 a–e.
26. Antike Helme, 1988, S. 487–489, K 86, Abb. K 86 a–f.
27. Zevi, 1993, p. 431–434, fig. 10. Antike Helme, S. 251–252, Abb. 28.
28. Antike Helme, 1988. S. 253, Abb. 29.
29. Antike Helme, 1988. S. 254.
30. Connolly, 1998, pp. 107, 111.
31. Antike Helme, 1988, S. 145–146.
32. The Greek style of helmet, which was often taken as a template by Roman sculptors of the Republican era and even the Imperial period for the helmets of soldiers, is usually referred to as Attic. However, closer examination of samples of these Attic or pseudo-Attic Roman helmets plunges us into a chaos of typological terminology for Greek and Hellenistic helmets. First of all, this deals with mixed shapes which combine elements of different helmet traditions. This phenomenon can be seen in some Roman helmet types. This symbiosis allows adjusting the typological classification to the purpose set by a particular researcher who distinguishes from those elements a single criterion to base his own classification on. Considering Attic helmets is especially complicated, as even the existence of their classical prototype is disputed, which may initially have been pure fiction. This helmet type was distinguished based on images in the vase paintings of the early Attic style, late black-figure vase painting and in early Attic coins. Based on the images, researchers describe a helmet with solid cheek-pieces (approximating these articles to Corinthian-type helmets) which are mounted on hinges. Then helmets of a slightly different shape were distinguished based on vase paintings, which became known as Chalcidian. Their main difference from the Attic helmet was declared to be cheek-pieces integral with the bowl. Subsequent researchers identified other features of a Chalcidian helmet, thanks to which it became barely distinguishable from the Attic one. All this led, as mentioned above, to great confusion which resulted in an ongoing discussion about how to refer to this type of helmet and whether the Attic helmet should be specifically distinguished.
33. Bottini, 1993, S. 54.
34. Dintsis, 1986, S. 38, № 54, Taf. 17, 5.
35. Schröder, 1912, S. 331, Beil. 10, 4–6.

36. Schröder, 1912, S. 332, Beil. 14, 1.
37. Schröder, 1912, S. 332, Beil. 14, 2–3.
38. Lipperheide, 1896, Abb. 302; Paddock, 1993, pp. 530–1, fig. 31.
39. Feugère, 2002, p. 74.
40. Bishop, Coulston, 2006, pp. 63–4.
41. Bishop, Coulston, 2006, p. 63.
42. Rüpke, 1990, S. 222.
43. Plut. Q. R. 37.
44. Suano, 1985, p. 19.
45. Burns, 2006, p. 32.
46. Cipriani, Longo, 1996, pp. 80–1.
47. Bendinelli, 1916, Tav. II; Proietti, 1980, p. 305, fig. 433; Stary, 1981, Taf. 55; Paddock, 1993, p. 64.
48. Paddock, 1993, p. 64.
49. Lipperheide, 1896, Abb. 516; Babelon, Blanchet, 1895, p. 659.
50. Greco, Guzzo, 1992, pp. 22–53.
51. Weege, 1909, p. 150.
52. Comstock, Vermuele, 1971, p. 408.
53. Merlin, 1909, pp. 125–38.
54. Bianco, 1996, pp. 253–4.
55. Schneider-Hermann, 1996, 4748
56. Jurgeit, 1999, pp. 106–8.
57. This cuirass is usually thought to belong to a Carthaginian soldier who brought it with him from Italy.
58. Zevi, 1993.
59. Greco, Guzzo, 1992, pp. 30–1.
60. Walters, 1915, plate XXXI; Zimmermann, 1979, p. 180.
61. Polyb. VI. 25.
62. The cuirasses were found in the first Prokhorovsky burial mound (Rostovtseff, 1918, pp. 13–14; Khazanov, 1971, p. 52) and in the Berdyanka burial (in the Southern Cis-Urals) (Morgunova, Meshherjakov, 1999, p. 126, fig. 4, 2). The burials with the cuirasses date from the late second century–first century BC. The goods found in the burials include silver phials with inscriptions in the Aramaic alphabet in the Parthian and Khwarezmian languages, which were transformed by their new owners in phalars. We can suppose that these items were brought as spoils from somewhere in Central Asia.
63. Particular attention should be paid to fastening clasps. Such clasps are never seen in Greek and Hellenistic cuirasses.
64. Maluquer de Motes, 1974.
65. Mielczarek, 1995, pp. 35–40.
66. Liv. II. 47. 6; VII. 26. 7.
67. Pyrrh. 16. 11.
68. Plut. Tib. Gr. 17. 2.
69. Richly-decorated greaves are depicted on the relief of Sant'Omobono, and a knee-piece from a bronze greave of the second–first centuries BC, which is decorated with a *gorgoneion*, has been excavated from a temple site at Ardea.
70. Sil. Ital. Pun. V, 132–148.
71. Coarelli, 1972, p. 48; Liberati, 1999, p. 27.
72. Robinson, 1975, p. 153, plate 434–435.
73. Rusu, 1969, S. 291, Abb. 10.
74. Liv. VII. 26. 3–5.
75. Amp. Liber Mem. XXII. 2.
76. Liv. VII. 26. 3–5.

77. Feugère, 1994, p. 64; Negin, 2013, pp. 182–3, fig. 5.
78. Wieser, 1894, Taf. 17, 88; Schröder, 1905, S. 23–24; Crawford, 1979, p. 480; Antike Helme, 1988, pp. 543–4; D'Amato, Sumner, 2009, p. 208; Negin, 2013, pp. 181–2.
79. Donner von Richter, 1894, p. 21, Abb. 29–35, Taf. 4; Robinson, 1975, p. 129, plates 376–377.
80. Toynbee, Clarke, 1948, pp. 20–7, plates 2–4; Robinson, 1975, pp. 130–1, plates 384–386.
81. Tagliamonte, 2002–2003, pp. 103–4, fig. 10–11.
82. Tagliamonte, 2002–2003, p. 103, fig. 12
83. Schäfer, 1979, pp. 243–50.
84. Sil. Ital. Pun. I. 176–179.
85. Trejster, 2009, pp. 120–34.
86. Kähler, 1958, Taf. 61.
87. Robinson, 1975, p. 190, fig. 197.
88. Liv. X. 44. 5; Aur. Vict. De vir. ill. LXXII. 3.
89. De Caro, 1983, pp. 71–4.
90. Paribeni, 2001, pp. 41ss.
91. Dion. Hal. V. 30.

CHAPTER 3

1. Liv. IX. 40. 4–6.
2. Plut. Caes. 42, Brut. 38. 5–6; Suet. Div. Iul. 67; Polyaen. VIII. 23. 20.
3. Drexel, 1924, S. 55–72; Garbsch, 1978.
4. Robinson, 1975, pp. 107–8.
5. However, it is necessary to point out that there was no uniform in the modern sense of the term in the Roman army. There was no absolute standardisation of protective armament; it also difficult to imagine that the clothing style, colouring and decoration could be strictly regulated throughout the Empire. A soldier's clothing and equipment, primarily his military belt, baldric – *balteus, cingulum militare* – were used to visually identify him (it is exactly weapons and a belt that Juvenal indicates as a distinctive feature of the military: *quos arma tegunt et balteus ambit* — Sat. XVI. 49). See: Bishop, Coulston, 2006, pp. 253ff.; Negin, 2009, pp. 119–23.
6. Bishop, 1990, pp. 21–2.
7. Fink, Hoey, Snyder, 1940, pp. 1–222.
8. Ios. B. Iud. V. 9. 1.
9. Holliday, 2002, pp. 22, 26; Künzl, 1988, pp. 7, 85–7.
10. Holliday, 2002, pp. 22, 26, 28.
11. Plut. Rom. XVI. 5–8.
12. Künzl, 1988, p. 85.
13. Künzl, 1988, pp. 38–44. But according to ancient authors to the first Tarquinius, see above.
14. Amm. Marc. XVI. 10. 5–8.
15. Serv. In eclogas 10.27; Dion. Hal. Ant. Rom. IV.74.1; Val. Max. IV.4.5; Iuv. X.43; Liv. V.23.5.
16. Ap. Lib. 9.66.
17. Künzl, 1988, pp. 85.
18. Liv. X. 7. 9, XXX. 15. 12.
19. Plin. HN. XXXIII. 11.
20. Holliday, 2002, p. 25; Künzl, 1988, p. 95.
21. Kuttner, 1995, pp. 47–8, 141.
22. Kuttner, 1995, p. 137.
23. Künzl, 1988, p. 90.
24. Vell. Pat. 2. 121. 3; Ap. Pun. 9; Lib. 9.66.
25. Holliday, 2002, pp. 36–42.
26. Holliday, 2002, p. 40, fig. 12.
27. Kuttner, 1995, pp. 140, 282, Np. 79; Künzl, 1988, pp. 38, 79.

28. Tac. Hist. II. 89.
29. Plin. HN. XX. 3.
30. Ios. B. Iud. V. 9. 1.
31. Ios. B. Iud. III. 5. 5; Tac. Hist. I. 38; Aur.Vict. Caes. XL. 25.
32. Leander Touati, 1987.
33. Rankov, 1994, p. 20.
34. Vermeule, 1960, pp. 8–11.
35. Dintsis, 1986, Taf. 48, 3.
36. Dehn, 1911, S. 252.
37. Schröder, 1905, S. 23, Abb. 9; Schröder, 1912, pp. 327, 344, Beil. 12, 4.
38. Rabinovich, 1941, Tabl. XXIII.
39. Toynbee, 1964, p. 293, plates 67 c, 68; Robinson 1975, pp. 132–4, plates 391–393; Garbsch, 1978, p. 73, Taf. 31, 1–2.
40. Klumbach, Wamser, 1976–1977, pp. 41–61; Garbsch, 1978, pp. 55–6, Taf. 10.
41. Déchelette 1913, pp. 253–8, plates XLIII–XLIV; Robinson 1975, pp. 132–4, plates 394–396.
42. Garbsch, 1978, p. 100, Abb. 6; Feugère, 1993, p. 112; D' Amato, Sumner, 2009, p. 185, fig. 268.
43. Klumbach, 1974, pp. 46–7, Taf. 33, pp. 61–2, Taf. 46; Robinson 1975, p. 98, plates 269–271; Negin, 2010a, p. 48, fig. 32.
44. Petrović, 1993, S. 97–106; D'Amato, Sumner, 2009, pp. 185–6, fig. 270.
45. Klumbach, 1974, pp. 47–8, Taf. 34, pp. 51–2, Taf. 37; Robinson 1975, p. 98, plates 269–271.
46. Langeveld, Graafstal, Swinkels, Künzl, 2010, pp. 297–304.
47. Senzacionno, 2013; Unikalni artefakti, 2013, p. 7.
48. Klumbach, 1974, pp. 52–3, Taf. 37; Robinson 1975, pp. 138–9, plates 417–420.
49. Junkelmann, 1992, pp. 190–1, Abb. 169.
50. Sharp, James, 2012, pp. 38–41.
51. Wieser, 1894, Taf. 17, 88; Schröder, 1905, pp. 23–4; Crawford, 1979, p. 480; Antike Helme, 1988, pp. 543–4.
52. Antike Helme, 1988, p. 543.
53. Ibid.
54. D'Amato, Sumner, 2009, p. 208.
55. Antike Helme, 1988, p. 543; Negin, 2013, pp. 181–2.
56. Menendez Arguin, 2006, pp. 91–2; Polito, 1998, fig. 135, p. 197.
57. According Dio Cassius (LXXV. 1) and Herodian (II. 13, 9), the Praetorians' arms and armour were richly decorated with gold and silver, as they received a much higher salary than ordinary legionaries, and, therefore, they could acquire such expensive things as a muscle cuirass.
58. Written sources contain no direct indications that the scorpion is the emblem of the Praetorians. But there is some indirect evidence linking this symbol with the Praetorian Guard. Researchers believe that the scorpion became the emblem of the Praetorian Guard as it was the zodiac sign of the Emperor Tiberius who completed the formation of these units started by Octavian Augustus (ILS 2662; Domaszewski, 1885. pp. 32, 57; Durry, 1938, pp. 203–6; Rankov, 1994, pp. 19, 24–7; Keppie, 1996. p. 122). We should also mention the standard of the third Praetorian cohort from the tombstone of Marcus Pompeius Asper, which depicts a scorpion (Domaszewski, 1885, p. 31. fig. 5; Rankov, 1994. p. 25). On the mosaic of Palestrina (ancient Praeneste) we can see two alleged Praetorians with rectangular shields which also have a scorpion emblem (Rankov, 1994. p. 25).
59. DAGR, 1873–1917, T. III. p. 2, col. 1315, fig. 4553; Avvisati, 2003, fig. 11; D'Amato, Sumner, 2009, p. 141, fig. 187.
60. Dio. Cass. LXXV; Herod. II. 13, 9.
61. Ios. B.Iud. III. 5. 1.
62. Junkelmann, 1991, pp. 142–51.

63. Junkelmann, 1991, p. 142.
64. Virg. Aen. V. 553–603.
65. Petrikovits, 1939. Abb. 3; Harmon, 1988. p. 250.
66. Junkelmann, 1991, S. 147.
67. The version that the *hippika gymnasia* originated from the *Lusus Troiae* was offered by H. von Petrikovits (Petrikovits, 1952, pp. 137–8) and supported by A. Hyland (Hyland, 1993, pp. 92, 96, Not. 18).
68. Arr. Tact. 33. 1.
69. Arr. Tact. 33. 1; 34. 7; 35. 3; 42. 4.
70. Ios. B.Iud. 3. 5. 1.
71. Davies, 1968, pp. 73–100; Lawson, 1980, pp. 173–6; Horsmann, 1991, pp. 75ff.; Hyland, 1993, pp. 19–23; Junkelmann, 1996, pp. 57–58.
72. Hyland, 1993, p. 21.
73. Junkelmann, 1996. pp. 57–8.
74. Arr. Tact. 35. 1–2; 35.7.
75. Arr. Tact. 34. 2–4.
76. Arr. Tact. 34. 5.
77. Arr. Tact. 34. 6. It could be a shortened chiton adapted for horsemen or a Scythian-Sarmatian type of linen or leather shirts. For more information on the Cimmerian chiton, see: Kiechle, 1965, S. 91, 118ff.; Robinson, 1975, p. 161; Junkelmann, 1996, pp. 71–3. M. Junkelmann suggests that this was the 'Cimmerian' chiton in which Amazons were depicted in the artworks of the classical period. See Junkelmann, 1996, p. 71
78. Arr. Tact. 34. 7.
79. Arr. Tact. 36. 1.
80. Arr. Tact. 36. 2.
81. Arr. Tact. 36. 3.
82. Dummy javelins (*pila praepilata, hastilia*) were usually used in training in gladiatorial schools (Liv. 26.51.4; Caes. BAfr. 72; Plin. HN. 8.17; Veg. 1.14). Apparently, spears used in the 'Cantabrian attack' were neither javelins nor usual spears (*lanceae*), but pointed sticks (*xyston*). Probably, they are those spears ala I Pannoniorum threw at the manoeuvres in Lambesis (*hastae brues et durae*), in contrast to light javelins of cavalrymen of the legio III Augusta (CIL. VIII. 18042, ILS. 2487). See: Davies, 1968, p. 90. Based on Josephus, A. Hyland supposed there was a quiver for javelins (Hyland, 1993, p. 143). Another point of view is offered by M. Junkelmann who believes that javelins were handed to them by special servants (*calones*) (Junkelmann, 1996, p. 64).
83. Arr. Tact. 36. 4–6.
84. Arr. Tact. 37. 2, 3.
85. Arr. Tact. 38. 1–5.
86. Arr. Tact. 39.1.
87. Arr. Tact. 39. 1.
88. Junkelmann, 1996, p. 60.
89. Arr. Tact. 39. 1–3.
90. Arr. Tact. 41. 1–7.
91. Arr. Tact. 41. 1.
92. Lawson, 1980.
93. Hyland, 1993; Junkelmann, 1996.
94. Connolly, 1975, pp. 64–5.
95. Connolly, 1988, pp. 22–3.
96. Lawson, 1980, pp. 176–9.
97. Hyland, 1993, pp. 122–3.
98. Arr. Tact. 36. 1.
99. Hyland, 1993, pp. 122–3.

100. Junkelmann, 1996, p. 59.

Chapter 4
1. See, for instance, MacMullen, 1960, p. 25.
2. Koch, Sichtermann, 1982, Taf. 76–78.
3. Robinson, 1975, p. 105, plate 300.
4. Herod. II. 13. 10.
5. Künzl, 1988, pp. 125, 131; Künzl, 1996.
6. Um, Deschler-Erb, 1997, p. 62, No. 2401, 2402.
7. See, for example: Robinson, 1975: 'Cavalry sport Helmet I'.
8. Born, Junkelmann, 1997, p. 66.
9. Born, Junkelmann, 1997, pp. 63–6.
10. Feugère, 1994, p. 114; Junkelmann, 2000a, pp. 87–90.
11. Junkelmann, 2000a, p. 90.
12. Born, Junkelmann, 1997, p. 160.
13. Robinson, 1975: 'Auxiliary Infantry D'.
14. Szabo, 1986, pp. 421–5.
15. Negin, 2012a. pp. 53–5.
16. Velkov, 1928, Taf. III–V.
17. Popović, Mano–Zisi, Veličkovic, Jeličič, 1969, № 206; Robinson, 1975, p. 85, plate 237.
18. Künzl, 2004, pp. 400–1.
19. Interpretation of the inscription on the helmet: t(urma) Maxi(mi) Macedo(nis) t(urma) Maxi(mi) Constanti(s). Probably, this refers to two cavalrymen who served in the squadron (*turma*) of the decurion Maximus (Szabo, 1986, p. 424).
20. Simonenko, 2009, pp. 141–2. ris. 115.
21. Klumbach, 1960; Klumbach, 1971; Thomas, 1971, pp. 29–44.
22. Connolly, 1981, p. 244, Fig. 8.
23. See, for example: Bishop, Coulston, 1993, p. 150, fig. 106, 2.
24. Bracessi, 1987, pp. 53–65; Cresci Marrone, 1987, pp. 66–77.
25. Junkelmann, 1996, p. 27. Abb. 42.
26. Künzl, 1999, p. 157.
27. Willems, 1992, p. 132, fig. 6.
28. Waurick, 1994, p. 645.
29. Künzl, 1999, p. 157; Junkelmann, 1996, S. 27.
30. Fairon, Moreau-Marechal, 1983; Junkelmann, 1996, p. 49, Abb. 48.
31. Feugère, 1994, p. 110.
32. Arr. Tact. 34.6.
33. Garbsch, 1978, pp. 10–11, Abb. 5, P 27, P 7, P 3, P 6, E 6, D 1–2, P 23.
34. Borhy, 1990; Born, Junkelmann, 1997, pp. 72–5.
35. Garbsch, 1978, p. 8.
36. Petru, 1974, pp. 225ff.
37. Künzl, 2001.
38. Garbsch, 1984, p. 68, Taf. 31. 2.
39. Garbsch, 1978, p. 80, P 28, Taf. 37; Junkelmann, 1996, p. 70, Abb. 144.
40. Garbsch, 1978, p. 85, R 16, Taf. 13. 2.
41. Ruprechtsberger, 1981, Taf. 4; Junkelmann, 1996, p. 70, Abb. 143.
42. Künzl, 2004, p. 392.
43. Künzl, 2004, pp. 389–94.
44. Künzl, 2001.
45. Garbsch, 1978, p. 8.
46. Negin, 2005, p. 62.
47. Pitts, 1987, p. 26; Borhy, 1990.

48. Bishop, 2002, pp. 62–3, fig. 7, 1.
49. Bishop, Coulston, 2006, p. 141.
50. Bishop, 2002, pp. 57, 62.
51. Arr. Tact. 41. 1.
52. Junkelmann, 1996, pp. 70–2.
53. Robinson 1975, p. 147, plate 423.
54. Robinson, 1975, pp. 147–8.
55. Robinson, 1975, p. 147, plate 421–422; Richardson, 1996, pp. 91–120.
56. For a detailed analysis of the iconography of the anatomical cuirasses of the Hellenistic and Roman statues, see: Vermeule, 1959.
57. Garbsch, 1978, pp. 29–30.
58. On spolia see: Picard, 1957, pp. 131–3; Latte, 1967, pp. 204–5; Rüpke, 1990, pp. 217–22.
59. Van Keuren, 1985, pp. 177–87; Jucker, 1977, pp. 16–37.
60. Rose, 2005, pp. 24–7.
61. Niemeyer, 1968, p. 97, No. 53, Taf. 17, 2.
62. Ando, 2000, pp. 278–92.
63. See, for example: Vermeule, 1959; Stemmer, 1978.
64. Ando, 2000, p. 304.
65. Rose, 2005, p. 53.
66. Greg. Naz. Or. IV. 80.
67. Christie's, 2004, p. 159 (Lot. 163).
68. Babelon, Blanchet, 1895, pp. 297–8, no. 686.
69. D'Amato, Sumner, 2009, p. 224, fig. 29.
70. Maluquer de Motes, 1974, pp. 321–2.
71. This cuirass probably dated from late Republican period. See Chapter 2.
72. Fischer, 2004, pp. 131–41.
73. Hom. Il. XVIII. 613.
74. Fortenberry, 1991, pp. 623–7.
75. Connolly, 1981, pp. 98, 100, 103, 109, 110.
76. Negin, 2005, p. 10; Robinson, 1975, p. 187.
77. Arr. Tact. 3. 5; Veget. I. 20; Garbsch, 1978, p. 9.
78. Bishop, Coulston, 1993, p. 143, fig. 101, 1.
79. Keim, Klumbach, 1951.
80. Kellner, 1978.
81. Garbsch, 1978, p. 12.
82. Kellner, 1978, pp. 28–33, Taf. 37.
83. Garbsch, 1978, p. 12.
84. Robinson 1975, p. 187, fig. 192, plate 505–507; Garbsch, 1978, p. 11, Abb. 5.
85. Garbsch, 1978, p. 81, Q 8, Taf. 38, 5.
86. Arr. Tact. 34. 5.
87. Ios. B. Iud. V. 9. 1.
88. James, 2004, pp. 176–9.
89. Plin. HN. XXXV. 30.
90. See: Born, Junkelmann, 1997, pp. 76–9.
91. Steiner, 1905, pp. 1–98; Lammert, 1938, p. 1660; Schuppe, 1937, p. 1880; Büttner, 1957, pp. 127–80; Maxfield, 1981; Petrovic, 1991, pp. 63–78; Kolobov, 1998.
92. Maxfield, 1981, pp. 239, 243.
93. Negin, 2005, p. 11.
94. Maxfield, 1981, p. 94.
95. Lehner, 1904, p. 367, Abb. XXX A.
96. Jahn, 1860.
97. Curle, 1911, p. 174.

98. Maxfield, 1981, p. 64.
99. Maxfield, 1981, p. 117.
100. Maxfield, 1981, p. 141.
101. Tertul. De coron. 1. 1; Tac. Hist. II. 89.
102. Robinson, 1975, p. 190, fig. 196–187; Connolly, 1981, pp. 112–13.
103. Garbsch, 1978, p. 13.
104. Garbsch, 1978, p. 11, Taf. 47, 1.
105. Garbsch, 1978, p. 10, Taf. 47, 2.
106. Curle, 1911, plate XXI.
107. Driel–Murray van, 1989, pp. 283–92, fig. 2–6.
108. Winterbottom, 1989, pp. 330–4, fig. 5–6.
109. Garbsch, 1978, p. 86, p 7, Taf. 46, 2–3.
110. Garbsch, 1978, p. 86, p 8, Taf. 46, 4.
111. Garbsch, 1978, p. 14.
112. Lehner, 1904, p. 372, Taf. 29; Garbsch, 1978, p. 1, Taf. 44.
113. Gamber, 1968, pp. 16–17, Abb. 15.
114. Robinson, 1975, pp. 191–2.
115. Holscher, 2003, p. 7, plate III, 2.
116. Labus, 1838, p. 197, Tav. LIII.
117. Domaszewski, 1888, pp. 138–45.
118. Sacken, 1883, pp. 56–60, Taf. IV.
119. Lindenschmit, 1881.
120. Benndorf, 1878, p. 65.
121. Lindenschmit, 1881, p. 5.
122. About Parthian face–mask helmets: Amm. Marc. XXV. 1. 12; Heliod. Aethiop. IX, 15; Iul. Orat. 1. 37C–38A. About Roman face–mask helmets: Amm. Marc. XVI. 10. 8.
123. Robinson, 1975, pp. 107–35.
124. Arr. Tact. 34.3.
125. Abdul-Hak, 1954–1955, pp. 163–88.
126. Doublet, 1890, p. 90, plate XIV, 1–2.
127. It could be helmets depicting wreaths on the bowl. See: Maxfield, 1981, pp. 73–4.
128. Face-mask helmets are probably shown on the Triumphal Arch of Orange (D' Amato, Sumner, 2009, p. 233, fig. 315 m–p). However, this image can be interpreted otherwise: piles of captured weapons were decorated with more sinister trophies in the form of cut–off enemy heads, which was a common thing for the Celts, but could be done by Roman auxiliaries, too. Helmets with anthropomorphic masks are depicted among other weapons on the reliefs of the first century AD in Teramo (Negin, 2010a, s. 115, fig. 135), the remains of the support pillar of Vesunna (now in the museum of Vesunna in Perigueux) (Robinson, 1975, p. 136, plate 411), as well as in the later monuments of the second–fifth centuries: the sarcophagus of Portonaccio (ca. 185) (Robinson, 1975, p. 111, fig. 136) and, judging by the pictures of the sixteen century, on the lost Column of Emperor Arcadius (Nicolle, 1995, pp. 16–17).
129. Lindenschmit, 1881, S. 2.
130. Robinson, 1975, p. 105, plate 300.
131. For example, tombstones of Tiberius Claudius Maximus and Gaius Marius. See Maxfield, 1981, plate 8a, 10a.
132. Arr. Tact. 34. 3.
133. Hanel, Wilbers-Rost, Willer, 2004.
134. Garbsch, 1978, p. 64, O 9, Taf. 18, 3.
135. Garbsch, 1978, p. 73, O 57, Taf. 25, 4.
136. Arr. Tact. 34.8.
137. Déchelette, 1903, pp. 235–58; Beck, Chew, 1991, p. 26.

138. Klumbach, 1949–1950, p. 28.
139. Junkelmann, 1996, p. 51.
140. Junkelmann, 2000a, pp. 124–7.
141. Junkelmann, 1996, p. 51.
142. Kern, 1982, p. 63.
143. Kellner, 1978, pp. 9–16.
144. Junkelmann, 1996, pp. 106. Anm. 173.
145. Junkelmann, 1996, pp. 51–2.
146. Geiß, Willer, 2007, pp. 61–7. An iron sheet was folded three times to form eight layers. The metal layers were united by forge welding, and then the resulting multilayer sheet was reduced to the desired thickness by cold forging.
147. Meijers, Schalles, Willer, 2007, pp. 68–76.
148. Meijers, Schalles, Willer, 2007, p. 72. In this experiment arrows 34cm long with 1.5cm thick 35g iron heads were used.
149. Meijers, Schalles, Willer, 2007, p. 74. As noted by the experimenters, such a result would not lead to a serious injury, but, however, could put a soldier out of action for some time because of shock.
150. The mask was found with the helmet in the burial in what is now Bulgaria. The mask is the Kalkriese type, the helmet is the Weisenau type. Both the mask and the helmet were forged from copper alloy (bronze or brass). The metal thickness of the mask and cheek pieces is approx. 1 mm, the metal thickness of the helmet is approx. 2mm. Currently, the helmet with the mask are in the Leon Levy and Shelby White collection in the Metropolitan Museum of Art in New York, inv. No. 686. See: Junkelmann, 1996, pp. 54–5, O 88; Born, Junkelmann, 1997, pp. 19–21.
151. Conclusions drawn from his personal experience of wearing a face-mask helmet in the role of a Roman signifer were offered by Aleksander Kirichenko, member of the re-enactors club of Legio XI CPF, Atlanta, USA.
152. This method of attachment is typical for most Roman helmets.
153. Jurjen Draaisma, a member of the re-enactor club Ala I Batavorum, Netherlands, shared his experience of wearing a cavalryman's mask in personal correspondence.
154. The original mask and helmet were found at Kops Plateau in Nijmegen, at the location of a fort of auxiliary cavalry. The mask was covered with a thin silver sheet, the helmet had a wig. Currently, the helmet with the mask is in collection of the Museum Het Valkhof, Nijmegen. Inv. KH.401/199. See: Junkelmann, 1996, p. 29, O 85; Meijers, Willer, 2007, pp. 21–2.
155. The helmet from Homs has figure–shaped vent–holes under the eye sockets on the mask cheeks (Seyrig, 1952, pp. 210–27, plate XXI). Similar holes are made on one of the masks found on the Kops Plateau in Nijmegen (Meijers, Willer, 2007, S.33).
156. Comparing Roman masks with medieval great helms, M. Junkelmann points out that the former had a big advantage in terms of visibility as eye slits in the Roman face-mask helmets are located close to the eyes, in contrast to medieval great helms. See: Junkelmann, 1996, p. 53.
157. Kalkriese-type masks covered the front of the face only. However, as seen from the example of the face-mask helmet from the Leon Levy and Shelby White collection, a soldier's ears were covered by the helmet cheek-pieces.
158. Holes on imitated ear auricles, which helped to enhance hearing, are made on the masks from Nijmegen and Reinheim. See: Meijers, Willer, 2007, p. 33; Negin, 2010a, p. 104.
159. Lindenschmit, 1881, p. 9.
160. Amm.Marc. XVI. 10. 8.
161. See: Junkelmann, 2000b, pp. 40–2; Junkelmann, 1996, p. 56. M. Junkelmann also highlights differences between masks of the early Imperial period and masks of the second–third centuries AD – the former had wider holes for the eyes and the mouth and nostrils, which

he believes to be an additional argument supporting that such masks were used in battle.

162. Berger, Franzius, Schlüter, 1991, p. 229, Abb. 20; Franzius, 1993, pp. 131–5, Abb. 24 a, b.
163. Kropatscheck, 1911, p. 351, № 12, Taf. 39. 2; Garbsch, 1978, O 1, p. 62.
164. Negin, 2005, pp. 60–3.
165. Amm. Marc. XXV. 1, 12; XVI. 10. 5–8.
166. Nicolle, 1995, pp. 16–17.
167. Ilkić, Miletić, Mrav, Radman-Livaja, Sanader, Tončinić, Zaninović, 2010, p. 211, No. 10.
168. Robinson 1975, p. 136, fig. 411.
169. Lindenschmit, 1881, p. 5.
170. Benndorf, 1878, p. 59.
171. Junkelmann, 1991, p. 138; Junkelmann, 1996, p. 20, Abb. 30.
172. Junkelmann, 1991, p. 138; Junkelmann, 1996, p. 21, Abb. 31.
173. Heliod. Aethiop. 9. 15; Amm. Marc. XXV. 1. 12.
174. Jaeckel, 1965, pp. 94–122.
175. Rostovtseff, 1935, fig. 46.
176. Drexel, 1924, p. 69.
177. Venedikov, 1960.
178. Krier, Reinert, 1993, p. 63.
179. Liv. I. 35. 9.
180. Petrikovits, 1952, p. 137.
181. Kohlert, 1976, S. 514.
182. Benndorf, 1878, p. 29; Robinson, 1975, p. 107, fig. 128.
183. Waurick, 1988, pp. 163–9.
184. Liv. X. 44. 5.
185. Turnure, 1965, p. 44.
186. Born, 1993, Taf. XXII; Junkelmann, 1996, p. 102.
187. Robinson, 1975, pp. 107–35.
188. Benndorf, 1878, p. 17.
189. Antika, 1954, p. 16; Pjatysheva, 1964, p. 27.
190. Robinson, 1975, p. 108.
191. Jaeckel, 1965, pp. 94–122.
192. If the Kostol helmet had an aventail, then it can be considered a remodelling of a Roman helmet to the tastes of a soldier of non-Roman origin.
193. Garbsch, 1978, pp. 19–27.
194. Namur, 1854; Benndorf, 1878, p. 325, № 18, Taf. 12. 1; Lindenschmidt, 1881, № 11, Taf. 2. 2; Lipperheide, 1896, p. 321, Abb. 482–483; Espérandieu, 1913, p. 332, № 4189; Beck, Chew, 1991, pp. 134–42; Krier, Reinert, 1993.
195. Towneley, 1799, pp. 1–12; Robinson, 1975, pp. 112–13, plate 310–313; Garbsch, 1978, I. 1, p. 58, Taf. 12, 1.
196. Curle, 1915, p. 81, plate 6; Ypey, 1966, p. 189, Abb. 4; Robinson, 1975, p. 118, plates 339–340; Garbsch, 1978, O 6, p. 63, Taf. 19, 1.
197. Born, Junkelmann, 1997, pp. 16–67.
198. Kropatscheck, 1911, p. 351, № 12, Taf. 39. 2; Garbsch, 1978, O 1, p. 62.
199. Berger, Franzius, Schlüter, 1991, S. 229, Abb. 20; Franzius, 1993, pp. 131–5, Abb. 24 a, b.
200. Benndorf, 1878, p. 39, № 28, Taf. 13. 1; Robinson, 1975, p. 123, plate 358; Garbsch, 1978, O 7, p. 64, Taf. 18, 2.
201. Willems, 1992, pp. 57–60, fig. 1, 2; Junkelmann, 1996, O 82, p. 54, Abb. 104.
202. Benndorf, 1878, p. 338, № 31, Taf. 14, 3; Robinson, 1975, p. 123, fig. 138; Garbsch, 1978, O 8, S. 64.
203. Junkelmann, 1996, O 88, pp. 54–5, Abb. 105–108.
204. Born, Junkelmann, 1997, pp. 84–8, Abb. 67, Taf. VIII– XI.
205. Curle, 1915, p. 81, plate 6; Kam, 1915, p. 261, Abb. 3–5; Braat, 1939, p. 35, Abb. 29, 37;

Robinson, 1975, pp. 118, 123, plates 339, 340, 357; Willems, 1992, pp. 57–66; Enckevort, Willems, 1994.

206. Djakovič, 1906–1907, pp. 1–55; Filov, 1923, p. 139; Venedikov, 1960, pp. 145–6, Abb. 9–10; Garbsch, 1978, O 2, p. 62, Taf. 17, 1–2.

207. Abdul-Hak, 1951, p. 167, plate 59; Klengel, 1971, pp. 102–3; Robinson, 1975, p. 122, plates 349–351; Garbsch, 1978, O 4, p. 63, Taf. 17, 3–4.

208. Mansel, 1938; Klumbach, 1949–1950, S. 30, Abb. 3; Robinson, 1975, pp. 118–19, plates 341–344; Garbsch, 1978, O 3, p. 62.

209. Robinson, 1975, pp. 112–13.

210. Born, Junkelmann, 1997, p. 32.

211. Born, Junkelmann, 1997, pp. 32–3.

212. Born, Junkelmann, 1997, S. 36.

213. Curle, 1911, pp. 168–9, plate XXIX; Garbsch, 1978, H 1; Robinson, 1975, p. 114, plates 318–319.

214. Garbsch, 1978, L 1, Taf. 14.

215. Garbsch, 1978, O 23, Taf. 21. 3.

216. Braccesi, 1987; Cresci Marrone, 1987; Künzl, 1999.

217. Born, Junkelmann, 1997, pp. 32–7.

218. Venedikov, 1960, pp. 143–5; Kohlert, 1976, p. 512, Abb. 79; Garbsch, 1978, p. 68, Taf. 22, 4.

219. De Agostino, 1958; Garbsch, 1978, p. 60, Taf. 15.

220. Kellner, Zahlhaas, 1993, pp. 80ff, Nr. 40; Junkelmann, 1996, p. 94, Abb. 75.

221. Garbsch, 1978, p. 60, Taf. 15, 1–2.

222. Garbsch, 1978, p. 69, Taf. 24, 1.

223. Garbsch, 1978, p. 70, Taf. 24, 4.

224. Benndorf, 1878, p 24, № 16, Taf. 9, 3–4; Garbsch, 1978, p. 71, Taf. 25, 1–2.

225. Keim, Klumbach, 1951; Garbsch, 1978, p. 48, Taf. 1, 1; 2, 3–4.

226. Keim, Klumbach, 1951.

227. But we should not forget that Herzogenburg-type masks (depicting male faces) found there date from an earlier stage of the development of Roman face-imitating masks than the Straubing-type female masks found in the same place, which can point to the secondary use of the former.

228. Arr. Tact. 33–39.

229. James, 2004, pp. 176–9.

230. Ap. Mithr. 69, 103; Plut. Pomp. 35.

231. SHA. Aurel. XXXIV, 1.

232. SHA. Comm. XI, 9.

233. Worrell, Pearce, 2011, pp. 355–93; Worrell, Jackson, 2011, pp. 20–7; Breeze, Bishop, 2013.

234. The Mithraic nature of the helmet decoration can also be supported by a griffin and a bowl depicted on it, cf. the images of a griffin, a lyre and a cup for drink offering on the altar stone, recently found in Musselburgh, East Lothian (Scotland). The front of the altar has an inscription saying that the altar is dedicated to Mithras (BBC, 2011).

235. Künzl, 1999, p. 157.

236. Lucan. Phars. II, 358; Iuv. VI, 503; Varro. VII, 44.

237. A crescent symbol is quite common in ancient graphic sources. Diana, goddess of the Moon, was portrayed with a crescent on her forehead in Roman mythology. The symbols of the sun and the crescent are popular in many Eastern peoples and associated with one of the oldest cults of celestial bodies – worshipping the Sun and the Moon. The Moon was associated with the feminine principle and the Sun with the masculine one. A crescent symbolised the beginning of a new life cycle. The image of the crescent kind of ensured a further prosperous development of life. For comparison, see a crescent-shaped gold pendant from the British Museum (Walker, Bierbrier, 1997, pp. 164–5, Nr. 190).

238. Iuv. VI, 120. Wigs (*galeri modum*) were reported by Tertullian. Blond female hair was found

in burials of the Roman period in Les Martres–de–Veyre (Audollent, 1923, pp. 275–328, especially 284, plate 8; Bartman, 2001, p. 7, fig. 5).

239. Benndorf, 1878, pp. 24ff, № 17, Taf. 10; Vlădescu, 1981.
240. Benndorf, 1878, p. 15, № 12, Taf. 3; Garbsch, 1978, S. 70, Taf. 24, 3.
241. Vermeule, Neuerburg, 1973, p. 36; Garbsch, 1978, p. 70, Taf. 25, 3.
242. Radulescu, 1963, p. 538, fig. 3–7; Garbsch, 1978, p. 73, Taf. 27.
243. Garbsch, 1978, p. 69, Taf. 24, 1.
244. Garbsch, 1978, p. 70, Taf. 24, 4.
245. Junkelmann, 1996, p. 95, Abb. 89.
246. Kohlert, 1976, p. 512, Abb. 80; Garbsch, 1978, p. 70.
247. Stojchev, 2005, pp. 303–6.
248. Dragotă, 1987, pp. 276–80.
249. Isac, Barbulescu, 2008, pp. 215–16; Isac, 2009.
250. Kocsis, 1993, pp. 281–2.
251. Garbsch, 1978, p. 55, Taf. 9, 1–4.
252. Garbsch, 1978, p. 73, Taf. 25, 4; Matešić, 2010, pp. 54–8.
253. Negin, 2012b, pp. 292–4, fig. 2–4.
254. Bartman, 2005, pp. 113–15.
255. Bartman, 2005, p. 115.
256. Bartman, 2005, p. 116.
257. Ricciardi, 2007.
258. Künzl, 2008, pp. 115–17.
259. Dio Cass. LXXII, 10; SHA. Marc. Aurel. XXVI. 8.
260. Dio Cass. LXXII, 10; Dio Cass. LXXV, 1; BGU II 362, 13, 15ff.
261. Künzl, 2008, p. 115.
262. See the hypothesis by J. Oliver (Oliver, 1941, pp. 540–1) criticised by O. Fink. For the criticism by O. Fink, see: Fink, 1944, pp. 17–19.
263. Garbsch, 1978, pp. 66, Taf. 21, 1–2.
264. Medusa was given snakes instead of hair due to the curse of Minerva. Her image was used both as a talisman warding off evil and as an 'evil eye', frightening the enemy with its malicious force (Ovid. Met. IV, 783–803) (Boschung, 1987, pp. 255–8). This function of a *gorgoneion* can be seen as early as in ancient Greek protective armour. Over time, however, a terrifying grimace on images of the Medusa disappears and the facial features initially frightening transformed into amazingly beautiful ones and a scary grin was replaced by calmness and tranquillity, so only the snakes and wings reminded one that it was a monster.
265. Belson, 1980, p. 377.
266. Kohlert, 1976, p. 513, Abb. 81; Garbsch, 1978, p. 70.
267. Negin, 2012b, pp. 295–6, fig. 5, 8.
268. Benndorf, 1878, p. 22, № 15, Taf. 7, 8; Lindenschmit, 1881, S. 7; Lipperheide, 1896, p. 346, Abb. 263; Robinson, 1975, pp. 126–7, plates 367–369; Negin, 2010a, pp. 138–40, figs 187–188.
269. Benndorf, 1878, p. 65.
270. Pjatysheva, 1964, p. 27.
271. De Agostino, 1958.
272. Kellner, Zahlhaas, 1993, pp. 80ff, Nr. 40; Junkelmann, 1996, p. 94, Abb. 75.
273. Junkelmann, 1996, p. 101.
274. Tončeva, 1964, p. 53, fig. 8; Garbsch, 1978, p. 68, Taf. 23, 1.
275. Garbsch, 1978, pp. 51–2, Taf. 7, 2, 4.
276. Garbsch, 1984, p. 67, Nr 4; Junkelmann, 1996, pp. 95–6.
277. Garbsch, 1984, p. 67, Nr 2a–b; Junkelmann, 1996, p. 96.
278. Boube–Piccot, 1994, pp. 45–8, plates 55–56.

279. Plut. Sol. 8–9; Hdt. IV. 145–146.
280. Bartman, 2005, p. 115.
281. Cool, 2004, p. 317.
282. Cool, 2004, pp. 2–23.
283. Cool, 2004, p. 461.
284. Bartman, 2005, p. 111.
285. Negin, 2010a, pp. 55–7, figs 44–47.
286. Garbsch, 1978, p. 48, Taf. 3; Negin, 2010a, pp. 55–7, fig. 68.
287. Garbsch, 1978, pp. 83–4, Taf. 42, 1–2; Negin, 2010a, pp. 173–4, figs 249, 251.
288. Junkelmann, 1996, pp. 77–8; Negin, 2010a, pp. 169–75.
289. Sim, Kaminski, 2012, p. 75, fig. 47; Fischer, 2012, p. 169, Abb. 216.
290. Garbsch, 1978, p. 72, Taf. 28, 3–4; Negin, 2010a, p. 148, figs 203–204.
291. Garbsch, 1978, p. 72, Taf. 28, 1–2; Negin, 2010a, p. 147, fig. 202, 2.
292. Born, Junkelmann, 1997, pp. 106–8, Taf. I–III.
293. Negin, 2010a, p. 114, fig. 133.
294. Isac, Barbulescu, 2008, pp. 217–18, Abb. 5, 27.
295. Achter het Zilveren Masker, 2007.
296. Geiß, Willer, 2007, pp. 61–7.
297. Mitschke, 2007, pp. 81–100.
298. Flor. II. 26. 16.
299. Garbsch, 1978, R 9, p. 84, Taf. 43, 3.
300. Junkelmann, 2000a, pp. 202–3, Abb. 112, Taf. XXIV.
301. Mansel, 1938; Klumbach, 1949–1950, p. 30. Abb. 3; Robinson, 1975, pp. 118–19, plates 341–344; Garbsch, 1978, O 3, S. 62.
302. Junkelmann, 1996, p. 50.
303. Maxfield, 1981, p. 81.
304. Robinson, 1975, pp. 112–13.
305. Junkelmann, 1996, p. 50.
306. Maxfield, 1981, p. 74.
307. Garbsch, 1978, M 1–2, pp. 59–60, Taf. 1–3.
308. Robinson, 1975, p. 114, plates 318–319.
309. Ibid., p. 114, plate 320.
310. Ibid., p. 115, plates 321–322.
311. Abdul-Hak, 1954–1955.
312. Garbsch, 1978, pp. 26–7.
313. Ibid., p. 27.
314. Suet. Aug. 100. 3.
315. Chernyshov, 1994.
316. Abdul-Hak, 1954–1955.
317. Curle, 1911, p. 166, plates XXVII, XXVIII.
318. Robinson, 1975, pp. 112–13.
319. Benndorf, 1878, pp. 328, № 23, Taf. 12, 3; Robinson, 1975, p. 113, plate 317; Garbsch, 1978, O 16, p. 65, Taf. 19, 4.
320. CIL. II. 4083.
321. Klumbach, 1960.
322. Beck, Chew, 1991, № 27, 29, p. 63; Bishop, Coulston, 2006, p. 108; Um, Deschler–Erb, 1997, № 2415–2421, p. 63.
323. Klumbach, 1960.
324. Neverov, 1996, p. 119.
325. Boschhung, 1987, pp. 255–8.
326. Schröder, 1905, p. 21, Abb. 8; Antike Helme, 1988, p. 362, K 118, p. 537.
327. Renel, 1903, p. 212.

328. Garbsch, 1978, p. 31.
329. Künzl, 2004, pp. 398–402.
330. Garbsch, 1978, G 1, S. 56, Taf. 11, 1.

Chapter 5
1. Dautova Ruševlian, Vujović, 2011, p. 41, 90, cat. 3 (Liebenau); Sommer, 1984, plate 76 n. 12; Schorsch, 1986, fig. 1, 2, 3 (Vermand).
2. Böhme,1974, plate 21.14; Thompson, 2004, p. 75, Kazanski, Mastikova, 2007, plate 23,7.
3. Altheim, 1943, plate 64; Dickinson & Harke, 1992, p. 19; Visy, 2000, p. 17.
4. Feugère, 2002, p. 191; excavated in 1957; Lebedinsky, 2001, p. 182.
5. Kazanski, Mastikova, 2007, p. 20, graves of local Roman *Phoederati* or garrison troops in Tsibilium.
6. Bishop, Coulston, 2006, p. 217.
7. Cracco Ruggini, Cassola, 1982, p. 305.
8. Sommer,1984, p. 96, plate 74; Schorsch, 1986, p. 18 fig. 1, p. 19, fig. 2, 3.
9. Schorsch, 1986, p. 19.
10. Schorsch, 1986, pp. 32, 35; on the Roman origin of all the Vermand staff see idem, p. 27.
11. Wilcox, 1982, p. 13.
12. Schorsch, 1986, pp. 24, 33; maybe a Frankish chieftain identified as the *Praefectus Laetorum*.
13. Ščukin, 1993, p. 327.
14. Schorsch, 1986, p. 34; Bishop-Coulston, 2006, pp. 199–200; Halsall, 2003, pp. 163ff.
15. Ščukin, 1993, fig. 5, n. 6; Lebedinsky, 2001, p. 182.
16. Zieling 1989, pp. 160–2; Kazanski, 1994, pp. 447–8. Ivaniševič-Kazanski, 2007, p. 118.
17. Kazanski, 1988, figs 6–7: Sapka Abgidzrahu, Budesti, Ujhartyan, Musov, Dobrodzien, Krikstonys;
18. Kazanski, 1988, p. 76; Kazanski-Mastykova, 2007, plate 3, 2, p. 14.
19. Kazanski, 1988, fig. 10, nn. 1, 14.
20. Kazanski, 1988, fig. 8, n. 1, 2; Milano Capitale, 1990, fig, 1f6A4.
21. Wilpert, 1916, plates 18; Hack, 1967, plate 138.
22. Piccirillo, Alliata, 1998, pp. 278–80, figs 23, 25, 28.
23. See my hypothesis in D'Amato, 2005, p. 46.
24. Wilcox, 1982, p. 20; Harrison, 1993, plate F and p. 53; Lebedinski, 2001, pp. 182–3.
25. Sommer,1984, pp. 95–6 and plate 56, 3; Bishop & Coulston, 2006, p. 216.
26. Kazanski, 1988, p. 77, figs 13,*1*, 14,*1*, 14,*5*, 13, 2–5.
27. DAI Rome photo archives, nn. 1937–581 and 1937–582.
28. Jorge, 2015, fig. 3 p. 45; Jorge, 2015b, fig. 13 p. 47.
29. Kiilerich, Torp, 1989, p. 321; Milano Capitale, 1990, cover and p. 78.
30. Kaus, 1996, p. 46, fig. 3.22.
31. Biscottini, Sena Chiesa, 2012, pp. 200–1, cat. 50, 52.
32. Ravegnani, 1989, fig. 5; Roma ed I Barbari, 2008, p. 352, cat. IVa (*solidi* of Justinian).
33. Goethert, 1996, pp. 115–26; Bishop & Coulston, 2006, p. 217.
34. Junkelmann, 1996, pp. 115ff.
35. Ibid., fig. 193.
36. This *deigmaton*, although in different colours, is visible many times on the *Notitia Dignitatum* Shields: s. for instance Barker, 1981, nn. xvii, cxxiv, cxl, clxii, clxx, clxxvi.
37. Junkelmann, 1996, figs 192–193.
38. Ibid., fig. 199.
39. See for instance Soupault, 1995, plates 4 n. 16; 5 nn. 1,11; 6 n. 5; 10 nn. 7,8.
40. Brogiolo, Chavarría Arnau, 2007, cat. 1.1.1 (Honorius Dyptich).
41. The shield 3 (the one with battlescenes) has been possible identified as a shield bearing the portrait of Florus, *Comes Aegipti* and *Praefectus Augustalis* of the Emperor Marcianus, see Junkelmann, 1996, pp. 124 and 126 n. 49.

42. Junkelmann, 1996, fig. 197.
43. Soupault, 1995, plate 4, 15.
44. Maspero, 1912, pp. 44, 50–2; Lloyd, 2010, p. 459.
45. Flinders Petrie, 1917, p. 38, plate XLII, 133.
46. The *Ala I Francorum* was stationed, according to the *Notitia*, at Contra Apollinopolis and the *Cohors I Francorum* at Diospolis (AD 425).
47. Goethert, 1996, p. 124; Sumner, 2003, p. 23; D'Amato, 2005, p. 35.
48. Carandini, Ricci, De Vos, 1982, figs 126, 130; Catullo, 2000, pp. 56–7.
49. Bianchi Bandinelli, 1970, p. 358 fig. 338; Hetherington, Forman, 1981, p. 62; Feugère, 2002, p. 194 fig. 256.
50. Racinet, 1888–2003, plates EC, 36–37, nr. 34.
51. Hottenroth, 1883, II, plate 25 nr. 3.
52. Newark, 1987, plate I.
53. Like those found on the Vermand shield and visible also in the Patera of Parabiago and anfora of Baratti, s. Milano Capitale, 1990, pp. 80–1, 184–5, cat. 1g.1d, 1g.1e.
54. Cascarino, Sansilvestri, 2009, p. 71.
55. Δρανδάκι & Ζιβα, 1997, fig. 296.
56. Nicolle, 1996, p. 67, fig. C.
57. D'Amato, 2009, pp. 37–8.
58. Δρανδάκι & Ζιβα, 1997, fig. 298.
59. Bianchi–Bandinelli, 1985, fig. 333.
60. Grabar, 1966, fig. 171.
61. Barker, 1981, p. 82; D'Amato, 2005, p. 45, plate C2; Künzl, 2008, p. 135 fig. 182.
62. Morillo, 2006, cover.
63. Barker, 1981, p. 83 figs 58, 107 fig. 60 nn. clxliv to cciii; Cascarino, Sansilvestri, 2009, p. 84 (Plate of Kertsch).
64. Di Dario, 2005, pp. 112–13, figs 11 and 11bis, 20 and 20bis; Künzl, 2008, p. 130.
65. Bishop & Coulston, 2006, p. 18; Brogiolo, Chavarría Arnau, 2007, p. 25; Cascarino, Sansilvestri, 2009, p. 142 fig. 5.35.
66. Pseudo-Modestus. De Voc. 9. 11 (*galea*, speaking of the Centurion's helmet); Pseudo–Modestus, 1523, p. 132 (*cassis*, speaking of the Centurion's helmet); Veget. I. 20 (*Galea*, helmet of the infantry; *gravis galea*, heavy helmet); I. 16, I. 20, II. 11, II. 13, II. 15. 4–6 (*cassis*, in general or referred to the infantry, and to the heavy infantrymen – *gravis armatura*); II. 13 (*cassis, galea*, both referred to the Centurion's helmet); II. 14. 3 (cassis, referring to the cavalry helmets); II. 16. 2 (*galea*, helmet of the *antesignani* and standard–bearers); III. 23 (*cassis*, helmets of infantrymen fighting against elephants); IV. 44 (*milites galeati*); Jul. Afr. Fragm. I. 1, 50–52 (*kranos* of the Roman infantry); *Cassis* and *Galea*, in Isid. Or. XVIII. 14. 1.
67. Bishop & Coulston, 2006, pp. 144ff. and fig. 113; Feugère, 1994, pp. 117–18; Cascarino, Sansilvestri, 2009, pp. 123ff.
68. For the place where it was found, see Künzl, 2008, p. 96 fig. 96; the Niederbieber specimen, in iron with bronze fittings, is 30.5cm tall.
69. It comprises the helmets and the fragments from Rainau-Buch, Niederbieber, Friedburg, Frankfurt-Hedderneim, Kalkar-Hönnepel, Amerongen, Donauwörth, Öhringen, Mainhardt, Bodegraven, Novae, Caerleon, Corbridge, Saalburg and those from unknown places, see Antike Helme, 1988, beilage 2 after p. 350 nn. 21–26, cat. 116 p. 533; Dyczek, 1992, p. 369 (early third century); Bishop. Coulston, 2006, p. 176 fig. 113; Junkelmann, 2000, p. 146 plate XVIII, cat. AG 543, p. 158; RR, 1975, pp. 90, 96–9, plates 258–268 and fig. 91; Stephenson, 1999, pp. 25ff., fig. 4, plates 7, 10, 12,13, 14; Kemkes, Scheuerbrand,Willburger, 2005, p. 85 fig. 76.
70. Such helmets are visible on various gravestones, like that of Iulius Aufidius, of the *Legio XVI Claudia* from Veria, or Marcus Aurelius Avitianus, of the *Legio I Adiutrix*, in Budapest; see Bishop, Coulston, 2006, pp. 173ff., p. 174 fig. 111; Coulston, 1990, p. 141 fig. 1; Cascarino,

Sansilvestri, 2009, p. 125 fig. 5.5.

71. RR,1975, p. 129, plates 376–377; Dixon, Southern, 1992, plate 26; Bishop, Coulston, 2006, p. 177 fig. 114 n. 4.

72. Visy, 2000, p. 15; he dated the relief around the second and third century; I would propose a later date for the relief, dated at the turn of the third–fourth century; but an early date is also possible, see Sumner, 1997, p. 33.

73. We should remember as the eagle was the legionary symbol of devotion to Jupiter.

74. RR, 1975, col. plates IV–V, figs. 130–132.

75. Sumner, 1997, p. 72; Stephenson, Dixon, 2001, p. 23; Cascarino, Sansilvestri, 2009, plate 1C.

76. RR, 1975, plates 378–380.

77. Giuliano, 1955, plate 37; Cowan 2015, p. 42.

78. Pautasso, 1984–1985, p. 56 fig. 1.

79. Abelterium, 2015, I/II, cover; fig. 3, p.55.

80. MacDowall, 1994, plates E, L, p. 58.

81. RR, 1975, pp. 130–1, plates 384–386 (Worthing); plates 391–396, pp. 132–3 (Guisborough, Chalon-sur-Saône); D'Amato, 2009, p. 185 (Alba Julia); Feugère, 1990, pp. 112–13, fig. 97 (Catate Razboieni–Alba Julia, Chalon-sur-Saône).

82. Giuliano, 1955, plates 36, 38–39, 59.

83. Lyne, 1994, fig. 1; reconstruction in D'Amato, 2005, plate A2; Lyne, 1994, fig. 2.

84. Racinet, who copied the upper bronze part of the standard of his cavalry *vexillarius* and the helmet from two originals at that time preserved in Madrid and Paris, said that 'during the Late Empire, the bronze helmet with horse-hairs continued the shape of the Greek helmet'.

85. It is the same clothing and armour worn by Euryale and Nisus consulting with the Trojans in the *fol. 73v* of the *Virgilius Vaticanus*, cod. Vat. Lat. 3225; s. Biblioteca Apostolica Vaticana, 1980, p. 70; the only difference is that the shoes (*campagi raeticulati*) here are white with red strings, while in the reconstruction of Racinet and Hottenroth are yellow with red strings.

86. Hottenroth, 1883, I, plate 64 n. 18.

87. Flinders Petrie, 1927, plate IV, nr. 32; reconstruction in D'Amato, 2005, plate C3.

88. James, 1986, p. 128; Lusuardi Siena, Perassi, Facchinetti, Bianchi, 2002, pp. 22, 37.

89. James, 1986, pp. 111–12; Bishop, Coulston, 2006, p. 210; Connolly, 2006, p. 260.

90. James, 1986, pp. 131ff.

91. Lusuardi Siena, Perassi, Facchinetti, Bianchi, 2002, p. 50 and plate VII, nr. 2, 3 and 5 to 10; Negin, 2007, fig. 2 nr. 2–7; fig. 3 nr. 2–3.

92. Klumbach, 1973, p. 97; Negin, 2010b, plate XIV, 1–2.

93. Wieczorek, Perin, Welck, Menghin, 1996, fig. 5, p. 828, where the helmet is dated to AD 400 and it is considered belonging to the elite troops of the *Dux Mogontiacensis* or to the *Praefectus Militum Secundae Flaviae*, due to traces of silvering on the surface of the bowl.

94. Southern, Dixon, 1996, plates 1–2; James, 1986, fig. 1 n. 2; Klumbach, 1973, pp. 111ff., plates 59–60.

95. Idem, 1973, pp. 103ff, plates 45–57; Thomas, 1971, pp. 13–19; James, 1986, fig. 1 nn. 3–6; Bishop, Coulston, 1993, p. 169, fig. 122 nn. 1–2.

96. Klumbach, 1973, pp. 95–101, plates 38–44; Southern-Dixon, 1996, plate 3; helmet 1 is of iron, covered by a sheath of gilded silver 0.1–0.3mm thick and 24cm long (only the bowl) and 14.8cm tall. Like the usual helmets of this type it is composed of two iron halves iron, linked through the metal crest. Between the iron parts and the silver sheath a black mastic was inserted (probably pitch or resin). This material also filled (internally) the punched ornaments. The iron crest was about 1mm thick, its peak is 2.2cm in height and it extended to the front and other back for 0.8cm. The frontal corner of the crest runs scutched, probably to the point at which the nose protection was inserted. The back side of the crest

was rectangular. The decorations of the crest sheath are positioned at intervals of 6–7cm The ridge of the crest is decorated with silver globes, 2–2.5cm apart. They have an oval shape and 1–1.3mm thick. The holes on the edges were decorated with small *s*; they were used to sewn the leather lining, as well as the fittings for the neck, nose and cheek-guards; the rear sideand the neck protection was about 13cm long, of which 9.7 x 11.1cm still survives. It is straight for 3cm, then bends. The two central holes of the upper border are 2.5cm apart. They were used for the fastening of the leather lining, which was probably allocated on the upper part. Two silver nails are co-located 6cm from the right side. The leather lining, which surrounded the whole bowl, was also fastened to them. The decoration is placed at these distances: 0.9–1cm. wide band inside, contoured by punched pearls. Other pearled bands run inside, at intervals of 1–1.5cm. The nose guard was directly attached to the bowl; two conical nails are still visible on it; the surviving lower part measures 8.3 x 2.7 x 0.6cm. Also it was backed from leather. The cheek-guards and the neck protection were fastened to the bowl by means of leather laces.

97. Klumbach, 1973, plate 42, 1; Wilhelmi, 1992, p. 5; Travis, 2014, fig. 58.
98. Southern, Dixon, 1996, p. 92, fig. 10; Negin, 2007, p. 351 n. 4; Negin, 2010b, plate XIII, n. 3.
99. Colt Hoare, 1829, p. 53; the God Mars is represented wearing a Intercisa-style helmet and his spear in his hand; for illustration s. Witts, 2007, p. 3; Duthy, 1839, pp. 32–3; the silver colour, the fake apotropaic eyes and the iron crest of the helmet are clearly visible.
100. Veget. II. 16: '… *galeas ferreas, sed transversis et argentatis cristis, ut celerius agnoscerentur a suis* … ' i.e. 'iron helmets, but fitted with silvered and transversal crests, that they might be more easily distinguished by their men …' .
101. The name of the dead is recorded in the *tabula inscriptionis* painted over the grave: '*D(is) M(anibus). Fl(avius) Maximianus, de n(umero) Ma … a …s vi(xit) an(nos) XXI. Carinus frater pientissimus fecit*' i.e. 'To the shades of the departed. Fl. Maximianus, of the Numerus of Ma … a … s (?), lived 21 years. The brother Carinus with great pity made it'. The symbols painted (crosses painted around him and on the *Tabula Inscriptionis*, peacocks, grape–vine and vine branches) reveals his Christian faith, notwithstanding the inscription *Dis Manibus*. For the employment of the formulary DM also by the Christians. Ahlqvist, 1995, p. 221 n. 649.
102. See Ahlqvist, 1995, plate 50; Bishop, Coulston, 1993, plate 7b, pp. 128–9; arcosolio 1, grave 1; the fresco is actually in very bad conditions of preservation; I should thank the Dr.ssa Maria Rita Sgarlata, Inspector of the *Commissione di Archeologia Sacra* at Siracusa and her assistant, the Dr.ssa Tatiana Bommara, without whose help I could not have had the chance to see it and publish the photos in this book.
103. The helmet came from the former collection of Axel Guttman; unfortunately only half of it is preserved, in iron with gilded copper overlay, still preserving the peaked crest decorated with shallow edges. The rim is pierced for the lining attachment, and the bowl is 22.2 cm. tall. See also Christie's, 2004, p. 159 cat. 163.
104. Bishop, Coulston, 1993, plate 7a, soldier from the *Catacombae* of Via Latina.
105. Bishop, Coulston, 2006, p. 211 n. 2.
106. Bishop, Coulston, 2006, p. 209 fig. 133, 2; Negin, 2010b, fig. 6.
107. Lusuardi Siena, Perassi, Facchinetti, Bianchi, 2002, p. 51 nn. 1, 2, 3, 4, 6; Negin, 2010b, plate XIV, nn. 3, 4, 5, 6, 7; plate XV, nn. 1, 2, 3, 4.
108. For example in Berkasovo I, Deurne and Concesti, see Bishop, Coulston, 2006, p. 212 fig. 4; MacDowall, 1995, p. 47 and plate F1.
109. Klumbach, 1973, plates 1–5; Demant, Egemann, 2007, p. 150 cat. 1.12.18; Biscottini, Sena Chiesa, 2012, p. 235 cat. 124.
110. Klumbach, 1973, p. 37.
111. Klumbach, 1973, p. 17.18; Bishop & Coulston, 2006, p. 212, n. 4.
112. James, 1986, p. 111, fig. 4; Dautova Ruševljan, Vujović, 2011, plate 1; Travis, 2012, fig. 59.
113. James, 1986, p. 110, fig. 3 n. 1; Negin, 2007, p. 350, fig. 1 n. 6 (coin of Constantine I).

114. MacDowall, 1994, p. 13.
115. Klumbach, 1973, plates 6–9; Negin, 2010b, plate XIV, n. 5.
116. Dautova Ruševljan, Vujović, 2011, p. 97.
117. Klumbach, 1973, plates 12–18.
118. Klumbach, 1973, plates 19–21 (Deurne) and 30–31 (San Giorgio of Nogara).
119. Klumbach, 1973, plates 32–37; Negin, 2010b, plate XV, 3.
120. Negin, 2007, pp. 336, 339 and 359 fig. 12.
121. Lusuardi Siena, Perassi, Facchinetti, Bianchi, 2002, plate VI, 2.
122. Klumbach, 1973, pp. 11–12; Lusuardi Siena, Perassi, Facchinetti, Bianchi, 2002, p.57.
123. Lusuardi Siena, Perassi, Facchinetti, Bianchi, 2002, p. 58.
124. Negin, 2007, fig. 5 n. 2; Negin, 2010b, plate XV, 1.
125. Donati, Gentili, 2005, p. 236; Negin, 2010b, fig. 5, n. 7; Biscottini, Sena Chiesa, 2012, p. 238, cat. 131.
126. Demandt, Engemann, 2007, p. 154 cat. 1. 13. 124 (München); Negin, 2010b, fig. 8 nn. 1 (Alsoheteny); 2, 4 (Sisak); 3 (Savaria), 5 – Private Collection; fig. 9 n. 2, system of application of the Chi–Ro to the crest of the helmet; Demandt-Engemann,2007, p. 154 cat. 1.13.124 (München).
127. Donati, Gentili, 2005, p. 235 cat, 49a–b.
128. Euseb. Vit. Const. I. 31. 1; IV. 9; Prudent. Contra Symm. I. 489; Lact. De mort. pers. 44. 5; the sources also mention plumed crests and gems on the Emperor's helmet.
129. Demandt, Engemann, 2007, p. 206, cat. 1. 13. 220; Tiussi, Villa, Novello, 2013, p. 30 n. 3.
130. Donati, Gentili, 2005, p. 235 cat, 48.
131. Volbach, 1952, cat. 48; Grabar, 1980, p. 280, fig. 321; Panella, 2011, p. 52.
132. Biscottini, Sena Chiesa, 2012, p. 149 cat. 49 (Constantine I); Lusuardi Siena, Perassi, Facchinetti, Bianchi, 2002, p. 35, nn. 10, 11, 12 (Constans II and Justinian I); Panella, 2011, p. 99, n. 100 (Theodosius II).
133. Lusuardi, Perassi, Facchinetti, Bianchi, 2002, p. 21, plate II, p. 25.
134. Pan. VI. 6. 2; Lusuardi, Perassi, Facchinetti, Bianchi, 2002, p. 32; Tiussi, Villa, Novello, 2013, p. 30 and fig. 4.
135. Pan. X. 29. 5: '*fulget nobilis galea et corusca luce gemmarum divinum verticem monstrat*'.
136. Especially the famous one minted in AD 315 from the Ticinum Mint; s. Lusuardi Siena, Perassi, Facchinetti, Bianchi, 2002, plate III, 7 and p. 56; Bishop, Coulston, 2006, p. 213, fig. 136; the attribution to the Ticinum Mint has been proposed by Alföldi.
137. Biscottini, Sena Chiesa, 2012, p. 270, cat. 199.
138. Alfoldi, 1932, p.19 n. 1; Lusuardi Siena, Perassi, Facchinetti, Bianchi, 2002, plate III, 8 and p. 56; Negin, 2007.
139. Amm. Marc. XXVII. 10–11; Lusuardi, Perassi, Facchinetti, Bianchi, 2002, p. 33; Dautova Ruševljan, Vujović, 2011, p. 97.
140. Bastien, 1992–1994, III, plate 205 n. 2.
141. *De Consulatu Stilichonis* II. 90.
142. Isid. Or. XVI. 9. 3.
143. Alföldi, 1932.
144. Eutr. IX. 25; IX. 27.
145. Bastien, 1992–1994, pp. 201, 204–6; Lusuardi, Perassi, Facchinetti, Bianchi, 2002, plate 3 nn. 1–6; it is not true what later authors said about the non-existence of the Attic or Corinthian types at the time of the production of the coins; they existed in the form of pseudo-Attic and pseudo-Corinthian, and it is in fact the type which is represented gemmed and decorated with precious stones, or embossed and decorated by a laurel wreath on the heads of the Emperors from Gallienus and Postumus up to Constantine.
146. See the pseudo-Corinthian and pseudo-Attic helmets of Crispus, in Bastien, 1982, nn. 42, 51, 52, 60; but in the mint of Lyon Crispus is covered by a ridge-helmet crown of Persian type, and this is not a mistake, as suggested by Lusuardi, Perassi, Facchinetti, Bianchi,

2002, p. 37 n. 65; simply Faustus wore also such helmet as well, and to the Gallic provinces he wanted to show himself as the new Augustus. Anyway the pseudo-Attic helmet can be seen on Constantine's head on coins minted up until AD 326; Bastien, 1992–1994, I, pp. 147, 216.

147. Lusuardi, Perassi, Facchinetti, Bianchi, 2002, plate 3 nn. 10 and 11.

148. Kraft, 1978, pp. 137–14; Bastien, 1992–1994, I, p. 210; Lusuardi, Perassi, Facchinetti, Bianchi, 2002, pp. 37–40.

149. Lusuardi, Perassi, Facchinetti, Bianchi, 2002, pp. 21, 24.

150. Ibid., plate III, 12.

151. James, 1986, p. 133, n. 61; Feugère, 1994, p. 151; Lusuardi, Perassi, Facchinetti, Bianchi, 2002, p. 53.

152. Lipinsky, 1975, pp. 231–5; Hughes & others,1989, p. 28; Lusuardi, Perassi, Facchinetti, Bianchi, 2002, p. 53 n. 3.

153. Braat, 1973, pp. 56–7 (Deurne Helmet); Klumbach, 1973, p. 87 (Berkasovo I); Skalon, 1973, p. 92 (Concesti).

154. Cor. Ioh. IV. 561: '… high helmets shining for crests and spikes …'; Anon. De Re Strat. XVI; Ravegnani, 1988, p. 47.

155. Werner, 1989, p. 426; Vogt, 2006, p. 10; Bavant has demonstrated that main four arma factories identified by M. Vogt are from the territories of the Eastern Roman Empire. Three of them could have been located in Constantinople or in area around the Sea of Marmara, in Nicomedia or Cyzicus. As for the fourth '*fabrica*', the western group of M. Vogt, B. Bavant has suggested locating it in Thessaloniki. The author explains the stability of the Baldenheim type by the centralised control of production exercised by the *comes sacrarum largitionum* (see Bavant 2008, 327ss); we know from the Theodosian Code (X. 22. 1) that the bronzing, silvering and gilding of the *Cassides* and *bucculae* (helmets and cheeckpiece) was reserved for the *Fabricae* of Antioch and Constantinople. The constitution (of AD 374, Valentinian I, Valens and Gratianus) allows us also to know the number of helmets and check–pieces that were produced each year there: eight bronze-coated helmets and eight cheek-pieces in both the workshops; eight gilded and silvered helmets and eight cheek-pieces in the Antioch *fabrica*; three gilded and silvered helmets and three cheek-pieces in the Constantinople *fabrica*.

156. For a nearly complete list and illustration of the different types of *Spangen-helme*, see Vogt, 2006 and Böhner, 1994, pp. 471–2; the *Spangen-helme* pertinent to the Roman military context are those from the Danube (ibid., figs. 23b, 24–25), Dolnie Semerovce (figs 26–27), Batajniza (fig. 29), Salona (fig. 30), Sinj (fig. 31), St. Vid (figs 32), Novae (see Widawnictwa Uniwersytetu Warszawskiego, 1993, p. 136, plate XXV nr. 136), Caricin Grad (see Bavant-Ivanisevic, 2003, kat. 40–41), Heraclea Lyncestis (Böhner, 1994 fig. 33; Werner, 1989, pp. 424–5); a Byzantine origin is also ascribed to the helmets of Torricella Peligna (Böhner fig. 22), Krefeld Gellep (figs 1–3), Morken (figs 4–5), Vézeronce (fig. 20), Planig (figs 8–10) and Leptis Magna (fig. 34); also the for *spangen-helme* coming from the Saône River (see Bailly, 1990, p. 120, figs 124–126), although used by Burgundian warriors, were probably an artwork of some Eastern Roman workshop.

157. James, 1986, p. 113; Vogt, 2006, pp. 18, 24ff.

158. Vogt, 2006, p. 182ss.; Glad, 2012, p. 356.

159. Werner, 1989, p. 427 (Torricella Peligna); Bailly, 1990, p. 141 (Saône-Allerey), fig. 126 (Saône-Saint Bernard, today in the Metropolitan Museum).

160. Werner, 1989, p. 421 (Krefeld-Gellep); Bailly, 1990, pp. 141ff, fig. 124 (Saône-La Truchère), fig. 125 (Saint Petersburg helmet, originally from Saône).

161. Bailly, 1990, fig. 123 cat. 186.

162. Like the helmets of Caricin Grad (figs 312–313).

163. Bailly, 1990, fig. 124, helmet from Saône-La Truchère (fig. 297); the impressive decoration of this band shows not Germanic, but Eastern Roman soldiers hunting, clad in a uniform

that corresponds to the iconography of the sixth century mosaics from Mount Nebo and Antiochia: an archer horseman armed with a composite bow; a foot hunter with a winged spear, dressed in a knee-length tunic, Phrygian cap and floating mantel; a second horseman using his spear against a lion; and a third cavalryman holding an early specimen of military flag or *bandon*. Other cavalrymen and infantrymen are represented hunting lions on the lower part of the band, and one of the cavalryman is even holding a *flammoulon* (i.e. a *bandon* with pennons) in his hand. The iconography embossed on the helmet shows as it could have only been produced in a Eastern workshop, and maybe it was originally destined for a Roman officer. We cannot today know how the helmet arrived in the Burgundy territory, i.e. as war booty, a purchase or as a gift.

164. Holmquist Olausson, 2007, p. 235.
165. Vogt, 2006, pp. 112–18.
166. Ibid., pp. 118–34.
167. The decoration of the birds with the tree of the life reminded the warrior his heavenly reward after death (see Vogt 2006, p. 134ss.; Holmquist Olausson 2007, 236).
168. Robinson 1975, p. 137, plates 413–414; D'Amato 2009, pp. 182–3, 185.
169. Werner, 1989, p. 423; Böhner, 1994, pp. 511, 515, 517, 519, 523.
170. Like in the Vezéronce specimen (see Musée du Louvre, 1992, cat. 74).
171. Like in the silver and gold-plated iron Dolné Semerovce specimen (see Dekan, 1981, plate 2).
172. Bihalji-Merin, 1974, plates 156–157; Burns, 1984, p. 158.
173. Vogt, 2006, pp. 78ff.
174. Amm. Marc. XXIV. 2.
175. Claud. Carm. Min. 1.1; Fesc. XIII.1.
176. Claud. Eutr. II.106; Amm.Marc. XVI. 12. 54.
177. Amm. Marc. XXIV. 6; Veg. II. 13. 4 and 16. 3; Lusuardi, Perassi, Facchinetti, Bianchi, 2002, p. 28.
178. Anth. Pal. IX. 322; DAGR (Daremberg-Saglio), s.v. *Galea*, vol. II. 2, col. 1434.
179. Isid. Or. XVIII.14. 2: *curvatura quae in galea prominet, super quam cristae sunt*; *conus* is also used by Claudianus (VII, 523).
180. Claud. Rapt. Pros. III. 216.
181. For the word *toupha* see also Lydus. De Mag. I. 8. which indicates this word like the Germanic counterpart of the Latin *iouba* and of the Greek λοφία; see also Lusuardi Siena, 1998, p. 23.
182. Cor. Ioh. IV. 480, 534; Ravegnani, 1988, p. 47; further descriptions of *Excubitores* in Corippus (Cor. In laud. Just. III. 168, 239, 241–242;) and Lydus (De Mag. I. 12) evidence bronze helmets (*cassides*) with red plumes, gold javelins (*pila*), axes (*secures*), round shields (*clipei*), and red *cothurni* as boots.
183. Veget. II. 13. 4; 16. 3.
184. Paneg. for the sixth Consulate. XVIII. 575–576 (see description on plates 17–19).
185. Cor. Ioh. IV. 495; s. also the Cavalryman of Isola Rizza, in Cascarino, 2012, p. 196.
186. Lusuardi, Perassi, Facchinetti, Bianchi, 2002, pp. 29–30.
187. Cor. Ioh. IV. 459–460.
188. Syvanne, 2015, fig. 2.
189. Coussin, 1926, plate VI, n. 32; Barker, 1981, p. 66 fig. 9, p. 77 fig. 46.
190. Hottenroth, 1888, I, plate 46 n. 15.
191. Visy, 2000, p. 15; but on the date see my personal opinion in note 72, *supra*.
192. Stephenson, 2006, p. 21, n. 12.
193. See the reconstructions of the German archaeologists in Freeden, Schnurbein, 2002, fig. 541; Forestier, 1928, p. 131; see also the sarcophagus of a Tetrarchic officer from Sid (fig. 319), in Dautova Ruševljan, Vujović, 2011, p. 99.
194. Giuliano, 1955, plates 37–38 (*Cornuti Seniores*).

195. Hartley, Hawkes, Henig, Mee, 2006, pp. 53–4, 57, 116, 122, 126, 141, 143 (Constantius Chlorus and Constantine); Ilkić, Čelhar, 2007, pp. 336–8, fig. 2 (Constantine II).

196. Giglioli, 1952, fig.7 (original fragments), 24–49 (Freshfield drawings of Renaissance); Mendel, 1914–1966, cat. 660 (346), vol. II, p. 442.

197. D'Amato, 2009, p. 137; Nicolle, 2002, p. 180.

198. Shadrake, 1994, p. 28; Shadrake, 1997, pp. 34–5; Travis & Travis, 2012, cap. V.

199. See for instance the aforementioned officer represented on his sarcophagus from Sid (fig. 319), where the typical baldric of the early fourth century and the round tab of a late sword Roman belt are clearly visible, illustrating the decoration of semi-precious stones or glass paste that we know from some representations of Late Roman swords or from the swords themselves, see Pop-Lazić, 2008, pp. 168–9 figs. 7, 8; or the scene of the conquest of Verona, on the Arch of Constantine, where pseudo-Attic helmets and muscled armour are represented beside Intercisa and Hedderneim helmets, see Negin, 2010b, fig. 2.

200. Pavia, 1999, p. 223.

201. Wilpert, 1916, plates 19, 23, 24, 26.

202. Hottenroth, 1888, I, plate 54 nn. 18–21; idem, II, plate 25, n. 3; Racinet, 1888–2003, plate EC, pp. 36–7, nr. 34.

203. Giglioli, 1952, fig, 54 (Probus Dyptich, Emperor Honorius); a small bronze head of the Gorgon was preserved in the collection of Axel Guttmann, see Christie's 2002 p. 129; another one has been recovered in Zeugma, see Başgelen, Ergeç, 2000, p. 24.

204. Hartley, Hawkes, Henig, Mee, 2006, p. 139; Stephenson, 2009, fig. 53 (the author suggests that the boy represented on the chariot with Constantine and Fausta is Constantius II and not Crispus); Bardill, 2012, pp. 170–1, fig. 107.

205. Petculescu, 2003, cat. 329 (specimen from Gherla).

206. Brogiolo, Chavarría Arnau, 2007, p. 46 cat. 1. 1. 1.

207. Villa, 2002, p. 165 plate I n. 12 (boss shaped like a lion head, probably boss of a breastplate); see reconstruction in D'Amato, 2012, plate H3 and p. 47.

208. Kemkes, Scheuerbrand, Willburger, 2005, p. 105, fig. n. 109, from Stuttgart Bad-Cannstatt.

209. DAGR (Daremberg-Saglio), 1877–1919, vol. III, 2, col. 1312–1313, sub voce *Lorica*; D'Amato, 2009, pp. 39, 51, 123, 135, 142, 145, 226, 246, 248, 250.

210. Humer, 2004, figs. 122–123, specimens from late second–early third century AD.

211. Humer, 2004, cat. 41, fig. 122.

212. Christie's, 2004, fig. 163.

213. Compare for instance with the mosaic of the seasons from Argos, s. D'Amato, 2005, p. 45 and plate B3; McDowall, 2001, p. 77.

214. Nicolle, 1992, p. 22.

215. I would like also recall the comparison of the Guttman specimen with the muscled armours represented on the mosaic from Abelterium (extra fig. 3), one of which is in polished bronze; with the armour represented on the altar of the Church of Prutting (fig. 315); with the many armours represented on the base of the Column of Arcadius, both represented in the iron and leather variant (fig. 277).

216. Hartley, Hawkes, Henig, Mee, 2006, p. 3.

217. Valentinian I according other authors, see Grabar, 1971, pp. 16–17; Nicolle, 1992, p. 9.

218. Stephenson, 2006, p. 95 (Diptych of Probus representing the Emperor Honorius); see also Kunzl, 2008, p. 133.

219. Panella, 2011, p. 107 (Constantius II); 109 (Constantine I).

220. Evangelatou, Papastavrou, Skotti, 2001, pp. 22–3, fig. 3–4.

221. *De Consulatu Stylichonis*. II. 90.

222. Hartley, Hawkes, Henig, Mee, 2006, p. 43; here in the Tetrarchic monument in Venice the *cinctorium* is a leather belt with fitted metal elements, fastened on the armour breast, like the model already seen for Favonius Facilis in classical age; see also Humer, 2004, cat. nn. 41–42, p. 130.

223. Amm. Marc. XXV. 3. 3 (Julian is *oblitus loricae* i.e. he forgot his cuirass); Zonaras (XIII. 13. 17) says that Julian had taken off his cuirass (θώραξ) because of its weight, and because of the heat; Charles, 2015, p. 143.

224. I.e. the responsible of the Imperial *Fabrica* (workshop) producing armours; see Rocco, 2012, p. 561.

225. Amm. Marc. XXVII. 7. 4; XXX. 6. 3 and XXX. 8. 2.

226. Amm. Marc. XXIV. 3. 4.

227. *Politus* in late antique Latin means pure, *purus*, without decorations, see Du Cange et al, 1883–1887, t. 6, col. 396c.; Drijvers & Hunt, 1999, p. 29; see also in figurative meaning Amm.Marc. XXIII. 5.

228. The description corresponds also to the images of Valentinian I on the coins: see King, 1987, p. 151 n. 58a; Plant, 2006b, p. 78; Plant, 2006a, p. 69.

229. Robinson, 1975, p. 147.

230. Gamber, 1966, pp. 269ff, plate L, LIV and LVII.

231. Ravegnani, 1988, plates 1–2; probably Justinian and Belisarius, although other identifications are also possible.

232. Bavant, Ivanisevic, 2003, kat. 3.

233. Ravegnani, 1988, p. 46 n. 40.

234. Dixon, Southern, 1996, jacket illustration; Bianchi, Munzi, 2006, p. 298, fig.1; Facchinetti, 2003, figs 5–6 p. 756.

235. Klawans, 1959, p. 92; Plant, 2006a, p. 63 n. CRB48; Ilkić, Čelhar, 2007, pp. 336–8 fig. 2.

236. Pavia, 1999, p. 139; see also Plant, 2006a, p. 68, n.CRB544; the coin shows the emperor with the diadem helmet and the shield, armed with a spear.

237. Sid. Carmina. II, 142–143: '… with the weight of the long spear (*contus*) dressing the steel chain armour … '.

238. *De Quartu Consulatu Hon.*, 523–524 *'quis decor, incedis quotiens clipeatus et auro squameus et rutilus cristis et casside maior'*; Charles, 2015, p. 144; the scale armour of Honorius is visible in coins minted by the Mint of Constantinople, see Diegi, 2010, p. 14 photo 14.

239. Sid. Carmina. V. 221–224: '… Time after time his helmet rang with blows, and his cuirass with its protecting scales kept off the thrust of spears, until the enemy was forced to turn and flee …'

240. Sid. Carmina. VII. 242–243: '… Wearing his scale–armour, his face still bearing the mark of the burnished helmet, scarce had he brought home his stained arms from the field when there came fresh wars and a battle this time under the very walls of his own city, stirred up by a faithless foe …'

241. Klawans, 1959, p. 99 (coins of Anthemius and Majorian).

242. Mendel, 1914–1966, cat. 653 (1094), vol. II p. 424; MacDowall, 2001, p. 89.

243. Horvat, 2002, p. 147; Kos, 2014, fig. 252.

244. Cor. Ioh. IV. 493–495; 535–536; Ravegnani, 1988, 44–47.

245. Wilpert, 1916, plates 20, 27.

246. Wilpert, 1916, pp. 473ff, age of the Pope Sixtus III.

247. Wilpert, 1916, plates 8, 13, 18–20, 23–28.

248. Sid. Carmina. VII. 260–266.

249. Hartley, Hawkes, Henig, Mee, 2006, p. 133, cat. 63.

250. Units of heavy armoured cavalry multiplied in the Late Empire and were known as both *Clibanarii* and *Cataphractarii* or *Cataphracti*. The terms could be used almost interchangeably, the term *cataphractarius* just meaning only 'armoured' and the term *clibanarius* coming from the military 'slang' with reference to the metallic body of a stove. In the later empire perhaps the word *clibanarius* meant the completely armoured cavalryman. See Baur, Rostovtzeff, 1933, p. 218 n. 16 and pp. 271ff; the technical term *ippeus kataphraktarios* was still widely employed in Egypt in the fourth century AD.

251. Charles, 2015, p.147; their main weapon, the heavy *contus* is described by Servius as a long

spear with short iron point (Serv. In eclogas. VII. 664). It is well represented in the Dura Europos graffiti and frescoes (Baur, Rostovtzeff, 1933, p. 185) where it is adorned with ribbons.

252. The most important and known world-wide from the tower 17 of Dura, see Baur, Rostovtzeff, 1933, p. 216 and. plate XXII, 2.

253. Pan. IV. 22: Amm. Marc. XVI. 10. 8ff. (description of the triumph of Constantius II with his *Clibanarii*); Jul. Or. in Constantii laudem I. 37ff.

254. Claud. De Sesto Consulatu. 570–575.

255. Amm. Marc. XXV. 1, 12–13; XVI.10. 8.

256. Amm. Marc. XVI. 10. 8: '… *Equites cataphracti*, the so-called *Clibanarii* from the Persians, protected by armoured coverings and tightened in belts of steel, that you could reckon statues chiseled by the hand of Praxiteles, not men; thin circular plates fitted to the curves of the body covered entirely their limbs in so cunningly an articulated way that it adapted itself to any movement the wearer needed to make …'

257. A fragment of such column, showing a clash between Roman and Goths heavy cavalry equipped like the Roman Imperial Guardsmen, is still preserved in the Archaeological Museum of Istanbul, see Mendel, 1914–1966, vol. III, 1315–1316 (2705); unfortunately the museum is closed for restoration and it was not possible to take a picture of it.

258. Wilhelmi, 1992, p.10.

259. Jul. Or. in Constantii laudem I. 37ff.: '… Your cavalry was almost unlimited in numbers and they all sat on their horses like statues, while their limbs were fitted with armour that followed closely the human shape. It covers the arms from wrist to elbow and thence to the shoulder, while a plated armour [θωραξ εκ τμηματων] protect the breast, the back and the shoulders. The head and face are covered by a metal helmet forming a unit with a mask (κρανος αυτω πρωσωπω), which makes its wearer look like a glittering statue, for not even the thighs and legs and the very ends of the feet lack this armour. It is attached to the cuirass by fine chain–armour like a web, so that no part of the body is visible and uncovered, for this woven covering protects the hands as well, and is so flexible that the wearers cab bend even their fingers …'.

260. See reconstruction in D'Amato, 2007, plate 3.

261. Nikonorov, 1997, p. 59.

262. For iconographic evidence of a complete horse protection see MacDowall, 2001, p. 69; Cristina, Lechilli, 2015, figs 4, 7; the covered horses of the Pompeianus Bathrooms, here represented, echoed the covered horses of the Imperial Guardsmen of Theodosius in the Freshfield drawings of the Arcadius Column, see Giglioli, 1952, figs 28, 29, 33, 36, 37, 38, 41; some of them are also covered with scale armours like the Dura Europos suites.

263. An. Peri Strat. 17.

264. Eadie, 1967, p. 169; MacDowell, 1995, p. 18; Schuckelt, 2015, fig. 5.

265. Veget. II. 15.

266. Nicolle, 1996, p. 21.

267. Stephenson, 2001, p. 111.

268. Junkelmann, 1992, fig. 2.

269. Petculescu, 2003, cat. 335.

270. Pinterovic, 1978, plate VII, 1.

271. Schuckelt, 2015, cat. 40.

272. Stepehsnson, 2001, pp. 115ff; James, 2004, pp. 129–34, plate 13.

273. Justin. XLI. 2. 10.

Bibliography

ABBREVIATIONS USED

AJA	*American Journal of Archaeology*
ARA	*Association for Roman Archaeology*
JdI	*Jahrbuch Deutschen Archaeologischen Instituts*
JRMES	*Journal of Roman Military Equipment Studies*
JRS	*Journal of Roman Studies*
MEFRA	*Mélanges de l'École française de Rome*
Op.Rom	*Opuscola Romana*
ParPass	*La parola del passato*
PBF	*Prähistorische Bronzefunde*
RR	Russell Robinson 1975
VAMZ	*Vjesnik Arheološkog muzeja u Zagrebu*

PRIMARY SOURCES

Amm. Marc. – Ammianus Marcellinus, *The Histories - Res Gestae*, Latin text and English translation by J. C. Rolfe, 3 vols., Loeb Classical Library, London, 1939–50.

An. peri strat. – 'The Anonymous Byzantine Treatise on strategy, Peri Strategias', in G. T. Dennis (ed.), *Three Byzantine Military Treatises*, CFHB, Washington, 1985.

Anth. Pal. – *The Greek Anthology*, with an English translation by W. R. Paton, Vol. 3, London, 1915.

App. Lib.; Mithr.; Pun. – Appianus, *Appiani Historia Romana* ed. P. Viereck et A.G. Roos. Editio stereotypa correctior addenda et corrigenda adiecit E. Gabba. Vols 1–2, Teubner, Leipzig, 1962.

Aristot. Hist. Anim. – Aristotle, *Historia Animalium*, Vol. I, Books I–X, ed. by D. M. Balme, Cambridge, 2011.

Arr. An. – Arrianus, Flavius, *Arriani De expeditione Alexandri libri septem*, rec. R. Geier, Teubner, Leipzig, 1873.

Arr. Tact. – Arrianus, Flavius, *Scripta minora*, ed. R. Hercher et A. Ehehard, Teubner, Leipzig, 1887.

Aul.Gell. – Aulus Gellius, *Attic Nights*, Vol. II, Books 6–13, Loeb Classical Library, London, 1927.

Aur. Vict. Caes.; De vir. ill. – *Sexti Aurelii Victoris Liber de Caesaribus; praecedunt Origo gentis Romanae et Liber de viris illustribus urbis Romae; subsequitur Epitome de Caesaribus*, recensuit

Franciscus Pichlmayr, Teubner, Leipzig, 1911.

BGU – Berliher griechische Urkunden, *Aegyptische Urkunden aus den königlichen Museen zu Berlin*, Bd. 1–9, Berlin, 1892–1937.

Caes. BAfr. – C. Iulii Caesaris, *Commentarii rerum gestarum*, ed. O. Seel. Vol. III. P. I: de bello Alexandriano, de bello Africano, Rec. E. Woelfflin, Teubner, Leipzig, 1896.

Cic. De Divin.– Cicero M.T., *On Divination – De Divinatione (Divin.); On Old Age – On Friendship – On Divination*, Loeb Classical Library, Harvard University Press, Cambridge, MA, 1923.

Cic. De Natura Deor. – Cicero, M.T., *On the Nature of the Gods – De Natura Deorum (De Nat.); On the Nature of the Gods – Academics*, Loeb Classical Library, Harvard University Press, Cambridge, MA, 1933.

CIL. – 'Corpus inscriptionum Latinarum'. in A. Degrassi (Hrsg.), *Corpus inscriptionum Latinarum*, Berlin, 1863 – ...; N. S.: 1981 – ...

Claud. – *Claudian,* ed. G. P. Goold , 2 Vols., Loeb Classical Library, Cambridge-London, 1922 (1990).

Cod. Th. – *Codex Theodosianus*, Latin text in *Theodosiani libri XVI cum constitutionibus Sirmondianis*, ed. Th. Mommsen, P.M. Meyer and P. Krueger, 1–2, Berlin, 1954–62.

Cor. Ioh. – Flavii Cresconii Corippi, *Iohannidos seu De Bellis Libycis, Libri VIII*, ed. by I. Diggle and F. R. D., Goodyear, Cambridge, 1970.

Cor. In Laud Just. – Flavius Cresconius Corippus. *In laudem Iustini Augusti minoris* (in praise of Justin II), ed. A. Cameron, London, 1976.

DAGR (Daremberg, Saglio) – Ch. Daremberg and E. Saglio, *Dictionnaire des antiquités grecques et romaines*, Paris, 1877–1919.

Dio Cass. – *Dio's Roman History. In 9 volumes with an English translation by E. Cary. On the basis of the version of Herbert Baldwin Foster*, Heinemann, London, 1914–27.

Diod. – Diodorus Siculus, *Bibliotheca historica*, ed. primam curavit Imm. Bekker, alteram L. Dindorf. Rec. F. Vogel, Vols I–V, Teubner, Leipzig, 1883–1906.

Dion. Hal. – Dionysii Halicarnessensis, *Antiquitatum Romanorum quae supersunt*, ed. C. Jacoby, Vols I–II, Teubner, Leipzig, 1887–8; Vol. III–IV, Rec. A. Kiessling, Teubner, Leipzig, 1867–70.

Euseb. Vit. Const. – Eusebius of Caesarea (Eus.), *Life of Constantine – Vita Constantini (Vita Const.)* Greek text in *Eusebii Pamphili de vita Constantini libri IV et panegyricus, atque Constantini ad sanctorum coetum oratio*, Leipzig, 1830.

Eutr. – Eutropius, *Abridgment of Roman History,* translated with notes by the Rev. J. S. Watson, London, 1853.

Fest. – Sexti Pompei Festi, *De verborum significatione quae supersunt cum Pauli Epitome*, ed. K. O. Muller Leipzig, 1880 (1839). Hildesheim, Olms, 1975.

Flor. – Florus, L., *Annaeus. Epitome of Roman history with an English translation by E.S. Forster*, Harvard Univ. Press, London, 1928.

Front. Strat. – Frontin, *Kriegslisten*. Lateinisch und Deutsch von Gerhard Bendz. 3., unveränderte Auflage, Akademie-Verlag, Berlin, 1987.

Greg. Naz. Or. – Gregorius av Nazianzenus, *Patrologiae Cursus Completus*. Series Graeca, ed. Jacques Paul Migne, Vols 35–36, Paris, 1857.

Hdt. – Herodotus, *Herodoti Historiarum libri IX*, ed. H. R. Dietsch. Editio altera. Curavit H. Kallenberg. Vols I–II, Teubner, Leipzig, 1885–1887.

Heliod. Aethiop. Heliodorus, *The Aethiopica literally and completely translated from the Greek, with introduction and notes*, priv. print. for the Athenian Society, Athens, 1897.

Herod. – Herodianus, *Herodiani Ab excessu divi Marci libri octo*, ed. K. Stavenhagen, Teubner, Leipzig, 1922.

Hom. Il. – Homeri Ilias, Volumen alterum rhapsodias XIII–XXIV continens, recensuit Martin L. West. K. G. Saur, Munich, 2000.

ILS – Inscriptiones Latinae selectae. In: Dessau, H. (Hrsg.). *Inscriptiones Latinae selectae* 1–3. 1892–1916. Berolini: apud Weidmannos.

Ios. B. Iud. – Iosephus Flavius. *Flavii Iosephi Opera*. Bd. 1–7. Berlin: Weidmann, 1885–95.

Isid. Or. –Isidori *Hispanensis Episcopi Etymologiarum sive Originum* Libri XX, ed. Lindsay W.M., Vols I–II, Oxford, 1911.

Iul. Orat. – Julianus Apostata. *The works of the Emperor Julian*: In three volumes. With an English translation by W. C. Wright. Cambridge (Mass.); London, 1979–80.

Iuv. – Juvenalis Decimus Julius, Persius Aulus Flaccus. *Works*, With an English translation by G. G. Ramsay. Cambridge (Mass.); London, 1940.

Jul. Afr. Fragm. – Julius Africanus, *Embroideries- Kestoi* (Fragm.) in Vieillefond, J. R., *Les cestes de Julius Africanus, étude sur l'ensemble des fragments avec édition, traduction et commentaries*, Florence, 1970.

Jul. Or. in Constantii Laudem – *Juliani Imperatoris in Constantii Laudem Oratio*, Schäfer G. H. (ed.), Leipzig, 1802 (2011).

Justin. – Marcus Junianus Justinus. *Epitoma Historiarum Philippicarum*. Watson G. S. (ed.), London, 1853.

Lact. De mort. pers. – Lactantius (Lact.). *De Mortibus Persecutorum – Of The Manner in Which The Persecutors Died* (Mort.Pers.). Latin and English text in *De Mortibus Persecutorum*, edited and translated by J.L. Creed. Oxford Early Christian Texts series. Oxford, 1984.

Lib. – Libanii Opera / Rec. R. Forster. Vols I–IV. Leipzig: Teubner, 1903–8.

Liv. – Livius Titus. *History*: in 13 volumes, with an English translation by B. O. Fister, Cambridge (Mass.); London: Havard Univ. Press, 1926–43.

Lucan. Phars. – Lucanus, M. Annaeus, *The Civil War (Pharsalia)*, with an English translation by J. D. Duff. Cambridge (Mass.); London: Havard Univ. Press, 1977.

Lucret. De Rer. Nat., – Lucretius, *De Rerum Natura*, Loeb Classical Library. Harvard University Press, 1924.

Lyd. De Mag. – Ioannis Lydi, *De Magistratibus Populi Romani Libri Tres*, Wunsch R. (ed.), Leipzig, 1903.

Ovid. Met. – Ovidius. P. Ovidi Nasonis *Opera / Ex rec. Merkelii*. Vol. I–III, Leipzig: Teubner, 1867–1871.

Pan. – *In praise of later Roman Emperors. The Panegyrici Latini*, introduction, translation and historical commentary, ed. C. E. V. Nixon and B. S.Rodgers, with Latin text of R. A. B. Mynors, Berkeley and Los Angeles, 1994.

Plin. HN. – Plinius, C. Secundus (Maior), *Natural History*: In 10 volumes, with an English translation by H. Rackham, Cambridge (Mass.); London, 1969–79.

Plut. Brut.; Caes.; Numa; Pomp.; Phyl.; Pyrrh.; Rom.; Sol.; Sulla.; Tib. Gr.; Aem. Paul. – *Plutarchi Vitae parallelae* / Rec. Cl. Lindskog et K. Ziegler. Vols I–IV. Leipzig: Teubner, 1960–8.

Plut. Q. R. – Plutarchus, *Quaestiones Romanae. Plutarch's Moralia*: in fifteen volumes, with an English translation by F. C. Babbitt. Vol. IV. London: Harvard Univ. Press, 1957.

Polyaen. – Polyaeni *Strategematon libri octo*, ed. E. Nolfflin and J. Meller. Leipzig: Teubner, 1887.

Polyb. – Polybii *Historia*, ed. L. Dindorfius. Vols I–IV. Leipzig: Teubner, 1866–8.

Proc. Build – Procopius, *Buildings*. Loeb Classical Library, vol. VII, Harvard University Press, 1940 (1996).

Prop. El. – Propertius, *Elegies*, ed. G.P. Goold, Harvard University Press, 1990.

Prudent. Contra Symm. – Prudentius, *Contra Symmachum*, with an English translation by H. J. Thomson, Vols I–II, Loeb Classical library, London-Cambrigde, 1949–53.

Pseudo Modestus – 'Modesti libellus de vocabulis rei militaris ad Tacitum Augustum' in Reeve M. D., *Vegetius. Epitoma rei militaris*, Oxford, 2004.

Serv. In eclogas – Servii Gramatici Qui feruntur in Vergilii carmina commentarii / Rec. G. Thilo et H. Hagen. Vols I–III. Leipzig: Teubner, 1883–7.

SHA. Aurel.; Comm.; Marc. Aurel. – *Scriptores Historiae Augustae*, ed. E. Hohl, Vols I–II, Leipzig: Teubner, 1955–65.

Sid. Carmina – Sidonius, *Poems and Letters*, ed. Anderson W.B., 2 vols, Loeb Classical Library, London, 1936 (1973).

Sil. Ital. Pun – Silius Italicus. *Punica*: In two volumes, with an English translation by J. D. Duff.

Cambridge (Mass.); London: Harvard Univ. Press, 1983–9.

Suet. Aug.; Div. Iul.; Tib.;– Suetonius, *C Suetonii Tranquilli Caesares*, ed. M. Ihm, Leipzig: Teubner, 1908.

Suidas. *Suidae Lexicon: ex recognitione Immanuelis Bekker*, ed. A. I. Bekker A.I, Berlin, 1854.

Tac. Ann. – Tacitus P. Cornelius, *The Histories* – Historiae (Hist.) Tacitus II, Histories 1–3; Tacitus III, Histories 4–5, Annals 1–3, Loeb Classical Library, Harvard University Press, 1925–31.

Tac. Hist. – Tacitus, P. Cornelius, *P. Corneli Taciti Libri qui supersunt*, ed. E. Koestermann, Vols I–II, Leipzig: Teubner, 1957–69.

Tertul. De coron. – Tertullianus. Q. S. Florentis Tertulliani *Opera*. Partes I–IV / Rec. A. Reifferscheid et G. Wissowa, H. Hoppe, Ae. Kroymann, V. Bulhart, J. Borleffs. Vindobonae, 1890–1957.

Val. Flac.Argon. – Valerius Flaccus, *Argonautica*, Loeb Classical Library, Harvard University Press, 1934.

Val. Max. – Valerii Maximi, *Factorum et dictorum memorabilium libri novem. Julii Pari et Januarii Nepotiani epitomis adiectis*, Rec. C. Halm. Leipzig: Teubner, 1865.

Varro. L. L. – M. Terentii Varronis, *de lingua latina librorum quae supersunt*, Leipzig; Weidmann, 1833.

Veget. – Vegetius. Flavii Vegetii Renati, *Epitoma rei militaris*, Rec. C. Lang, Leipzig: Teubner, 1869.

Vell. Pat. – Vellei Paterculi, *Historiarum ad M. Vinicium consulem*, Rec. W. S. Watt, Leipzig: Teubner, 1988.

Virg. Aen. – P. Vergilii Maronis, *Opera omnia*, ed. A. Forbiger, Partes I–III. Leipzig: Teubner, 1873–5.

Zonaras – Zonaras Iohannes. Annales, [in:] Patrologie grecque, vol. 134–135, 137, ed. J. P. Migne, Paris, 1864.

SECONDARY SOURCES

Abdul-Hak, 1951 – Abdul-Hak, S., *Catalogue illustre du Departement des Antiquites Greco-Romaines au Musee de Damas*, Damascus, 1951.

Abdul-Hak, 1954–1955 – Abdul-Hak, S., 'Rapport préliminaire sur des objets provenant de la nécropole romaine située a proximité de Nawa (Hauran)', *Les Annales Archéologiques de Syrie*, 4–5, 1954–5, pp. 163–88.

Abelterium, 2015, II/I – Município de Alter do Chão, *Abelterium*, Vol. I. n. 2. Majo, 2015.

Achter het Zilveren Masker, 2007 – *Achter het Zilveren Masker: nieuw onderzoek naar de productietechnieken van Romeinse ruiterhelmen (= Hinter der silbernen Maske: neue Untersuchungen zur Herstellungstechnik römischer Reiterhelme)*, ed. R. Meijers, F. Willer, Nijmegen-Bonn: Museum het Valkhof–Rheinisches Landesmuseum des Landschaftsverbandes Rheinland, 2007.

Ahlqvist, 1995 – Ahlqvist, A., *Pitture e mosaici nei cimiteri Paleocristiani di Siracusa*, Venice, 1995.

Aigner-Foresti, 1994 – Aigner-Foresti, L., 'Movimenti etnici nella Roma dell' VIII secolo a.C.', *Contributi dell' Istituto di Storia Antica* XX, 1994, pp. 3–10.

Alföldi, 1932 – Alföldi, A., 'The helmet of Constantine with the Christian monogram', *JRS*, 22, 1932, pp. 9–23.

Altheim, 1943 – Altheim, F., *Die Krise der alten Welt*, Berlin, 1943.

Anderson, 1970 – Anderson J. K., *Military Theory and Practice in the Age of Xenophon*. Berkeley-Los Angeles, 1970.

Ando, 2000 – Ando, C., *Imperial Ideology and Provincial Loyalty in the Roman Empire*, Los Angeles, 2000.

Annali dell'Istituto di Corrispondenza Archeologica, 'Rapporto del Signor Carlo Avvolta intorno le tombe di Tarquinia', *Annals de l'Institut de Correspondance Archéologique pour l'an 1829*, Rome, 1829, pp. 91–101.

Antika, 1954 – *Antika u Narodnom muzeju u Beogradu*, Beograd, 1954.

Antike Helme, 1988 – *Antike Helme: Sammlung Lipperheide und andere Bestände des Antikenmuseums Berlin. 1988*, Mainz: Verlag des Römisch-Germanischennak Zentralmuseum, Mainz, 1988.

Audollent, 1923 – Audollent, A., 'Les tombes gallo-romaines a inhumation des Martres-de-Veyre (Puy-de-Dome)', *Mémoires présentés par divers savants à l'Académie des Inscriptions et Belles-Lettres de l'Institut de France*, XIII, 1923, pp. 275–328.

Aurino, Gobbi, 2012 – Aurino, P., and Gobbi A., 'Pontecagnano prima dei principi: il tumulo dei guerrieri e la fine della prima età del ferro', in *L'Etruria dal Paleolitico al primo ferro, lo stato delle ricerche. Atti del decimo incontro di studi di Preistoria e Protostoria in Italia*, Vol. II, Milano, 2012, pp. 801–36.

Avvisati, 2003 – Avvisati, C., *Pompei, mestieri e botteghe 2000 anni fa*, Rome, 2003.

Babbi, Peltz, 2013 – Babbi A., and Peltz, U., *La tomba del guerriero di Tarquinia, Romisch-Germanisches Monographien*, Bd. 109, 2013.

Babelon, Blanchet, 1895 – Babelon, E., and Blanchet J.-A., *Catalogue des bronzes antiques de la Bibliothèque nationale*, Paris, 1895.

Bailly, 1990 – Bailly A., *Les armes des 6e et 7e siècles // Du silex à la poudre . . . 4000 ans d'armement en Val de Saône, catalogue d'exposition*, ed. Bonnamour, L., Chalon-sur-Saône, 1990, pp. 119–46.

Bardill, 2012 – Bardill, J., *Constantine, Divine Emperor of the Christian Golden Age*, Cambridge, 2012.

Barker, 1981 – Barker, P., *The Armies and the Enemies of Imperial Rome, 150 BC – 600 AD*, Worthing, 1981.

Bartman, 2001 – Bartman, E., 'Hair and the Artifice of Roman Female Adornment', *AJA*, 105.1, 2001, pp. 1–25.

Bartman, 2005 – Bartman, E., 'The mock face of battle', *Journal of Roman Archaeology*, 18.1, 2005, pp. 99–119.

Bartoloni, 2003 – Bartoloni, G., *Le società dell'Italia primitiva. Lo studio delle necropoli e la nascita delle aristocrazie*, Rome, 2003.

Başgelen, Ergeç, 2000 – Başgelen, N., Ergeç, R., *Belkis-Zeugma, Halfeti, Rumkale, a last look at history*, Istanbul, 2000.

Bastien, 1992–1994 – Bastien, P., *Les bustes monétaires des Empereurs Romains*, T. I–III, Wetteren, 1992–1994.

Baur, Rostovtzeff , 1933 – Baur, P. V. C., and Rostovtzeff, M., *The Excavations at Dura-Europos*, Report IV, London, 1933.

Bavant, Ivanisevic, 2003 – Bavant B., and Ivanisevic, V., *Iustiniana Prima – Caričin Grad*, Leskovac, 2003.

BBC 2011 – 'Rare Roman altar stones uncovered in Musselburgh'. *BBC News (online news article)*: http://www.bbc.co.uk/news/uk-scotland-edinburgh-east-fife-12771243 (accessed: 17 Mar 2011).

Beck, Chew, 1991 – Beck F., and Chew, H., *Masques de fer. Un officier romain du temps de Caligula*. Musée des Antiquités Nationales, St. Germain en Laye, Paris, 6 Nov 1991 – 4 Feb 1992, Paris, 1991.

Bedini, 1990 – Bedini, A., 'Abitato protostorico in località Acqua Acetosa Laurentina', in *Archeologia a Roma – la materia e la tecnica nell'arte antica*, Rome, 1990, pp. 48–58.

Bedini, Cordano, 1977 – Bedini A., and Cordano F., 'L'VIII secolo nel Lazio e l'inizio dell'orientalizzante antico alla luce di recenti scoperte nella necropoli di Castel di Decima', *ParPass*, 32, 1977, pp. 274–311.

Belson, 1980 – Belson, J. P., 'The Medusa Rondanini: A New Look', *AJA*, 84.3, 1980, pp. 373–8.

Bendinelli, 1916 – Bendinelli, G., 'Tomba con vasi e bronzi del V secolo avanti Cristo: scoperta nella necropoli di Todi', *Monumenti antichi*, 24, 1916, Sl. 841–914.

Benndorf, 1878 – Benndorf, O., 'Antike Gesichtshelme und Sepulcralmasken', *Denkschrift der philosophisch-historischen Classe der kaiserlichen Akademie der Wissenschaften zu Vienna*, 28, Vienna, 1878.

Berger, Franzius, Schlüter, 1991 – Berger, F., Franzius G., Schlüter, W., and Wilbers-Rost, S., 'Archäologische Quellen zur Varusschlacht? Die Untersuchungen in Kalkriese, Stadt Bremische, sowie Venne und Schwagstorf, Gemeinde Ostercappeln, Landkreis Osnabrück', *Antike Welt*, 22/4, 1991, pp. 221–34.

Bergonzi, 1992 – Bergonzi, G., 'Etruria – Piceno – Caput Adriae: guerra e aristocrazia nell'Età del Ferro', *La civiltà picena nelle Marche. Studi in onore di Giovanni Annibaldi*, Ripatransone, 1992, pp. 60–88.

Bianchi Bandinelli, 1970 – Bianchi Bandinelli, R., *Roma, la fine dell'arte antica*, Milan, 1970.

Bianchi Bandinelli, 1985 – Bianchi Bandinelli, R., *Roma, la fine dell'arte antica*, Milan, 1985.

Bianchi, Munzi, 2006 – Bianchi, B., and Munzi, M., 'L'elmo-diadema, una insegna tardo-antica di potere tra oriente ed occidente', *MEFRA*, 118/1, 2006, pp. 297–313.

Bianco, 1996 – Bianco, S., *Greci, Enotri e Lucani nella Basilicata Meridionale*, Naples, 1996.

Biblioteca Apostolica Vaticana, 1980 – Biblioteca Apostolica Vaticana, *Vergilius Vaticanus – Codex Vaticanus Latinus 3225*, special postcard colour edition, Graz, 1980.

Bihalji-Merin, 1974 – Bihalji-Merin, O., *Umetničko Blago Jugoslavije*, Beograd, 1974.

Biscottini, Sena Chiesa, 2012 – Biscottini, P., and Sena Chiesa, G., *Costantino 313 d.C.: l'editto di Milano e il tempo della tolleranza*. Milan, 2012.

Bishop, 1990 – Bishop, M. C., 'On Parade: Status, Display and Morale in the Roman Army', *Akten des 14. Internationalen Limeskongresses 1986 in Carnuntum*, T. 1, Vienna, 1990, pp. 21–30.

Bishop, 2002 – Bishop, M.C., 'Lorica Segmentata vol. I: A Handbook of Articulated Roman Plate Armour', *JRMES* Monograph 1, Chirnside, 2002.

Bishop, Coulston, 1993 – Bishop, M. C., and Coulston, J. C. N., *Roman Military Equipment. From the Punic Wars to the Fall of Rome*, 1st ed London, 1993.

Bishop, Coulston, 2006 – Bishop, M. C., and Coulston J. C. N., *Roman Military Equipment. From the Punic Wars to the Fall of Rome*, 2nd ed London, 2006.

Böhme, 1974 – Böhme, H.W., 'Germanische Grabfunde des 4. bis 5. Jahrhunderts zwischen unterer Elbe und Loire, Munich', *Münchner Beiträge zur Vor- und Frühgeschichte*, 19, Munich: Beck, 1974.

Böhner, 1994 – Böhner, K., 'Die frühmittelalterlichen Spangenhelme und die nordischen Helme der Vendelzeit', *Jahrbuch des Römisch-Germanischen Zentralmuseums Mainz*, Bd. 41, 1994, pp. 471–549.

Bohry, 1990 – Borhy, L., 'Zwei neue Parade-Brustplatten im Ungarischen Nationalmuseum', *Bayerische Vorgeschichtsblätter*, 55, 1990, pp. 299–307.

Boitani F., 2001 – Boitani, F., *Veio, Cerveteri, Vulci, Città d'Etruria a confronto, Roma Catalogo della Mostra (Roma 2001)*, ed. A.M. Moretti Sgubini, Rome, 2001, p. 112.

Bonfante Warren, 1970 – Bonfante Warren. L., 'Roman Triumphs and Etruscan Kings: The Changing Face of the Triumph', *JRS*, 60, 1970, pp. 49–66.

Borgna, 1993 – Borgna, E., 'Ancile e arma ancilia. Osservazioni sullo scudo dei Salii', *Ostraka*, 2, 1993, pp. 9–42.

Born, 1993 – Born H., *Restaurierung antiker Bronzewaffen*, Mainz, 1993.

Born, Junkelmann, 1997 – Born, H., and Junkelmann, M., *Römische Kampf- und Turnierrüstungen*, Mainz, 1997.

Born, Hansen, 1992 – Born, H., and Hansen, S., 'Ein urnenfelderzeitlicherGlockenhelm aus der Sammlung Zschille', *Acta Praehistorica et Archaeologica*, 24, 1992, pp. 339–56.

Boschung, 1987 – Boschung, D., 'Römische Glasphalerae mit Porträtbüsten', *Bonner Jahrbücher*, 187, 1987, pp. 193–258.

Bottini, 1993 – Bottini, A., *Armi. Gli strumenti della guerra in Lucania*, Bari, 1993.

Boube-Piccot, 1994 – Boube-Piccot, C., *Les bronzes antiques du Maroc. IV. L'equipement militaire et l'armement*, Paris, 1994.

Braat, 1973 – Braat, W. C., Van Buchem, H. J. H., Zadoks-Josephus Jitta, A. N., and Leene, J.E., 'Der Fund von Deurne, Holland', *Spätrömische Gardehelme*, Munich, 1973, pp. 51–83.

Braat, 1939 – Braat, W. C., 'Romeinsche helmen in het Rijksmuseum van Oudheden',

Oudheidkundige Mededelingen, 20, 1939, pp. 29–46.

Braccesi, 1987 – Braccesi, L., 'Germanico e l'imitatio Alexandri in occidente', *Germanico. La persona, la personalita, il personaggio nel bimillenario dalla nascita. Atti del convegno Macerata-Perugia 9–11 Maggio 1986. Università degli Studi di Macerata. Pubblicazioni della Facoltà di Lettere e Filosofia 39*, Roma, 1987, pp. 53–65.

Breeze, Bishop, 2013 – Breeze, D. J., and Bishop, M. C., *The Crosby Garrett Helmet*, Pewsey, 2013.

Brennan, 2000 – Brennan, T. C., *The Praetorships in the Roman Republic*, Vols 1–2, Oxford, 2000.

Brogiolo, Chavarría Arnau, 2007 – Brogiolo, G.P., and Chavarría Arnau, A., *I Longobardi, dalla caduta dell'Impero all'alba dell'Italia*, Milan, 2007.

Bröndsted, 1836 – Bröndsted, P. O., *The bronzes of Siris: now in the British Museum*, London, 1836.

Burns, 1984 – Burns, T. S., *History of the Ostrogoths*, Bloomington and Indianapolis, 1984.

Burns, 2006 – Burns, M., *South Italic military equipment: the cultural and military significance of the warrior's panoply from the 5th to the 3rd centuries B.C.*, PhD thesis, University College London, 2006.

Bury, 1923 – Bury, J. B., *History of the Later Roman Empire*, London, 1923.

Büttner, 1957 – Büttner, A., 'Untersuchungen über Ursprung und Entwiklung von Auszeichnungen in roemischen Heer', *Bonner Jahrbücher*, 157, 1957, pp. 127–80.

Buzzi, 1976 – Buzzi, G., *Giulio Cesare*, Milan, 1976.

Caccioli, 2009 – Caccioli, D. A., and Peck, H. W., *The Villanovan, Etruscan and Hellenistic collections in the Detroit Institute of Arts*, Boston, 2009.

Cairo, 2009 – Cairo G., *Roma, tra storia ed archeologia: religione, istituzioni, territorio nell'epoca delle origini. Tesi di Laurea*, Bologna, 2009.

Camerin, 2000 – Camerin, M., 'La ricostruzione dei carri nella storia dei ritrovamenti', *Carri da Guerra e principi Etruschi, catalogo della mostra*, ed. A. Emiliozzi, Rome, 2000. pp. 87–94.

Camporeale, 2001 – Camporeale, G. (ed.), *The Etruscans outside Etruria*, Los Angeles, 2001.

Carandini, Ricci, De Vos, 1982 – Carandini, A., Ricci, A., and De Vos, M., *Filosofiana: la villa di Piazza Armerina*, Palermo, 1982.

Cascarino, 2007 – Cascarino, G., *L'esercito romano. Armamento e organiszazione. Vol. I: dalle origini alla fine della Repubblica*, Città di Castello, 2007.

Cascarino, 2012 – Cascarino, G., *L'esercito romano. Armamento e organiszazione. Vol. IV: l'Impero d'Oriente e gli ultimi Romani*, Città di Castello, 2012.

Cascarino, Sansilvestri, 2009 – Cascarino, G., and Sansilvestri, C., *L'esercito romano. Armamento e organiszazione. Vol. III: dal III secolo alla fine dell'impero d'Occidente*, Città di Castello 2009.

Cassola, 1973 – Cassola, P. G., *Le armi defensive dei Micenei nelle figurazioni*, Rome, 1973.

Catullo, 2000 – Catullo, L., *L'Antica Villa Romana del Casale di Piazza Armerina nel passato e nel presente*, Messina, 2000.

Cerchiai, 1995 – Cerchiai, L., *I Campani*, Milan, 1995.

Charles, 2015 – Charles, M. B., 'Imperial Cuirasses in Latin Verse: from Augustus to the Fall of the West', *L'antiquité classique*, 73, 2004, pp. 127–48.

Cherici, 2008 – Cherici, A., 'Armati e tombe con armi nella società dell'Etruria Padana: analisi di alcuni monumenti', *La colonizzazione Etrusca in Italia, Atti del XV convegno internazionale di Studi sulla Storia e l'Archeologia dell'Etruria*, in *Annali della Fondazione per il Museo 'Claudio Faina'*, Vol. XV, Orvieto, 2008, pp. 187–246.

Cherici, 2009 – Cherici, A., 'Etruria e Roma: per una storia del rapporto tra impegno militare e capienza politica nelle comunità antiche', *Gli Etruschi e Roma, fasi monarchica ed alto-repubblicana, Atti del XVI convegno internazionale di Studi sulla Storia e l'Archeologia dell'Etruria*, in *Annali della Fondazione per il Museo 'Claudio Faina'*, Vol. XVI, Orvieto, 2009, pp. 155–75.

Chernyshov, 1994 – Chernyshov, Ju. G., *Social'no-utopicheskie idei i mif o «zolotom veke». Chast' 2: Rannij principat*, Novosibirsk, 1994.

Chiarucci, 2003 – Chiarucci, P., *L'esercito romano*, Albano, 2003.

Christie's, 2002 – *The Axel Guttmann Collection of Ancient Arms and Armour*, Part 1, London, 2002.

Christie's, 2004 – *The Axel Guttmann Collection of Ancient Arms and Armour*, Part 2: Auction

Wednesday 28 April 2004 at 10.30 am, Lots 1–179 & 2 pm, Lots 200–478, South Kensington, London, 2004.

Cialdea, 1940 – Cialdea, U., 'Nuovi rivelamenti di oggetti antichi', *Atti V Congr. Int. St. Romani*, Rome, 1940, pp. 91–6.

Cipriani, Longo, 1996 – Cipriani, M., and Longo, F., *Poseidonia ei Lucani*, Naples, 1996.

Cirilli, 1913 – Cirilli, R., *Les prêtres danseurs de Rome*, Paris, 1913.

Coarelli & others, 1975 – Coarelli, F., Lucignani, L., Tamassia, R., and Torelli, M., *Le grandi avventure dell'archeologia, I misteri delle civiltà scomparse* Vol. IV, Rome, 1975.

Coarelli, 1972 – Coarelli, F., 'Il sepolcro degli Scipioni', *Dialoghi di Archeologia*, 16, 1972, pp. 36–106.

Colivicchi, 2009 – Colivicchi, F., 'Warriors and citizens, model of self-representation in native Basilicata', *Verso la città, forme insediative in Lucania e nel mondo italico fra IV e III sec. A.C.*, Venosa, 2009, pp. 69–88.

Colonna, 1977 – Colonna, G., 'Un aspetto oscuro del Lazio antico: le tombe del VI–V secolo a.C', *ParPass*, XXIII, 1977, pp. 131–65.

Colonna, 1987 – Colonna, G., 'Maestro dell'Ercole e della Minerva; nuova luce sull'attività dell'officina veiente', *Op.Rom*, 44, 1987, pp. 7–42.

Colonna, 1991 – Colonna, G., 'Gli scudi bilobati nell'Italia Centrale e l'ancile dei Salii', *Archeologia Classica*, 43, 1991, pp. 55–122.

Colonna, 1996 – Colonna, G., 'Roma arcaica, i suoi sepolcreti e le vie per i Colli Albani', in *Alba Longa. Mito, storia, archeologia (Atti dell'incontro di studio, Roma – Albano Laziale 27–29 gennaio 1994)*, Rome, 1996, pp. 335–54.

Colonna, 2000 – Colonna, G., 'L'Italia antica: Italia centrale', *Carri da guerra e principi Etruschi, catalogo della mostra*, ed. A. Emiliozzi, Rome, 2000, pp. 15–23.

Colt Hoare, 1829 – Colt Hoare, R., 'Observations upon four mosaic pavements discovered in the County of Hants [Thruxton, Bramdean and Crondall]', *Archaeologia*, 22, 1829, pp. 49–54.

Comis, Re, 2009 – Comism L., and Re, C., 'Riti guerrieri nel contesto funerario della cultura Villanoviana/Orientalizzante, una ricerca integrata', in *Pagani e Cristiani. Forme ed attestazioni di religiosità del mondo antico in Emilia*, Vol. VIII, Castelfranco Emilia, 2009, pp. 47–94.

Comstock, Vermuelle, 1971 – Comstock, M., and Vermuelle, C. C., *Greek Etruscan and Roman Bronzes in the Museum of Fine Arts, Boston*, Boston, 1971.

Connolly, 1981 – Connolly, P., *Greece and Rome at War*, London, 1981.

Connolly, 2006 – Connolly, P., *Greece and Rome at War*, London, 2006.

Cool, 2004 – Cool, H. E. M., 'The Roman Cemetery at Brougham, Cumbria: Excavations 1966–67', *Britannia Monograph* 21, London, 2004.

Coulston, 1990 – Coulston, J. C. N., 'Later Roman armour, 3rd-6th centuries AD', *JRMES*, 1, 1990, pp. 139–60.

Courbin, 1957 – Courbin, P., 'Une tombe géométrique d'Argos (planches I–V)', *Bulletin de correspondance hellénique*, Vol. 81, No. 1, 1957, pp. 322–86.

Coussin, 1926 – Coussin, P., *Les Armes Romaines*, Paris, 1926.

Cowan, 2013 – Cowan, R., 'The art of the Etruscan Armourer', in MacIntosh Turfa, J. (ed.), *The Etruscan World*, London & New York, 2013, pp. 747–58.

Cowan, 2015 – Cowan, R., *Roman Legionary, AD 284–337*, Oxford, 2015.

Cracco Ruggini, Cassola, 1982 – Cracco Ruggini, L., and Cassola, F., *Storia antica delle Grandi civiltà, II*, Florence, 1982.

Crawford, 1979 – Crawford, J. S., 'A Portrait of Alexander the Great at the University of Delaware', *AJA*, 83, 1979, pp. 477–81.

Cresci Marrone, 1987 – Cresci Marrone, G., 'Germanico e l'imitatio Alexandri', *Germanico. La persona, la personalità, il personaggio nel bimillenario dalla nascita. Atti del convegno Macerata-Perugia 9–11 Maggio 1986. Universita degli Studi di Macerata. Pubblicazioni della Facolta di Lettere e Filosofia 39*, Rome, 1987, pp. 67–77.

Cristina, Lechilli, 2015 – Cristina, A., and Lechilli, E., 'Les différentes représentations et symboliques du cheval à travers l'iconographie de la région de Cirta du Ier à la fin du IIIe siècle après J.-C.', *In Situ*, 27, 2015, pp. 2–14.

Cristofani, 1990 – Cristofani, M. (ed.), *La grande Roma dei Tarquini*, Rome, 1990.

Curle, 1911 – Curle, J., *A Roman Frontier Post and its People. The Fort at Newstead*, Glasgow, 1911.

Curle, 1915 – Curle, J., 'On a Roman visor helmet recently discovered near Nijmegen, Holland', *JRS*, 5, 1915, pp. 81–6.

D'Amato, 2005 – D'Amato, R., *Roman Military Clothing 400–640 AD*, Oxford, 2005.

D'Amato, 2011 – D'Amato, R., *Roman Centurions 753–31 BC: The Kingdom and the Age of the Consuls*, Oxford, 2011.

D'Amato, 2012 – D'Amato, R., *Roman Centurions 31 BC–AD 500: The Classical and Late Empire*, Oxford, 2012.

D'Amato, Sumner, 2009 – D'Amato, R., and Sumner, G., *Arms and Armour of the Imperial Roman Soldier: From Marius to Commodus, 112 BC–AD 192*, London, 2009.

D'Amato, Salimbeti, 2011 – D'Amato, R., and Salimbeti, A., *Bronze Age Greek Warrior, 1600–1100 BC*, Oxford, 2011.

D'Amato, Salimbeti, 2014 – D'Amato, R., and Salimbeti, A., *The Carthaginians 6th–2nd Century BC*, Oxford, 2014.

Dautova-Ruševljan, Vujović, 2011 – Dautova-Ruševljan V., and Vujović M., *Kasnoantički šlem iz Jarka*, Supičić, 2011.

Davies, 1968 – Davies, R.W., 'The Training Grounds of the Roman Cavalry', *Archaeological Journal*, Vol. 125, 1968, pp. 73–100.

De Agostino, 1958 – De Agostino, A., 'Gli Elmi di Rapolano', *Archeologia Classica*, Vol. 10, 1958, pp. 84–6.

De Caro, 1983 – De Caro, S., 'Una nuova tomba dipinte da Nola', *Rivista dell'Istituto Nazionale d'Archeologia e storia dell' Arta*, 1983, 1–3, VI–VII, pp. 71–95.

De Grossi Mazzorin, 1995 – De Grossi Mazzorin, J., 'Ricerche zooarcheologiche in alcuni insediamenti protostorici dell'Etruria meridionale', *Preistoria e Protostoria in Etruria* Vol. 2, Milan, 1995, pp. 17–26.

De Marinis, 1976 – De Marinis, G., 'Pettorali metallici a scopo difensivo nel villanoviano recente', *Atti e Memorie dell'Accademia La Colombaria XLI*, Florence, 1976, pp. 1–30.

De Puma, 2013 – De Puma, R. D., *Etruscan Art in the Metropolitan Museum of Art*, New York, 2013.

Déchelette, 1903 – Déchelette, J., 'La sépulture de Chassenard et les coins monétaires de Paray-le-Monial', *Revue Archéologique* 4ème serie, 1, 1903, pp. 235–58.

Déchelette, 1913 – Déchelette, J., *La collection Millon: antiquités pré-historiques et gallo-romaines*, Paris, 1913.

Dehn, 1911 – Dehn, G., 'Die Bronzefunde bei Ponte Sisto', *Mittheilungen des Kaiserlich Deutschen Archäologischen Instituts. Römische Abteilung = Bullettino dell'Imperiale Istituto archeologico germanico. Sezione romana*, Bd. 26, 1911, pp. 238–59.

Dekan, 1981 – Dekan, J., *Moravia Magna, The Great Moravian Empire*, Bratislava, 1981.

Demandt, Engemann, 2007 – Demandt, A., and Engemann, J. (eds), *Konstantin der Grosse, Austellungkatalog*, Mainz, 2007.

Dennis, 1848 – Dennis, G., *The Cities and Cemeteries of Etruria*, London, 1848.

Dewing, 1940 (1996) – Dewing, H. B., 'The Equestrian Statue of Justinian in the Augustaeum', in Procopius, *Buildings*, Loeb Classical Library. Vol. VII. Harvard University Press, 1940 (1996), p. 3968.

Di Dario, 2005 – Di Dario, B. M., *La Notitia Dignitatum, immagini e simboli del Tardo Impero Romano*, Padua, 2005.

Di Mino and Bertinetti, 1990 – Di Mino, M. R., and Bertinetti, M. (ed.), *Archeologia a Roma*, Rome, 1990.

Dickinson, Härke, 1992 – Dickinson, T., and Härke, H., *Early Anglo-Saxon Shields*, London, 1992.

Diegi, 2010 – Diegi, R., 'Le monete di Costanzo Gallo. Giuliano l'Apostata e Gioviano', *Panorama Numismatico*, 2010, pp. 17–24.

Dintsis, 1986 – Dintsis, P., *Hellenistische Helme*, Rome, 1986.

Dixon-Southern, 1992 – Dixon, K. R., and Southern, P., *The Roman Cavalry*, London, 1992.

Djakovič, 1906–1907 – Djakovič, B., T'rakijska grobnica pri Plovdiv i nekropolt na drevnija grad', *Sbornik s narodni umotvorenija*, 22–23, 1906–7, pp. 1–55.

Domaszewski, 1885 – Domaszewski, A. von, *Die Fahnen im römischen Heere*, Vienna, 1885.

Domaszewski, 1888 – Domaszewski, A. von, 'Römischer Pferdeschmuck aus Siebenbürgen', *Archäologisch-epigraphische Mitteilungen aus Österreich-Ungarn*, 12, 1888, pp. 138–45.

Donati, Gentili, 2005 – Donati, A., and Gentili, G. (eds), *Costantino il Grande, la civiltà antica al bivio tra Occidente ed Oriente*, Cinisello Balsamo, 2005.

Donner von Richter, 1894 – Donner von Richter, O., 'Die Heddernheimer Helme: die etruskischen und der griechische Helm des frankfurter historischen Museums in ihrer Bedeutung für die Geschichte antiker Helmformen', *Mitteilungen über Römischen Funde in Heddernheim*, Frankfurt (Main), 1, 1894, pp. 21–50.

Doublet, 1890 – Doublet, G., *Musée d'Alger*, Paris, 1890.

Drago, 2009 – Drago, L. (ed.), *Il Lazio dai Colli Albani ai Monti Lepini tra preistoria ed età moderna*, Rome, 2009.

Dragotă, 1987 – Dragotă, G., 'Masca romană de bronz de la Cincsor (jud. Brasov)', *Studii şi cercetări de istorie veche*, 38, 3, 1987, pp. 276–80.

Drexel, 1924 – Drexel, F., 'Römische Paraderüstung', *Strena Buliciana*, Zagreb-Split, 1924, pp. 55–72.

Driehaus, 1968 – Driehaus, J., 'Die Panzer von Augsburg und Vize (Thrakien), zwei Meisterwerke antiker Brünnenmacherkunst', *Mitteilungen der Berlinner Gesellschaft für Anthropologie, Ethnologie und Urgeschichte*, Band 2, Heft 1, 1968, pp. 14–16.

Driehaus, Raub, Bakker, 2010 – Driehaus, J., Raub, Ch., and Bakker, L., 'Die Panzer von Augsburg und Vize. Eine Untersuchung zur Metalltechnologie im 1. Jahrhundert n. Chr.', *Bericht der Römisch-Germanischen Kommission*, 91, 2010, pp. 339–408.

Driel-Murray, 1989 – Driel-Murray, C. van, 'The Vindolanda chamfrons and miscellaneous items of leather horse gear', *Roman Military Equipment: the Sources of Evidence. Proceedings of the Fifth Roman Military Equipment Conference, British Archaeological Reports*, International Series 476, Oxford, 1989, pp. 281–318.

Drijvers & Hunt, 1999 – Drijvers, G. W., Hunt, D., *The Late Roman World and its Historian*, London & New York, 1999.

Du Cange et.al. – Du Cange, Mons., et al., *Glossarium mediæ et infimæ latinitatis*. Niort, 1883–7.

Durry, 1938 – Durry, M., *Les Cohortes prétoriennes*, Paris, 1938.

Duthy, 1839 – Duthy, J., Esq., *Sketches of Hampshire*, Winchester, 1839.

Dyczek, 1992 – Dyczek, P., 'Bronze finds from the site of the valetudinarium at Novae (Moesia inferior)', *Acta of the 12th Congress on ancient bronzes*, Nijmegen, 1992, pp. 365–72.

Eadie, 1967 – Eadie, J., 'The development of the Roman mailed cavalry', *JRS*, Vol. 57, No. 1/2, 1967, pp. 161–73.

Emiliozzi, 2000 – Emiliozzi, A. (ed.), *Carri da Guerra e principi Etruschi, catalogo della mostra*, Rome, 2000.

Emiliozzi, 1997 – Emiliozzi, A. (ed.), *Carri da Guerra e principi Etruschi, catalogo della mostra*, Rome, 1997.

Enckevort, Willems, 1994 – Enckevort, H. L. H. van, and Willems, W. J. H., 'Roman cavalry helmets in ritual hoards from the Kops Plateau at Nijmegen, The Netherlands', *JRMES*, 5, 1994, pp. 125–37.

Espérandieu, 1913 – Espérandieu, E., *Recueil général des bas-reliefs, statues et bustes de la Gaule Romaine*, T. 5, Paris, 1913.

Evangelatou, Papastavrou, Skotti, 2001 – Evangelatou, M., Papastavrou H., and Skotti, P.-T. (eds), *Byzantium: An Oecumenical Empire, exhibition catalogue, October 2001–January 2002*, Athens, 2001.

Facchinetti, 2003 – Facchinetti, G., 'Monete ed insigne del potere: la raffigurazione di elmi fra

IV e VI secolo d.C.', *Actas del XIII Congreso Internacional de Numismatica, Madrid 15–19 Septiembre 2003*, Madrid, 2003, pp. 747–58.

Fairon, Moreau-Maréchal, 1983 – Fairon, G., and Moreau-Maréchal, J., 'La tombe au casque de Weiler, commune d'Autelbas, près d'Arlon', *Germania*, 61, 1983, pp. 551–64.

Feugère, 1990 – Feugère, M., 'Les armes romaines', in Bonnamour, L. (ed.), *Du silex à la poudre . . . 4000 ans d'armement en Val de Saône, catalogue d'exposition*, Chalon-sur-Saône, 1990, pp. 93–118.

Feugère, 1993 – Feugère, M., *Les armes des romains de la République à l'Antiquité tardive*, Paris, 1993.

Feugère, 1994 – Feugère, M., *Casques antiques. Les visages de la guerre de Mycènes à la fin de l'Empire romain*, Paris, 1994.

Feugère, 2002 – Feugère, M., *Weapons of Romans*, Stroud, 2002.

Fields, 2011 – Fields, N., *Early Roman Warrior, 753-321 BC*, Oxford, 2011.

Filov, 1923 – Filov, B., 'Shlemt maska v muzeja pri Plovdiskata Narodna Biblioteka', *Godishnik Narodna Biblioteka v Plovdiv*, 1923, pp. 123–39.

Fink, 1944 – Fink, R. O., 'Feriale Duranum I, 1 and Mater Castrorum', *AJA*, 48, 1, 1944, pp. 17–19.

Fink, Hoey, Snyder, 1940 – Fink, R. O., Hoey, A. S., and Snyder, W. F., 'The Feriale Duranum', *Yale Classical Studies*, Vol. 7, 1940, pp. 1–222.

Fischer, 2004 – Fischer, Th., 'Bemerkungen zu Grab 622 von Kemnitz, Kreis Potsdam in Brandenburg', in Friesinger H. and Stuppner A. (Hrsg.), *Zentrum und Peripherie – Gesellschaftliche Phänomene der Frühgeschichte*, Vienna, 2004, pp. 131–41.

Fischer, 2012 – Fischer, Th., *Die Armee der Caesaren. Archäologie und Geschichte*, Regensburg, 2012.

Flinders Petrie, 1917 – Flinders Petrie, W. M., *Tools and Weapons*, Warminster-Encino, 1917.

Flinders Petrie, 1927 – Flinders Petrie, W. M., *Objects of Daily Use*, London, 1927.

Forestier, 1928 – Forestier, A., *The Roman Soldier*, London, 1928.

Fossati, 1987 – Fossati, I., *Gli eserciti Etruschi*, Milan, 1987.

Franzius, 1993 – Franzius, G., 'Die römischen Funde aus Kalkriese', *Kalkriese – Römer im Osnabrücker Land. Archäologische Forschungen zur Varusschlacht*, Bramsche, 1993, pp. 107–82.

Frazer, 1894 – Frazer, J. G., *The Golden Bough: a Study in Comparative Religion*, New York & London, 1894.

Fulminante, 2003 – Fulminante, F., *Le sepolture principesche nel Latium vetus tra la fine della prima età del ferro e l'inizio dell'età orientalizzante*, Rome, 2003.

Furtwängler, 1905 – Furtwängler, A., 'Bronzewagen von Monteleone', in Brunn, H., and Bruckmann, F. (eds), *Denkmäler griechischer und römischer Skulptur*, 2nd ed. Munich, 1905, pp. 314–30.

Fuss, 1840 – Fuss, J. D., *Roman Antiquities*, London, 1840. Reprint London: Forgotten Books, 2013.

Galieti, 1938 – Galieti, A., 'Contributo alla conoscenza dell'armatura dei Prisci Latini', *Atti IV Congr. Int. St. Romani*, II, Rome, 1938, pp. 281–2.

Gamber, 1966 – Gamber, O., 'The Sutton-Hoo military equipment, an attempted reconstruction', *The Journal of the Arms & Armour Society*, 6, 1966, pp. 265–89.

Gamber, 1968 – Gamber, O., 'Kataphrakten, Clibanarier, Normannenreiter', *Jahrbuch der kunsthistorischen Sammlung in Vienna*, 64, 1968, pp. 7–44.

Garbsch, 1978 – Garbsch, J., *Römische Paraderüstungen*, Munich, 1978.

Geiger, 1994 – Geiger, A., *Treibverzierte Bronzerundschilde der italischen Eisenzeit aus Italien und Griechenland (Prähistorische Bronze Funde III, 1)*, Munich, 1994.

Geiß, Willer, 2007 – Geiß, E., and Willer, F., 'Experientele archeologie: smeedexperimenten met betrekking tot de Romeinse gezichtsmaskers uit Nijmege', *Achter het Zilveren Masker: Nieuw onderzoek naar de productietechnieken van Romeinse ruiterhelmen (Hinter der silbernen Maske: neue Untersuchungen zur Herstellungstechnik römischer Reiterhelme)*, Hrsg. R. Meijers, F. Willer, Nijmegen, 2007, pp. 61–7.

Georgiev, Bacharov, 1987 – Georgiev, P., and Bachvarov, I., 'Rimski bronzov shlem ot kolektsiyata na okruzhaniya istoricheski muzej, Silistra', *Archeologia*, 2, 1987, pp. 18–24.

Giglioli, 1952 – Giglioli, G. Q., *La colonna di Arcadio a Costantinopoli*, Naples, 1952.

Gilliver, 2007 – Gilliver, K., 'Display in Roman Warfare: The Appearance of Armies and Individuals on the Battlefield', *War in History*, 14, 2007, 1, pp. 1–21.

Giuliano, 1955 – Giuliano, A., *Arco di Costantino*, Milan, 1955.

Gjerstad, 1956 – Gjerstad, E., *Early Rome II. The Tomb*, Lund, 1956.

Glad, 2012 – Glad, D., 'The Empire's influence on barbarian elites from the Pontus to the Rhine (5th–7th centuries); a case study of lamellar weapons and segmental helmets', in Vujadin, I., and Kazanski, M., *The Pontic Danubian Realm in the Period of the Great Migration*, Paris-Beograd, 2012, pp. 349–62.

Goethert, 1996 – Goethert, K .P., 'Neue römische Prunkschilde', in Junkelmann, M., *Reiter wie Statuen aus Erz*, Mainz, 1996, pp. 115–26.

Grabar, 1966 – Grabar, A., *L'âge d'or de Justinien: de la mort de Théodose à l'Islam*, Paris, 1966.

Grabar, 1971 – Grabar, A., *L'empereur dans l'art byzantine*, London, 1971.

Grabar, 1980 – Grabar, A., *L'età d'oro di Giustiniano: dalla morte di Teodosio all'Islam*, Milan, 1980.

Greco, Guzzo, 1992 – Greco, E., and Guzzo, P. G., *Laos II. La Tomba a Camera Di Marcellina*, Taranto, 1992.

Guzzo, 2000 – Guzzo, P. G., 'La tomba 104 del Fondo Artiaco o sia dell'ambiguità del segno', *Damarato, Studi di antichità classica offerti a Paola Pelagatti*, Milan, 2000, pp. 135–47.

Hack, 1967 – Hack, B., *I mosaici di Santa Maria Maggiore in Roma*, Baden, 1967.

Halsall, 2003 – Halsall, G., *Warfare and Society in the Barbarian West 450-900* (Warfare and History), London and New York, 2003.

Hanel, Wilbers-Rost, Willer, 2004 – Hanel, N., Wilbers-Rost, S., and Willer F., 'Die Helmmaske von Kalkriese', *Bonner Jahrbücher*, Bd. 204, 2004, pp. 71–92.

Harmon, 1988 – Harmon, D. P., 'The Religious Significance of Games in the Roman Age', *The Archaeology of the Olympics: The Olympics and Other Festivals in Antiquity*, Madison, 1988, pp. 236–55.

Harrison, 1993 – Harrison, M., *Anglo-Saxon Thegn AD 449-1066*, Oxford, 1993.

Hartley, Hawkes, Henig, 2006 – Hartley E., Hawkes J., Henig, M., and Mee, F., *Constantine the Great. York's Roman Emperor*, York, 2006.

Helbig, 1905 – Helbig, W., *Sur les attributs des Saliens*, Paris, 1905.

Helbig, 1912 – Helbig, W., and Amelung, W., *Führer durch die Sammlungen in Rom*. Vol. I. 3rd ed., Lipsia, 1912.

Hencken,1968 – Hencken, H., *Tarquinia, Villanovans and Early Etruscans*, 2 vols in American School of Prehistoric Research, Peabody Museum, Harvard University, Bulletin 23, Cambridge, 1968.

Hetherington, Forman, 1981 – Hetherington P., and Forman, W., *Byzantium, City of Gold, City of Faith*, London, 1981.

Holliday, 2002 – Holliday, P. J., *The Origin of Roman Historical Commemoration in the Visual Arts*, Cambridge, 2002.

Holmquist Olausson, 2007 – Holmquist Olausson, L., 'Curious birds, two Helmet (?) mounts with a Christian motif from Birka's Garrison', in eds. Fransson, U., *et al* (eds), *Cultural interaction between east and west. Archaeology, artefacts and human contacts in northern Europe*, Stockholm Studies in Archaeology 44, Stockholm, 2007, pp. 231–7.

Holscher, 2003 – Holscher, T., 'Images of War in Greece and Rome: Between Military Practice, Public Memory and Cultural Symbolism', *JRS*, 93, 2003, pp. 1–17, Pl. III, 2.

Horsmann, 1991 – Horsmann, G., 'Untersuchungen zur militärischen Ausbildung im republikanischen und kaiserzeitlichen Rom', *Wehrwissenschaftliche Forschungen. Abteilung Militärwissenschaftliche Studien*, 35. Boppard am Rhein, 1991.

Horvat, 2002 – Horvat, J., 'The hoard of Roman Republican Weapons from Grad near Šmihel', *Arheološki vestnik*, 53, 2002, pp. 117–92.

Hottenroth, 1888 – Hottenroth, F., *Il Costume, Le Armi, Gli Utensili dei Popoli Antichi e Moderni* Vol. I–II, Rome, 1887–92.

Hughes and others, 1989 – Hughes, M., and others, 'Technologie de l'argenterie romaine', *Trésors d'orfèvrerie gallo-romains, catalogue of the exhibition*, Lyon, 1989, pp. 21–8.

Humer, 2004 – Humer, F., *Marc Aurel und Carnuntum*, Horn, 2004.

Hyland, 1993 – Hyland, A, *Training the Roman Cavalry from Arrian's Ars Tactica*, Stroud, 1993.

Ilkić, Miletić, Mrav, Radman-Livaja, Sanader, Tončinić, Zaninović, 2010 – Ilkić, M., Miletić, Ž., Mrav, Z., Radman-Livaja, I., Sanader, M., Tončinić, D., Zaninović, M., *Nalazi rimske vojne opreme u Hrvatskoj* [Finds of Roman military equipment in Croatia]: [katalog izložbe], Zagreb, 2010.

Ilkić, Čelhar, 2007 – Ilkić, M., and Čelhar, M., 'Two rare Roman Imperial coins found in Roman Liburnia'. *VAMZ*, 3, XL, 2007, pp. 333–8.

Isac, 2009 – Isac, D., 'The cavalry parade mask from Gilău', *Ephemeris Napocensis*, XIX, 2009, pp. 191–8.

Isac, Barbulescu, 2008 – Isac, D., and Barbulescu, M., 'Neue Paraderustungen aus Dakien', *Acta Musei Napocensis*, 43–44, 1, 2008, pp. 211–31.

Isler-Kerényi, 2009 – Isler-Kerényi, C., 'Antefisse Sileniche fra Grecia ed Etruria', *Ocnus*, 17, 2009, pp. 55–64.

Ivanišević, Kazanski, 2007 – Ivanišević, V., and Kazanski, M., 'Nouvelle Nécropole des grandes Migrations de Singidunum', *Starinar*, 57, 2007, pp. 113–35.

Jaeckel, 1965 – Jaeckel, P., 'Pergamenische Waffenreliefs', *Waffen und Kostümkunde*, siebenter Band, 2, 1965, pp. 94–122.

Jahn, 1860 – Jahn, O., *Die Lauersforter Phalerae. Fest-Programm zu Winckelmanns Geburtstage*, Bonn, 1860.

James, 1986 – James, S., 'Evidence from Dura-Europos for the origins of late Roman helmets', *Syria*, T 63, 1986, pp. 107–34.

James, 2004 – James, S., *The Excavations at Dura-Europos conducted by Yale University and the French Academy of Inscriptions and Letters 1928 to 1937. Final Report VII: The Arms and Armour and other Military Equipment*, London, 2004.

Jarva, 1995 – Jarva, E., 'Archaiologia on Archaic Greek Body Armour', *Studia Archaeologica Septentrionalia 3. Rovianiemi: Societas Historica Finlandiae Septentrionalis*, Helsinki, 1995.

Jorge, 2015 – Jorge, A., 'Alexandre, o Grande e a batalha de Hidaspes o Mosaico do Triclinium da casa de Medusa', *Abelterium* Vol. II, n. 1, Alter do Chão, 2015, pp. 52–71.

Joy, 1997 – Joy, R. J. T., 'Historical Aspects of Medical Defence Against Chemical Warfare', in Sidell, F. R. (ed.), *Medical Aspects of Chemical and Biological Warfare*, Washington, 1997, pp. 111–28.

Jucker, 1977 – Jucker, H., 'Dokumentationen zur Augustusstatue von Primaporta', *Hefte des Archäologisches Seminars der Universität Bern*, 3,1977, pp. 16–37.

Junkelmann, 1991 – Junkelmann, M., *Die Reiter Roms. Teil 2: Der militärische Einsatz*, Mainz, 1991.

Junkelmann, 1992 – Junkelmann, M., *Die Reiter Roms. Teil 3: Zubehör, Reitweise, Bewaffnung*, Mainz, 1992.

Junkelmann, 1996 – Junkelmann, M., *Reiter wie Statuen aus Erz*, Mainz am Rhein, 1996.

Junkelmann, 2000a – Junkelmann, M., *Römische helme*, Mainz, 2000.

Junkelmann, 2000b – Junkelmann, M., 'Familia Gladiatoria: The Heroes of the Amphitheatre', in E. Köhne, E., and C. Ewigleben, C. (eds), *Gladiators and Caesars*, Berkeley, 2000, pp. 31–74.

Jurgeit, 1999 – Jurgeit, F., *Die etruskischen und italischen Bronzen sowie Gegenstande aus Eisen, Blei und Leder im Badischen Landesmuseum Karlsruhe*, Vols. I, II, Rome, 1999.

Kähler, 1958 – Kähler, H., *Rom und Seine Welt: bilder zur Geschichte und Kultur*, München, 1958.

Kam, 1915 – Kam, G. M., 'Antieke helmen in het museum "Kam"', *Bulletin van den Nederlandschen Oudheidkundigen Bond* ser. 2, 1915, 8, pp. 258–66.

Katalog Budapest, 2003 – *Führer durch die archäologische Ausstellung des ungarischen Nationalmuseums (400 000 v. Chr. – 804 n. Chr.)*, Budapest, 2003.

Kaus, 1996 – Kaus, K., 'Das spätantike Pannonien', in *Reitervölker aus dem Osten – Hunnen + Awaren. Katalog der Burgenländischen Landesausstellung 1996 im Schloß Halbturn, 26. April – 31*.

Oktober 1996, Eisenstadt, 1996, pp. 39–64.

Kazanski, 1988 – Kazanski, M., 'Quelques paralleles entre l'armement en Occident et à Byzance (Ive-VIIe s.)', *Gaule Mérovingienne et monde méditerranéen. Les derniers Romains en Septimanie Ive-VIIIe s.*, Lattes, 1988, pp. 75–87.

Kazanski, 1994 – Kazanski, M., 'Les éperons, les umbo, les manipules de boucliers et les haches de l'époque romaine tardive dans la région pontique: origine et diffusion, *Beiträge zur römischer und barbarischer Bewaffnung in der ersten vier nachchristlichen Jahrhunderten*, Lubin-Marburg, 1994 (1995), pp. 429–85.

Kazanski-Mastykova, 2007 – Kazanski M., (in collaboration with A. Mastykova, with contributions by Akhmedov, I., Cheynet, J.-C., Domzalski, K., Malachev, V., Sodini, J.-P., and Soupault, V.) *Tsibilium*, Vol. 2. La nécropole apsile de Tsibilium (Caucase, Abkhazie). Etude du site, BAR International Series –1721–II. Oxford, 2007.

Keim, Klumbach, 1951 – Keim, J., and Klumbach, H., *Der römische Schatzfund von Straubing*, Munich, 1951.

Kellner, 1978 – Kellner, H. J., 'Der römische Verwahrfund von Eining', *Münchner Beiträge zur Vor- und Frühgeschichte* 29, Munich, 1978.

Kellner, Zahlhaas, 1993 – Kellner, H.J., and Zahlhaas, G., *Der römische Tempelschatz von Weißenburg i. Bay*, Mainz, 1993.

Kemkes, Scheuerbrand, Willburger, 2005 – Kemkes, M., Scheuerbrand, J., and Willburger, N., *Der Limes. Grenze Roms zu den Barbaren*, Ostfildern, 2005.

Keppie, 1996 – Keppie, L. J. F., 'The Praetorian Guard Before Seianus', *Athenaeum*, 84, 1996, pp. 101–24.

Kern, 1982 – Kern, G. von, *Die Stilentwicklung des Riefelharnisches*, Munich, 1982.

Khazanov, 1971 – Khazanov, A. M., *Ocherki voennogo dela sarmatov*, Moscow, 1971.

Kiechle, 1965 – Kiechle, F., 'Die "Taktik" des Flavius Arrianus', *Bericht der Römisch-Germanischen Kommission*, 45, 1965, pp. 87–129.

Kiilerich, Torp, 1989 – Kiilerich, B., and Torp, H., 'Hic est: hic Stilicho, the date and interpretation of a notable dyptich, the Stilicho Dyptich at Monza', *Jahrbuch des Deutschen Archäologischen Instituts*, Bd. 104, 1989, pp. 319–71.

Kilian, 1977 – Kilian, K., 'Das Kriegergrab von Tarquinia', *JdI*, 92, 1977, pp. 24–98.

King, 1987 – King, C. E., *Roman Silver Coins*, London, 1987.

Klawans, 1959 – Klawans, H. Z., *Reading and Dating Roman Imperial Coins*, Racine, 1959.

Klengel, 1971 – Klengel, H., *Syria Antiqua*, Leipzig, 1971.

Klumbach, 1949–1950 – Klumbach, H., 'Römische Gesichtshelme aus Mainz', *Mainzer Zeitschrift*, Bd. 44–45, 1949–1950, pp. 28–33.

Klumbach, 1960 – Klumbach, H., 'Ein Paradeschildbuckel aus Miltenberg', *Bayerische Vorgeschichtsblätter*, 25, 1960, pp. 125–32.

Klumbach, 1973 – Klumbach, H., *Spätrömische gardehelme*, Munich, 1973.

Klumbach, 1974 – Klumbach, H., *Römische Helme aus Niedergermanien. Katalog einer Ausstellung in Rheinischen Landesmuseums Bonn, 1974*, Köln, 1974.

Klumbach, Wamser, 1976–1977 – Klumbach, H., and Wamser, L., 'Ein Neufund zweier außergewöhnlicher Helme der römischen Kaiserzeit aus Theilenhofen, Landkreis Weißenburg-Gunzenhausen. Ein Vorbericht', *Jahresbericht der Bayerischen Bodendenkmalpflege*, 17–18, 1976-7, pp. 41–61.

Koch, Sichtermann, 1982 – Koch, G., and Sichtermann, H., *Römische Sarkophage*, Munich, 1982.

Kocsis, 1993 – Kocsis, L.,' A recently identified cavalry sports helmet from Aquincum', *Budapest régiségei: a főváros területén talált műemlékek és történelmi nevezetességű helyek leírása*, 30, 1993, pp. 281–292.

Kohlert, 1976 – Kohlert, M., 'Zur Entwicklung, Funktion und Genesis römischer Gesichtsmasken in Thrakien und Niedermösien', *Wissenschaftliche Zeitschrift der Humboldt-Universität zu Berlin, Gesellschafts- und Sprachwissenschaftliche Reihe*, 25, 1976, pp. 509–16.

Kolobov, 1998 – Kolobov, A. V., 'Boevye nagrady rimskih legionerov jepohi principata', *Vestnik*

Permskogo universiteta. Ser. «Istorija», 2, 1998, pp. 27–34.

Kools, 2013 – Kools, S., *The Apulo-Corinthian Helmet: A south-east Italic helmet type and what it can say about the social and cultural context in which it was used*, Leiden, 2013.

Kos, 2014 – Kos, P., 'Ad Pirum, Hrušica, in Claustra Alpium Iuliarium', *Vestnik*, XXVI, Ljubljana, 2014.

Kraft, 1978 – Kraft, K., 'Der Helm des Römischen Kaisers', *Gesammelte Aufsz zur antike Geldgeschichte und Numismatik I*, Darmstadt, 1978, pp. 133–44.

Kreilinger, 1996 – Kreilinger, U., *Römische Bronzeappliken: historische Reliefs im Kleinformat*, Heidelberg, 1996, Taf. 1–9.

Krier, Reinert, 1993 – Krier, J., and Reinert, F., *Das Reitergrab von Hellingen. Die Treverer und das römische Militär in der frühen Kaiserzeit*, Luxemburg, 1993.

Kropatscheck, 1909 – Kropatscheck, G., 'Ausgrabungen bei Haltern. Die Fundstücke der Jahre 1905–1907', *Mitteilungen der Altertumskommission für Westfalen*, 5, 1909, pp. 323–58.

Künzl, 1988 – Künzl, E., *Der römische Triumph: Siegesfeiern im antiken Rom*, Munich, 1988.

Künzl, 1996 – Künzl, E., 'Gladiusdekorationen der frühen römischen Kaiserzeit: Dynastische Legitimation, Victoria und Aurea Aetas', *Jahrbuch des Römisch-Germanischen Zentralmuseums Mainz* 43, 1996, pp. 383–474.

Künzl, 1999 – Künzl, E., 'Fellhelme. Zu den mit organischem Material dekorierten römischen Helmen der frühen Kaiserzeit und zur imitatio Alexandri des Germanicus', *Rom, Germanien und die Ausgrabungen von Kalkriese. Internationaler Kongress der Universität Osnabrück und des Landschaftsverbandes Osnabrücker Land e. V. vom 2. bis 5. September 1996. Osnabrücker Forschungen zu Altertum und Antike-Rezeption 1*, Bramsche, 1999, pp. 149–68.

Künzl, 2001 – Künzl, E., 'Die Ikonographie der römischen Panzerplatte von Ritopek, Serbien /YU', *Belgian Archaeology in a European Setting. Album Amicorum Joseph Remi Mertens I. Acta Archaeologica Lovaniensia Monographiae* 12, 2001, pp. 71–83.

Künzl, 2004 – Künzl, E., 'Sol, Lupa, Zwillingsgottheiten und Hercules: Neue Funde und Bemerkungen zur Ikonographie römischer Paradewaffen', *Archäologisches Korrespondenzblatt*, 34, 2004, pp. 389–406.

Künzl, 2008 – Künzl, E., *Unter den goldenen Adlern: Der Waffenschmuck des römischen Imperiums*, Mainz, 2008.

La Regina, 1992 – La Regina, A. (ed.), *Roma 1000 anni di civiltà. Catalogo della Mostra. Palais de la Civilisation, Montreal, 7 maggio – 12 ottobre 1992*, Milan, 1992.

La Regina, 2003 – La Regina, A. (ed.), *Nike, il gioco e la vittoria*, Rome, 2003.

La Rocca, 1976 – La Rocca, E., 'Il sepolcreto dell'Esquilino', in Acanfora, M. O. (ed.), *Civiltà del Lazio primitivo*, Rome, 1976.

Labus, 1838 – Labus, G., *Museo Bresciano illustrato*. Brescia, 1838.

Lammert, 1938 – Lammert, F., 'Phalerae', *Paulys Realencyclopädie der classischen Altertumswissenschaft*, Bd. XIX, 1938, Sp. 1660.

Langeveld, Graafstal, Swinkels, Künzl, 2010 – Langeveld, M., Graafstal, E., Swinkels, L., and Künzl, E., 'Een voorhoofdband van een ruiterhelm uit de inheemse nederzetting', *Basisrapportage archeologie*, 19, 2010, pp. 297–304.

Latte, 1967 – Latte, K., 'Römische Religionsgeschichte', *Handbuch der Altertumswissenschaft*. Abt. 5. Tl. 4. Munich, 1967.

Lawson, 1980 – Lawson, A. K., 'Zu den römischen Reiterspielen', *Archäologisches Korrespondenzblatt*, 10, 1980, pp. 173–84.

Leander Touati, 1987 – Leander Touati, A. M., 'The Great Trajanic Frieze: The Study of a Monument and the Mechanism of Message Transmission in Roman Art', *Acta Instituti Romani Regni Sueciae* XLV, Stockholm, 1987.

Lebedinsky, 2001 – Lebedinsky, I., *Armes et guerriers barbares*, Paris, 2001.

Lehner, 1904 – Lehner, H., 'Die Einzelfunde von Novaesium', *Bonner Jahrbücher*, 111–112, 1904, pp. 243–418.

Liberati, 1997 – Liberati, A. M., 'L'esercito di Roma nell'età delle guerre puniche, ricostruzioni e plastici del Museo della Civiltà Romana di Roma', *JRMES*, 8, 1997, pp. 25–40.

Lindenschmit, 1881 – Lindenschmit, L., 'Masken und Visirhelme aus Erz und Eisen', *Alterthümer unserer heidnischen Vorzeit*, Bd. III, Beilage zu Heft 11, 1881, 1–10.

Lipinsky, 1975 – Lipinsky, A., 'Oro, argento, gemme e smalti, Tecnologia delle arti dalle origini alla fine del Medioevo, 3000 a.C. – 1500 d.C.', *Arte e Archeologia, Studi e Documenti*, 8, Florence, 1975.

Lipkin, 2014 – Lipkin, S., 'The belt in the Prehistoric Central Tyrrhenian Italy', *Monographs of the Archaeological Society of Finland* 2, Oulu, 2014, pp. 35–58.

Lipperheide, 1896 – Lipperheide, F. F. von, *Antike helme*, Munich, 1896.

Lloyd, 2010 – Lloyd, A. B., *A Companion to Ancient Egypt*, Oxford, 2010.

Lusuardi Siena, 1998 – Lusuardi Siena, S. L'identità materiale e storica della corona: un enigma in via di risoluzione?, *La corona ferrea nell'Europa degli Imperi, 2/II Alla scoperta del prezioso oggetto, scienza e tecnica*, Milan, 1998, pp. 173–249.

Lusuardi, Perassi, Facchinetti, Bianchi, 2002 – Lusuardi Siena, S., Perassi, C., Facchinetti,G., and Bianchi, B., 'Gli elmi tardo-antichi (IV-VI sec.) alla luce delle fonti letterarie, numismatiche ed archeologiche: alcune considerazioni ' in Buora, M., *Miles Romanus, Dal Po al Danubio nel Tardoantico*, Pordenone, 2002, pp. 21–62.

Luzzatto, Pompas, 1988 – Luzzatto, L., and Pompas, R., *Il significato dei colori nelle civiltà antiche*, Milan, 1988.

Lyne, 1994 – Lyne, M., 'Late Roman Helmet Fragments from Richborough', *JRMES*, 5, 1994, pp. 97–105.

MacDowall, 1994 – Macdowall, S., *Late Roman Infantryman 236-565 AD*, Oxford, 1994.

MacDowall, 1995 – Macdowall, S., *Late Roman Cavalryman 236-565 AD*, Oxford, 1995.

MacDowall, 2001 – MacDowall, S., *Adrianople AD 378*, Oxford, 2001.

MacMullen, 1960 – MacMullen, R., 'Inscriptions on armor and the supply of arms in the Roman Empire', *AJA*, 64, 1960, pp. 23–40.

Maluquer de Motes, 1974 – Maluquer de Motes, J., 'La Coraza Griega de Bronce, del Museo de Granada', *Zephyrvs*, XXV, 1974, pp. 321–7.

Mansel, 1938 – Mansel, A. M., 'Grabhügelforschung in Ostthrakien', *Bulletin de l'Institute d'Archéologie Bulgare*, 12, 1938, pp. 154–89.

Martinelli, 2004 – Martinelli, M., *La lancia, la spada ed il cavallo, il fenomeno guerra nell'Etruria e nell'Italia centrale tra età del bronzo ed età del ferro*, Florence, 2004.

Martinelli, Paolucci, 2006 – Martinelli, P., and Paolucci, G., *Etruscan Places*, Florence, 2006.

Maspero, 1912 – Maspero, J., *Organisation militaire de l'Égypte byzantine*, Paris, 1912.

Mastrocinque, 1993 – Mastrocinque, A., *Romolo, la Fondazione di Roma tra storia e leggenda*, Este, 1993.

Matešić, 2010 – Matešić, S., 'Der germanische Helm aus dem Thorsberger Moor', *Archäologische Nachrichten aus Schleswig-Holstein*, 16, 2010, pp. 54–8.

Maxfield, 1981 – Maxfield, V. A., *The Military Decorations of the Roman Army*, London, 1981.

McCartney, 1917 – McCartney, E. G., 'The military indebtedness of Early Rome to Etruria', *Memoirs of the American Academy in Rome*, Vol. I, Rome, 1917, pp. 121–67.

Meijers, Schalles, Willer, 2007 – Meijers, R., Schalles, H.-J., and Willer, F., 'Schietproeven met een reconstructie van een Romeins geschut op specifieke Metaalplaten (Schussexperimente mit einer rekonstruierten römischen Torsionswaffe auf definierte Metallbleche)', *Achter het Zilveren Masker: Nieuw onderzoek naar de productietechnieken van Romeinse ruiterhelmen (Hinter der silbernen Maske: neue Untersuchungen zur Herstellungstechnik römischer Reiterhelme)*, Hrsg. R. Meijers, F. Willer, Nijmegen, 2007, pp. 68–76.

Meijers, Willer, 2007 – Meijers, R., and Willer, F., 'Catalogus van de onderzochte ijzeren gezichtshelmen uit Nijmegen (Katalog der untersuchten eisernen Gesichtshelme aus Nijmegen)', *Achter het Zilveren Masker: Nieuw onderzoek naar de productietechnieken van Romeinse ruiterhelmen (Hinter der silbernen Maske: neue Untersuchungen zur Herstellungstechnik römischer Reiterhelme)*, Hrsg. R. Meijers, F. Willer, Nijmegen, 2007, pp. 21–30.

Mendel, 1914–1966 – Mendel, G., *Catalogue des sculptures grecques, romaines et byzantines*, 3 vols, Rome, 1914–66.

Menendez Arguin, 2006 – Menendez Arguin, A. R., *Pretorianos la guardia imperial de l'antigua Roma*, Madrid, 2006.

Menichelli, Magno, Orsingher, 2008 – Menichelli, S., Magno, F., and Orsingher, G. P., *Etruschi guerrieri*, Viterbo, 2008.

Merlin, 1909 – Merlin, A., 'Découverte d'une cuirasse italiote près de Ksour-Es-Saf (Tunisie)', *Monuments et mémoires de la Fondation Eugène Piot*, 17.2, 1909, pp. 125–38.

Mielczarek, 1995 – Mielczarek, M., 'Armes greques, scythes et sarmates du littoral septentrional de la mer noire dans la collection du Musée de l'Armée Polonaise à Varsovie', *Monumenta Antiqua Orae Septentrionalis Ponti Euxini Reperta Locisque Externis Deposita, Toruń*, 1995, pp. 35–40.

Milano Capitale, 1990 – *Milano capitale dell'Impero romano, 286-402 d.c.*, Milano, 1990.

Mitschke, 2007 – Mitschke, S., 'Die organischen Auflagerungen an den Reiterhelmen aus Nijmegen und Xanten–Wardt', *Achter het Zilveren Masker: nieuw onderzoek naar de productietechnieken van Romeinse ruiterhelmen (= Hinter der silbernen Maske: neue Untersuchungen zur Herstellungstechnik römischer Reiterhelme)*, Hrsg. R. Meijers, F. Willer, Nijmegen–Bonn, 2007, pp. 81–100.

Montanaro, 2009 – Montanaro, A. C., 'La tomba 131 di Salapia (Cerignola, Foggia) appunti e riconsiderazioni', *Archeologia Classica*, LX, 2009, pp. 1–27.

Mora, 1995 – Mora, F., *Il pensiero storico-religioso antico. Autori greci a Roma. 1. Dionigi d'Alicarnasso*, Rome, 1995.

Moretti Sgubini, 2001 – Moretti Sgubini, A. M., *Veio, Cerveteri, Vulci, Città d'Etruria a confronto. Catalogo della mostra, Roma, Museo nazionale etrusco di Villa Giulia. Villa Poniatowski, 1 ottobre-30*, Rome, 2001.

Morgunova, Meshherjakov, 1999 – Morgunova, N. L., and Meshherjakov, D. V., '"Prohorovskie" pogrebenija V Berdjanskogo mogil'nika', *Arheologicheskie pamjatniki Orenburzh'ja*, Vyp. III, Orenburg, 1999, pp. 124–46.

Morillo, 2006 – Morillo, A. C. (ed.). Arqueología Militar Romana en Hispania, production y abastecimiento en el ámbito militar. Leon, 2006.

Moscati, 1976 – Moscati, S., *Vita sociale nell'antichità*, Milan, 1976.

Müller Karpe, 1962 – Müller-Karpe, H., 'Zur Stadtwerdung Roms', *Bullettino dell'instituto archeologico Germanico, Sezione Romana*, Ottavo supplement, Heidelberg, Kerle, 1962.

Musée du Louvre, 1992 – Musée du Louvre, *Byzance. L'art byzantin dans les collections publiques françaises*, Paris, 1992.

Namur, 1854 – Namur, A., *Une sépulture druidique du commencement de l'ère gallo- romaine, découverte entre Hellange et Souftgen en 1853*, Luxembourg, 1854.

Naue, 1896 – Naue, J., 'Armi Italiane della collezione Naue in Monaco', *Bullettino di Paletnologia Italiana*, Anno XXII, Parma, 1896, pp. 94–104.

Negin, 2004. – Negin, A. E., 'K voprosu o zashhitnom vooruzhenii rimskih katafraktariev i klibanariev', *«IX Chtenija pamjati professora Nikolaja Petrovicha Sokolova». Nizhny Novgorod, NNGU, 29-30 oktjabrja 2004 g*, Nizhny Novgorod, pp. 45–9.

Negin, 2005 – Negin, A. E., 'Klady rimskogo paradnogo vooruzhenija v provincii Recija', *Aktual'nye problemy istoricheskoj nauki i tvorcheskoe nasledie S.I. Arhangel'skogo: XIV chtenija pamjati chlena-korrespondenta AN SSSR S.I. Arhangel'skogo, 25-26 fevralja 2005g*, Chast' 1, Nizhny Novgorod, 2005, pp. 60–3.

Negin, 2007 – Negin, A. E., 'Pozdnerimskie shlemy: problemy genezisa', *Antiqvitas Aeterna. Povolzhskij antikovedcheskij zhurnal: Vyp. 2: Vojna, armija i voennoe delo v antichnom mire*, Saratov, 2007, pp. 335–59.

Negin, 2008 – Negin, A. E., 'Ob jekonomicheskih aspektah oruzhejnogo proizvodstva v Rime jepohi Principata', *Vestnik NNGU*, 6, 2008, pp. 171–7.

Negin, 2009 – Negin, A. E., 'Vooruzhenie kak identifikator voennogo i social'nogo statusa rimskogo voennosluzhashhego', *Vremja, sobytie, istoricheskij opyt v diskurse sovremennogo istorika: XVI chtenija pamjati chlena-korrespondenta AN SSSR S.I. Arhangel'skogo, 15-17 aprelja 2009 goda*, Nizhny Novgorod, 2009, pp. 119–23.

Negin, 2010a – Negin, A. E., *Rimskoe ceremonial'noe i turnirnoe vooruzhenie*, Sankt-Peterburg, 2010.

Negin, 2010b – Negin, A. E., 'Pozdnerimskie shlemy s prodol'nym grebnem', *Germania-Sarmatia II*, Kaliningrad-Kursk, 2010, pp. 343–58.

Negin, 2012a – Negin, A. E., 'Sferokonicheskie shlemy v rimskoj armii jepohi Antoninov: vzaimovlijanija oruzhejnyh tradicij Sredizemnomor'ja', *Sredizemnomorskij mir v antichnuju i srednevekovuju jepohi: kross-kul'turnye kommunikacii v istorricheskom prostranstve i vremeni. XIII chtenija pamjati professora Nikolaja Petrovicha Sokolova: Materialy Mezhdunarodnoj nauchnoj konferencii (Nizhny Novgorod, 25-27 sentjabrja 2012 g.)*, Nizhny Novgorod, 2012, pp. 53–5.

Negin, 2012b – Negin, A. E., 'Mater castrorum, amazonki, gorgona Meduza i shlemy-lichiny s zhenskimi chertami lica v rimskoj imperatorskoj armii', *Stratum plus*, No. 4, 2012, pp. 283–300.

Negin, 2013 – Negin, A .E., 'Dekorativnye rimskie shlemy', *Stratum plus*, No. 4, 2013, pp. 179–86.

Neverov, 1996 – Neverov, O. Ya., 'Rimskie nagradnye znaki – falery iz kollekcii Jermitazha', *Problemy istorii, filologii, kul'tury*, 3, Moscow-Magnitogorsk, 1996, pp. 116–20.

Newark, 1987 – Newark, T., *Medieval Warlords*, Hong Kong, 1987.

Nicolle, 1995 – Nicolle, D., *Medieval Warfare Source Book. Vol. I: Warfare in Western Christendom*, London, 1995.

Nicolle, 1996 – Nicolle, D., *Medieval Warfare Source Book. Vol 2: Christian Europe and its Neighbours*, London, 1996.

Nicolle, 2002 – Nicolle, D., *Romano-Byzantine armies 4th – 9th centuries*, London, 1992.

Niemeyer, 1968 – Niemeyer, H. G., *Studien zur statuarischen Darstellung der römischen Kaiser*, Berlin, 1968.

Nikonorov, 1997 – Nikonorov, V. P., *The Armies of Bactria 700 BC – 450 AD*, 2 vols, Stockport, 1997.

Nizzo, 2008 – Nizzo, V., 'Riflessioni sulla pratica del rituale inceneratorio nel Lazio Meridionale della III e IV fase', *Aristonothos*, 2008, 3, pp. 111–70.

Nizzo, 2012 – Nizzo, V., 'Aspetti della ideologia guerriera a Roma e nel Latium Vetus durante l'età di Romolo' in Libera, R., and Carosi S., *L'esercito e la cultura militare di Roma antica, Atti 29 Corso di Archeologia e Storia Antica del Museo Civico di Albano (Albano 2010)*, Albano Laziale, 2012, pp. 59–91.

Oliver, 1941 – Oliver, J. H., 'Notes on Documents of the Roman East', *AJA*, 1941, 45.4, pp. 537–43.

Paddock, 1985 – Paddock, J., 'Some changes in the manufacture and supply of Roman bronze helmets under the Late Republic and Early Empire', *Proceedings of the Second Roman Military Equipment Research Seminar* (ed. M. C. Bishop). BAR. 275, Oxford, 1985.

Paddock, 1993 – Paddock, J., *The Bronze Italian Helmet: the development of the cassis from the last quarter of the sixth century BC to the third quarter of the first century AD*, Vols. I, II, PhD thesis, University College London, 1993.

Pallottino, 1952 – Pallottino, M., *Etruscan Painting*, Geneva, 1952.

Pandolfini Angeletti 2006 – Pandolfini Angeletti, M. (ed.), *Archeologia in Etruria meridionale. Atti delle giornate di studio in ricordo di Mario Moretti*, Rome, 2006.

Panella, 2011 – Panella, C., *I segni del potere, realtà ed immaginario della sovranità nella Roma Imperiale*, Bari, 2011.

Paribeni, 1928 – Paribeni, R., 'Capodimonte. Ritrovamento di tombe arcaiche', *Notizie di scavi di Antichità*, Rome, 1928, pp. 434–67.

Paribeni, 2001 – Paribeni, E., *Guerrieri dell'età del Ferro in Lunigiana*, La Spezia, 2001.

Pautasso, 1984–1985 – Pautasso, A., 'i simboli cristiani nella monetazione di Roma e Bisanzio', *Ad Quintum*, 1984–1985, 7.

Pavia, 1999 – Pavia, C., *Guida dei Mitrei di Roma Antica*, Rome, 1999.

Pellegrini, 1899–1901 – Pellegrini, G., 'Fregi arcaici Etruschi in terracotta a piccole figure', *Studi e Materiali di Archeologia Numismatica*, 1899–1901, pp. 87–118.

Pensabene, 2001 – Pensabene, P., *Le terrecotte del Museo Nazionale Romano II. Materiali dai depositi votivi di Palestrina: Collezioni Kircheriana e Palestrina, Rome*, 2001.

Pericoli, Conde, 1976 – Pericoli, U., and Conde, R., *Las Legionas Romanas*, Barcelona, 1976.

Petculescu, 2003 – Petculescu, L., *Antique Bronzes in Romania*, Bucharest, 2003.

Petrikovits, 1939 – Petrikovits, H. von, 'Troiae lusus', *Klio*, 32, 1939, pp. 209–20.

Petrikovits, 1952 – Petrikovits, H. von, 'Troiaritt und Geranostanz', *Beiträge zur älteren europäischen Kulturgeschichte (Festschrift R. Egger)*, 1952, I, pp. 126–43.

Petrovic, 1991 – Petrovic, P., 'Dona Militaria', *Starinar*, 42, 1991, pp. 63–78.

Petrović, 1993 – Petrović, P., 'Rimski paradni šlem iz Brze Palanke (Egeta)', *Zbornik Narodnog muzeja, H-1. Arheologija*, Beograd, 1993, pp. 97–106.

Picard, 1957 – Picard, G. Ch., *Les trophées romains: Contribution à la historie de la religion et de l'art triomphal de Rome*, Paris, 1957.

Piccirillo, Alliata, 1998 – Piccirillo, M., and Alliata, E., *Mount Nebo. New Archaeological Excavations, 1967–1997. Studium Biblicum Franciscanum. Collectio Maior 28*, Jerusalem, 1998.

Pinterovic, 1978 – Pinterovic, D., 'Limesstudien in der Baranja und in Slawonien', *Archaeologia Iugoslavica* IX, Beograd, 1978, pp. 55–82.

Pinza, 1905 – Pinza, G., 'Monumenti primitivi di Roma e del Lazio', *Monumenti Antiche* XV, Milano, 1905, pp. 39–403.

Pitts, 1987 – Pitts, L., 'Musov – a Roman military station', *Archaeology Today*, April 1987, pp. 22–6.

Pjatysheva, 1964 – Pjatysheva, N. V., *Zheleznaja maska iz Hersonesa*, Moscow, 1964.

Plant, 2006a – Plant, R., *Roman Base Metal Coins, a Price Guide*, Stockport, 2006.

Plant, 2006b – Plant, R., *Roman Silver Coins, a Price Guide*, Stockport, 2006.

Polito, 1998 – Polito, E., *Fulgentibus Armis: Introduzione allo studio dei fregi d'armi antichi*, Rome, 1998.

Pop-Lazić, 2008 – Pop-Lazić, S., 'Late Roman Necropolis Beljnjača in Šid', *Starinar*, LVIII, 2008pp. 163–73.

Popović, Mano-Zisi, Veličkovic, Jeličič, 1969 – Popović, B., Mano-Zisi, D., Veličkovic, M., and Jeličič, B., *Anticka bronza u Jugoslaviji, 1844–1969*, Beograd, 1969.

Potter, 1818 – Potter, J. D. D., *Archaeologia Graeca or the Antiquities of Greece*, 2 vols, Edinburgh, 1818.

Proietti, 1980 – Proietti, G., *I1 Museo Nazionale Etrusco di Villa Giulia*, Rome, 1980.

Rabinovich, 1941 – Rabinovich, B. Z., 'Shlemy skifskogo perioda', *Trudy Otdela Istorii Pervobytnoj Kul'tury Gosudarstvennogo Ermitazha. T. I.*, Leningrad, 1941, pp. 99–171.

Racinet, 1888 – Racinet, A., *Le Costume Historique*, 6 vols, Paris, 1888.

Racinet, 2003 – Racinet, A., *The Complete Costume History*, Koln, 2003.

Radulescu, 1963 – Radulescu, A., 'Elmi bronzei di Ostrov', *Dacia*, 7, 1963, pp. 543–51.

Rankov, 1994 – Rankov, B., *The Praetorian Guard*, Oxford, 1994.

Ravegnani, 1988 – Ravegnani, G., *Soldati di Bisanzio in età Giustinianea*, Rome, 1988.

Ravegnani, 1989 – Ravegnani, G., *La Corte di Giustiniano*, Rome, 1989.

Renel, 1903 – Renel, Ch., *Cultes militaiers de Rome. Les ensigns*, Lyon, 1903.

Reuter, 1999 – Reuter, M., 'Zwei Reiterhelmfragmente aus einer römischen Altmetallwerkstatt des 3. Jhs. n. Chr. in Herten, Kreis Lörrach', in Kemkes, M., and Scheuerbrandt, J. (Hrsg.), *Fragen zur römischen Reiterei. Kolloquium zur Ausstellung 'Reiter wie Statuen aus Erz. Die römische Reiterei am Limes zwischen Patrouille und Parade' im Limesmuseum Aalen am 25./26.02.1998*, Stuttgart, 1999, pp. 44–8.

Ricciardi, 2007 – Ricciardi, R. A., *Where Did All the Women Go: The Archaeology of the Soldier Empresses*, Dissertation, University of Cincinnati, 2007.

Richter, 1915 – Richter, G. M.A., *Greek, Etruscan and Roman Bronzes*, New York, 1915.

Robinson, 1975 – Robinson, H. R., *The Armour of Imperial Rome*, London, 1975.

Rocco, 2012 – Rocco, M., *L'esercito romano tardo-antico: persistenze e cesure dai Severi a Teodosio I*, Padua, 2012.

Roma ed i Barbari, 2008 – *Roma e i Barbari*. La nascita di un nuovo mondo. *Catalogo* della Mostra (Venezia, Palazzo Grassi), Milano, 2008.

Rose, 2005 – Rose, Ch. B., 'The Parthians in Augustan Rome', *AJA*, 109, 1, 2005, pp. 21–76.

Rostovtseff, 1918 – Rostovtseff, M. I., 'Kurgannye nahodki Orenburgskoj oblasti jepohi rannego i pozdnego jellinizma', *Materialy po arheologii Rossii*, 37, 1918, pp. 3–102.

Rostovtseff, 1935 – Rostovtseff, M. I., 'Dura and the Problem of the Parthian Art', *Yale Classical Studies*, 5, 1935, pp. 157–304.

Rüpke, 1990 – Rüpke, J., *Domi militiae. Die Religiöse Konstruktion des Krieges in Rom*, Stuttgart, 1990.

Ruprechtsberger, 1981 – Ruprechtsberger, E. M., 'Zum Dolichenusfund von Mauer an der Url', *Jahrbuch des Oberösterreichischen Musealvereins*, 106, 1981, pp. 45–54.

Sabbatini, 2008 – Sabbatini, T., 'La società attraverso l'organizzazione delle necropoli', *Potere e splendore. Gli antichi Piceni a Matelica (catalogo della mostra)*, Rome, 2008, pp. 51–70.

Sacken, 1883 – Sacken, E. von, 'Über einige römische Metall- und Emailarbeiten', *Jahrbuch der Kunsthistorischen Sammlungen des Allerhöchsten Kaiserhauses*, 1, 1883, pp. 41–60.

Salmon, 1967 – Salmon, E. T., *Samnium and the Samnites*, Cambridge, 1967.

Salvetti, Sommella, 1994 – Salvetti, C., and Sommella, A. M., *Antiquarium comunale: storia di un museo romano e delle sue raccolte archeologiche*, Rome, 1994.

Sannibale, 1998 – Sannibale, M., *Le armi della collezione Gorga al Museo Nazionale Romano*, Rome, 1998.

Sannibale 2008 – Sannibale, M., *La raccolta Giacinto Guglielmi. II. bronzi e materiali vari*, Rome, 2008.

Saulnier, 1980 – Saulnier, C., *L'armée et la guerre dans le monde etrusco-romain*, Paris, 1980.

Schäfer, 1979 – Schäfer, Th., 'Das Siegesdenkmal vom Kapitol', *Die Numider. Reiter und Könige nördlich der Sahara, Ausstellungskatalog Bonn 1979/1980*, Bonn, 1979, pp. 243–50.

Schliemann, 1880, – Schliemann, H., *Mycenae*, New York, 1880.

Schneider-Herrmann, 1996 – Schneider-Herrmann, G., *The Samnites of the Fourth Century B. C.: as depicted on Campanian vases and other sources*, London, 1996.

Schorsch, 1986 – Schorsch, D., 'The Vermand treasure: A testimony to the presence of the Sarmatians in the Western Roman Empire', *Metropolitan Museum Journal*, 21, 1986, pp. 17–40.

Schröder, 1905 – Schröder, B., 'Die Freiherrlich von Lipperheidesche Helmsammlung in den Kgl. Museen zu Berlin', *Archäologischer Anzeiger*, 1905, pp. 15–30.

Schröder, 1912 – Schröder, B., 'Thrakische Helme', *Jahrbuch des deutschen archäologischen Institut*, Bd XXVII, 1912, pp. 317–44.

Schuckelt, 2015 – Schuckelt, S., *Evidence for horse armour in Roman Army and the use of chamfrons by Roman cavalry*, Cardiff diss., 2015.

Schuppe, 1937 – Schuppe, E., 'Torques', *Paulys Realencyclopädie der classischen Altertumswissenschaft*, Bd. XVI, 1937, Sp.1880.

Scott, 2005 – Scott, R. T., 'The contribution of archaeology to early Roman History' in Raaflaub, K.A. (ed.), *Social Struggles in Archaic Rome*, Oxford, 2005, pp. 98–106.

Scubla, 2012–2013 – Scubla, M. A,. *Lo scudo bilobato nei contesti archeologici dell'Italia Antica*. Materiali e questioni connesse, tesi di laurea of Università degli Studi di Milano, 2009.

Ščukin, 1993 – Ščukin, M. B., 'A propos des contacts militaires entre les Sarmates et les Germains à l'èpoque romaine (d'après l'armement et spécialment les umbo de boucliers et les lances', *L'Armée romaine et les barbares du IIIe au VIIe siècle*, Paris, 1993, pp. 323–33.

Sekunda, 1986 – Sekunda, N., *The Ancient Greeks*, London, 1986.

Sekunda, Northwood, 1995 – Sekunda, N., and Northwood, S., *Early Roman Armies*, Oxford, 1995.

Senzacionno, 2013 – 'Senzacionno: zlatni nakiti v Brestovica' , *Vestnik Rodopi*. Informacionen bjuletin – broj 7. August 2013. URL: http://www.calameo.com/books/ 0022208821cf81756a9e1 (accessed: 23 Nov 2013).

Seyrig, 1952 – Seyrig, H., 'Antiquités de la nécropole d'Emèse'. *Syria*, Vol. 29, No. 3/4, 1952, pp. 204–50.

Shadrake, 1997 – Shadrake, D., and Shadrake, S., *Barbarian Warriors. Saxons, Vikings, Normans*, Singapore, 1997.

Shadrake, 1994 – Shadrake, D., 'Britannia and Arthur', *Ancient Warriors*, I, 1994, pp. 26ff.

Sharp, James, 2012 – Sharp, H., and James, S., 'Reconstructing the Hallaton helmet', *Current Archaeology*, No. 264, 2012, pp. 38–41.

Sim, Kaminski, 2012 – Sim, D., and Kaminski, J., *Roman imperial armour: the production of early imperial military armour*, Oxford, 2012.

Simonenko, 2009 – Simonenko, A. V., *Sarmatskie vsadniki Severnogo Prichernomor'ja*, St. Petersburg, 2009.

Skalon, 1973 – Skalon, K. M., 'Der Helm von Concesti in Rumänien', *Spätrömische Gardehelme*, Munich, 1973, pp. 91–4.

Snodgrass, 1967 – Snodgrass, A. M., *Arms and Armor of the Greeks*, Baltimore & London, 1967.

Sommella, 1973–1974 – Sommella, P., 'La necropoli protostorica rinvenuta a Pratica di Mare', *Rendiconti della Pontificia Accademia*, XLVI, 1973–4, pp. 33–48.

Sommer, 1984 – Sommer, M., *Die Gürtel und Gürtelbeschläge des 4. und 5. Jahrhunderts im römischen Reich (Bonner Hefte zur Vorgeschichte, 22)*, Bonn, 1984.

Soupault, 1995 – Soupault, V., 'Les tombes à épée au nord-est et à l'Est de la mer Noire au Bas Empire', *La noblesse Romaine et les chefs barbares*, Paris, 1995, pp. 227–45.

Southern-Dixon, 1996 – Southern, P., and Dixon, K. R., *The Late Roman Army*, London, 1996.

Spence, 2002 – Spence, I. G., *Historical Dictionary of Ancient Greek Warfare*, Lanham, 2002.

Spineto, 1997 – Spineto, N., 'The King of the wood, oggi: una rilettura di James George Frazer alla luce dell'attuale problematica storico religiosa', in Brandt, G. R., Zander Touati, A. M., Zahle, J., *Nemi, Status Quo. Recent research at Nemi and the Sanctuary of Diana*, Rome, 2000, pp.17–24.

Stary, 1981 – Stary, P. F., 'Zurfruheisenzeitlichen Bewaffnung und Kampfesweise', *Mittelitalien Marburger Studien zur Vor-und Frühgeschichte*, Band 3, Mainz, 1981.

Stauffer, 2006 – Stauffer, A., 'L'abito della tomba B/1971' in Bentini, L., Boiardi, A., Eles, P. von, Poli, P., and Rodriguez, E., *Il Potere e la Morte. Aristocrazia, guerrieri e simboli*, Verucchio, 2006.

Steiner, 1905 – Steiner, P., 'Die Dona Militaria', *Bonner Jahrbücher*, 114/115, 1905, pp. 1– 98.

Stemmer, 1978 – Stemmer, K., *Untersuchungen zur Typologie, Chronologie und Ikonographe der Panzerstatuen*, Berlin, 1978.

Stephenson, 1999 – Stephenson, I. P., *Roman Infantry Equipment: The Later Empire*, Stroud, 1999.

Stephenson, 2006 – Stephenson, I. P., *Romano-Byzantine Infantry Equipment*, Stroud, 2006.

Stephenson, Dixon, 2001 – Stephenson, I. P., and Dixon, K. R., *Roman Cavalry Equipment*, Stroud, 2001.

Stojchev, 2005 – Stojchev, S., 'Shlem-maska ot Madara', *Trakija i okolnijat svjat. Nauchna konferencija – Shumen 2004*, Sofia, 2005, pp. 303–6.

Strøm, 1971 – Strøm, I., *Problems Concerning the Origin and Early Development of the Etruscan Orientalizing Style*, Odense 1971.

Suano, 1986 – Suano, M., 'Sabellian-Samnite Bronze Belts in the British Museum', *British Museum Occasional Paper* No. 57, London, 1986.

Sumner, 1997 – Sumner, G., *Roman Army, Wars of the Empire*, London, 1997.

Sumner, 2003 – Sumner, G., *Roman Military Clothing II, AD 200-400*, Oxford, 2003.

Sumner, 2009 – Sumner, G., *Roman Military Dress*, Stroud, 2009.

Syvanne, 2015 – Syvanne, L., *Military History of Late Rome, 284-361 AD*, Barnsley, 2015.

Szabo, 1986 – Szabo, K., 'Le casque romain d'Intercisa – récente trouvaille du Danube', *Studien zu den Militärgrenzen Roms III. – 13. Internationaler Limeskongress – Aalen 1983*, Stuttgart, 1986, pp. 421–5.

Tagliamonte, 2002–2003 – Tagliamonte, G., 'Dediche di armi nei santuari sannitici', *Cuadernos de prehistoria y arqueología*, 28–29, 2002–3, pp. 95–125.

Term, 1983 – Term, M., *The Representation of Greek Hoplite Body-Armour in the art of the fifth and fourth centuries B.C.*, 2 vols, Oxford, 1983.

Thomas, 1971 – Thomas, E., *Helme, Schilde, Dolche. Studien über Römische-pannonische Waffenkunden*, Budapest, 1971.

Thompson, 2004 – Thompson, L., *Ancient Weapons in Britain*, Barnsley, 2004.

Tiussi, Villa, Novello, 2013 – Tiussi, C., Villa, L., and Novello, M. (eds.), *Costantino e Teodoro. Aquileia nel IV secolo*, Milano, 2013.

Tomedi, 2000 – Tomedi, G., 'Italische Panzerplatten und Panzerscheiben' *PBF*, III.3, Stuttgart, 2000.

Tončeva, 1964 – Tončeva, G., 'Novootkriti grobnici okolo Odesos', *Izvestija na Narodnija muzej – Varna*, 1964, XVI, 1, pp. 51–60.

Torelli & others, 2000 – Torelli, M. (ed.), *Gli Etruschi*, Cinisello Balsamo, 2000.

Touring Club, 1981 – Touring Club, Lazio, *Guida d'Italia del Touring Club Italiano*, Milan, 1981.

Towneley, 1799 – Towneley, Ch., 'Account of Antiquities discovered at Ribchester', *Vetusta Monumenta*, 4, 1815, pp. 1–12.

Toynbee, Clarke, 1948 – Toynbee, J. M. C., and Clarke, R. R., 'A Roman decorated helmet and other objects from Norfolk', *JRS*, 38, 1948, pp. 20–7.

Travis & Travis, 2012 – Travis, H., and Travis, R., *Roman Body Armour*, Stroud, 2012.

Travis & Travis, 2014 – Travis H., and Travis, R., *Roman Helmets*, Stroud, 2014.

Trejster, 2009 – Trejster, M. Ju,. 'Bronzovyj nagrudnik pancirja s izbrazheniem golovy Meduzy iz kurgana u st. Elizavetinskoj v Prikuban'e', *Bosporskie issledovanija. 2009. 21*, Simferopol'-Kerch', 2009, pp. 120–34.

Tuck, 2015 – Tuck, S. L., *A History of Roman Art*, Oxford, 2015.

Turfa, 2011 – Turfa, J. M., *Catalogue of the Etruscan Gallery of the University of Pennsylvania Museum of Archaeology and Anthropology*, Philadelphia, 2011.

Turnure, 1965 – Turnure, J. H., 'Etruscan Ritual Armor: Two Examples in Bronze', *AJA*, 69, 1965, pp. 39–48.

Um, Deschler-Erb, 1997 – Um, K., and Deschler-Erb, E., *Katalog der Militaria aus Vindonissa*, Brugg, 1997.

Unikalni artefakti, 2013 – Unikalni artefakti otkriha na Pamuk mogila plovdivski arheolozi // Trakijski agrovesti Plovdiv. Godina XIX. Broj 27 (807), 25–31.07.2013 g. URL: http://www.sgb-bg.org/docs/presa/807.pdf (accessed: 23 Nov 2013).

Van Keuren, 1985 – Van Keuren, F., 'Cosmic Symbolism of the Pantheon on the Cuirass of the Prima Porta Augustus' in Winkes, R. (ed.), *The Age of Augustus*, Providence, 1985, pp. 177–87.

Various, 1990 – Various Authors, *Roma e l'Italia*, Milan, 1990.

Velkov, 1928 – Velkov, I., 'Neue Grabhügel aus Bulgarien', *Bulletin de l'Institut d'Archéologie Bulgare*, 5, 1928, pp. 13–55.

Venedikov, 1960 – Venedikov, I., 'Der Gesichtsmaskenhelm in Thrakien', *Eirene*, 1, 1960, pp. 143–51.

Vermeule, 1959 – Vermeule, C. C., 'Hellenistic and Roman Cuirassed Statues', *Berytus*, Vol. 13, 1959, pp. 1–82.

Vermeule, 1960 – Vermeule, C. C., 'A Roman silver helmet in the Toledo (Ohio) Museum of Art', *JRS*, 50, 1960, pp. 8–11.

Vermeule, Neuerburg, 1973 – Vermeule, C., and Neuerburg, N., *Catalogue of the Ancient Art in the J. Paul Getty Museum*, Malibu, 1973.

Versnel, 1970 – Versnel, H. S., *Triumphus. An Inquiry into the Origin. Development and Meaning of the Roman Triumph*, Leiden, 1970.

Villa, 2002 – Villa L., 'Militari e militaria nel Veneto Orientale', *Miles Romanus: dal Po al Danubio nel tardoantico; atti del Convegno internazionale, Pordenone-Concordia Sagittaria, 7-19 marzo 2000*, ed. M. Buora, Pordenone, 2002, pp. 163–73.

Visconti, 1796 – Visconti, E .Q., *Il Museo Pio Clementino descritto. Bassirilievi del Museo Pio Clementino. T. V.*, Rome, 1796.

Visy, 2000 – Visy, Z., *Historischer Uberblick, in Limesmuseum Aalen. Von Augustus bis Attila: Leben am ungarischen Donaulimes. Zweigmuseum des Wurttembergischen Landesmuseums Stuttgart. Schriften des Limesmuseums Aalen*, Aalen, 2000, pp. 11–18.

Vlădescu, 1981 – Vlădescu, CR. M., 'Masca de paradă de la Romula si incercarea de reconstituire a coifului de cavalerie romană', *Studii şi cercetări de istorie veche*, 32, 2, 1981, pp. 195–203.

Vogt, 2006 – Vogt, M., *Spangenhelme. Baldenheim und verwandte Typen. Kataloge vor – und frühgeschichtlicher Altertümer 39*, Mainz, 2006.

Volbach, 1952 – Volbach, W. F., *Elfenbeinarbeiten der Spätantike und des frühen Mittelalters*, Mainz, 1952.

Walker, Bierbrier, 1997 – Walker, S., and Bierbrier, M., *Ancient Faces: Mummy Portraits from Roman Egypt*, London, 1997.

Walters, 1915 – Walters, H. B., *Select bronzes, Greek, Roman and Etruscan: in the departments of antiquities, seventy-three plates*, London, 1915.

Waurick, 1988 – Waurick, G., 'Helme der hellenistischen Zeit und ihre Vorläufer, *Antike Helme. Handbuch mit Katalog. Monographien des Römisch-Germanischen Zentralmuseums*, Band 14, Mainz, 1988, pp. 151–80.

Waurick, 1994 – Waurick, G., 'Römischer Eisenhelm aus Windisch, Kt. Aargau/Schweiz (1. Jahrhundert n. Chr.)', *Jahrbuch des Römisch-Germanischen Zentralmuseums*, 41, 1994, p. 645'.

Weege, 1909 – Weege, F., 'Oskische Grabmalerei', *Jahrbuch des Kaiserlich Deutschen Archaologischen Instituts*, 24, 1909, pp. 99–162.

Werner, 1989 – Werner, J., 'Nuovi dati sulle origini degli spangen-helme alto-medioevali del tipo Baldenheim', *XXXVI corso di cultura sull'arte Ravennate e Bizantina. Ravenna e l'Italia fra Goti e Longobardi*, Ravenna, 1989.

White, DeVries, Romano, Romano, Stolyarik, 1995 – White, D., DeVries, K., Romano, D. G., Romano, I. B., and Stolyarik, Y., *The Ancient Greek World. The Rodney S. Young Gallery, University of Pennsylvania Museum of Archaeology and Anthropology*, Philadelphia, 1995.

Widawnictwa Uniwersytetu Warszawskiego, 1993 – Widawnictwa Uniwersytetu Warszawskiego, 'Novensia, Badania Ekspedycji archeologicznej Uniwersytetu Warszawskiego w Novae', *Studia i materialy pod redakcja naukowa*, 5, 1993, Warsaw, 1993.

Wieczorek, Perin, Welck, Menghin, 1996 – Wieczorek, A., Perin, P., Welck, K. von, and Menghin, W. (Hrsg.), *Die Franken – Wegbereiter Europas*, Mainz, 1996.

Wieser, 1894 – Wieser, F. R. von, *Die Freiherrlieh von Lipperheidesche Sammlung antiker Bronzen. Mit 50 Tafeln in Lichtdruck*, Berlin-Innsbruck, 1894.

Wilcox, 1982 – Wilcox, P., *Rome's Enemies (1). Germanics and Dacians*, London, 1982.

Wilhelmi, 1992 – Wilhelmi, K., Isa pantae tois prosohpois. Die bronzeeisenversilberte Helmmaske aus der frühen Kaiserzeit am Kalkrieser Berg. Germanische Beute aus römischer Paraderüstung "haerentia corpori" tegmina? Ein status quaestionis', *JRMES*, 3, 1992, pp. 1–36.

Willems, 1992 – Willems, W. J. H., 'Roman Face-masks from the Kops Plateau, Nijmegen, The Netherlands', *JRMES*, 3, 1992, pp. 57–66.

Wilpert, 1916 – Wilpert, J., *Die Römische Mosaiken und Malereien der Kirchlichen Bauten vom IV. bis XIII. Jahrundert*, IV Banden, Freiburg im Breisgau, 1916.

Winterbottom, 1989 – Winterbottom, S., 'Saddle covers, chamfrons and possible horse armour from Carlisle', *Roman Military Equipment: the Sources of Evidence. Proceedings of the Fifth Roman Military Equipment Conference*, British Archaeological Reports, International Series 476, Oxford, 1989, pp. 319–36.

Witts, 2007 – Witts, P., 'The lost mosaics of Bramdean', *ARA*, 2007, pp. 3–8.

Woodard, 2006 – Woodard, R. D., *Indo-European Sacred Space. Vedic and Roman Cult*, Urbana and Chicago, 2006.

Worrell, Jackson, 2011 – Worrell, S., Jackson, R., Mackay, A., Bland, R., and Pitts, M., 'The Crosby Garrett Roman Helmet', *British Archaeology*, 116, 2011, pp. 20–7.

Worrell, Pearce, 2011 – Worrell, S., and Pearce, J., 'Finds Reported under the Portable Antiquities Scheme', *Britannia*, 42, 2011, pp. 355–93.

Ypey, 1966 – Ypey, J., 'Twee viziermaskerhelmen uit Nijmegen', *Numaga*, 13, 1966, pp. 187–99.

Zevi, 1993 – Zevi, F., 'La tomba del Guerriero di Lanuvio', *Spectacles sportifs et scéniques dans le monde étrusco-italique. Actes de la table ronde de Rome (3–4 mai 1991)*, Rome, 1993, pp. 409–42.

Zieling, 1989 – Zieling, N., 'Studien zu Germanischen Schilden der Spätlatène-und der römischen Kaiserzeit im Freien Germanien', *British Archaeological Report International*, Series 505, Oxford, 1989.

Zimmermann, 1979 – Zimmermann, J., 'Une cuirasse de Grande Grece', *Museum Helveticum*, 36, 1979, pp. 177–84.

Δεληβορριάς Ά. - Φωτόπουλος Δ., *Η Ελλάδα του Μουσείου Μπενάκη*, Μουσείο Μπενάκη, Αθήνα 1997.